International Series in Operations Research & Management Science

Volume 327

The book series **International Series in Operations Research and Management Science** encompasses the various areas of operations research and management science. Both theoretical and applied books are included. It describes current advances anywhere in the world that are at the cutting edge of the field. The series is aimed especially at researchers, doctoral students, and sophisticated practitioners.

The series features three types of books:

- Advanced expository books that extend and unify our understanding of particular areas.
- Research monographs that make substantial contributions to knowledge.
- Handbooks that define the new state of the art in particular areas. They will be entitled Recent Advances in (name of the area). Each handbook will be edited by a leading authority in the area who will organize a team of experts on various aspects of the topic to write individual chapters. A handbook may emphasize expository surveys or completely new advances (either research or applications) or a combination of both.

The series emphasizes the following four areas:

Mathematical Programming: Including linear programming, integer programming, nonlinear programming, interior point methods, game theory, network optimization models, combinatorics, equilibrium programming, complementarity theory, multiobjective optimization, dynamic programming, stochastic programming, complexity theory, etc.

Applied Probability: Including queuing theory, simulation, renewal theory, Brownian motion and diffusion processes, decision analysis, Markov decision processes, reliability theory, forecasting, other stochastic processes motivated by applications, etc. Production and Operations Management: Including inventory theory, production scheduling, capacity planning, facility location, supply chain management, distribution systems, materials requirements planning, just-in-time systems, flexible manufacturing systems, design of production lines, logistical planning, strategic issues, etc. Applications of Operations Research and Management Science: Including telecommunications, health care, capital budgeting and finance, marketing, public policy, military operations research, service operations, transportation systems, etc.

This book series is indexed in Scopus.

More information about this series at https://link.springer.com/bookseries/6161

Makoto Tanaka • Antonio J. Conejo
Afzal S. Siddiqui

Economics of Power Systems

Springer

Makoto Tanaka
National Graduate Institute for Policy Studies (GRIPS)
Tokyo, Japan

Antonio J. Conejo
Department of Integrated Systems Engineering
The Ohio State University
Columbus, OH, USA

Afzal S. Siddiqui
Department of Computer and Systems Sciences
Stockholm University
Kista, Sweden

Department of Mathematics and Systems Analysis
Aalto University
Espoo, Finland

ISSN 0884-8289 ISSN 2214-7934 (electronic)
International Series in Operations Research & Management Science
ISBN 978-3-030-92870-4 ISBN 978-3-030-92871-1 (eBook)
https://doi.org/10.1007/978-3-030-92871-1

This Springer imprint is published by the registered company Springer Nature Switzerland AG
The registered company address is: Gewerbestrasse 11, 6330 Cham, Switzerland

To Naomi, Rei, and Shou

In memory of my mother María, for the many gentle lessons she gave me

To Niraj Patel

Preface

The purpose of this book is to provide an up-to-date and detailed description of the microeconomic concepts and operations research techniques needed to comprehend the design and operation of power markets and the actions of their agents: producers, consumers, prosumers (i.e., agents that are both producers and consumers such as residential customers with solar photovoltaic systems), operators, and regulators. This is critical to address issues in a continuously evolving power-system environment that incorporates an increasing number of no-marginal-cost renewable energy sources such as solar and wind, increasingly competitive storage facilities, increasingly responsive demands, an increasing need for decarbonization, and widespread communication channels that enable distributed decision making. Such an evolving environment calls for revisiting the microeconomic concepts and operations research techniques needed by students and practitioners in the power-systems field.

The book is intended for advanced undergraduate and graduate students, researchers, and practitioners in the power-market community that encompasses engineering, operations research, economics, and business. We provide a tutorial-style book written in an accessible manner, including many illustrative examples, from stylized to more detailed ones, for the reader to understand the economic concepts and operations research procedures used by power-market professionals. We expand such concepts and procedures envisioning a renewable-dominated marketplace.

This book consists of seven chapters. Chapter 1 describes the general theory of demand with a focus on electricity markets. It covers key concepts of microeconomics, including utility functions, demand functions, price elasticity of demand, and consumer surplus. It also discusses the effect of demand response induced by time-varying prices and the decision making of prosumers with distributed generation units.

Chapter 2 explores the economic foundations of electricity supply, starting with a discussion of operating costs in the short run and, then, investment costs in the long run. It discusses a firm's short- and long-run profit-maximization decisions. It also examines the interaction of conventional generation technologies and variable renewable energy sources (VRES) with null operating costs. Energy storage that may mitigate spatio-temporal imbalances is also explored.

Chapter 3 describes electricity market auctions, i.e., clearing algorithms for electricity markets, focusing on the day-ahead market. It starts with an analysis of single-node single- and multi-period auctions and, then, discusses network-constrained single- and multi-period auctions.

Chapter 4 considers marginal prices for energy in power markets. It first describes the long- and short-term properties of such prices, i.e., investment-cost recovery and short-term efficiency under perfect competition. In turn, it considers marginal prices pertaining to non-convexities (e.g., start-up cost and minimum power output). Stochastic and multi-period market-clearing algorithms are also examined.

Chapter 5 discusses market power observed in electric-power markets. It describes how to measure the degree of market power and market concentration. Based on game theory, it presents oligopoly models with simultaneous and sequential decision makers. An extended framework of a leader-follower oligopoly model is presented with multiple leaders including both producers and consumers who submit offer/bid prices strategically.

Chapter 6 addresses the issue of negative environmental externalities present in power markets. It examines the effects of market-based mechanisms, such as environmental taxation, emission-permit schemes, and renewable portfolio standards. It also presents detailed network-constrained operational models with externalities to accommodate realistic spatial, technological, and temporal factors along with the market power of producers in power systems.

Chapter 7 explores investment decisions in a decentralized electricity industry with VRES penetration. It first investigates transmission planning, required by both the remote locations of promising VRES sites and variability management. It then examines investment in generation capacity, mirroring the structure of transmission planning. It presents detailed models with realistic spatial, technological, and temporal factors as well as the market power of producers.

The book provides a blend of theoretical analysis and practical applications. It includes GAMS codes for numerical examples that can be readily used. These features make the book of interest to students, researchers, and practitioners in the power-market community. We hope that this book will facilitate research and commercial advances in power markets.

To conclude, we would like to thank our colleagues and students for their insightful observations and valuable comments. Particularly, we are grateful to Carlos Batlle for his shrewd observations pertaining to Chap. 4. We are also grateful to Camille Price for encouraging us to write this book, as well as to the editorial staff of Springer, for their help throughout the writing process.

Tokyo, Japan — Makoto Tanaka
Columbus, OH, USA — Antonio J. Conejo
Stockholm, Sweden — Afzal S. Siddiqui
September 2021

Contents

1 Demand ... 1
- 1.1 Introduction ... 1
- 1.2 Utility ... 2
  - 1.2.1 Utility Function ... 3
  - 1.2.2 Quadratic Utility Function ... 5
- 1.3 Demand for Goods ... 7
  - 1.3.1 Utility Maximization and Demand Function ... 7
  - 1.3.2 Linear Demand Function ... 8
  - 1.3.3 Substitutes and Complements ... 12
- 1.4 Elasticity ... 13
  - 1.4.1 Price Elasticity of Demand ... 14
  - 1.4.2 Elasticity for Linear Demand ... 15
  - 1.4.3 Various Cases of Elasticity ... 17
- 1.5 Consumer Surplus ... 19
  - 1.5.1 Gross Benefit and Consumer Surplus ... 19
  - 1.5.2 Maximizing Consumer Surplus ... 21
- 1.6 Demand Aggregation ... 22
  - 1.6.1 Market Demand ... 23
  - 1.6.2 Aggregation of Consumer Surplus ... 24
- 1.7 Demand Response ... 27
- 1.8 Prosumer ... 30
- 1.9 Summary ... 32
- 1.10 End-of-Chapter Exercises ... 33
- References ... 34

2 Supply ... 35
- 2.1 Introduction ... 35
- 2.2 Operating Costs ... 36
  - 2.2.1 Calculating Operating Costs ... 37
  - 2.2.2 Short-Run Supply Stack ... 38
  - 2.2.3 Economic Dispatch ... 39

2.3 Investment Costs 47
2.3.1 Calculating Levelized Costs 47
2.3.2 Screening Curves 48
2.3.3 Investment Planning 55
2.4 Profit Maximization 60
2.4.1 Short-Run Profit Maximization 60
2.4.2 Long-Run Profit Maximization 66
2.5 Variable Renewable Energy Sources 70
2.6 Energy Storage 75
2.7 Summary 81
2.8 End-of-Chapter Exercises 82
2.9 GAMS Codes 83
References 95

3 Market Clearing 97
3.1 Introduction 97
3.2 Day-Ahead Market 98
3.2.1 Single-Node Single-Period Auction 98
3.2.2 Single-Node Multi-Period Auction 101
3.2.3 Network-Constrained Single-Period Auction 105
3.2.4 Network-Constrained Multi-Period Auction 108
3.2.5 Stochastic Auction 112
3.3 Intra-Day Market 112
3.4 Futures Market 112
3.5 Summary 113
3.6 End-of-Chapter Exercises 113
3.7 GAMS Codes 114
References 115

4 Marginal Pricing 117
4.1 Introduction 117
4.2 Marginal Pricing and Investment-Cost Recovery 117
4.2.1 Optimal Control and Perfect Knowledge 118
4.2.2 Perfect Competition 122
4.3 Marginal Pricing and Short-Term Efficiency 124
4.3.1 Un-congested Clearing 124
4.3.2 Congested Clearing 127
4.3.3 General Formulation 129
4.4 Non-convexities and Marginal Pricing 131
4.4.1 Non-convexities: Illustrative Example 132
4.4.2 Non-convexities: General Formulation 135
4.5 Uncertainty: Two-Stage Marginal Pricing 137
4.5.1 Uncertainty: Illustrative Example 138
4.5.2 Uncertainty: General Formulation 143

4.6 Multi-Period Marginal Pricing 145
4.6.1 Multi-Period: Illustrative Example 146
4.6.2 Multi-Period: General Formulation 148
4.7 Summary 150
4.8 End-of-Chapter Exercises 151
4.9 GAMS Codes 151
References 153

5 Market Power 155
5.1 Introduction 155
5.2 Concept of Market Power 156
5.2.1 Monopoly 156
5.2.2 Lerner Index 158
5.2.3 Monopsony 158
5.3 Oligopoly 160
5.3.1 Game Theory 160
5.3.2 Cournot Oligopoly 161
5.3.3 Herfindahl-Hirschman Index 168
5.3.4 Stackelberg Oligopoly 170
5.4 Multiple Leaders 172
5.4.1 Market Clearing: Primal Problem, Dual Problem, and Optimality Conditions 172
5.4.2 Producer 1 Exercising Market Power 176
5.4.3 Producer 2 Exercising Market Power 178
5.4.4 Consumer 1 Exercising Market Power 179
5.4.5 Consumer 2 Exercising Market Power 182
5.4.6 Multiple Agents Exercising Market Power 183
5.5 Summary 187
5.6 End-of-Chapter Exercises 188
5.7 GAMS Codes 189
References 194

6 Environmental Externalities 197
6.1 Introduction 197
6.2 Negative Externalities 198
6.3 Market-Based Mechanisms for Pollution Control 200
6.3.1 Taxation and Permit Schemes 200
6.3.2 Renewable Portfolio Standards 204
6.4 Network-Constrained Models with Externalities 206
6.4.1 First-Best Policy for CO_2 Emissions 207
6.4.2 CO_2 Taxation in a Deregulated Electricity Industry 213
6.4.3 Renewable Portfolio Standard in a Deregulated Electricity Industry 223

6.5 Summary 235
6.6 End-of-Chapter Exercises 236
6.7 GAMS Codes 237
References 253

7 Investment 255
7.1 Introduction 255
7.2 Transmission Expansion 256
7.2.1 Transmission Expansion Under Central Planning 257
7.2.2 Bi-Level Transmission Expansion 267
7.3 Generation Expansion 277
7.3.1 Generation Expansion Under Central Planning 277
7.3.2 Bi-Level Generation Expansion 281
7.4 Summary 292
7.5 End-of-Chapter Exercises 293
7.6 GAMS Codes 294
References 312

Index 315

Chapter 1
Demand

1.1 Introduction

The restructured electricity industry relies on markets rather than regulation in generation and retail sectors, whereas transmission and distribution sectors have been kept regulated. For example, wholesale electricity prices are determined by supply and demand conditions in wholesale power markets [10]. Thus, it is important to understand the mechanisms of both supply and demand in the markets. This chapter focuses on the demand side, particularly consumer behavior, while Chap. 2 explores the supply side.

Electricity is supplied to consumers mainly comprising households, commercial buildings, and industrial facilities. For instance, the industrial sector amounts to 40% of all power consumption, while the household and commercial sectors account for 30% of consumption, respectively, in the EU [5]. In deregulated power markets, consumers tend to face variation in electricity prices since retailers try to pass on the volatile energy prices to their customers. Consumers of electricity would respond to changing prices by altering the quantities demanded.

Microeconomic theory explains the general mechanism of demand [13, 15]. It explores basic factors such as consumer preferences, choices, and welfare. Particularly, we are interested in consumer behavior facing market prices. In other words, our interest lies in the quantities of goods that consumers are willing to buy at various levels of prices in the market. With a focus on electricity markets, this chapter primarily discusses the general theory of demand that is applicable to any market including other energy markets (e.g., gas and oil).

We begin with the basic concept of utility, which measures the level of satisfaction or pleasure from consuming goods. The general form of utility is represented as a function of various goods such as electricity, gas, and water. In applications, it is useful to consider specific functional forms for utility including a Cobb–Douglas utility function and a quadratic utility function.

M. Tanaka et al., *Economics of Power Systems*, International Series
in Operations Research & Management Science 327,
https://doi.org/10.1007/978-3-030-92871-1_1

With facing market prices, a consumer maximizes utility from consuming the goods under his/her own budget constraint. The solutions for the utility-maximization problem yield the optimal levels of the quantities for consumption. These solutions are called demand functions, which are functions of prices and, hence, exhibit the relationship between the quantities demanded and the market prices. Particularly, we derive linear demand functions, often used for the analysis of electricity markets.

As characterized by demand functions, consumers react to variation in prices by changing the quantities demanded. In power markets, if the electricity price were to rise in some periods, then customers would decrease their consumption by adjusting the usage of their electric equipment. We discuss the concept of the price elasticity of demand to measure the degree of consumer reaction to price changes. The price elasticity for linear demand is of particular interest for applications.

Furthermore, we evaluate the monetary value of power consumption. Based on demand functions, we introduce the general concepts of the gross benefit and consumer surplus in welfare analysis. Specifically, consumer surplus measures the net gain from consuming the good after paying for it at the market price. We demonstrate that utility maximization is closely related to surplus maximization.

The analysis for a single consumer is then extended to a number of consumers in the market. We examine the aggregation of individual consumer demand into the overall market-demand function. In the same vein, individual consumer surplus is aggregated for all customers in the market. We also investigate the maximization of aggregate consumer surplus from the perspective of a public entity such as a system operator in power markets.

Finally, we pick up two issues pertinent to the recent advancement of technologies in the electric power industry. One issue is demand response of consumers equipped with the advanced smart meters that can record near real-time electricity consumption. Time-varying prices would induce demand response of consumers, thereby improving economic efficiency. Another issue is an increase in consumers with distributed generation units such as rooftop solar photovoltaic (PV) systems. Such customers are regarded as "prosumers" who sell and buy electricity in the market. We describe the decision making of prosumers.

In the rest of this chapter, after introducing the concept of utility in Sect. 1.2, demand functions are derived in Sect. 1.3. Sections 1.4 and 1.5 explain the concepts of price elasticity of demand and consumer surplus, respectively, while Sect. 1.6 demonstrates how to aggregate demand in the overall market. Sections 1.7 and 1.8 discuss the issues of demand response and prosumer, respectively. Section 1.9 summarizes this chapter, while Sect. 1.10 gives end-of-chapter problems.

1.2 Utility

Customers in power markets obtain some level of satisfaction or pleasure by consuming electricity. In economics, the level of satisfaction or pleasure is measured by utility. This section explains the general form of utility as a function of various goods such as electricity, gas, and water. We also discuss specific functional forms for utility, i.e., a Cobb–Douglas utility function and a quadratic utility function.

1.2.1 Utility Function

We begin with a general description of utility from consuming a bundle of n goods. The quantities of goods are denoted by a non-negative $n \times 1$ vector, $\mathbf{x}$. For example, households consume a number of goods such as electricity, gas, water, food, and clothes. Consumers obtain some level of satisfaction from their consumption. The overall satisfaction is measured by the concept of utility. A utility function represents an individual's preference ordering over a set of alternatives. More specifically, we consider a utility function of the form:

$$U(\mathbf{x}) \tag{1.1}$$

where $U : \mathbb{R}^n \to \mathbb{R}$.

When a consumer changes the quantities of each good, his/her satisfaction level and, hence, utility would change as well. Particularly, when the quantity of one specific good i changes with the quantities of other goods held constant, we measure the marginal utility, $MU_i(\mathbf{x})$, with respect to x_i:

$$MU_i(\mathbf{x}) = \frac{\partial U(\mathbf{x})}{\partial x_i} \tag{1.2}$$

$MU_i(\mathbf{x}) \geq 0$ may be assumed since a *ceteris paribus* increase in the consumption of one good would usually bring additional satisfaction or, at least, maintain the same level of satisfaction.

Utility functions can take a variety of functional forms. One typical example is a Cobb–Douglas utility function of the form:

$$U(\mathbf{x}) = \prod_{j=1}^{n} x_j^{s_j} = x_1^{s_1} x_2^{s_2} x_3^{s_3} \cdots x_n^{s_n} \tag{1.3}$$

where $0 < s_j < 1$ and $\sum_{j=1}^{n} s_j = 1$. For a Cobb–Douglas utility function, the marginal utility with respect to x_i is derived as follows:

$$MU_i(\mathbf{x}) = \frac{s_i \prod_{j=1}^{n} x_j^{s_j}}{x_i} \tag{1.4a}$$

$$= \frac{s_i U(\mathbf{x})}{x_i} \tag{1.4b}$$

Illustrative Example 1.1 *Cobb–Douglas utility function.*

We here consider a numerical example of a Cobb–Douglas utility function for two goods, $i = 1, 2$, with $s_1 = \frac{2}{5}$ and $s_2 = \frac{3}{5}$:

$$U(x_1, x_2) = x_1^{\frac{2}{5}} x_2^{\frac{3}{5}} \tag{1.5}$$

The two goods can be, for example, electricity and gas. Figure 1.1 illustrates the utility level over a set of alternatives for (x_1, x_2). Overall, if the quantities of both goods increase, then the consumer's utility also increases, which would be understandable.

As an illustration, Fig. 1.2 depicts the level of utility with respect to x_1 while fixing the quantity of good 2 at $x_2 = 10$. Specifically, Fig. 1.2 shows a function, $U(x_1, 10) = x_1^{\frac{2}{5}} 10^{\frac{3}{5}}$. When the customer can consume more quantity of good 1, e.g., electricity, he/she would get more satisfaction using appliances such as air conditioners.

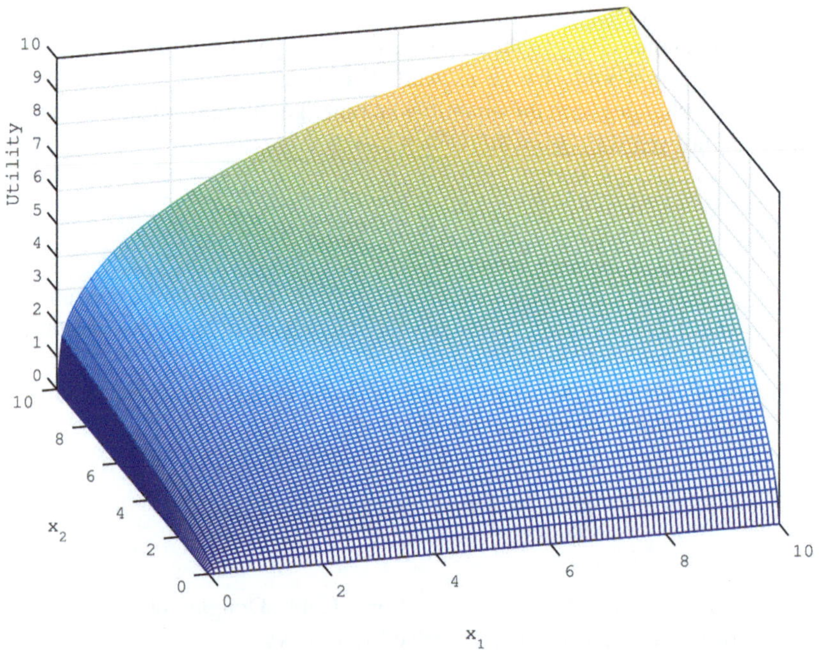

Fig. 1.1 Cobb–Douglas utility function for two goods

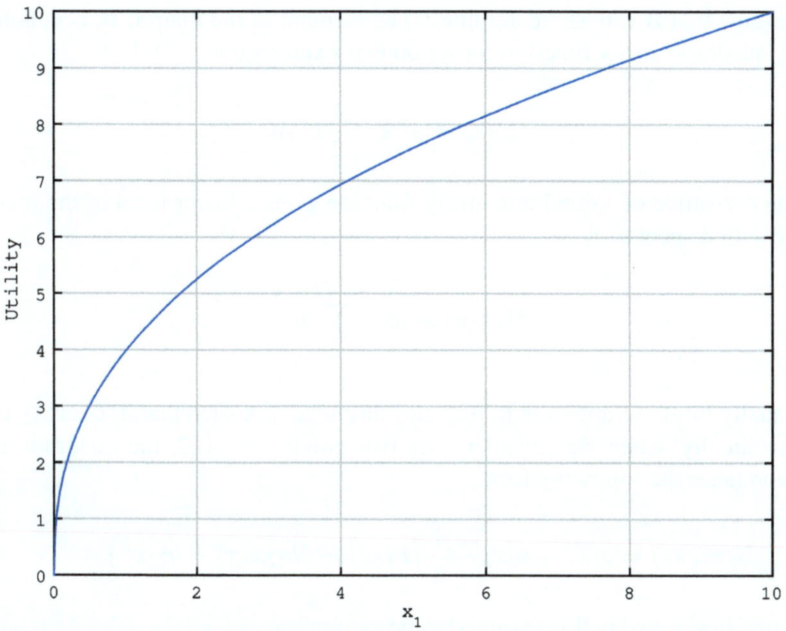

Fig. 1.2 Quantity consumed and utility

Furthermore, the marginal utility for good 1, with x_2 held constant, can be derived as follows:

$$MU_1(x_1, x_2) = \frac{2}{5} x_1^{\frac{2}{5}-1} x_2^{\frac{3}{5}} \tag{1.6a}$$

$$= \frac{2}{5} \frac{x_1^{\frac{2}{5}} x_2^{\frac{3}{5}}}{x_1} \tag{1.6b}$$

$$= \frac{2}{5} \frac{U(x_1, x_2)}{x_1} \tag{1.6c}$$

With x_2 fixed at $x_2 = 10$, the marginal utility, $MU_1(x_1, 10) = \frac{2}{5}\frac{U(x_1,10)}{x_1}$, corresponds to the gradient of $U(x_1, 10)$ in Fig. 1.2.

1.2.2 Quadratic Utility Function

Another popular functional form for utility is a quadratic utility function. Let **a** and **B** denote a strictly positive $n \times 1$ vector and a symmetric $n \times n$ matrix, respectively.

We assume that **B** is positive definite.[1] The element of the matrix, **B**, is denoted by b_{ij}. A quadratic utility function for n goods is expressed as:

$$U(\mathbf{x}) = \mathbf{a}^\top \mathbf{x} - \frac{1}{2}\mathbf{x}^\top \mathbf{B}\mathbf{x} \tag{1.7}$$

The derivative of a quadratic utility function gives a linear form of the marginal utility with respect to x_i:

$$MU_i(\mathbf{x}) = a_i - \sum_{j=1}^{n} b_{ij} x_j \tag{1.8}$$

We usually limit our attention to the relevant range of $\mathbf{x}$ such that $MU_i(\mathbf{x}) \geq 0$.

Specifically, when we consider only two goods $i = 1, 2$, the quadratic utility function takes the following form:

$$U(x_1, x_2) = a_1 x_1 + a_2 x_2 - \frac{1}{2}\left(b_{11}x_1^2 + 2b_{12}x_1x_2 + b_{22}x_2^2\right) \tag{1.9}$$

Note that $b_{12} = b_{21}$ as **B** is assumed to be symmetric.

Then, the linear form of the marginal utilities with respect to x_1 and x_2 are, respectively, derived as follows:

$$MU_1(x_1, x_2) = a_1 - b_{11}x_1 - b_{12}x_2 \tag{1.10a}$$

$$MU_2(x_1, x_2) = a_2 - b_{12}x_1 - b_{22}x_2 \tag{1.10b}$$

Illustrative Example 1.2 *Quadratic utility function.*

We consider a simple numerical example of a quadratic utility function for two goods, $i = 1, 2$, such as electricity and gas. Assume that $a_1 = a_2 = 20$, $b_{11} = b_{22} = 1$, and $b_{12} = b_{21} = \frac{1}{2}$. Then, the quadratic utility function is represented as:

$$U(x_1, x_2) = 20(x_1 + x_2) - \frac{1}{2}\left(x_1^2 + x_1x_2 + x_2^2\right) \tag{1.11}$$

We then obtain the linear marginal utilities with respect to x_1 and x_2, respectively:

$$MU_1(x_1, x_2) = 20 - x_1 - \frac{1}{2}x_2 \tag{1.12a}$$

$$MU_2(x_1, x_2) = 20 - \frac{1}{2}x_1 - x_2 \tag{1.12b}$$

---

[1] A symmetric $n \times n$ matrix, **B**, is called positive definite if $\mathbf{x}^\top \mathbf{B}\mathbf{x} > 0$ for all $\mathbf{x} \neq \mathbf{0}$.

1.3 Demand for Goods

Consumers of electricity respond to changes in prices by altering the quantities demanded. This decision is characterized by the demand function, which is a function of prices. Generally, demand functions are derived from utility maximization of consumers under their budget constraints. Our focus is to derive linear demand functions, which are often used for the analysis of power markets.

1.3.1 Utility Maximization and Demand Function

We investigate consumer behavior to know the most preferred bundle of goods, chosen from the set of alternatives. Specifically, we examine the quantities of goods, $\mathbf{x}$, that a consumer chooses for consumption, facing the market prices of those goods. Each consumer needs to make a decision under his/her own budget constraint. Let $\mathbf{p}$ and m be a non-negative $n \times 1$ vector of prices and a fixed amount of strictly positive budget (e.g., income) that can be allocated to goods, respectively. With the prevailing prices, the consumer chooses the quantities of n goods, $\mathbf{x}$, to maximize utility from consuming those goods under his/her budget constraint:

$$\underset{\mathbf{x}\geq\mathbf{0}}{\text{Maximize}}\ U(\mathbf{x}) \tag{1.13a}$$

$$\text{s.t. } \mathbf{p}^\top \mathbf{x} = m \ : \ \lambda \tag{1.13b}$$

We here treat the budget constraint (1.13b) as an equality with the Lagrange multiplier, λ. This can also be expressed as an inequality, $\mathbf{p}^\top \mathbf{x} \leq m$.

Setting the Lagrangian, $L = U(\mathbf{x}) + \lambda\left(m - \mathbf{p}^\top \mathbf{x}\right)$, and assuming interior solutions (i.e., non-zero consumption) for $\mathbf{x}$, the first-order condition for good i is obtained as:

$$MU_i(\mathbf{x}) = \lambda p_i \tag{1.14}$$

The first-order conditions for the utility-maximization problem (1.13) imply that the consumer chooses the quantities of goods by balancing his/her marginal utility and the market price adjusted by λ.

To better understand the implication of consumer behavior, we can rearrange the first-order conditions for any two goods i and j:

$$\frac{MU_i(\mathbf{x})}{p_i} = \frac{MU_j(\mathbf{x})}{p_j} = \lambda, \quad \forall i, j \tag{1.15}$$

This condition states that the consumer decides the quantities of goods such that the marginal utilities per money unit (e.g., dollar) spent are equalized among all goods.

For example, the marginal utility per dollar for electricity should be equal to that for gas at the optimum.

Similarly, (1.15) can be rewritten as:

$$\frac{MU_i(\mathbf{x})}{MU_j(\mathbf{x})} = \frac{p_i}{p_j}, \quad \forall i, j \tag{1.16}$$

This indicates that the ratio of the marginal utilities for any two goods is equal to the ratio of the corresponding prices at the optimum.

The solutions for the utility-maximization problem (1.13) yield the optimal levels of the quantities for goods, i.e., the vector-valued demand functions, $\mathbf{x} = X(\mathbf{p})$, where $X : \mathbb{R}^n \to \mathbb{R}^n$. The demand function for good i is written as:

$$x_i = X_i(\mathbf{p}) \tag{1.17}$$

The quantity for one good demanded by the consumer generally depends on not only its own price but also the prices of all other goods.

If the quantity demanded decreases as its own price increases, i.e., $\frac{\partial x_i}{\partial p_i} < 0$, then the "law of demand" holds in the classical sense. A monotonically decreasing demand function implies an inverse relationship between the price and the quantity demanded. For typical commodities such as food and gasoline, consumers tend to reduce their consumption if prices rise. Likewise, customers in power markets would decrease their usage of electricity during peak periods with high prices.

Furthermore, when the vector-valued demand functions have their inverses, i.e., $\mathbf{p} = P(\mathbf{x})$, where $P : \mathbb{R}^n \to \mathbb{R}^n$, then the inverse-demand function for good i can be expressed as follows:

$$p_i = P_i(\mathbf{x}) \tag{1.18}$$

1.3.2 Linear Demand Function

In this subsection, we derive linear demand functions, which are often used for the analysis of power markets. Such demand functions are linear (or affine) in prices. Here, we consider n goods with the quantities of $\mathbf{x}$ and a numeraire good with the quantity of x_0. A numeraire good can be regarded as a composite commodity that consists of all other goods outside the markets under consideration. The price of a numeraire good is normalized to $p_0 = 1$. It is often convenient to introduce a composite commodity since we can then concentrate on the analysis of the goods of our interest, e.g., electricity.

Specifically, we are interested in the maximization of a quadratic utility function of the form:

$$U(x_0, \mathbf{x}) = \mathbf{a}^\top \mathbf{x} - \frac{1}{2}\mathbf{x}^\top \mathbf{B}\mathbf{x} + x_0 \tag{1.19}$$

where **a** and **B** are a strictly positive vector and an $n \times n$ positive definite matrix, respectively, as in (1.7). It is worth noting that the utility function (1.19) has the form of $U(x_0, \mathbf{x}) = V(\mathbf{x}) + x_0$, which is sometimes called a quasilinear utility function in the sense that it is linear in the quantity of one good, i.e., a numeraire good, x_0, although $V(\mathbf{x})$ may be non-linear.

The utility-maximization problem of a consumer under the budget constraint, including a numeraire good, is represented as:

$$\underset{x_0, \mathbf{x} \geq \mathbf{0}}{\text{Maximize}}\ \mathbf{a}^\top \mathbf{x} - \frac{1}{2}\mathbf{x}^\top \mathbf{B}\mathbf{x} + x_0 \tag{1.20a}$$

$$\text{s.t. } \mathbf{p}^\top \mathbf{x} + x_0 = m \tag{1.20b}$$

With $x_0 = m - \mathbf{p}^\top \mathbf{x}$, we can then turn the problem (1.20) into an unconstrained maximization problem:

$$\underset{\mathbf{x} \geq \mathbf{0}}{\text{Maximize}}\ \mathbf{a}^\top \mathbf{x} - \frac{1}{2}\mathbf{x}^\top \mathbf{B}\mathbf{x} + m - \mathbf{p}^\top \mathbf{x} \tag{1.21}$$

Assuming interior solutions for **x**, the first-order conditions for the maximization problem (1.21) form a system of equations, $\mathbf{a} - \mathbf{B}\mathbf{x} - \mathbf{p} = \mathbf{0}$. It is straightforward to first derive the linear inverse-demand functions, which are linear (or affine) in quantities:

$$\mathbf{p} = \mathbf{a} - \mathbf{B}\mathbf{x} \tag{1.22}$$

The linear inverse-demand function for good i is expressed as follows:

$$p_i = P_i(\mathbf{x}) = a_i - \sum_{j=1}^{n} b_{ij} x_j \tag{1.23}$$

Next, we can represent the linear demand functions, which are linear (or affine) in prices, using the inverse matrix, $\mathbf{B}^{-1}$:

$$\mathbf{B}\mathbf{x} = \mathbf{a} - \mathbf{p} \tag{1.24a}$$

$$\mathbf{x} = \mathbf{B}^{-1}\mathbf{a} - \mathbf{B}^{-1}\mathbf{p} \tag{1.24b}$$

Let $\hat{b}_{ij}$ and $\hat{a}_i$ denote the elements of the matrix, $\mathbf{B}^{-1}$, and the vector, $\mathbf{B}^{-1}\mathbf{a}$, respectively. Then, the linear demand function for good i is written as follows:

$$x_i = X_i(\mathbf{p}) = \hat{a}_i - \sum_{j=1}^{n} \hat{b}_{ij} p_j \tag{1.25}$$

The derivative of x_i with respect to its own price, p_i gives:

$$\frac{\partial x_i}{\partial p_i} = -\hat{b}_{ii} < 0 \tag{1.26}$$

Since $\mathbf{B}$ is assumed to be positive definite, its inverse, $\mathbf{B}^{-1}$, is also positive definite. Hence, the diagonal elements of $\mathbf{B}^{-1}$ are strictly positive, i.e., $\hat{b}_{ii} > 0$. This indicates that the linear demand function (1.25) is monotonically decreasing in its own price, which implies the classical "law of demand."

Let us focus on one good such as electricity with the quantity of x_1, along with a numeraire good, consisting of all other goods, with the quantity of x_0. Assume a quadratic utility function, $U(x_0, x_1) = a_1x_1 - \frac{1}{2}b_1x_1^2 + x_0$, with strictly positive parameters, $a_1, b_1 > 0$. Again, this utility function has the form of $U(x_0, x_1) = V(x_1) + x_0$, which can be seen as a quasilinear utility function in that it is linear in x_0. Then, the utility-maximization problem of a consumer is described as:

$$\underset{x_0, x_1 \geq 0}{\text{Maximize}}\ a_1x_1 - \frac{1}{2}b_1x_1^2 + x_0 \tag{1.27a}$$

$$\text{s.t. } p_1x_1 + x_0 = m \tag{1.27b}$$

This problem is converted into an unconstrained maximization problem:

$$\underset{x_1 \geq 0}{\text{Maximize}}\ a_1x_1 - \frac{1}{2}b_1x_1^2 + m - p_1x_1 \tag{1.28}$$

Deriving an interior solution yields the linear inverse-demand function and the linear demand function, respectively:

$$p_1 = P_1(x_1) = a_1 - b_1x_1 \tag{1.29a}$$

$$x_1 = X_1(p_1) = \frac{a_1}{b_1} - \frac{1}{b_1}p_1 \tag{1.29b}$$

It is straightforward to observe an inverse relationship between the quantity and the price:

$$\frac{dx_1}{dp_1} = -\frac{1}{b_1} < 0 \tag{1.30}$$

Illustrative Example 1.3 *Linear demand for two goods with a numeraire.*

We show a numerical example of linear demand functions for two goods $i = 1, 2$, using the same parameters as in Illustrative Example 1.2. The utility-maximization problem with a numeraire good is formulated as:

$$\underset{x_0, x_1, x_2 \geq 0}{\text{Maximize}}\ 20(x_1 + x_2) - \frac{1}{2}\left(x_1^2 + x_1 x_2 + x_2^2\right) + x_0 \tag{1.31a}$$

$$\text{s.t. } p_1 x_1 + p_2 x_2 + x_0 = m \tag{1.31b}$$

Substituting $x_0 = m - p_1 x_1 - p_2 x_2$ into the objective function, interior solutions give the following linear inverse-demand functions for the two goods:

$$p_1 = P_1(x_1, x_2) = 20 - x_1 - \frac{1}{2} x_2 \tag{1.32a}$$

$$p_2 = P_2(x_1, x_2) = 20 - \frac{1}{2} x_1 - x_2 \tag{1.32b}$$

Correspondingly, the linear demand functions are derived as follows:

$$x_1 = X_1(p_1, p_2) = \frac{2}{3}(20 - 2p_1 + p_2) \tag{1.33a}$$

$$x_2 = X_2(p_1, p_2) = \frac{2}{3}(20 + p_1 - 2p_2) \tag{1.33b}$$

These linear demand functions are monotonically decreasing in their own prices:

$$\frac{\partial x_1}{\partial p_1} = \frac{\partial x_2}{\partial p_2} = -\frac{4}{3} < 0 \tag{1.34}$$

Illustrative Example 1.4 *Linear demand for one good with a numeraire.*

We further restrict our attention to one good, using the parameters, $a_1 = 20$ and $b_1 = 1$. The utility-maximization problem with a numeraire good is described as:

$$\underset{x_0, x_1 \geq 0}{\text{Maximize}}\ 20x_1 - \frac{1}{2} x_1^2 + x_0 \tag{1.35a}$$

$$\text{s.t. } p_1 x_1 + x_0 = m \tag{1.35b}$$

An interior solution yields the linear inverse-demand function and the linear demand function for one good, respectively:

$$p_1 = P_1(x_1) = 20 - x_1 \tag{1.36a}$$

$$x_1 = X_1(p_1) = 20 - p_1 \tag{1.36b}$$

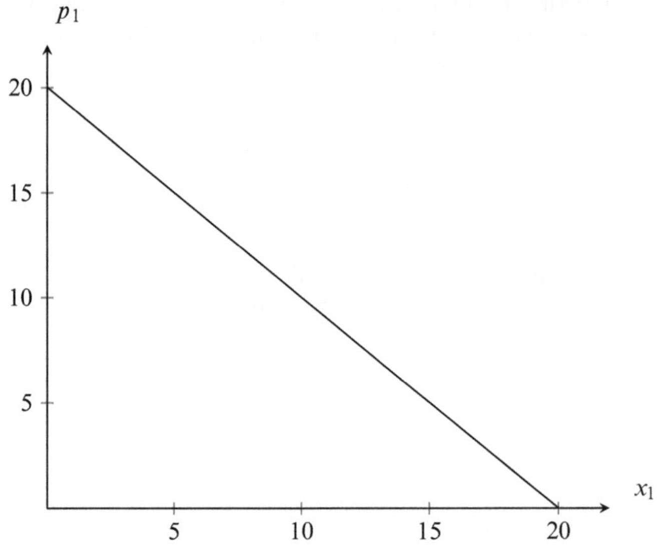

Fig. 1.3 Linear demand

Those functions are illustrated as a downward-sloping curve in Fig. 1.3, which is sometimes called a demand curve. Again, the linear demand function is monotonically decreasing in its own price:

$$\frac{dx_1}{dp_1} = -1 < 0 \tag{1.37}$$

1.3.3 Substitutes and Complements

As is seen in the demand function, $x_i = X_i(\mathbf{p})$, the quantity demanded for one good depends on not only its own price but also the prices of all other goods. Two goods are called substitutes if a rise in the price of one good leads to an increase in the purchase of another good, i.e., $\frac{\partial x_i}{\partial p_j} > 0$. For example, coffee and tea may be substitutes. If the price of coffee rises, then consumers may turn to consuming more tea because of the advantageous price of tea in a relative sense. In contrast, the goods are called complements if a rise in the price of one good leads to a decrease in the purchase of another good, i.e., $\frac{\partial x_i}{\partial p_j} < 0$. For instance, coffee and cream may be complements. When the price of coffee increases, people will consume less coffee along with cream.

Illustrative Example 1.5 *Substitutes.*

Consider the linear demand functions (1.33) for two goods with a numeraire in Illustrative Example 1.3. These demand functions exhibit the characteristics of substitutes:

$$\frac{\partial x_1}{\partial p_2} = \frac{\partial x_2}{\partial p_1} = \frac{2}{3} > 0 \tag{1.38}$$

Thus, an increase in the price of one good results in more consumption of another good.

Illustrative Example 1.6 *Complements.*

Next, we consider another example of linear demand functions for two goods with a numeraire, by slightly modifying the parameters of the utility function in (1.31). Assume that the quadratic utility function for two goods has the parameters of $a_1 = a_2 = 20$, $b_{11} = b_{22} = 1$, and $b_{12} = b_{21} = -\frac{1}{2}$. We then solve the maximization problem with the quadratic utility function, $U(x_0, x_1, x_2) = 20(x_1 + x_2) - \frac{1}{2}\left(x_1^2 - x_1x_2 + x_2^2\right) + x_0$, under the budget constraint as in (1.31). Simple calculation yields the linear inverse-demand functions:

$$p_1 = P_1(x_1, x_2) = 20 - x_1 + \frac{1}{2}x_2 \tag{1.39a}$$

$$p_2 = P_2(x_1, x_2) = 20 + \frac{1}{2}x_1 - x_2 \tag{1.39b}$$

The linear demand functions are also obtained as follows:

$$x_1 = X_1(p_1, p_2) = \frac{2}{3}(60 - 2p_1 - p_2) \tag{1.40a}$$

$$x_2 = X_2(p_1, p_2) = \frac{2}{3}(60 - p_1 - 2p_2) \tag{1.40b}$$

Now, the demand functions show the characteristics of complements:

$$\frac{\partial x_1}{\partial p_2} = \frac{\partial x_2}{\partial p_1} = -\frac{2}{3} < 0 \tag{1.41}$$

A rise in the price of one good leads to less consumption of another good.

1.4 Elasticity

If the electricity price were to increase in some periods, then customers would reduce power consumption by adjusting the usage of their electric equipment. For the analysis of power markets, it is useful to know the degree of the consumer response to price changes. This section introduces the concept of the price elasticity of demand to measure such response by consumers. We elaborate on the price elasticity for linear demand.

1.4.1 Price Elasticity of Demand

In the previous section, we have discussed that the market prices affect the consumer decision about the quantities demanded. Then, we are interested in the degree of the consumer response to changes in prices. To measure the responsiveness, the concept of elasticity is useful and often used. The price elasticity of demand, e_{ii}, is defined as:

$$e_{ii} = \frac{\partial x_i}{\partial p_i}\frac{p_i}{x_i} \tag{1.42}$$

The price elasticity of demand measures the percentage (proportionate) change in the quantity demanded in response to the percentage change in the price of a good, i.e., $\frac{\Delta x_i/x_i}{\Delta p_i/p_i} = \frac{\Delta x_i}{\Delta p_i}\frac{p_i}{x_i}$. In short, the elasticity shows the responsiveness of consumers reacting to price changes. If the demand function is monotonically decreasing in its own price, i.e., $\frac{\partial x_i}{\partial p_i} < 0$, then the price elasticity of demand is negative (non-positive), i.e., $e_{ii} \leq 0$, with non-negative prices and quantities.[2]

If a 1% rise in price leads to a fall of more than 1% in quantity demanded, then we state that demand is "elastic."

$$|e_{ii}| > 1 \text{ or } e_{ii} < -1 \tag{1.43}$$

By contrast, if a 1% rise in price causes a fall of less than 1% in quantity demanded, then we say that demand is "inelastic."

$$|e_{ii}| < 1 \text{ or } e_{ii} > -1 \tag{1.44}$$

Empirically, existing studies suggest that the price elasticities of the residential demand for electricity in the U.S. range from −0.1 to −0.4 [1, 14]. This implies that a 1% increase in the price results in decreases in the quantities demanded by 0.1% to 0.4%. According to such empirical works, the price elasticity of the residential demand is considered as inelastic. Households would be moderately responsive to changes in price.

[2] When $\frac{\partial x_i}{\partial p_i} < 0$ and $p_i > 0$, then strict inequality holds, i.e., $e_{ii} < 0$.

On the other hand, the cross-price elasticity of demand, e_{ij}, is defined as

$$e_{ij} = \frac{\partial x_i}{\partial p_j} \frac{p_j}{x_i} \tag{1.45}$$

This measures the percentage (proportionate) change in the quantity demanded in response to the percentage change in the price of another good. If two goods are substitutes, i.e., $\frac{\partial x_i}{\partial p_j} > 0$, then $e_{ij} \geq 0$. By contrast, if the goods are complements, i.e., $\frac{\partial x_i}{\partial p_j} < 0$, then $e_{ij} \leq 0$.[3]

1.4.2 Elasticity for Linear Demand

In this subsection, we focus on linear demand functions, particularly for one good with the quantity, x_1, with a numeraire to elaborate more on the (own-) price elasticity of demand. First, recall the linear inverse-demand function, $p_1 = a_1 - b_1 x_1$, in (1.29a), or the linear demand function, $x_1 = \frac{a_1}{b_1} - \frac{1}{b_1} p_1$, in (1.29b), with strictly positive parameters, $a_1, b_1 > 0$. Figure 1.4 shows the linear demand curve with the vertical intercept of a_1 and the horizontal intercept of $\frac{a_1}{b_1}$. The price elasticity of demand is obtained as:

$$e_{11} = -\frac{1}{b_1} \frac{p_1}{x_1} \leq 0 \tag{1.46}$$

The absolute values for the price elasticity of linear demand are classified as follows:

$$|e_{11}| = 1, \ \text{ if } x_1 = \frac{a_1}{2b_1} \tag{1.47a}$$

$$|e_{11}| > 1, \ \text{ if } 0 \leq x_1 < \frac{a_1}{2b_1} \tag{1.47b}$$

$$|e_{11}| < 1, \ \text{ if } \frac{a_1}{2b_1} < x_1 \leq \frac{a_1}{b_1} \tag{1.47c}$$

Simple calculation gives $|e_{11}| = 1$ at the midpoint, $x_1 = \frac{a_1}{2b_1}$, of the demand curve in Fig. 1.4. If the quantity demanded is less than the midpoint, $x_1 = \frac{a_1}{2b_1}$, then it is elastic, i.e., $|e_{11}| > 1$. By contrast, if the quantity demanded is greater than the midpoint, $x_1 = \frac{a_1}{2b_1}$, then it becomes inelastic, i.e., $|e_{11}| < 1$.[4]

[3] In both cases, strict inequalities hold when $p_j > 0$.

[4] At the horizontal endpoint of the demand curve, i.e., $x_1 = \frac{a_1}{b_1}$, the price, p_1, becomes 0. This yields $|e_{11}| = 0$, which is called a perfectly inelastic case. In contrast, the quantity demanded

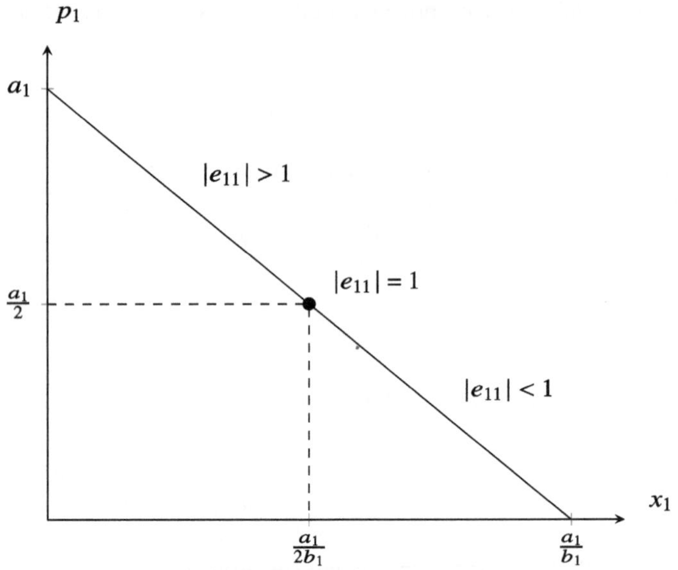

Fig. 1.4 Elasticity for linear demand

Illustrative Example 1.7 *Elasticity for linear demand.*

Recall the linear demand for one good with a numeraire in Illustrative Example 1.4. The linear inverse-demand function is $p_1 = 20 - x_1$ as in (1.36a), or the linear demand function is $x_1 = 20 - p_1$ as in (1.36b). The price elasticity of demand is derived as:

$$e_{11} = -\frac{p_1}{x_1} \leq 0 \tag{1.48}$$

To illustrate the results in (1.47), we calculate the absolute values for the price elasticity of demand at $x_1 = 5$, 10, and 15 as follows:

$$|e_{11}| = 1, \quad \text{if } x_1 = 10 \tag{1.49a}$$

$$|e_{11}| = \frac{15}{5} = 3 > 1, \quad \text{if } x_1 = 5 \tag{1.49b}$$

$$|e_{11}| = \frac{5}{15} = \frac{1}{3} < 1, \quad \text{if } x_1 = 15 \tag{1.49c}$$

Those results are also depicted in Fig. 1.5.

becomes 0 at the vertical endpoint of the demand curve. Then, $|e_{11}|$ becomes ∞, which is called a perfectly elastic case.

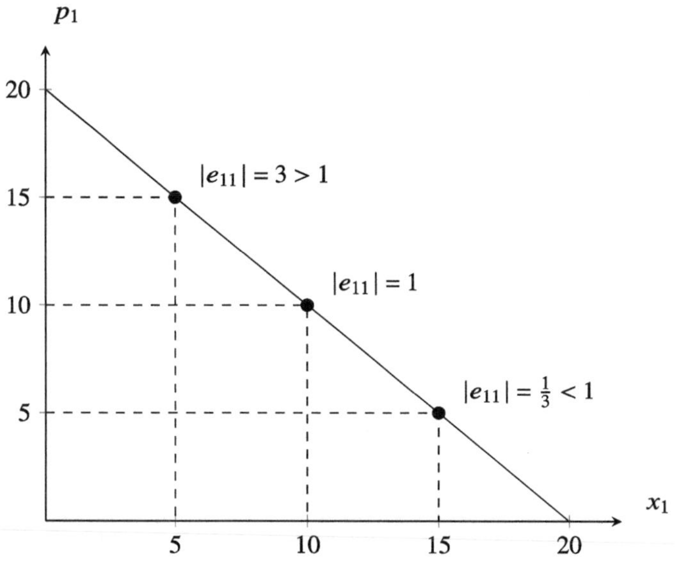

Fig. 1.5 Example of elasticity for linear demand

1.4.3 Various Cases of Elasticity

Demand for some goods and services (e.g., emergency services) may be very inelastic. The price elasticity of demand may be close to zero. At the extreme, we define perfectly inelastic demand with $e_{11} = 0$. Figure 1.6 illustrates a vertical demand curve of $x_1 = 10$, which shows an example of perfectly inelastic demand. The quantity demanded remains unchanged at $x_1 = 10$ regardless of the price level.

At the other extreme, we can define perfectly elastic demand with $e_{11} = -\infty$ or $|e_{11}| = \infty$ in absolute value. Figure 1.7 depicts a horizontal demand curve of $p_1 = 10$, which shows an instance of perfectly elastic demand. When the price rises above $p_1 = 10$, the quantity demanded drops off to zero.

On the other hand, we can consider a downward-sloping demand curve with a constant price elasticity of demand. A demand function of the form, $x_1 = d_1 p_1^{c_1}$, with $d_1 > 0$ and $c_1 \leq 0$, has a constant elasticity of c_1 at any point on the demand curve. Noting that $\frac{dx_1}{dp_1} = c_1 d_1 p_1^{c_1 - 1}$, the price elasticity of demand for this functional form is derived as follows:

$$e_{11} = c_1 d_1 p_1^{c_1 - 1} \frac{p_1}{d_1 p_1^{c_1}} \tag{1.50a}$$

$$= c_1 \tag{1.50b}$$

Figure 1.8 illustrates a demand function of the form, $x_1 = 20 p_1^{-1}$. This demand function has a constant elasticity, $e_{11} = c_1 = -1$ or $|e_{11}| = 1$ in absolute value.

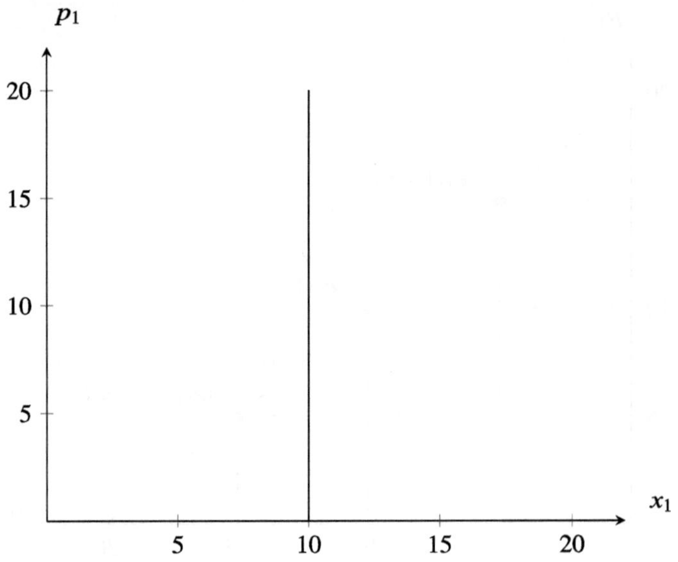

Fig. 1.6 Perfectly inelastic demand

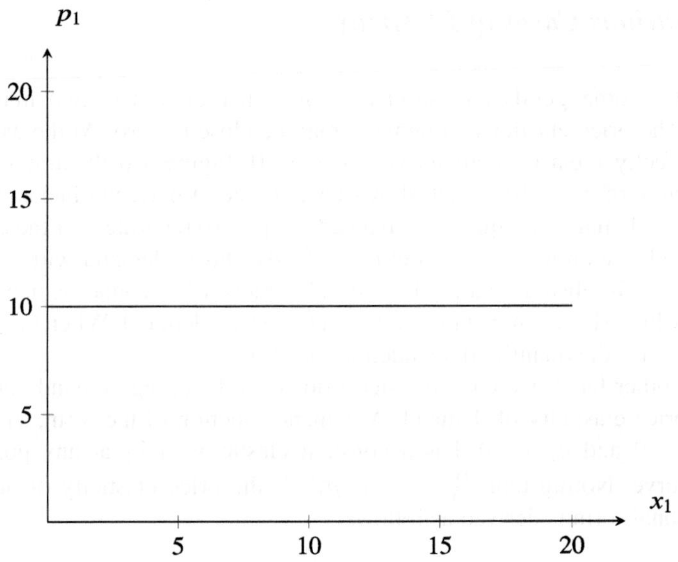

Fig. 1.7 Perfectly elastic demand

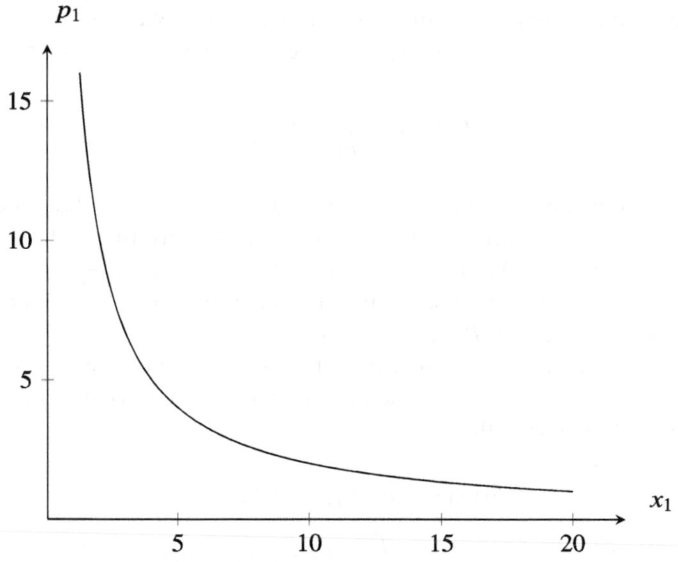

Fig. 1.8 Demand with constant elasticity

Note also that when $c_1 = 0$ in $x_1 = d_1 p_1^{c_1}$, this describes the case of perfectly inelastic demand. Indeed, the demand curve boils down to $x_1 = d_1$.

1.5 Consumer Surplus

It is useful to evaluate the monetary value of power consumption. Based on demand functions, we discuss the general concepts of welfare that measure the monetary value of consumption. Particularly, consumer surplus measures the net gain from consuming the good after the payment. We also examine the relationship between utility maximization and surplus maximization.

1.5.1 Gross Benefit and Consumer Surplus

In what follows in Sects. 1.5–1.8, we limit our attention to one good with the quantity, x_1, such as electricity with a numeraire good for the sake of brevity. However, the discussion can be extended to more goods.

The inverse-demand function, $p_1 = P_1(x_1)$, can be interpreted as the amount the consumer is willing to pay for an additional unit of the good. Hence, $P_1(x_1)$ can be regarded as the marginal willingness-to-pay (WTP) or the marginal benefit for this customer to consume the additional unit of the good. We can derive the gross or total benefit of the consumer, $B_1(x_1)$, by integrating the inverse-demand function:

$$B_1(x_1) = \int_0^{x_1} P_1(x_1')dx_1' \tag{1.51}$$

The gross benefit indicates the monetary value of consuming the good up to x_1 without considering the expense. By construction, the derivative of the gross benefit function is the marginal WTP or the marginal benefit, i.e., $\frac{dB_1(x_1)}{dx_1} = P_1(x_1)$. In Fig. 1.9, the area of a trapezoid below the demand curve up to the quantity, $x_1 = 12$, illustrates the gross benefit, $B_1(x_1) = B_1(12)$.

On the other hand, the consumer pays for the good to obtain the gross benefit. Consumer surplus, $CS_1(x_1)$, is defined by subtracting the payment, p_1x_1, from the gross benefit, $B_1(x_1)$, as follows:

$$CS_1(x_1) = B_1(x_1) - p_1x_1 \tag{1.52a}$$

$$= \int_0^{x_1} P_1(x_1')dx_1' - p_1x_1 \tag{1.52b}$$

Consumer surplus measures the monetary value of the net gain from consuming the good up to x_1 after the payment. In Fig. 1.9, consumer surplus is illustrated as the shaded area of the triangle between the demand curve and the horizontal line of the market price, $p_1 = 8$. This customer obtains an economic surplus, i.e., consumer

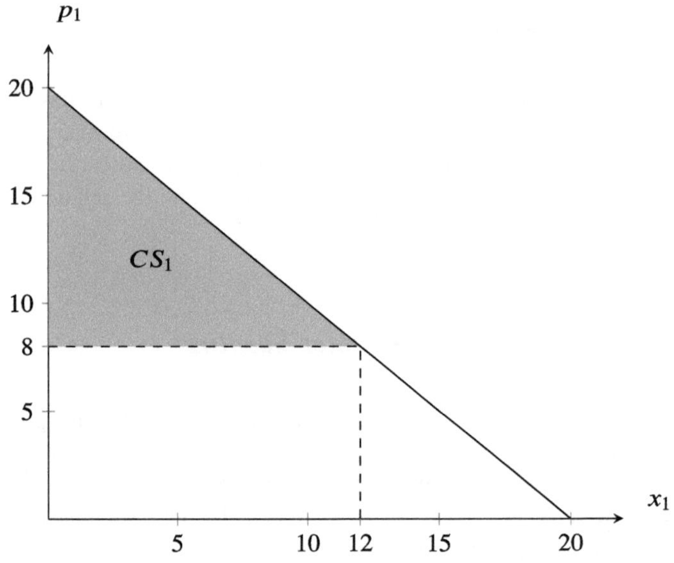

Fig. 1.9 Consumer surplus

surplus, $CS_1(x_1) = CS_1(12)$, after paying for its consumption, $x_1 = 12$, at the unit price of $p_1 = 8$. Consumer surplus can be also derived by integrating the demand function, $X_1(p_1)$, from p_1 to ∞, i.e., $\int_{p_1}^{\infty} X_1(p_1')dp_1'$.

Illustrative Example 1.8 *Consumer surplus.*

Recall again the linear inverse-demand function, $p_1 = 20 - x_1$, in (1.36a), which is considered in Illustrative Example 1.4. Consumer surplus for this customer is expressed as:

$$CS_1(x_1) = \int_0^{x_1} (20 - x_1')dx_1' - p_1 x_1 \tag{1.53a}$$

$$= 20x_1 - \frac{1}{2}x_1^2 - p_1 x_1 \tag{1.53b}$$

When the customer consumes $x_1 = 12$ at the unit price of $p_1 = 8$, consumer surplus is obtained as $CS_1(12) = 72$. This is illustrated as the shaded area of the triangle in Fig. 1.9. Suppose that the price rises to $p_1 = 10$, leading to a reduction of consumption to $x_1 = 10$. Then, consumer surplus decreases to $CS_1(10) = 50$. Obviously, less consumption with a higher price implies smaller consumer surplus for the customer.

1.5.2 Maximizing Consumer Surplus

With the concept of consumer surplus, we revisit the meaning of utility maximization. Specifically, we relate utility maximization to surplus maximization of a consumer, focusing on a quasilinear utility function, $U(x_0, x_1) = V(x_1) + x_0$, as discussed in Sect. 1.3.2.

For $V(x_1)$, we here consider a quadratic function, $a_1 x_1 - \frac{1}{2}b_1 x_1^2$, in (1.27a) as an illustration. But, the discussion in this subsection is not limited to a quadratic function for $V(x_1)$. Recalling the inverse-demand function, $p_1 = P_1(x_1) = a_1 - b_1 x_1$, in (1.29a), we can rearrange the utility function, $U(x_0, x_1)$, as follows:

$$U(x_0, x_1) = a_1 x_1 - \frac{1}{2}b_1 x_1^2 + x_0 \tag{1.54a}$$

$$= \int_0^{x_1} (a_1 - b_1 x_1')dx_1' + x_0 \tag{1.54b}$$

$$= \int_0^{x_1} P_1(x_1')dx_1' + x_0 \tag{1.54c}$$

$$= B_1(x_1) + x_0 \tag{1.54d}$$

Then, the utility-maximization problem (1.27) can be represented by using the gross benefit function:

$$\underset{x_0, x_1 \geq 0}{\text{Maximize}}\ U(x_0, x_1) = B_1(x_1) + x_0 \tag{1.55a}$$

$$\text{s.t. } p_1 x_1 + x_0 = m \tag{1.55b}$$

This problem is converted to an unconstrained maximization problem:

$$\underset{x_1 \geq 0}{\text{Maximize}}\ B_1(x_1) + m - p_1 x_1 \tag{1.56}$$

Since $CS_1(x_1) = B_1(x_1) - p_1 x_1$ as in (1.52a), the problem can be further reformulated as the maximization of consumer surplus:

$$\underset{x_1 \geq 0}{\text{Maximize}}\ CS_1(x_1) + m \tag{1.57}$$

The constant budget, m, can be disregarded in the maximization problem (1.57). Therefore, the maximization of consumer surplus, $CS_1(x_1)$, is equivalent to the maximization of utility, $U(x_0, x_1) = V(x_1) + x_0$, under the budget constraint, $p_1 x_1 + x_0 = m$.[5] This fact is useful for applications as consumer behavior can be simply characterized by surplus maximization, i.e., $\text{Maximize}_{x_1 \geq 0}\ CS_1(x_1)$, based on the information of the inverse-demand function.

1.6 Demand Aggregation

The demand side of electricity markets consists of a number of consumers such as households, commercial buildings, and industrial facilities. This section discusses how to aggregate individual consumer demand into the overall market-demand function. Likewise, individual consumer surplus can be aggregated for all customers in the market. We then investigate the maximization problem of aggregate consumer surplus from the viewpoint of a social planner (e.g., a system operator).

[5] Strictly speaking, this simple and convenient relationship between surplus maximization of consumer and utility maximization holds for quasilinear utility but not for more general forms of utility. See, for example, [15]. However, quasilinear utility is widely used for a variety of applications of consumer theory.

1.6.1 Market Demand

We extend the analysis for one consumer to many consumers in the market. Let $k = 1, \ldots, \ell$ denote the index of customers who consume one good with the quantity, $x_{1,k}$, such as electricity with a numeraire. The quantity, $x_{1,k}$, demanded by each consumer can be added up to the total quantity, q_1. Similarly, the individual demand function, $x_{1,k} = X_{1,k}(p_1)$, can be also aggregated to the market-demand function, $Q_1(p_1)$:

$$q_1 = \sum_{k=1}^{\ell} x_{1,k} \tag{1.58a}$$

$$= \sum_{k=1}^{\ell} X_{1,k}(p_1) = Q_1(p_1) \tag{1.58b}$$

In this way, we can construct the market-demand function, $q_1 = Q_1(p_1)$, which reflects the aggregate demand of all consumers facing the same market price, p_1.

Moreover, if $Q_1(p_1)$ is monotonically decreasing, then the market-demand function yields an inverse-market-demand function:

$$p_1 = Q_1^{-1}(q_1) = P_1(q_1) \tag{1.59}$$

Illustrative Example 1.9 *Aggregate demand.*

As a simple illustration, Fig. 1.10 shows the aggregate demand consisting of three identical consumers, each of whom has an identical demand as shown in Fig. 1.3 (Illustrative Example 1.4) or in Fig. 1.9 (Illustrative Example 1.8). Each customer $k = 1, 2, 3$ consumes $x_{1,k} = 12$ at the market price of $p_1 = 8$. The individual quantity is summed up to the total quantity, $q_1 = \sum_{k=1}^{3} x_{1,k} = 36$. In the same vein, the individual demand curve is horizontally summed to construct the market-demand curve illustrated in the outer solid line in Fig. 1.10. Furthermore, individual consumer surplus is also aggregated in the shaded area of the triangle between the market-demand curve and the horizontal line of the market price, $p_1 = 8$.

More specifically, the market-demand function can be derived by aggregating the individually identical demand function, i.e., $\sum_{k=1}^{3} X_{1,k}(p_1) = \sum_{k=1}^{3}(20 - p_1)$:

$$q_1 = Q_1(p_1) = 60 - 3p_1 \tag{1.60}$$

Then, the inverse-market-demand function is obtained by calculating $Q_1^{-1}(q_1)$:

$$p_1 = P_1(q_1) = 20 - \frac{1}{3}q_1 \tag{1.61}$$

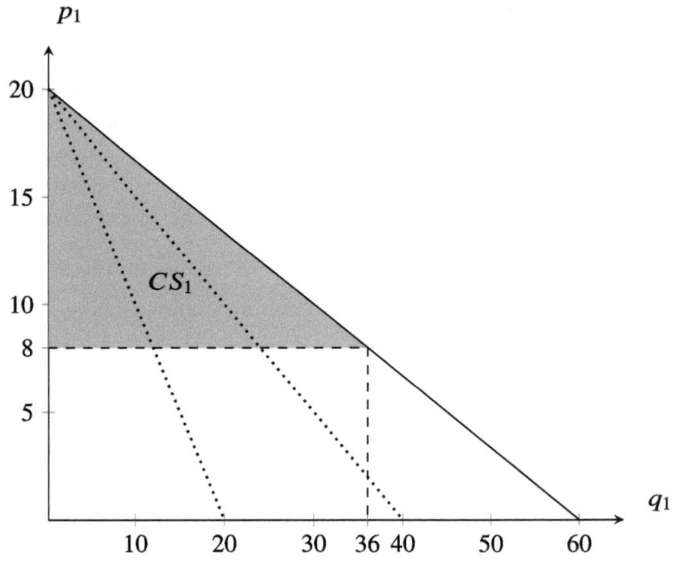

Fig. 1.10 Aggregate demand

1.6.2 Aggregation of Consumer Surplus

The individual gross benefit, $B_{1,k}(x_{1,k})$, can be also aggregated for all consumers in the market:

$$B_1(x_{1,1}, \ldots, x_{1,\ell}) = \sum_{k=1}^{\ell} B_{1,k}(x_{1,k}) \tag{1.62}$$

Then, aggregate consumer surplus is obtained by subtracting the payments of consumers from (1.62), or equivalently, by aggregating individual consumer surplus, $CS_1(x_{1,k})$:

$$CS_1(x_{1,1}, \ldots, x_{1,\ell}) = \sum_{k=1}^{\ell} B_{1,k}(x_{1,k}) - p_1 \sum_{k=1}^{\ell} x_{1,k} \tag{1.63a}$$

$$= \sum_{k=1}^{\ell} CS_{1,k}(x_{1,k}) \tag{1.63b}$$

In Sect. 1.5.2, we discussed the maximization of consumer surplus by individual customers. Since $CS_1(x_{1,1}, \ldots, x_{1,\ell})$ is an additively separable function, the individual maximization problem of consumer surplus (while disregarding the constant budget), i.e., Maximize$_{x_{1,k} \geq 0}$ $CS_{1,k}(x_{1,k})$, can be collected to form a maximization problem of aggregate consumer surplus in the market:

$$\underset{x_{1,1},\ldots,x_{1,\ell}\geq 0}{\text{Maximize}} \; CS_1(x_{1,1},\ldots,x_{1,\ell}) \tag{1.64}$$

Indeed, assuming interior solutions, the first-order conditions for (1.64) yield:

$$\frac{\partial CS_1(x_{1,1},\ldots,x_{1,\ell})}{\partial x_{1,k}} = \frac{dCS_{1,k}(x_{1,k})}{dx_{1,k}} = 0, \;\; \forall k \tag{1.65}$$

These conditions can be viewed as a collection of the individually optimal decision by each customer, who maximizes his/her consumer surplus, $CS_{1,k}(x_{1,k})$. The maximization problem (1.64) of aggregate consumer surplus may be regarded as representing the decision by a "social planner" (e.g., a system operator), which coincides with the decentralized decision making of individual consumers.[6]

Moreover, conditions (1.65) can be also expressed using the market price and the marginal benefit of each consumer:

$$p_1 = \frac{dB_{1,1}(x_{1,1})}{dx_{1,1}} = \cdots = \frac{dB_{1,\ell}(x_{1,\ell})}{dx_{1,\ell}} \tag{1.66a}$$

$$= P_{1,1}(x_{1,1}) = \cdots = P_{1,\ell}(x_{1,\ell}) \tag{1.66b}$$

These conditions imply that the marginal benefit or the marginal WTP of consuming the good is equated among all consumers through the market price. Figure 1.10 illustrates the case where the marginal benefit of three consumers are equalized at the market price of $p_1 = 8$.

So far, we have not considered the upper limit of the consumption. However, electric equipment and appliances have their own power rating limits. Thus, the upper limit of consumption, $x_{1,k}^{\max}$, for consumer k may be considered in the maximization problem of aggregate consumer surplus:

$$\underset{x_{1,1},\ldots,x_{1,\ell}\geq 0}{\text{Maximize}} \; CS_1(x_{1,1},\ldots,x_{1,\ell}) \tag{1.67a}$$

$$\text{s.t. } x_{1,k} \leq x_{1,k}^{\max} : \; \nu_{1,k}, \; \forall k \tag{1.67b}$$

Setting the Lagrangian function, $L = CS_1(x_{1,1},\ldots,x_{1,\ell}) + \sum_{k=1}^{\ell} \nu_{1,k} \left(x_{1,k}^{\max} - x_{1,k}\right)$, the Karush–Kuhn–Tucker (KKT) conditions are derived as follows:

$$\frac{dB_{1,k}(x_{1,k})}{dx_{1,k}} - p_1 - \nu_{1,k} \leq 0, \; \forall k \tag{1.68a}$$

$$0 \leq \nu_{1,k} \perp x_{1,k}^{\max} - x_{1,k} \geq 0, \; \forall k \tag{1.68b}$$

[6] This argument holds when consumers are price takers without any influence on the market price.

where $\perp$ denotes complementarity, i.e., $0 \leq a \perp b \geq 0$ is equivalent to $a \geq 0$, $b \geq 0$ and $ab = 0$. When consumer k uses electricity up to its maximum capacity, i.e., $x_{1,k} = x_{1,k}^{\max} > 0$, $\frac{dB_{1,k}(x_{1,k})}{dx_{1,k}} - p_1 - \nu_{1,k} = 0$ holds, and hence:

$$\frac{dB_{1,k}(x_{1,k})}{dx_{1,k}} \geq p_1 \tag{1.69}$$

This implies that the marginal benefit or the marginal WTP can be greater than or equal to the market price for a consumer who uses electricity at its maximum capacity.

Illustrative Example 1.10 *Consumers with a constant marginal benefit.*

We here assume that each consumer has a constant marginal benefit (or marginal utility), i.e., $\frac{dB_{1,k}(x_{1,k})}{dx_{1,k}} = u_{1,k} > 0$. Thus, each customer obtains the gross benefit of $u_{1,k}x_{1,k}$ by consuming the quantity $x_{1,k}$. The maximization problem of aggregate consumer surplus is represented as:

$$\underset{x_{1,1},\ldots,x_{1,\ell} \geq 0}{\text{Maximize}} \sum_{k=1}^{\ell} (u_{1,k} - p_1)x_{1,k} \tag{1.70a}$$

$$\text{s.t. } x_{1,k} \leq x_{1,k}^{\max} : \nu_{1,k}, \ \forall k \tag{1.70b}$$

The KKT conditions are derived as follows:

$$u_{1,k} - p_1 - \nu_{1,k} \leq 0, \ \forall k \tag{1.71a}$$

$$0 \leq \nu_{1,k} \perp x_{1,k}^{\max} - x_{1,k} \geq 0, \ \forall k \tag{1.71b}$$

Suppose that there are three consumers, $k = 1, 2, 3$, with constant marginal benefits, $u_{1,1} = 18$, $u_{1,2} = 12$, and $u_{1,3} = 5$, respectively. The upper bounds of their consumption are $x_{1,1}^{\max} = 14$, $x_{1,2}^{\max} = 20$, and $x_{1,3}^{\max} = 26$. Assume that the market price is $p_1 = 8$. In this case, the marginal benefits of consumers 1 and 2 are greater than the market price of 8, and they consume at their maximum capacity, i.e., $x_{1,1} = x_{1,1}^{\max} = 14$ and $x_{1,2} = x_{1,2}^{\max} = 20$, respectively. On the other hand, the marginal benefit of consumer 3 is less than the market price of 8, and $x_{1,3} = 0$. Thus, total quantity demanded in the market is $q_1 = \sum_{k=1}^{3} x_{1,k} = 34$. Moreover, aggregate consumer surplus is $CS_1(14, 20, 0) = 140 + 80 = 220$, which is illustrated in the shaded area in Fig. 1.11.

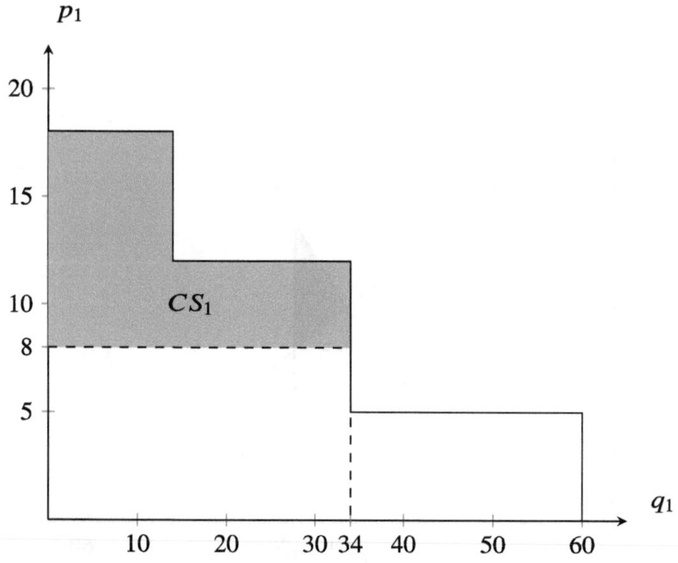

Fig. 1.11 Aggregate demand of consumers with constant marginal benefit

1.7 Demand Response

This section discusses the effect of demand response induced by time-varying prices. Demand for goods such as electricity and gas typically varies within a day or within a year. For example, electricity demand during the daytime, i.e., peak, is usually higher than that during the nighttime, i.e., off-peak. Correspondingly, the incremental costs of supplying power vary within a day, reflecting the merit order of power plants (e.g., coal-, gas-, and oil-fired power plants). When consumers face a constant price such as a flat rate for electricity, it causes economic inefficiency. Time-varying prices that reflect time-varying demand and, hence, costs would induce demand response by customers, thereby improving economic efficiency.

For illustration, we consider two levels of aggregate demand in the market, i.e., the peak period during the daytime and the off-peak period during the nighttime. The downward-sloping curve in Fig. 1.12 illustrates the peak demand, while Fig. 1.13 depicts the demand curve for the off-peak period in the market. Note that the vertical and horizontal intercepts for the peak demand are greater than those for the off-peak demand. The upward-sloping curves in both figures are the market supply curves of the goods. As is discussed in Chap. 2, the supply curve indicates the marginal cost, which is the incremental cost for supplying an additional unit of the output. For simplicity, we assume the same supply curves for the peak and off-peak periods.

Suppose that the price for this good is constant. Hence, consumers face the flat rate, p_1^{flat}, in both the peak and off-peak times. In Fig. 1.12 for the peak period, the flat rate of p_1^{flat} is lower than the level of p_1^{peak} at the intersection of the demand

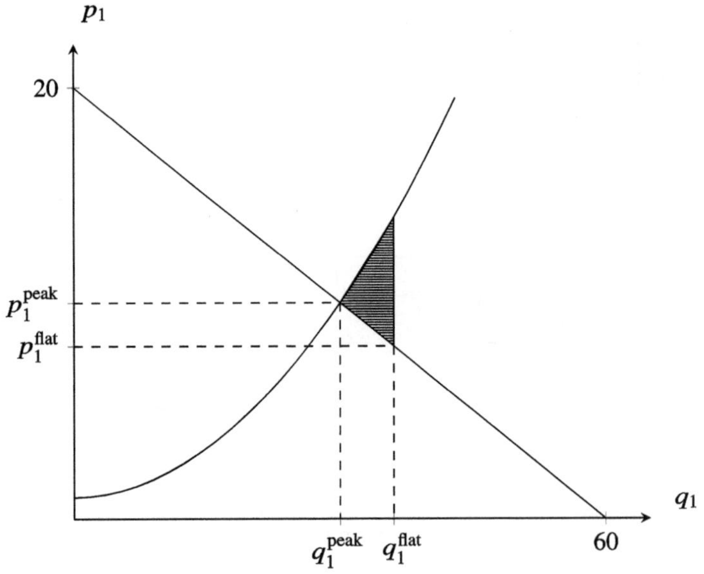

Fig. 1.12 Pricing for peak period

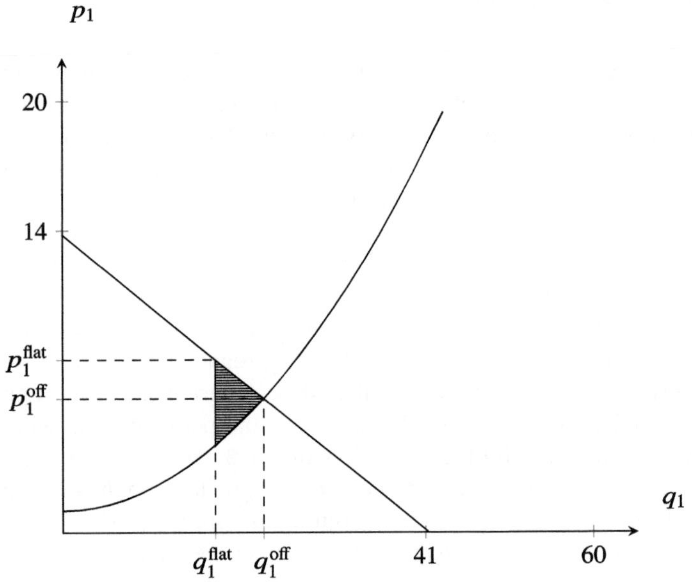

Fig. 1.13 Pricing for off-peak period

and supply curves. Correspondingly, the quantity demanded by the consumers who face p_1^{flat} is q_1^{flat}, which is greater than the quantity, q_1^{peak}, under the price level of p_1^{peak}. This outcome under the flat rate of p_1^{flat} is economically inefficient because the marginal cost of supplying this good is greater than the marginal benefit of consumers for q_1^{flat}. If customers were to consume q_1^{peak}, then the marginal cost would be just equal to the marginal benefit at the intersection of the demand and supply curves. However, customers actually consume up to q_1^{flat}, enlarging the deviation of the marginal cost and the marginal benefit. This is regarded as a social loss since an additional unit of the good beyond q_1^{peak} brings more cost compared to benefit. Specifically, the hatched area of the triangle between q_1^{peak} and q_1^{flat} in Fig. 1.12 is an efficiency loss, which is sometimes called a "deadweight loss."

On the other hand, the flat rate of p_1^{flat} is higher than the level of p_1^{off} at the intersection of the demand and supply curves in Fig. 1.13 for the off-peak period. Correspondingly, the quantity, q_1^{flat}, demanded by the consumers facing p_1^{flat} is now less than the quantity, q_1^{off}, under the price level of p_1^{off}. The outcome under the flat rate of p_1^{flat} is also economically inefficient in the off-peak period since the marginal benefit of consumers is greater than the marginal cost of supplying this good at q_1^{flat}. If customers were to consume q_1^{off}, then the marginal benefit would be exactly equal to the marginal cost at the intersection of the demand and supply curves. But, customers consume only q_1^{flat} with the large deviation between the marginal benefit and the marginal cost. This causes an inefficiency since an incremental decrease of the good below q_1^{off} yields more loss of benefit compared to cost saving. The hatched area of the triangle between q_1^{off} and q_1^{flat} in Fig. 1.13 is again a deadweight loss.

A natural way to avoid such an inefficiency is to utilize time-varying pricing (also called dynamic pricing) instead of a flat rate. In the peak period with high demand, the price is set at the higher level of p_1^{peak} at the intersection of the demand and supply curves. This induces a demand response by consumers to reduce the quantity from q_1^{flat} to q_1^{peak}. As a result, the social loss illustrated in the hatched area of the triangle in Fig. 1.12 is eliminated. Similarly in the off-peak period with low demand, the price is set at the lower level of p_1^{off} at the intersection of the demand and supply curves. Then, the social loss shown in the hatched area of the triangle in Fig. 1.13 disappears because of the demand response by consumers, raising the quantity from q_1^{flat} to q_1^{off}. Therefore, time-varying pricing that induces demand response of consumers is welfare enhancing.

Although time-varying electricity prices have some history for commercial and industrial customers, most electricity tariffs for residential customers have not recently reflected the time variation [2, 12]. One reason is that the electronic interval meters needed to record time-varying consumption were not installed at the household level. However, advanced smart meters that can record near real-time electricity consumption and communicate it to the suppliers have been widely installed for residential customers in many countries and regions over the past decade [9]. Along this line, an increasing number of pilot programs on time-varying pricing for households has been conducted in the U.S. [6, 7] and other countries [11].

1.8 Prosumer

Distributed generation units for residential customers have rapidly expanded for the last decade. Particularly, deployment of rooftop solar photovoltaic (PV) units has grown dramatically in the U.S., Europe, and other countries/regions [3]. Residential customers who own solar PV systems can be characterized by the concept of "prosumer" [4, 8]. The term prosumer refers to a market player that is both a producer and a consumer. As a producer, the PV prosumer generates power with his/her rooftop solar panel and may sell the excess electricity to the grid. On the other hand, the PV prosumer is a consumer who uses electricity for appliances in the residence. As a consumer, the prosumer may self-consume power provided by the solar panel or purchase electricity from the grid. Another traditional example of the prosumer is a farmer who raises plants and livestock such as crops and poultry. A farmer sells his/her produce to the market, while self-consuming part of them.

We examine a simple case of prosumer behavior. Consider a residential prosumer with a rooftop solar PV system that produces electricity, r_1, which is exogenous to him/her. Assume that the marginal cost of PV generation is zero in the short run. Also assume that the prosumer can sell or buy electricity at the market price of p_1. Then, the PV prosumer decides his/her consumption level, x_1, to maximize the sum of the gross benefit of consuming electricity, $B_1(x_1)$, and the transaction with the grid, $p_1(r_1 - x_1)$:

$$\underset{x_1 \geq 0}{\text{Maximize}}\ B_1(x_1) + p_1(r_1 - x_1) \tag{1.72}$$

If the PV output, r_1, is greater than the consumption, x_1, then the excess power is sold to the grid at p_1, bringing revenue to the prosumer. By contrast, if the PV output is less than the consumption, then the prosumer compensates for the shortage of power by purchasing electricity from the grid. Assuming an interior solution, the first-order condition of the prosumer's problem gives $\frac{dB_1(x_1)}{dx_1} = p_1$. This implies that the prosumer decides his/her electricity consumption such that the marginal benefit is just equal to the market price, regardless of the exogenous PV output, r_1. We discuss the implication using the following numerical examples.

Illustrative Example 1.11 *Prosumer with power sale.*

We consider a PV prosumer with the linear inverse-demand function for electricity, $p_1 = 20 - x_1$, as in (1.36a) of Illustrative Example 1.4. Suppose that the PV output is relatively large amounting to $r_1 = 21$ in sunny weather. The market price of power is $p_1 = 8$. With the gross benefit function, $B_1(x_1) = 20x_1 - \frac{1}{2}x_1^2$, the maximization problem of the PV prosumer is formulated as:

$$\underset{x_1 \geq 0}{\text{Maximize}}\ 20x_1 - \frac{1}{2}x_1^2 + 8(21 - x_1) \tag{1.73}$$

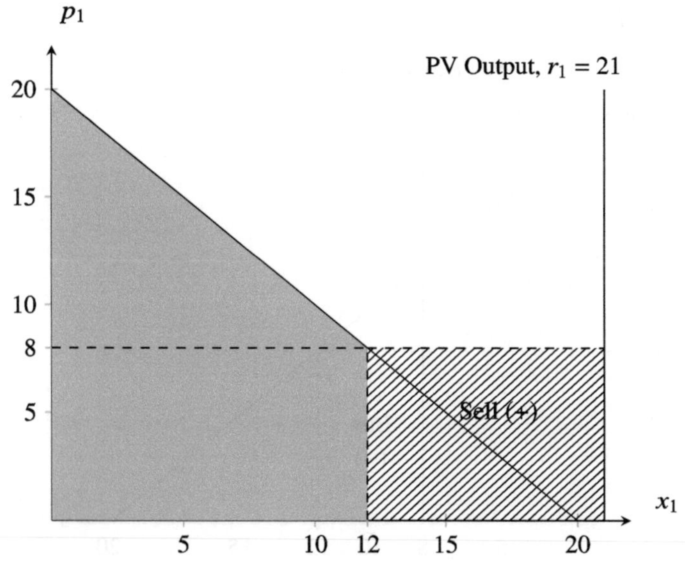

Fig. 1.14 Prosumer selling power

A simple calculation yields an interior solution, $x_1 = 12$. Figure 1.14 illustrates the optimal outcome for the PV prosumer selling the excess power to the grid. This prosumer consumes electricity up to $x_1 = 12$ until his/her marginal benefit is equalized with the market price of $p_1 = 8$. The quantity, $x_1 = 12$, is the self-consumption of the PV output as it is less than $r_1 = 21$. Since the short-run marginal cost of PV generation is assumed to be zero, it incurs no variable cost to the prosumer. Hence, the prosumer enjoys the gross benefit without any expense as shown in the shaded area under the demand curve up to $x_1 = 12$. On the other hand, the excess power, $r_1 - x_1 = 9$, is sold to the grid at $p_1 = 8$. The revenue from this sale is illustrated in the hatched area of the rectangle. This way, the prosumer maximizes the sum of the gross benefit of electricity consumption and the sale of the excess power.

Illustrative Example 1.12 *Prosumer with power purchase.*

We here assume that the PV output is $r_1 = 8$ in cloudy weather, which is relatively small compared to the PV output in the previous example. The PV prosumer's problem is now described as:

$$\underset{x_1 \geq 0}{\text{Maximize}}\ 20x_1 - \frac{1}{2}x_1^2 + 8(8 - x_1) \tag{1.74}$$

As in the previous example, we obtain a solution, $x_1 = 12$, where the marginal benefit equals the market price. However, in contrast to the previous example, the prosumer purchases power from the grid since the PV output is relatively small in

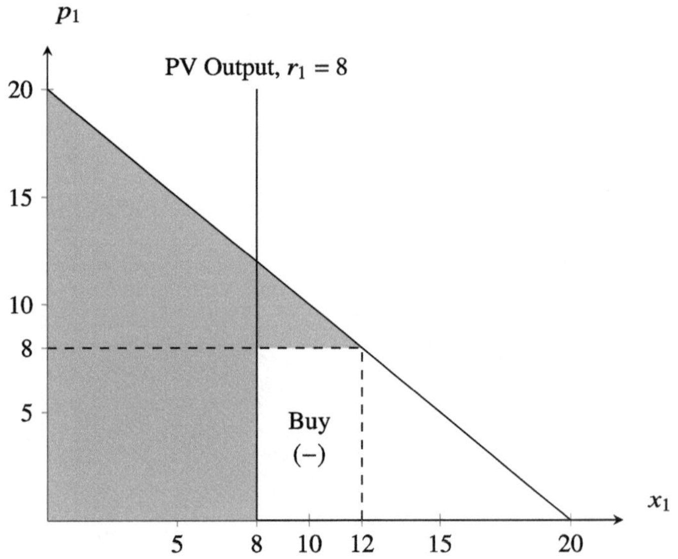

Fig. 1.15 Prosumer buying power

this case. Figure 1.15 shows the optimal outcome for the PV prosumer buying the shortage of power. The prosumer self-consumes electricity up to $r_1 = 8$. The shaded area under the demand curve up to $r_1 = 8$ exhibits the gross benefit of the self-consumption without any expense. Moreover, this prosumer purchases electricity from the grid at the market price of $p_1 = 8$ to compensate for the shortage of power, i.e., $r_1 - x_1 = -4$. With this transaction, the prosumer gains the shaded area of triangle between $x_1 = 8$ and 12 after subtracting the payment from the corresponding gross benefit. This triangular area can be regarded as an additional consumer surplus obtained by buying electricity for more consumption, which is not covered by the PV output.

1.9 Summary

In this chapter, we have discussed the general theory of demand that can be applied to electricity markets.

1. Consumer satisfaction for consuming goods can be measured by utility.
2. Facing market prices, a consumer maximizes utility from consuming the goods under his/her own budget constraint.
3. Demand functions are derived as the solutions to the utility-maximization problem of a consumer.

4. The price elasticity of demand measures the degree of the consumer response to price changes.
5. Consumer surplus measures the net gain from consuming the good after the payment.
6. Individual demand functions and consumer surplus can be aggregated for all customers in the market.
7. Based on the general theory of demand, we can analyze recent issues of electricity markets such as the effect of demand response and prosumers.

1.10 End-of-Chapter Exercises

1.1 Consider two goods with a numeraire. The utility function is given by $U(x_0, x_1, x_2) = 60(x_1 + x_2) - \left(x_1^2 + x_1x_2 + x_2^2\right) + x_0$ with the budget constraint, $p_1x_1 + p_2x_2 + x_0 = m$. Consider an arbitrary level of budget, m. Then, solve the utility-maximization problem and derive the linear demand functions for those two goods. Also, check whether the two goods are substitutes or complements.

1.2 Consider one good with a numeraire. The utility function is given by $U(x_0, x_1) = 40x_1 - 2x_1^2 + x_0$ with the budget constraint, $p_1x_1 + x_0 = m$. Consider an arbitrary level of budget, m. Then, solve the utility-maximization problem and derive the linear demand function for this good. Also, calculate the derivative of x_1 with respect to its own price, p_1, and check whether or not it is negative.

1.3 Consider a linear inverse-demand function, $p_1 = 40 - 2x_1$, or a linear demand function, $x_1 = 20 - \frac{1}{2}p_1$. Calculate the absolute values for the price elasticity of demand, $|e_{11}|$, at various points on the demand curve, e.g., $x_1 = 5$, 10, and 15. Check whether demand is elastic or inelastic at each point.

1.4 Consider a linear demand function of the form, $x_1 = f_1 - g_1p_1$. Suppose that the price elasticity of demand is $e_{11} = -0.2$ at the point, $(x_1, p_1) = (100, 20)$, on the demand curve. Then, derive the linear demand function, i.e., derive f_1 and g_1.

1.5 Consider a linear inverse-demand function, $p_1 = 40 - 2x_1$, as in Exercise 1.3. Suppose that the market price is $p_1 = 10$. Then, calculate the gross benefit and consumer surplus. Moreover, how do those values change if the price rises to $p_1 = 20$?

1.6 Consider three heterogenous consumers (instead of identical consumers) with heterogenous individual demand functions, $x_{1,k} = f_{1,k} - g_{1,k}p_1$, $k = 1, 2, 3$, in Illustrative Examples 1.9. Choose heterogenous values for $f_{1,k}$ and $g_{1,k}$, $k = 1, 2, 3$. Then, illustrate the market-demand curve by adding the individual demand curves horizontally. [Hint: the market-demand curve may be piecewise linear.]

1.7 Consider the prosumer in Illustrative Examples 1.11 and 1.12. Suppose that the PV output, r_1, varies depending on the weather, e.g., ranging from $r_1 = 0$ to 25. Calculate the sum of the gross benefit of consuming electricity and the transaction with the grid for various levels of r_1 to see how the welfare of the prosumer changes with the variation in the PV output.

References

1. Alberini, A., Filippini, M.: Response of residential electricity demand to price: the effect of measurement error. Ener. Econ. **33**, 889–895 (2011)
2. Borenstein, S.: Time-varying retail electricity prices: theory and practice. In: Griffin, J.M., Puller, S. (eds.) Electricity Deregulation: Choices and Challenges. University of Chicago Press, Chicago (2005)
3. Borenstein, S.: Private net benefits of residential solar PV: the role of electricity tariffs, tax incentives, and rebates. J. Assoc. Environ. Resour. Econ. **4**, S85–S122 (2017)
4. Chen, Y., Tanaka, M., Takashima, R.: Energy expenditure incidence in the presence of prosumers: can a fixed charge lead us to the promised land. IEEE Trans. Power Syst. Published online (2021). https://doi.org/10.1109/TPWRS.2021.3104770
5. European Environment Agency: Overview of electricity production and use in Europe (2016). https://www.eea.europa.eu/data-and-maps/indicators/overview-of-the-electricity-production-2/assessment
6. Faruqui, A., Sergici, S.: Household response to dynamic pricing of electricity: a survey of 15 experiments. J. Reg. Econ. **38**, 193–225 (2010)
7. Faruqui, A., Sergici, S.: Dynamic pricing of electricity in the Mid-Atlantic region: econometric results from the Baltimore gas and electric company experiment. J. Reg. Econ. **40**, 82–109 (2011)
8. Gautier, A., Jacqmin, J., Poudou, J.C.: The prosumers and the grid. J. Reg. Econ. **53**, 100–126 (2018)
9. Haney, A.B., Jamasb, T., Pollitt, M.G.: Smart metering and electricity demand: technology, economics and international experience. Cambridge Working Paper in Economics 0905, Cambridge (2009)
10. Hogan, W.W.: Market design practices: which ones are best? IEEE Power Energy Mag. **17**, 100–104 (2019)
11. Ito, K., Ida, T., Tanaka, M.: Moral suasion and economic incentives: field experimental evidence from energy demand. Am. Econ. J. Econ. Policy **10**, 240–267 (2018)
12. Jessoe, K., Rapson, D.: Commercial and industrial demand response under mandatory time-of-use electricity pricing. J. Ind. Econ. **63**, 397–421 (2015)
13. Nicholson, W., Snyder, C.: Microeconomic Theory: Basic Principles and Extensions. Cengage Learning, Boston (2016)
14. Paul, A.C., Myers, E.C., Palmer, K.L.: A partial adjustment model of US electricity demand by region, season, and sector. RFF DP 08-50, Washington (2009)
15. Varian, H.R.: Microeconomic Analysis. W.W. Norton & Company, New York (1992)

Chapter 2
Supply

2.1 Introduction

Historically, the power sector consisted of vertically integrated investor-owned utilities (IOUs) that controlled all functions of the industry, viz. generation, distribution, retailing, and transmission [48]. These IOUs were typically granted franchise monopolies in geographical areas and were subject to regulatory oversight, e.g., about the retail rates offered to consumers. Such a setup enabled IOUs to exploit the "natural monopoly" effect that is inherent to many network-based industries by internalizing operating complementarities, e.g., between generation and transmission expansion. In turn, consumers were guaranteed cost certainty [23], although power companies did not have the incentive to minimize costs as they were free from competitive pressure. Likewise, IOUs relied upon large-scale proven technologies such as coal-fired and nuclear power plants (or, hydropower where available) to cover baseload demand with gas- and oil-fired plants to meet peak demand as needed. Thus, generation technologies were installed in sufficient capacity to match demand growth along with a reserve margin, and the lack of competitive pressure or environmental regulation precluded the development of more energy-efficient technologies.

With the restructuring of the power sector in the 1980s, the electricity industry in most OECD countries is now deregulated with generation and retailing functions opened up to competition. Meanwhile, distribution and transmission are still largely handled by regulated entities because they are natural monopolies with long-run average costs that decrease with capacity size. Thus, it is not efficient to have competing network providers, although so-called merchant investors have been proposed [24, 26]. Under the deregulated paradigm, power companies and retailers compete for market share, while network planners anticipate their investments in making their own capacity additions. These competitive forces together with more recent legally binding obligations to meet climate targets by reducing greenhouse

M. Tanaka et al., *Economics of Power Systems*, International Series
in Operations Research & Management Science 327,
https://doi.org/10.1007/978-3-030-92871-1_2

gas emissions have led to a transformation of electricity supply by incentivizing the adoption of VRES [47]. Hence, power supply is now more dependent on VRES and market-based decisions than it was in the 1980s when it was marked by centralized decision making and thermal power plants, cf. the share of solar and wind electricity generation in Germany has gone from negligible in 1990 to 28.6% in 2019 [1].

Given the transformation of the power sector due to both economic and environmental drivers, it is worthwhile revisiting the underpinnings of industry supply. In contrast to the conventional thermal supply stack [40], the increased penetration of VRES could both lower the market-clearing price while amplifying its volatility [34]. Thus, somewhat paradoxically, although VRES generation will require more flexibility, its null operating cost renders thermal plants with high ramp rates, viz. gas turbines, less economic. In the short run, such intermittency will affect price formation and have ramifications for market design [27]. Consequently, economic incentives for short-run firm and industry operational decisions need methodical exposition in order to understand better the roles of flexible assets, e.g., ramping plants and storage, in integrating VRES. Similarly, long-run investment decisions will have to be reassessed so that they account for the intermittency of VRES. Indeed, conventional power-system planning models represent variability on the demand side via load segments [22] and could drastically overestimate VRES availability if not sufficiently modified [32].

This chapter explores the economic foundations of electricity supply starting with a discussion of the components of operating costs in Sect. 2.2. Taking a long-run view, Sect. 2.3 investigates investment costs using the levelized cost of investment and screening curves. The connection between operating costs and investment costs to firms' short- and long-run profit-maximization problems is the topic of Sect. 2.4. VRES and their implications for short-run operational dispatch, viz. in terms of ramping decisions, are analyzed in Sect. 2.5. Likewise, the impact of energy storage on VRES integration is examined in Sect. 2.6. Section 2.7 summarizes this chapter, while Sects. 2.8 and 2.9 provide end-of-chapter problems and GAMS codes for selected examples, respectively.

2.2 Operating Costs

In the short run, capacity levels are fixed, and a firm's production decision depends on whether or not its revenue covers its variable costs [44]. Such costs change only with the level of production, e.g., fuel, emissions, and other variable operations and maintenance (O&M) expenses such as water consumption. Of course, there may also be fixed O&M (or, quasi-fixed) costs related to regularly scheduled maintenance and general administration incurred by plants [17]. These fixed O&M costs do not vary with the level of operation. If plants are outright retired, then neither variable nor fixed O&M costs apply. For sake of this exposition, we will ignore fixed O&M costs and assume that operating costs are simply variable costs comprising fuel, emissions, and variable O&M costs.

2.2.1 *Calculating Operating Costs*

For thermal plants, e.g., those using coal, natural gas, or oil as fuel, the fuel cost depends on (i) the generator efficiency and (ii) fuel prices. In power-system economics, the heat rate, which is actually the inverse of the efficiency, is used and measured in BTU per kWh, where "BTU" is a non-SI unit that stands for "British thermal units" and refers to thermal energy content. A typical gas-fired combined-cycle turbine might have a heat rate of 7500 BTU/kWh, i.e., it takes 7500 BTU of thermal energy to yield 1 kWh of electrical energy. Consequently, a lower heat rate refers to a more efficient turbine. Moreover, since 1 kWh is equivalent to 3412 BTU, the efficiency of the aforementioned combined-cycle turbine, i.e., the proportion of thermal energy converted to electrical energy, is [15]:

$$\frac{3412\ \text{BTU}}{1\ \text{kWh}} \times \frac{1\ \text{kWh}}{7500\ \text{BTU}} = 0.4549 \tag{2.1}$$

In the U.S. and other OECD countries, fuel prices vary periodically because they are based on settled prices in commodity markets. For example, the U.S. Energy Information Administration (EIA) tabulates data on natural-gas prices paid by generators, which are typically quoted in \$ per MMBTU, i.e., dollars per million BTU. Using the preceding combined-cycle turbine with a heat rate of 7500 BTU/kWh, a natural-gas price of \$4.43/MMBTU yields a fuel cost (expressed in \$/MWh) of:

$$\frac{7500\ \text{BTU}}{1\ \text{kWh}} \times \frac{1\ \text{MMBTU}}{1000000\ \text{BTU}} \times \frac{1000\ \text{kWh}}{1\ \text{MWh}} \times \frac{\$4.43}{1\ \text{MMBTU}} = \$33.23/\text{MWh} \tag{2.2}$$

The cost of emissions for power plants depend on (i) pollutant, e.g., CO_2, content of the fuel, (ii) the heat rate, and (iii) the price of the pollutant.[1] As mentioned earlier, the heat rate is typically measured in BTU per kWh, whereas pollutant prices are measured in \$ per t, where "t" is the abbreviation for "tonne" and pollutant content is usually specified in lbs per MMBTU in the U.S., where "lbs" is the abbreviation for "pounds." Data for emission prices are available from relevant authorities or markets, e.g., the EU Emissions Trading System (ETS) [19] and the Regional Greenhouse Gas Initiative (RGGI) [31] for CO_2 prices. CO_2 contents of various fuels may be obtained from the U.S. EIA [14]. For example, the CO_2 content

[1] The pollutant price usually refers to a carbon tax or the price of CO_2 emission permits. An example of the former is the carbon price of C\$45/t in the Canadian province of British Columbia in 2021 [4], whereas the EU Emissions Trading System is an example of the latter with an approximate permit price of €50/t in 2021 [19].

of natural gas is 117 lbs/MMBTU. Given its heat rate of 7500 BTU/kWh and a CO_2 price of \$2.67/t, the cost of emissions for a gas-fired combined-cycle plant is:

$$\frac{117 \text{ lbs CO}_2}{1 \text{ MMBTU}} \times \frac{0.0005 \text{ t}}{1 \text{ lbs}} \times \frac{\$2.67}{1 \text{ t CO}_2} \times \frac{7500 \text{ BTU}}{1 \text{ kWh}} \times \frac{1 \text{ MMBTU}}{1000000 \text{ BTU}} \times \frac{1000 \text{ kWh}}{1 \text{ MWh}}$$
$$= \$1.17/\text{MWh} \tag{2.3}$$

As for variable O&M costs, they depend on the plant's configuration. For a combined-cycle gas-fired plant with an average capacity factor, they are estimated to be \$2.77/MWh [29]. Thus, for such a plant, the operating cost in the short run comprises the fuel cost from (2.2), the emission cost from (2.3), and the variable O&M costs of \$2.77/MWh:

$$\$33.23/\text{MWh} + \$1.17/\text{MWh} + \$2.77/\text{MWh} = \$37.17/\text{MWh} \tag{2.4}$$

Note that in (2.4), we treat the cost of CO_2 emissions as if it were a tax rather than endogenously determined via a cap-and-trade constraint as is the case in the EU ETS and RGGI. For now, the distinction is not important since we merely characterize the operating cost *ex post* for the purpose of constructing a short-run supply stack.

2.2.2 Short-Run Supply Stack

Following the aforementioned procedure, short-run supply stacks[2] for regions may be constructed. For example, the appendix to [11] describes how the short-run supply stack for New York during the year 2013 is constructed. Rather than one single supply stack, the seasonal variations in fuel prices, hydro inflows, and VRES availability cause both the operating costs and effective capacities to change periodically. Table 2.1 provides a snapshot of the supply stack during the summer months.[3] It is meant to be indicative of the generation potential and should not be interpreted as meaning that 807 MW of VRES and 4272 MW of ROR capacity are fully available during a typical summer period. In fact, these capacities along with some of the costs for the thermal plants will vary depending on the hour of the year, and, ideally, 8760 such supply stacks would give a full picture of New York's generation capacity. Methods for using representative days

[2] These are also referred to as short-run supply curves and are comprised of the short-run marginal costs.

[3] Following [11], the abbreviations for the plant types correspond to technologies and fuels (if used). Besides VRES, we have ST (steam turbine), CC (combined cycle), ROR (run-of-river hydro), IC (internal combustion), and GT (gas turbine) as technologies. The fuels are UR (uranium), BIT (bituminous coal), NG (natural gas), FO6 (residual fuel oil), FO2 (distillated oil 2), and KER (kerosene).

Table 2.1 Data for New York's short-run supply stack (summer 2013)

Plant type	Operating cost ($/MWh)	Capacity (MW)
VRES	0	807
ST-UR	5.16	5418
ROR	6	4272
ST-BIT	38.01	1495
CC-NG	38.76	8992
IC-NG	54.27	104
ST-NG	62.94	3570
GT-NG	67.60	1971
ST-FO6	174.10	5973
IC-FO2	233.21	111
GT-FO2	305.87	1902
GT-KER	323.32	959

or weeks to group similar periods in order to reduce the computational burden while simultaneously preserving the chronology of available resources can be done via statistical clustering [13, 32].

From the constructed short-run supply stack in Fig. 2.1, peak and off-peak market prices for typical summer periods may be obtained using corresponding quantities demanded, i.e., 23.05 GWh and 17.11 GWh, respectively [11, 30]. Intersecting these values with the short-run supply stack[4] yields indicative peak and off-peak prices of $62.94/MWh and $38.76/MWh, respectively. In effect, CC-NG is the off-peak marginal technology, while ST-NG is the peak one. While mean periodic summer prices observed for downstate New York during 2013 corresponded to these values, actual market-clearing prices will depend on other factors that we have ignored for now, viz. transmission constraints, net imports, pumped-hydro storage operations, hydropower and VRES availabilities, demand response, unit-commitment decisions, and ramping restrictions. We will address some of these real-world aspects in subsequent sections of this chapter and elsewhere in the book. Nevertheless, for now, suffice it to say that the short-run supply stack and average load conditions provide us with a useful snapshot of power-system operations.

2.2.3 Economic Dispatch

Indices and Sets

$s \in \mathcal{S}$ Seasons.

$t \in \mathcal{T}$ Time periods.

$u \in \mathcal{U}$ Generation technologies.

---

[4] Although the units of the horizontal axis in Fig. 2.1 are in GW, they may equivalently be interpreted as GWh per hour, i.e., reflective of the flow of energy per time.

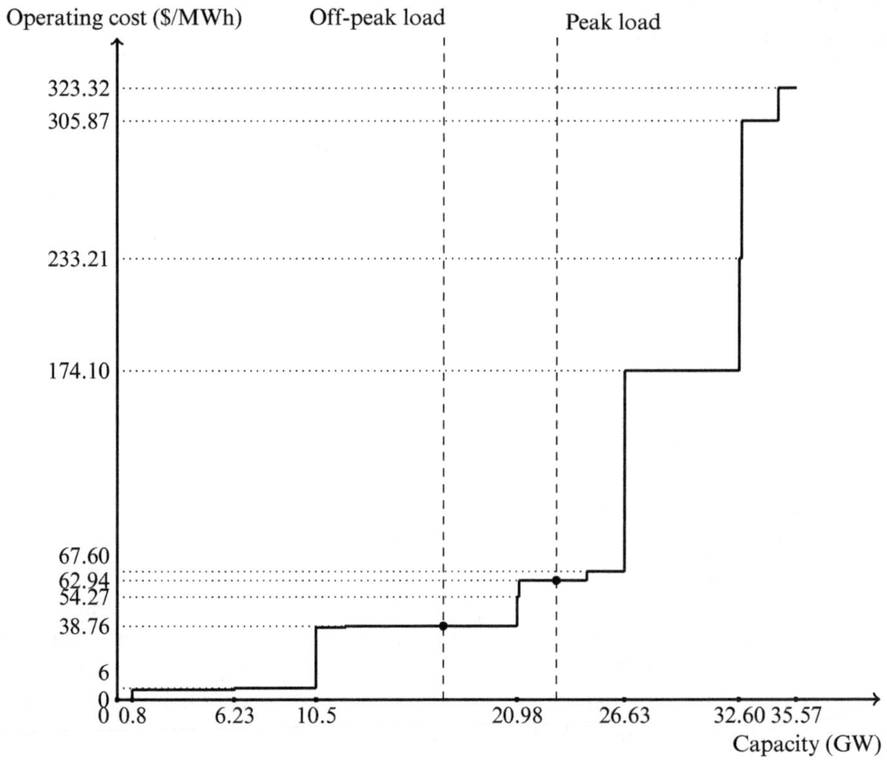

Fig. 2.1 New York's short-run supply stack (summer 2013)

Parameters

$A_{s,t,u}$	Maximum availability factor for technology u in season s and period t [–].
$C^{\text{opr}}_{s,t,u}$	Operating cost of technology u in season s and period t [$/MWh].
$C^{\text{lsh}}_{s,t}$	Load-shedding cost in season s and period t [$/MWh].
$D_{s,t}$	Demand in season s and period t [MWh].
K_u	Installed generation capacity of technology u [MW].
T_t	Length of period t [h].
W_s	Weight of season s [–].

Primal Variables

$d_{s,t}$	Load shed in season s and period t [MWh].
$y_{s,t,u}$	Generation from technology u in season s and period t [MWh].

Dual Variables

$\beta_{s,t,u}$	Marginal value of maximum generation in season s and period t for technology u [$/MWh].
$\lambda_{s,t}$	Marginal value of energy consumption in season s and period t [$/MWh].

$\phi^d_{s,t}$ Marginal value of non-negativity of load shedding in season s and period t [\$/MWh].

$\phi^y_{s,t,u}$ Marginal value of non-negativity of generation output in season s and period t for technology u [\$/MWh].

In the short run, operating costs are minimized by dispatching generation technologies to meet periodic demand. Load shedding may also be implemented in periods when generation capacity is insufficient to meet demand.[5] Note that this perspective assumes that all plants are price takers and the market is cleared by a system operator that balances supply and demand subject to the plants' capacity limits. For now, we ignore more realistic technical constraints, viz. ramp rates, hydro or storage balance, and unit commitment, as well as transmission congestion. Thus, the economic dispatch problem may be formulated as:

$$\underset{d_{s,t}, y_{s,t,u}}{\text{Minimize}} \sum_{s \in \mathcal{S}} W_s \sum_{t \in \mathcal{T}} \left(\sum_{u \in \mathcal{U}} C^{\text{opr}}_{s,t,u} y_{s,t,u} + C^{\text{lsh}}_{s,t} d_{s,t} \right) \tag{2.5a}$$

$$\text{s.t.} \sum_{u \in \mathcal{U}} y_{s,t,u} + d_{s,t} - D_{s,t} = 0 : \lambda_{s,t}, \forall s, t \tag{2.5b}$$

$$y_{s,t,u} \leq A_{s,t,u} T_t K_u : \beta_{s,t,u}, \forall s, t, u \tag{2.5c}$$

$$d_{s,t} \geq 0 : \phi^d_{s,t}, \forall s, t \tag{2.5d}$$

$$y_{s,t,u} \geq 0 : \phi^y_{s,t,u}, \forall s, t, u \tag{2.5e}$$

where (2.5a) is the season-weighted operating cost of the power system to be minimized by a central planner. Here, $\sum_{u \in \mathcal{U}} C^{\text{opr}}_{s,t,u} y_{s,t,u}$ and $C^{\text{lsh}}_{s,t} d_{s,t}$ are the costs of operating the generation technologies and load shedding, respectively, for period $t \in \mathcal{T}$ during season $s \in \mathcal{S}$. For example, a period may correspond to an hour and $|\mathcal{T}|$, i.e., the cardinality of $\mathcal{T}$, may be 168 if we use representative weeks in our model, i.e., $|\mathcal{T}| = \frac{24\text{ h}}{\text{day}} \times \frac{7\text{ days}}{\text{week}}$. Thus, each season is reflected by a representative week with cost $\sum_{t \in \mathcal{T}} \left(\sum_{u \in \mathcal{U}} C^{\text{opr}}_{s,t,u} y_{s,t,u} + C^{\text{lsh}}_{s,t} d_{s,t} \right)$, which is multiplied by the seasonal weight, W_s, indicating the number of weeks of type s in the year and summed over all $s \in \mathcal{S}$ to render the season-weighted operating cost as in (2.5a).

The operational problem is constrained by:

- Energy balance, i.e., generation plus load shedding equals energy demand (2.5b).
- Maximum generation bounds based on installed capacity (2.5c).
- Non-negativity constraints on load shedding and generation (2.5d)–(2.5e).

[5] The load-shedding cost is either the societal cost of lost load, i.e., the value of lost load (VOLL), or a price cap. The former is typically assumed to be \$10,000/MWh, while the latter is usually \$1200/MWh in U.S. markets [3].

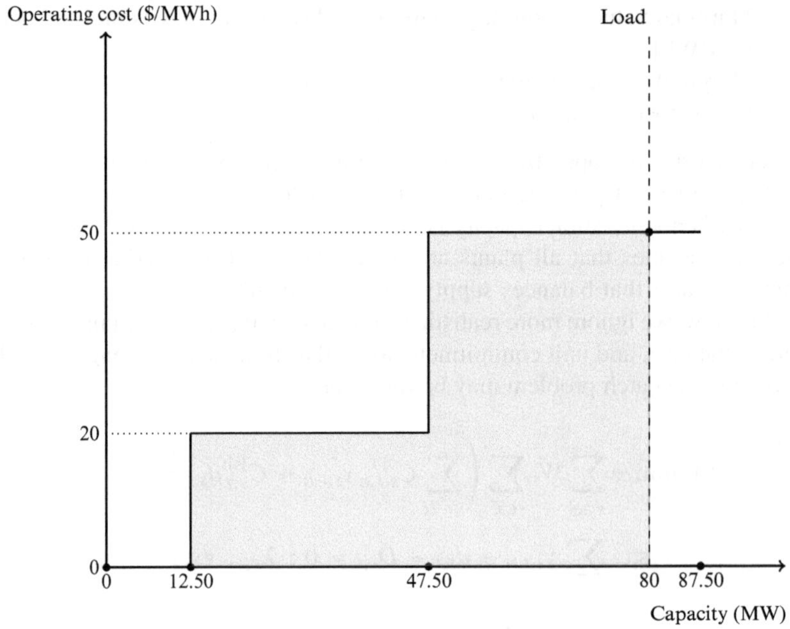

Fig. 2.2 Least-cost operational dispatch

Note that the unitless parameter, $A_{s,t,u}$, is relevant only for run-of-river hydro and VRES because it reflects the seasonal resource availabilities.[6] For thermal technologies, $A_{s,t,u} = 1$. Since the objective function (2.5a) is linear in the variables along with the constraints (2.5b)–(2.5e), (2.5a)–(2.5e) is a linear programming (LP) problem. Furthermore, given the absence of constraints that link decisions across periods, e.g., ramping or storage, the LP (2.5a)–(2.5e) is effectively separable across time periods, i.e., it may be solved separately for every period $t \in \mathcal{T}$ during season $s \in \mathcal{S}$. Nevertheless, we will proceed with the current exposition and add real-world features in subsequent sections. Finally, the lower-case Greek letters adjacent to the colons in each constraint are the dual variables for this problem.

Intuitively, the LP (2.5a)–(2.5e) matches the demand in each period with the available generation capacity plus load shedding (if necessary). A graphical representation of the least-cost solution is given in Fig. 2.2. For example, with a demand of 80 MWh and three technologies with operating costs $0/MWh, $20/MWh, and $50/MWh and installed capacities 25 MW, 35 MW, and 40 MW, respectively, the optimal dispatch is 12.50 MWh, 35 MWh, and 32.50 MWh, respectively, as long as the zero-cost technology has 50% resource availability. In effect, the installed capacity is sufficient to meet the demand, and load shedding is not required. The shaded region in Fig. 2.2 has an area that is equal to the minimized cost (2.5a), which happens to be $2325 in this case.

[6] This assumes that VRES output may be curtailed, which may not have been possible in the nascent years of renewable support via feed-in tariffs.

The significance of the dual variables, especially $\lambda_{s,t}$, i.e., the marginal value of energy consumption, becomes clearer once the first-order necessary conditions (FONCs) of the LP (2.5a)–(2.5e) are inspected. This is because the dual variables provide information about the marginal cost of generation, which is used to set the market-clearing price. In order to understand this connection, we first formulate the Lagrangian function, L, for the LP (2.5a)–(2.5e):

$$\begin{aligned} L = &\sum_{s \in \mathcal{S}} W_s \sum_{t \in \mathcal{T}} \left(\sum_{u \in \mathcal{U}} C^{\text{opr}}_{s,t,u} y_{s,t,u} + C^{\text{lsh}}_{s,t} d_{s,t} \right) \\ &- \sum_{s \in \mathcal{S}} \sum_{t \in \mathcal{T}} \lambda_{s,t} \left(\sum_{u \in \mathcal{U}} y_{s,t,u} + d_{s,t} - D_{s,t} \right) \\ &- \sum_{s \in \mathcal{S}} \sum_{t \in \mathcal{T}} \sum_{u \in \mathcal{U}} \beta_{s,t,u} \left(A_{s,t,u} T_t K_u - y_{s,t,u} \right) - \sum_{s \in \mathcal{S}} \sum_{t \in \mathcal{T}} d_{s,t} \phi^d_{s,t} \\ &- \sum_{s \in \mathcal{S}} \sum_{t \in \mathcal{T}} \sum_{u \in \mathcal{U}} y_{s,t,u} \phi^y_{s,t,u} \end{aligned} \tag{2.6a}$$

Consequently, the FONCs, or Karush–Kuhn–Tucker (KKT) conditions, are that the partial derivatives of the Lagrangian function in (2.6a) equal zero for each primal variable (2.7a)–(2.7b) along with the primal constraints (2.7c)–(2.7f), complementarity conditions for inequality constraints (2.7g)–(2.7i), and non-negativity constraints on dual variables associated with inequality constraints (2.7j)–(2.7l):

$$W_s C^{\text{lsh}}_{s,t} - \lambda_{s,t} - \phi^d_{s,t} = 0, \ \forall s, t \tag{2.7a}$$

$$W_s C^{\text{opr}}_{s,t,u} - \lambda_{s,t} + \beta_{s,t,u} - \phi^y_{s,t,u} = 0, \ \forall s, t, u \tag{2.7b}$$

$$\sum_{u \in \mathcal{U}} y_{s,t,u} + d_{s,t} - D_{s,t} = 0, \ \forall s, t \tag{2.7c}$$

$$A_{s,t,u} T_t K_u - y_{s,t,u} \geq 0, \ \forall s, t, u \tag{2.7d}$$

$$d_{s,t} \geq 0, \ \forall s, t \tag{2.7e}$$

$$y_{s,t,u} \geq 0, \ \forall s, t, u \tag{2.7f}$$

$$\beta_{s,t,u} \left(A_{s,t,u} T_t K_u - y_{s,t,u} \right) = 0, \ \forall s, t, u \tag{2.7g}$$

$$\phi^d_{s,t} d_{s,t} = 0, \ \forall s, t \tag{2.7h}$$

$$\phi^y_{s,t,u} y_{s,t,u} = 0, \ \forall s, t, u \tag{2.7i}$$

$$\beta_{s,t,u} \geq 0, \ \forall s, t, u \tag{2.7j}$$

$$\phi^d_{s,t} \geq 0, \ \forall s, t \tag{2.7k}$$

$$\phi^y_{s,t,u} \geq 0, \ \forall s, t, u \tag{2.7l}$$

In the context of the market clearing depicted in Fig. 2.2, assuming $W_s = 1, \forall s$, $A_{s,t,u} = 0.50, \forall s, t, u$, and $T_t = 1, \forall t$, KKT condition (2.7a) becomes $C^{\text{lsh}}_{s,t} \geq \lambda_{s,t}$ because $\phi^{d}_{s,t} \geq 0$ as load shedding is not deployed, i.e., $d_{s,t} = 0$. Intuitively, the marginal cost of load shedding is greater than or equal to its marginal benefit, $\lambda_{s,t}$, which is also the market-clearing price. Next, KKT condition (2.7b) is $C^{\text{opr}}_{s,t,u} = \lambda_{s,t}$, i.e., the marginal cost of generation equals the marginal value of energy consumption, for the marginal technology with an operating cost of \$50/MWh because $K_u > y_{s,t,u}$ and $y_{s,t,u} > 0$, which imply $\beta_{s,t,u} = 0$ and $\phi^{y}_{s,t,u} = 0$, respectively, via KKT conditions (2.7g) and (2.7i), respectively. Thus, $\lambda_{s,t} = 50$ is the market-clearing price and equals the operating cost of the marginal technology, which also means that a *ceteris paribus* increase in the quantity demanded by 1 MWh will increase the minimized cost by \$50. By contrast, KKT condition (2.7b) is $C^{\text{opr}}_{s,t,u} + \beta_{s,t,u} = \lambda_{s,t}$ for the inframarginal technologies with operating costs of \$0/MWh and \$20/MWh that are deployed at capacity, i.e., $A_{s,t,u} T_t K_u = y_{s,t,u}$ and $y_{s,t,u} > 0$, which imply $\beta_{s,t,u} \geq 0$ and $\phi^{y}_{s,t,u} = 0$, respectively, via KKT conditions (2.7g) and (2.7i), respectively. Consequently, $\beta_{s,t,u}$ equals \$50/MWh and \$30/MWh for the two inframarginal technologies with operating costs of \$0/MWh and \$20/MWh, respectively. These $\beta_{s,t,u}$ values reflect the marginal values of capacity for the two technologies, e.g., a *ceteris paribus* increase in 1 MW of capacity for the technology with an operating cost of \$0/MWh lowers the minimized cost by \$25 for the analyzed period. Formally, the envelope theorem links the minimized cost to the right-hand sides of the constraints via the Lagrange multipliers [44]:

$$\frac{\partial L}{\partial D_{s,t}} = \lambda_{s,t}, \ \forall s, t \tag{2.8a}$$

$$\frac{\partial L}{\partial K_u} = -\sum_{s \in \mathcal{S}} \sum_{t \in \mathcal{T}} A_{s,t,u} T_t \beta_{s,t,u}, \ \forall u \tag{2.8b}$$

Hence, the dual variables, $\lambda_{s,t}$ and $\beta_{s,t,u}$, obtained as a result of solving instances of LP (2.5a)–(2.5e) enable us to conduct comparative statics on the objective function value, i.e., the minimized cost.

Illustrative Example 2.1 *Cost-minimizing LP for economic dispatch.*

We implement LP (2.5a)–(2.5e) for a stylized example with two seasons, three time periods, and three technology types. If we use representative days, then this means that each day consists of three time periods each of length $T_t = 8$ h, i.e., $\sum_{t \in \mathcal{T}} T_t = 24$. We further assume that the seasons have equal shares, i.e., $W_s = 183$ assuming a 366-day year.[7] The technology operating costs, $C^{\text{opr}}_{s,t,u}$, are as in Fig. 2.2 for all

[7] We could equivalently use representative weeks, in which two equally weighted seasons would result in $W_s = 26$ assuming a 52-week year. In that case, with three time periods, we would have $T_t = 56$ h, i.e., $\sum_{t \in \mathcal{T}} T_t = 168$.

Table 2.2 Demand parameters, $D_{s,t}$ (MWh)

	Period		
Season	$t = 1$	$t = 2$	$t = 3$
$s = 1$	280	600	720
$s = 2$	880	640	420

Table 2.3 Availability parameters for VRES technology, $A_{s,t,1}$

	Period		
Season	$t = 1$	$t = 2$	$t = 3$
$s = 1$	0.20	0.10	0.05
$s = 2$	0.25	0.50	0.75

Table 2.4 Load-shedding decisions, $d_{s,t}$ (MWh)

	Period		
Season	$t = 1$	$t = 2$	$t = 3$
$s = 1$	0	0	110
$s = 2$	230	0	0

Table 2.5 Operational decisions, $y_{s,t,u}$ (MWh)

		Period		
Technology	Season	$t = 1$	$t = 2$	$t = 3$
$u = 1$	$s = 1$	40	20	10
	$s = 2$	50	100	150
$u = 2$	$s = 1$	240	280	280
	$s = 2$	280	280	270
$u = 3$	$s = 1$	0	300	320
	$s = 2$	320	260	0

Table 2.6 Marginal value of demand, $\lambda_{s,t}$ ($/MWh)

	Period		
Season	$t = 1$	$t = 2$	$t = 3$
$s = 1$	3660	9150	91,500
$s = 2$	91,500	9150	3660

s, t, while the load-shedding cost, $C^{\text{lsh}}_{s,t}$, equals \$500/MWh for all s, t. Likewise, the installed capacities, K_u, for the three technologies are as in Fig. 2.2, i.e., 25 MW, 35 MW, and 40 MW. The main difference here from the illustration in Fig. 2.2 is that we allow for variation in load, $D_{s,t}$, in Table 2.2 and the availability of the zero-cost VRES technology, $A_{s,t,u}$, in Table 2.3 by season and period. The availabilities of the two other technologies are set to 1 for all seasons and periods. Given these data, the minimized operating cost is \$48,055,800 for the entire year. The optimal solutions for the primal and dual variables are given in Tables 2.4, 2.5, 2.6, and 2.7.[8]

[8] In order to save space, the values of the dual variables for the non-negative constraints, $\phi^d_{s,t}$ and $\phi^y_{s,t,u}$, are not presented. However, they can be verified to be zero in instances when the corresponding primal variables are strictly positive.

Table 2.7 Marginal value of capacity, $\beta_{s,t,u}$ ($/MWh)

Technology	Season	Period $t = 1$	$t = 2$	$t = 3$
$u = 1$	$s = 1$	3660	9150	91,500
	$s = 2$	91,500	9150	3660
$u = 2$	$s = 1$	0	5490	87,840
	$s = 2$	87,840	5490	0
$u = 3$	$s = 1$	0	0	82,350
	$s = 2$	82,350	0	0

For example, during season $s = 2$ and period $t = 2$, it is evident from Tables 2.4 and 2.5 that no load shedding occurs and technologies $u = 1$, $u = 2$, and $u = 3$ generate 100 MWh, 280 MWh, and 260 MWh, respectively. Dividing each of these values by $T_t = 8$, we observe that the operations in any given hour are 12.50 MWh, 35 MWh, and 32.50 MWh, which matches the dispatch in Fig. 2.2. From Table 2.6, we obtain that the marginal value of demand is $9150/MWh, i.e., a *ceteris paribus* increase in load by 1 MWh during season $s = 2$ and period $t = 2$ would increase minimized cost by $9150 annually,[9] cf. (2.8a). Since there are 183 days of this type, the impact of such an increase in a typical hour during season $s = 2$ and period $t = 2$ is $9150 divided by 183, i.e., $50. In other words, the marginal value of demand in a typical hour during season $s = 2$ and period $t = 2$ is $50/MWh, which is also the market-clearing price as indicated in Fig. 2.2. From (2.7b), this is also the operating cost of the marginal technology plus the marginal value of capacity, i.e., for technology $u = 3$ during season $s = 2$ and period $t = 2$, we have $\lambda_{s,t} = W_s C^{\text{opr}}_{s,t,u} + \beta_{s,t,u} - \phi^{y}_{s,t,u} = 183 \times 50 + 0 - 0 = 9150$, where the values for $\beta_{s,t,u}$ and $\phi^{y}_{s,t,u}$ are zero because neither the capacity-limit constraint nor the non-negativity constraint is binding. By contrast, (2.7b) for the two inframarginal technologies reveals the same $\beta_{s,t,u}$ values as in Table 2.7, viz. $\beta_{s,t,u} = -183 \times 0 + 9150 + 0 = 9150$ for technology $u = 1$ and $\beta_{s,t,u} = -183 \times 20 + 9150 + 0 = 5490$ for technology $u = 2$. The interpretation of the $\beta_{s,t,u}$ values for each technology is facilitated via (2.8b), viz. that they indicate the marginal impact of additional capacity of technology u on the annual minimized cost. In particular, for $u = 1$, we note that $-\sum_{s \in \mathcal{S}} \sum_{t \in \mathcal{T}} A_{s,t,u} T_t \beta_{s,t,u} = -0.20 \times 8 \times 3660 - 0.10 \times 8 \times 9150 - 0.05 \times 8 \times 91500 - 0.25 \times 8 \times 91500 - 0.50 \times 8 \times 9150 - 0.75 \times 8 \times 3660 = -291336$. Hence, a *ceteris paribus* increase in the installed capacity of technology $u = 1$ by 1 MW would decrease the annual minimized cost by $291,336.[10]

[9] This assumes that the *ceteris paribus* increase in the load is within the allowable increase.

[10] This assumes that the *ceteris paribus* increase in the installed capacity of technology $u = 1$ is within the allowable increase.

2.3 Investment Costs

In the long run, it is possible to modify installed capacity, e.g., via investment in new plants or decommissioning of existing ones. If investment occurs, then capital costs need to be incorporated into the total cost. These costs are typically amortized over the lifetime of the plant in order to have a basis for comparison with operating cost. Using publicly available data, we will explain how to incorporate so-called levelized costs in least-cost planning models.

2.3.1 Calculating Levelized Costs

The costs of investment in new power plants are typically reported as overnight capital costs on a \$/kW basis. Such costs reflect the total cost to a developer including labor, material, transportation, project management, electrical and mechanical equipment, land, and utility interconnection costs, for example. In [17], overnight capital costs are reported for representative technology types, e.g., that of a 650 MW coal plant is \$3676/kW. Assuming a thirty-year lifetime for the plant and a 5%/a interest rate (where "a" stands for "annum"), the amortized fixed cost may be calculated as follows [9]:

$$\frac{\$3676}{\text{kW}} \times \left[\frac{0.05 \times 1.05^{30}}{1.05^{30} - 1}\right] = \frac{\$239.12}{\text{kW-a}} \tag{2.9}$$

Subsequently, the amortized fixed cost in (2.9) may be allocated over a given year (assuming 366 days or 8784 h in the year) in order to facilitate comparison with operating costs on a \$/MWh basis as follows:

$$\frac{\$239.12}{\text{kW-a}} \times \frac{1000\,\text{kW}}{1\,\text{MW}} \times \frac{1\,\text{a}}{8784\,\text{h}} = \frac{\$27.22}{\text{MWh}} \tag{2.10}$$

Combining the amortized fixed cost, $\overline{C}_u^{\text{gen}}$, in (2.9) with the variable cost, $\overline{C}_u^{\text{opr}}$, of \$20/MWh from Fig. 2.2, the levelized cost (in \$/MW-a) of the coal plant that operates for $\overline{H}$ hours per annum may be calculated as follows:

$$\begin{aligned} \overline{C}_u\left(\overline{H}\right) &= \overline{C}_u^{\text{gen}} + \overline{C}_u^{\text{opr}} \times \overline{H} \\ &= \frac{\$239120}{\text{MW-a}} + \frac{\$20}{\text{MWh}} \times \overline{H} \end{aligned} \tag{2.11}$$

Thus, such a plant that operates for 8784 hours per annum has a levelized cost of \$414,200/MW-a.

Likewise, in [17], overnight capital costs for a 430 MW combined-cycle gas-fired plant and a 200 MW on-shore wind plant are \$1084/kW and \$1265/kW, respectively. Assuming thirty-year lifetimes and 5%/a interest rates for both, (2.9) may be used to obtain amortized fixed costs of \$70.51/kW-a and \$82.29/kW-a, respectively. Via (2.10), this yields \$8.03/MWh and \$9.37/MWh, respectively. Finally, the levelized costs of these two technologies may be calculated from (2.11) as $\frac{\$70510}{\text{MW-a}} + \frac{\$50}{\text{MWh}} \times \overline{H}$ and $\frac{\$82290}{\text{MW-a}} + \frac{\$0}{\text{MWh}} \times \overline{H}$, respectively.

2.3.2 *Screening Curves*

In conventional energy-planning models [22, 40], the levelized costs calculated in (2.11) are used to trace out the minimum-cost technology combination to meet a given annual demand distribution. The latter is called a load-duration curve in which a cumulative frequency distribution of the annual demand is represented. By matching the least-cost technologies to the demand durations, the joint investment and operational decisions are rendered in an intuitive manner. We illustrate how to use screening curves with the load-duration curve in Illustrative Example 2.2 in the absence of VRES. However, it should be noted that this method for energy planning is based on the assumptions that supply output is not intermittent and that conventional technologies will not be ramp-constrained. Consequently, the chronology of energy demand may be neglected, which enables the load-duration curve to "slice" the annual energy demand into strata to be served by candidate technologies. Yet, the increased penetration of VRES undermines the validity of this framework because the intermittency of supply increases the need for flexibility, e.g., through ramping of conventional technologies or storage. Therefore, ignoring the time-dependence of such decisions in conventional energy-planning models based on the load-duration curve will distort the actual cost of serving energy demand. We will explore remedies to this framework, e.g., scaling VRES availability or using a so-called residual load-duration curve, but, first, we illustrate how conventional energy planning works in the absence of VRES.

Illustrative Example 2.2 *Investment planning and generation dispatch via screening curves and the load-duration curve.*

We ignore VRES and focus on energy planning with conventional technologies only. First, via (2.11), the screening curves for coal and gas have equations $\frac{\$239120}{\text{MW-a}} + \frac{\$20}{\text{MWh}} \times \overline{H}$ and $\frac{\$70510}{\text{MW-a}} + \frac{\$50}{\text{MWh}} \times \overline{H}$, respectively. These lines are plotted in the upper panel of Fig. 2.3. Note that the curves intersect when $\overline{H}$ equals 5626.33 h, which means that the lower envelope of levelized costs is traced out in bold. In effect, due to a higher amortized fixed cost and lower variable cost, coal's levelized cost is lower than that of gas if it is operated for more than 5626.33 h during the year, while gas is cheaper otherwise. Using this threshold, the load-duration curve is "sliced" into base and peak loads with the technologies' capacities scaled accordingly to satisfy them. In order to derive a load-duration curve using the demand data from Table 2.2 in Illustrative Example 2.1, we first define $\ell \in \mathcal{L}$ as the load slices for the year.

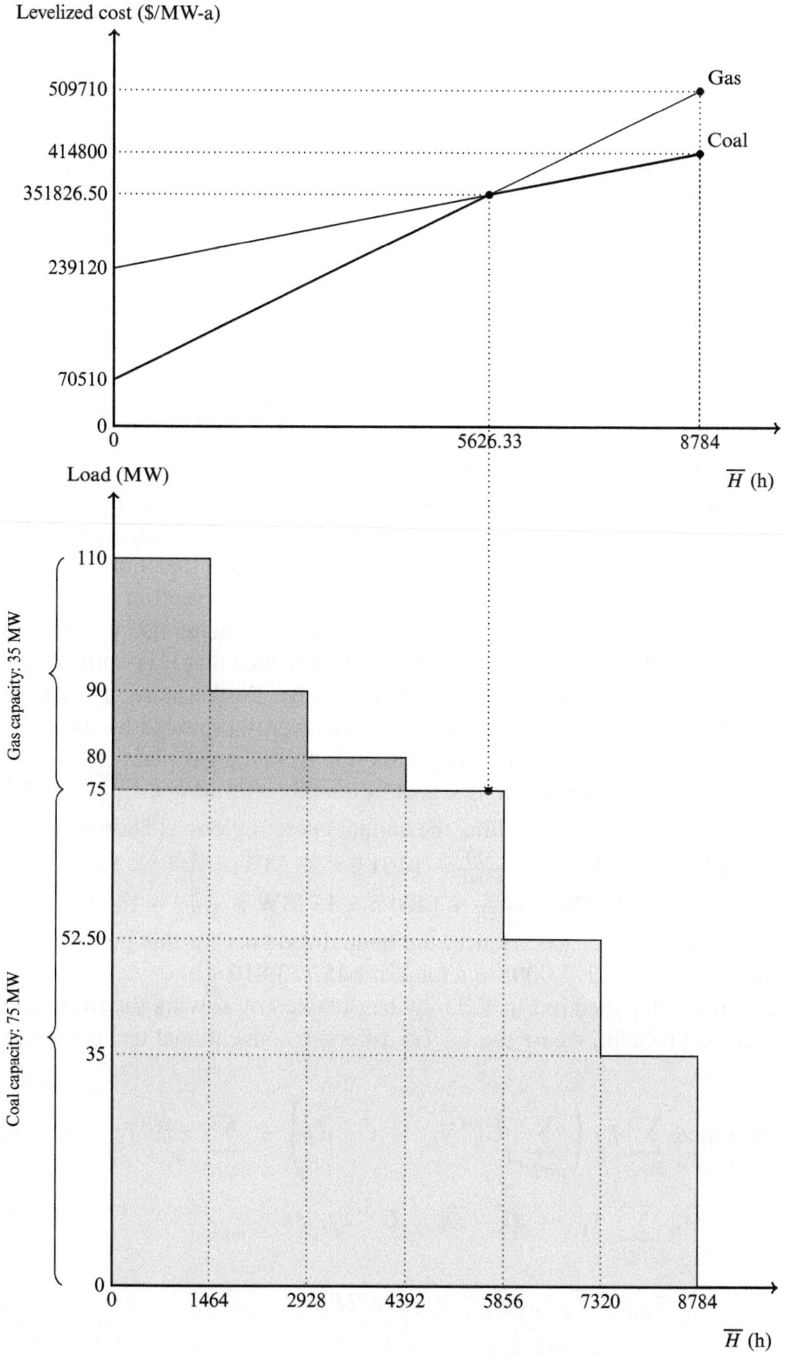

Fig. 2.3 Screening curves and load-duration curve without VRES

Table 2.8 Load levels, $\overline{D}_{(\ell)}$ (MW)

(1)	(2)	(3)	(4)	(5)	(6)
35	52.50	75	80	90	110

Given the six demand levels in Table 2.2, we conveniently use six load slices with load levels (in MW), $\overline{D}_{\ell}$, and load durations (in h), $\overline{T}_{\ell}$, defined as follows:

$$\overline{D}_{(\ell)} = \frac{D_{s,t}}{T_t}, \forall \ell : \ O(s,t) = O(\ell) \tag{2.12}$$

$$\overline{T}_{(\ell)} = W_s T_t, \forall \ell : \ O(s,t) = O(\ell) \tag{2.13}$$

where $\overline{D}_{(\ell)}$ is the ordered statistic for the load levels, $(\ell) = (1), (2), \ldots, (|\mathcal{L}|)$, and $O(s,t)$ is a mapping of the indices (s,t) to an ordinal ranking. For example, the demand data in Table 2.2 yield $O(1,1) = 1$, $O(2,3) = 2$, and $O(2,1) = 6$. Consequently, the load levels are calculated in Table 2.8, whereas $\overline{T}_{(\ell)}$ are all equal to 1464 h. Using $\overline{D}_{(\ell)}$ and $\overline{T}_{(\ell)}$, the corresponding load-duration curve appears in the lower panel of Fig. 2.3. Subsequently, as we trace down the point of intersection between the screening curves from the upper to the lower panel in Fig. 2.3, we end up at point (5626.33, 75) on the load-duration curve. Tracing this point to the left, we hit the vertical axis at point (0, 75), which indicates that it is optimal to install 75 MW of coal capacity and 35 MW of gas capacity. Furthermore, the light-shaded region of the load-duration curve represents the energy provided by the coal plant, and the dark-shaded region indicates production from the gas plant. The annualized investment cost corresponding to this generation mix is 75 MW$\times \frac{\$239120}{\text{MW-a}}$+35 MW$\times \frac{\$70510}{\text{MW-a}} = \$20{,}401{,}850$. Meanwhile, the annual operating cost is 5856 h $\times$ 75 MW $\times \frac{\$20}{\text{MWh}} + 1464$ h $\times$ 52.50 MW $\times \frac{\$20}{\text{MWh}} + 1464$ h $\times$ 35 MW $\times \frac{\$20}{\text{MWh}} = \$11{,}346{,}000$ for coal and 1464 h $\times$ 35 MW $\times \frac{\$50}{\text{MWh}} + 1464$ h $\times$ 15 MW $\times \frac{\$50}{\text{MWh}} + 1464$ h $\times$ 5 MW $\times \frac{\$50}{\text{MWh}} = \$4{,}026{,}000$ for gas. Hence, the annualized cost for this generation mix is \$20,401,850 plus \$15,372,000 for a total of \$35,773,850.

The solution depicted in Fig. 2.3 may be obtained by solving the following cost-minimization problem, where the set $\mathcal{U}^C$ refers to conventional technologies:

$$\underset{\overline{d}_{\ell}, \overline{y}_{\ell,u}, \overline{x}_u}{\text{Minimize}} \sum_{\ell \in \mathcal{L}} \overline{T}_{\ell} \left(\sum_{u \in \mathcal{U}^C} \overline{C}_u^{\text{opr}} \overline{y}_{\ell,u} + \overline{C}_{\ell}^{\text{lsh}} \overline{d}_{\ell} \right) + \sum_{u \in \mathcal{U}^C} C_u^{\text{gen}} \overline{x}_u \tag{2.14a}$$

$$\text{s.t.} \sum_{u \in \mathcal{U}^C} \overline{y}_{\ell,u} + \overline{d}_{\ell} - \overline{D}_{\ell} = 0 : \ \overline{\lambda}_{\ell}, \ \forall \ell \tag{2.14b}$$

$$\overline{y}_{\ell,u} \leq \overline{T}_{\ell} \overline{x}_u : \overline{\beta}_{\ell,u}, \forall \ell, u \in \mathcal{U}^C \tag{2.14c}$$

$$\overline{d}_{\ell} \geq 0 : \ \overline{\phi}_{\ell}^d, \ \forall \ell \tag{2.14d}$$

$$\overline{y}_{\ell,u} \geq 0 : \overline{\phi}^{y}_{\ell,u}, \forall \ell, u \in \mathcal{U}^{C} \tag{2.14e}$$

$$\overline{x}_{u} \geq 0 : \overline{\phi}^{x}_{u}, \forall u \in \mathcal{U}^{C} \tag{2.14f}$$

Similar to (2.5a)–(2.5e), it aims to minimize the annual operating cost of generation technologies subject to demand balance and capacity constraints. However, (2.14a)–(2.14f) includes the annualized investment cost in (2.14a), treats capacities as decision variables, $\overline{x}_u$, and uses the load-duration definitions (2.12)–(2.13) instead of energy demands. In addition, the operating cost of the generation mix in Illustrative Example 2.2 may be verified by inserting the fixed capacities for coal and gas plants into the problem instance of Illustrative Example 2.1 that solves (2.5a)–(2.5e).

In the absence of VRES, screening curves combined with the load-duration curve provide an adequate assessment of energy planning. A naïve extension of this approach to incorporate VRES would be simply to scale VRES capacity by the average availability factor for each technology, i.e., $\overline{A}_u \equiv \frac{\sum_{s \in \mathcal{S}} \sum_{t \in \mathcal{T}} W_s A_{s,t,u}}{|\mathcal{T}| \sum_{s \in \mathcal{S}} W_s}$. However, such a scaling ignores the chronology of VRES availability and does not capture its correlation with demand as Illustrative Example 2.3 demonstrates next.

Illustrative Example 2.3 *Investment planning and generation dispatch via screening curves and the load-duration curve with scaled VRES capacity.*

Using the data in Table 2.3 from Illustrative Example 2.1, we calculate $\overline{A}_u$ for VRES as $\frac{183 \times (0.20+0.10+0.05)+183 \times (0.25+0.50+0.75)}{3 \times (183+183)} = 0.308333$. Next, we scale the levelized cost of wind by this factor to make it $\frac{\$82290}{\text{MW-a}} \times \frac{1}{0.308333} = \frac{\$266887}{\text{MW-a}}$ as depicted in the upper panel of Fig. 2.4. In spite of this scaled levelized cost, coal is "screened out," i.e., it never has the lowest levelized cost for any capacity usage. Instead, the wind and gas screening curves intersect at 3927.52 h, thereby implying that wind functions as the baseload technology for nearly 5000 h during the year. Tracing this point of intersection down to the lower panel of Fig. 2.4, we find that it hits the load-duration curve at point (3927.52, 80). As we trace this point to the left, we hit the vertical axis at point (0, 80), which implies that the load is "sliced" such that the scaled capacity requirements are 80 MW of wind and 30 MW of gas. Note that the 80 MW of scaled wind capacity becomes $\frac{80\text{ MW}}{0.308333} = 259.46$ MW of nominal wind capacity. The annualized investment cost of this generation mix is 259.46 MW $\times \frac{\$82290}{\text{MW-a}} + 30$ MW $\times \frac{\$70510}{\text{MW-a}} = \$23,466,263$. Assuming a constant availability factor of 0.308333 for wind throughout the year, the annual operating cost is zero for wind (since it always has enough capacity to produce up to 80 MW of power) and is 1464 h $\times$ 30 MW $\times \frac{\$50}{\text{MWh}} + 1464$ h $\times$ 10 MW $\times \frac{\$50}{\text{MWh}} = \$2,928,000$ for gas. However, the implied annual cost of \$26,394,263 is overly optimistic for this generation mix once the actual wind availability factor is used. For example, fixing the wind and gas capacities to 259.46 MW and 30 MW, respectively, in the least-cost optimal dispatch problem, (2.5a)–(2.5e), we obtain an annual operating cost of \$66,038,112 for a total annual cost of \$89,504,333. In reality, the operating cost is higher because the wind resource is not available at its average, viz. during

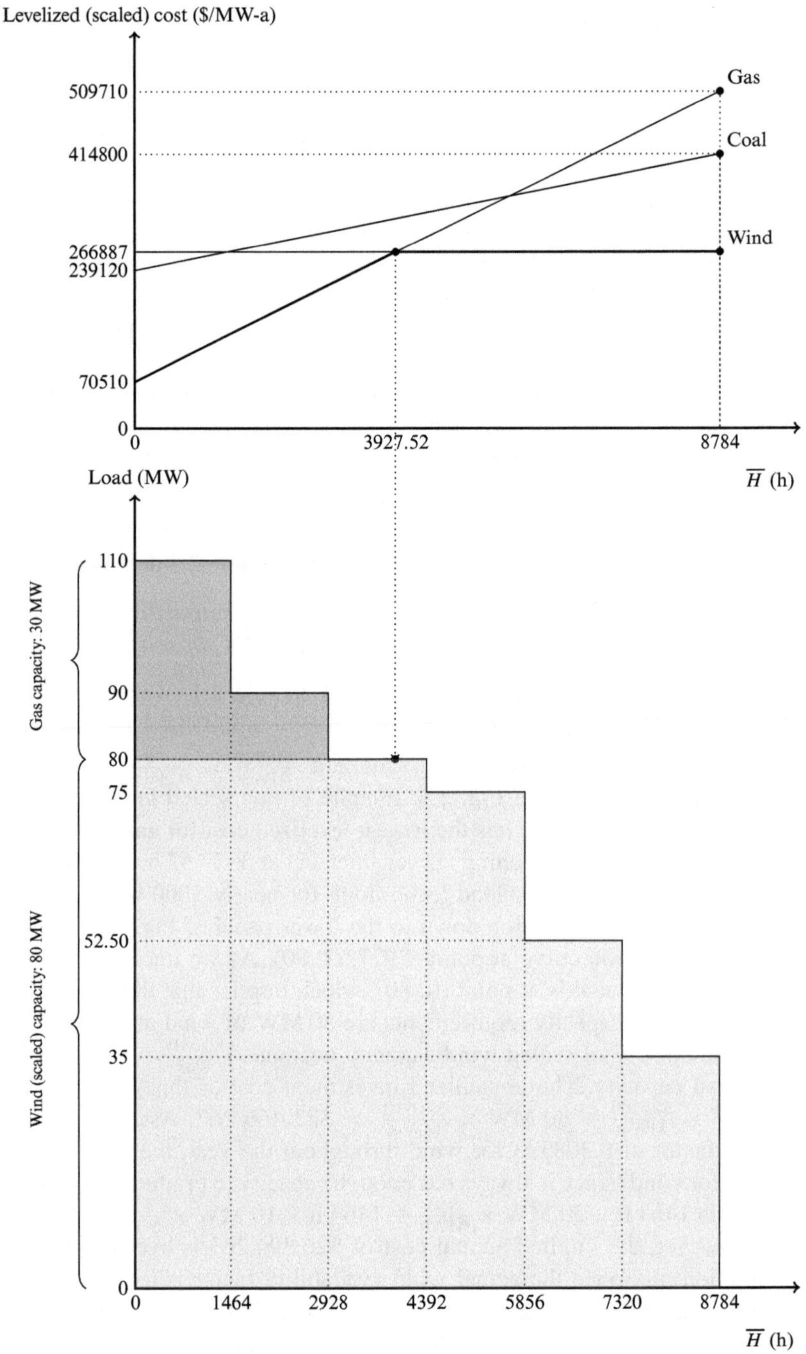

Fig. 2.4 Screening curves and load-duration curve with scaled VRES capacity

load slices (3), (5), and (6). These correspond to season and period combinations of (1, 2), (1, 3), and (2, 1), respectively. During these instances, the wind availability is relatively low compared to the load, thus necessitating load shedding together with increased gas dispatch.[11] Hence, the operating cost is actually $1464\text{ h} \times 30\text{ MW} \times \frac{\$50}{\text{MWh}} + 1464\text{ h} \times 19.054\text{ MW} \times \frac{\$500}{\text{MWh}} + 1464\text{ h} \times 30\text{ MW} \times \frac{\$50}{\text{MWh}} + 1464\text{ h} \times 47.027\text{ MW} \times \frac{\$500}{\text{MWh}} + 1464\text{ h} \times 30\text{ MW} \times \frac{\$50}{\text{MWh}} + 1464\text{ h} \times 15.135\text{ MW} \times \frac{\$500}{\text{MWh}} = \$66{,}038{,}112$.

The scaled solution depicted in Fig. 2.4 may also be obtained by solving (2.14a)–(2.14f) with the modifications that all technologies are included (and not only $u \in \mathcal{U}^C$) and (2.14c) becomes $\overline{y}_{\ell,u} \le \overline{T}_\ell \overline{A}_u \overline{x}_u : \beta_{\ell,u}, \forall \ell, u$. Nevertheless, the scaled approach typically underestimates system operating costs because it destroys the chronology of VRES output [32].

Given the commitment to VRES targets in many electricity industries, such technologies may be treated as must-run plants and netted out from load-duration curves [43, 49] as follows:

$$\hat{D}_{(\ell)} = \left\{ \overline{D}_{(\ell)} - \sum_{u \in \mathcal{U}^R} A_{s,t,u} K_u \right\}^+ , \forall \ell : O(s,t) = O(\ell) \tag{2.15}$$

where $\mathcal{U}^R$ is the set of all VRES technologies.[12] In effect, by fixing VRES capacity a priori, it is possible to derive a so-called residual load-duration curve that preserves the chronology. Subsequently, the optimal generation mix of conventional technologies may be determined on the basis of the residual load-duration curve.

Illustrative Example 2.4 *Investment planning and generation dispatch via screening curves and the residual load-duration curve with 10% VRES capacity.*

We use the same data as in Illustrative Example 2.2 with the exception that the jurisdiction has a 10% VRES capacity obligation, i.e., there should be enough VRES capacity to cover at least 10% of peak load. In this case, since peak load is 110 MW, 11 MW of wind capacity is assumed. As such, the screening curves in the upper panel of Fig. 2.5 are the same as those in Fig. 2.3. The main difference is in netting out the VRES output in each load slice as in (2.15), e.g., $\hat{D}_{(1)} = \{35 - 0.20 \times 11\}^+ = 32.80$, in order to create the residual load-duration curve in the lower panel of Fig. 2.5. Again, using the intersection at 5626.33 h for the screening curves in the upper panel of Fig. 2.5, we trace it down to the residual load-duration curve in the lower panel of Fig. 2.5. This time, we end up at point (5626.33, 73.90) on the residual load-duration curve, which means that it is optimal to install 73.90 MW of coal and 33.35 MW of gas in addition to the

[11] Although wind availability during (1, 1) is also below the average, the shortfall is mitigated by the fact this is also a low-demand instance.

[12] $\mathcal{U}^R \cup \mathcal{U}^C = \mathcal{U}$, $\mathcal{U}^R \cap \mathcal{U}^C = \emptyset$, $K_u, \forall u \in \mathcal{U}^R$ are fixed capacities, and $\{X\}^+$ refers to the positive part of X.

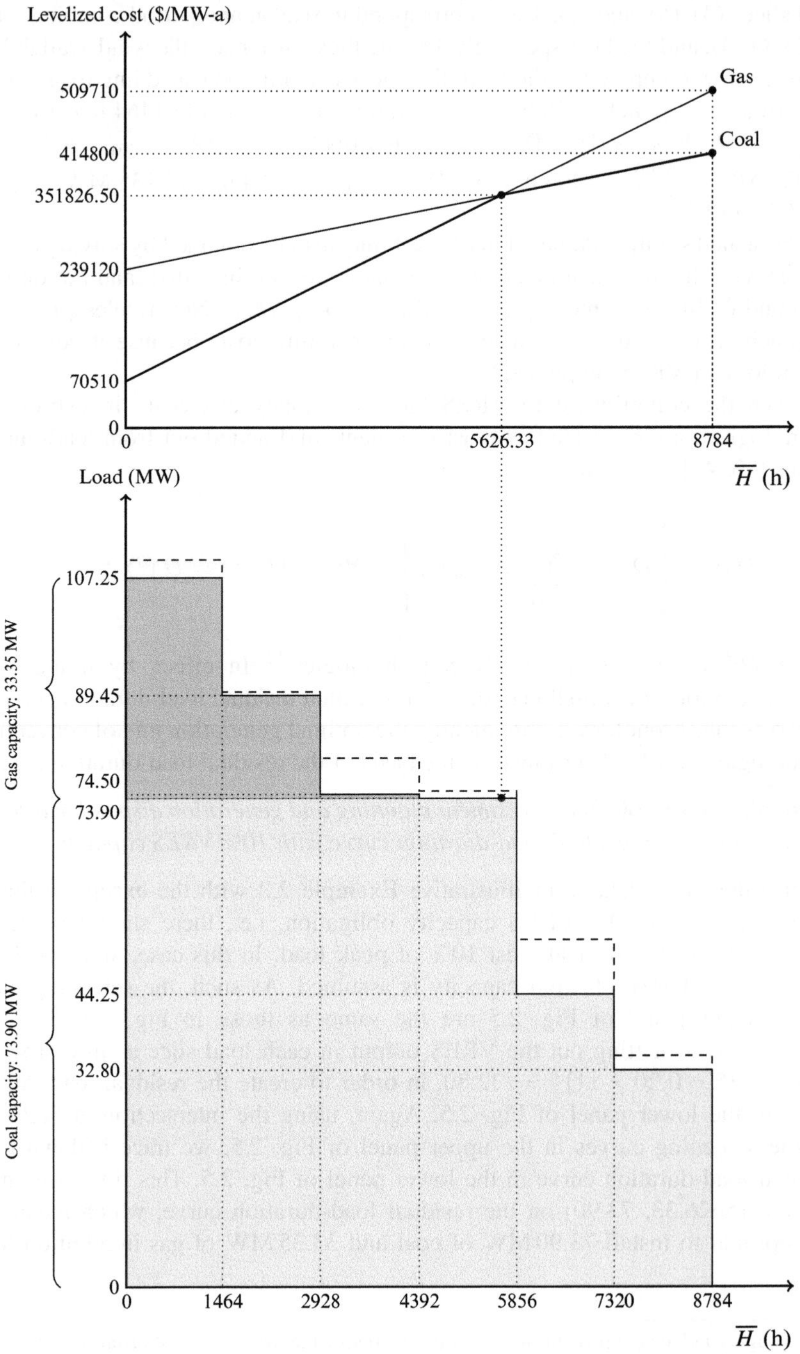

Fig. 2.5 Screening curves and residual load-duration curve with 10% VRES capacity

mandated 11 MW of wind capacity. Due to VRES output, the need for conventional capacity is trimmed to the reduced shaded areas in the lower panel of Fig. 2.5. As a result, the annualized investment cost corresponding to this generation mix is $73.90\ \text{MW} \times \frac{\$239120}{\text{MW-a}} + 33.35\ \text{MW} \times \frac{\$70510}{\text{MW-a}} + 11\ \text{MW} \times \frac{\$82290}{\text{MW-a}} = \$20{,}927{,}666.50$. Meanwhile, the annual operating cost is $5856\ \text{h} \times 73.90\ \text{MW} \times \frac{\$20}{\text{MWh}} + 1464\ \text{h} \times 44.25\ \text{MW} \times \frac{\$20}{\text{MWh}} + 1464\ \text{h} \times 32.80\ \text{MW} \times \frac{\$20}{\text{MWh}} = \$10{,}911{,}192$ for coal and $1464\ \text{h} \times 33.35\ \text{MW} \times \frac{\$50}{\text{MWh}} + 1464\ \text{h} \times 15.55\ \text{MW} \times \frac{\$50}{\text{MWh}} + 1464\ \text{h} \times 0.60\ \text{MW} \times \frac{\$50}{\text{MWh}} = \$3{,}623{,}400$ for gas. Hence, the annualized cost for this generation mix is \$20,927,666.50 plus \$14,534,592 for a total of \$35,462,258.50.

The annualized cost in Illustrative Example 2.4 may be verified by fixing capacities of all technologies and running the problem instance of (2.5a)–(2.5e) with the other data from Illustrative Example 2.1. Equivalently, the result may also be obtained by running the problem instance of (2.14a)–(2.14f) in which (2.14b) is modified such that $\overline{D}_\ell$ is replaced by $\hat{D}_\ell$.

In summary, although screening curves provide valuable intuition for generation planning in a power system without much variability, their use in modern power systems with a high penetration of VRES could grossly underestimate operating costs since load-duration curves do not preserve the chronology of energy production and consumption. While residual load-duration curves improve the representation of time vis-à-vis naïvely scaling VRES availability, they are still hampered by their exogenous treatment of VRES capacity. In practice, the analysis with residual load-duration curves in Illustrative Example 2.4 may be repeated for several VRES capacity levels [43].

Nevertheless, aspects such as unit commitment and ramping constraints are more prominent in power systems with high VRES penetration. In other words, unlike the traditional screening-curve approach with its assumption that all installed technologies are controllable and their capacity could be matched to load slices, the impact of short-term cycling of thermal plants on investment decisions cannot be ignored. While heuristics that adjust the screening-curve method [2, 49] enable a system-wide allocation of costs from cycling of conventional plants precipitated by increased VRES penetration, an optimization approach as outlined in Sect. 2.3.3 provides a comprehensive assessment of energy planning. Extensions to allow for ramping constraints and energy storage are provided in Sects. 2.5 and 2.6, respectively.

2.3.3 Investment Planning

The same nomenclature as in Sect. 2.2.3 is used here with the following additions.

Parameter

C_u^{gen} Annualized investment cost of technology u [\$/MW].

Primal Variable

x_u Capacity investment in technology u [MW].

Dual Variable

ϕ_u^x Marginal value of non-negativity of capacity investment for technology u [\$/MW].

As alluded to in Sect. 2.3.2, the use of screening curves with a load-duration curve may be limited in handling investment in generation capacity with VRES. Other aspects that such an approach may neglect are short-term operational constraints of thermal plants, energy storage, and market power. Furthermore, investment decisions are typically undertaken over a multi-year horizon for discrete units at specific locations. These facets are again difficult to incorporate in the approach with screening curves because it assumes that decisions are undertaken for a target year with continuous capacity sizing and no transmission constraints. We will investigate some of these features either in this chapter or later in this book, e.g., ramping constraints in Sect. 2.5, energy storage in Sect. 2.6, transmission constraints in Chap. 3, unit commitment in Chap. 4, market power in Chap. 5, externalities in Chap. 6, and transmission investment in Chap. 7. Investment planning over a multi-year horizon and with discrete units is explored in more detail in [9]. Instead, our focus in this section is to extend the cost-minimization LP for economic dispatch in Sect. 2.2.3 to allow for capacity expansion in a manner that accounts for VRES output.

Given these assumptions, the cost-minimization LP for generation expansion and operations is:

$$\underset{d_{s,t},y_{s,t,u},x_u}{\text{Minimize}} \sum_{s\in\mathcal{S}} W_s \sum_{t\in\mathcal{T}} \left(\sum_{u\in\mathcal{U}} C^{\text{opr}}_{s,t,u} y_{s,t,u} + C^{\text{lsh}}_{s,t} d_{s,t} \right) + \sum_{u\in\mathcal{U}} C^{\text{gen}}_u x_u \tag{2.16a}$$

$$\text{s.t.} \sum_{u\in\mathcal{U}} y_{s,t,u} + d_{s,t} - D_{s,t} = 0 : \lambda_{s,t}, \ \forall s,t \tag{2.16b}$$

$$y_{s,t,u} \leq A_{s,t,u} T_t x_u : \beta_{s,t,u}, \ \forall s,t,u \tag{2.16c}$$

$$d_{s,t} \geq 0 : \phi^d_{s,t}, \ \forall s,t \tag{2.16d}$$

$$y_{s,t,u} \geq 0 : \phi^y_{s,t,u}, \ \forall s,t,u \tag{2.16e}$$

$$x_u \geq 0 : \phi^x_u, \ \forall u \tag{2.16f}$$

where (2.16a) is the annualized investment and operating cost for a test year, i.e., similar to that in (2.5a) with the addition of the investment cost, $\sum_{u\in\mathcal{U}} C^{\text{gen}}_u x_u$. The energy-balance constraint (2.16b) is identical to that in (2.5b), while x_u substitutes for K_u in the right-hand side of (2.5c) to yield (2.16c) in the capacity constraint. Finally, (2.16f) is the non-negativity constraint for the investment decision, x_u.

Because of its intentional similarity to (2.5a)–(2.5e), the Lagrangian function for (2.16a)–(2.16f) differs from (2.6a) only in the terms involving x_u:

$$
\begin{aligned}
L = &\sum_{s\in\mathcal{S}} W_s \sum_{t\in\mathcal{T}} \left(\sum_{u\in\mathcal{U}} C^{\text{opr}}_{s,t,u} y_{s,t,u} + C^{\text{lsh}}_{s,t} d_{s,t} \right) + \sum_{u\in\mathcal{U}} C^{\text{gen}}_u x_u \\
&- \sum_{s\in\mathcal{S}} \sum_{t\in\mathcal{T}} \lambda_{s,t} \left(\sum_{u\in\mathcal{U}} y_{s,t,u} + d_{s,t} - D_{s,t} \right) \\
&- \sum_{s\in\mathcal{S}} \sum_{t\in\mathcal{T}} \sum_{u\in\mathcal{U}} \beta_{s,t,u} \left(A_{s,t,u} T_t x_u - y_{s,t,u} \right) \\
&- \sum_{s\in\mathcal{S}} \sum_{t\in\mathcal{T}} d_{s,t} \phi^d_{s,t} - \sum_{s\in\mathcal{S}} \sum_{t\in\mathcal{T}} \sum_{u\in\mathcal{U}} y_{s,t,u} \phi^y_{s,t,u} - \sum_{u\in\mathcal{U}} x_u \phi^x_u
\end{aligned} \tag{2.17a}
$$

Consequently, the KKT conditions of (2.16a)–(2.16f) are similar to those of (2.5a)–(2.5e). In particular, (2.7a)–(2.7c), (2.7e)–(2.7f), and (2.7h)–(2.7l) all hold as before, but (2.7d) and (2.7g) are modified as follows:

$$A_{s,t,u} T_t x_u - y_{s,t,u} \geq 0, \ \forall s, t, u \tag{2.18a}$$

$$\beta_{s,t,u} \left(A_{s,t,u} T_t x_u - y_{s,t,u} \right) = 0, \ \forall s, t, u \tag{2.18b}$$

Moreover, the following KKT conditions related to x_u are added:

$$C^{\text{gen}}_u - \sum_{s\in\mathcal{S}} \sum_{t\in\mathcal{T}} \beta_{s,t,u} A_{s,t,u} T_t - \phi^x_u = 0, \ \forall u \tag{2.19a}$$

$$x_u \geq 0, \ \forall u \tag{2.19b}$$

$$x_u \phi^x_u = 0, \ \forall u \tag{2.19c}$$

$$\phi^x_u \geq 0, \ \forall u \tag{2.19d}$$

Note that (2.19a) is simply the stationarity condition with respect to x_u, whereas (2.19c) and (2.19d) are the complementarity condition and the non-negativity condition, cf. (2.7i) and (2.7l).

From KKT conditions (2.7a)–(2.7c), (2.7e)–(2.7f), (2.7h)–(2.7l), (2.18a)–(2.18b), and (2.19a)–(2.19d), we obtain two important economic insights. First, suppose that a technology, u', has a strictly positive capacity installed, i.e., $x_{u'} > 0$, and is always dispatched at its available capacity, i.e., $y_{s,t,u'} > 0, \ \forall s, t$ and $y_{s,t,u'} = A_{s,t,u'} T_t x_{u'} \ \forall s, t$. From (2.19c), $x_{u'} > 0$ implies $\phi^x_{u'} = 0$, which renders $\sum_{s\in\mathcal{S}} \sum_{t\in\mathcal{T}} \beta_{s,t,u'} A_{s,t,u'} T_t = C^{\text{gen}}_{u'}$ from (2.19a). Next, $y_{s,t,u'} > 0, \ \forall s, t$ in (2.7i) yields $\phi^y_{s,t,u'} = 0, \ \forall s, t$ and $y_{s,t,u'} = A_{s,t,u'} T_t x_{u'} \ \forall s, t$ in (2.18b) yields $\beta_{s,t,u'} \geq 0, \ \forall s, t$. Multiplying both sides of (2.7b) for u' by $A_{s,t,u'} T_t$ and summing up over all s, t yields $\sum_{s\in\mathcal{S}}\sum_{t\in\mathcal{T}} W_s C^{\text{opr}}_{s,t,u'} A_{s,t,u'} T_t + \sum_{s\in\mathcal{S}}\sum_{t\in\mathcal{T}} \beta_{s,t,u'} A_{s,t,u'} T_t = \sum_{s\in\mathcal{S}}\sum_{t\in\mathcal{T}} A_{s,t,u'} T_t \lambda_{s,t}$, which boils down to

$$\sum_{s\in\mathcal{S}}\sum_{t\in\mathcal{T}} W_s C^{\text{opr}}_{s,t,u'} A_{s,t,u'} T_t + C^{\text{gen}}_{u'} = \sum_{s\in\mathcal{S}}\sum_{t\in\mathcal{T}} A_{s,t,u'} T_t \lambda_{s,t} \tag{2.20}$$

after use of (2.19a) for u'. In other words, a technology u' that is adopted and dispatched at its available capacity throughout the entire year earns precisely enough revenues to cover its annualized investment cost plus its annual operating cost. Here, the annualized investment cost plus the annual operating cost may be thought of as the long-run marginal cost.

Second, in contrast, suppose that a technology $\hat{u}$ is adopted, i.e., $x_{\hat{u}} > 0$ and $\phi^x_{\hat{u}} = 0$ from (2.19c), but never dispatched at its available capacity, i.e., $0 < y_{s,t,\hat{u}} < A_{s,t,\hat{u}} T_t x_{\hat{u}},\ \forall s, t$. From (2.18b) for $\hat{u}$, this implies that $\beta_{s,t,\hat{u}} = 0,\ \forall s, t$. However, if $C^{\text{gen}}_{\hat{u}} > 0$, then (2.19a) would not hold, i.e., it would contradict our supposition that $x_{\hat{u}} > 0$ and $\phi^x_{\hat{u}} = 0$. Hence, a technology $\hat{u}$ that is not dispatched at its available capacity in at least one (s, t) combination will never be adopted in the first place.

In summary, if a technology is adopted, then it must be dispatched at its available capacity in at least one (s, t) combination over the year. Thus, in any (s, t) combination such that the technology is dispatched at its available capacity, we have $\beta_{s,t,\hat{u}} \geq 0$ from (2.18b) and $W_s C^{\text{opr}}_{s,t,u} + \beta_{s,t,u} = \lambda_{s,t} \Rightarrow \lambda_{s,t} - W_s C^{\text{opr}}_{s,t,u} = \beta_{s,t,u} \geq 0$ from (2.7b), i.e., the revenue earned by the technology at least covers its operating cost. By contrast, if an adopted technology is dispatched at less than its available capacity in a given (s, t) combination, then we have $\beta_{s,t,u} = 0$ from (2.18b) and $\lambda_{s,t} = W_s C^{\text{opr}}_{s,t,u}$ from (2.7b), i.e., the revenue earned by the technology is just sufficient to cover its operating cost. Hence, for a technology to be adopted, it must earn revenues above its operating cost in at least one (s, t) combination over the year in order to be able to cover its annualized investment cost.

Illustrative Example 2.5 *Cost-minimizing LP for generation expansion.*

We revisit Illustrative Example 2.1 in which the capacities of wind, coal, and gas were arbitrarily fixed at 25 MW, 35 MW, and 40 MW, respectively. Here, we endogenously select the technologies' capacities, x_u, by executing a problem instance of (2.16a)–(2.16f) using demand and VRES availability data in Tables 2.2 and 2.3, respectively, along with annualized investment costs, C^{gen}_u, from Sect. 2.3.1. The latter, in particular, are \$82,290/MW, \$239,120/MW, and \$70,510/MW for wind, coal, and gas technologies, respectively. We obtain the result that the optimal investment in Table 2.9 is quite different from the arbitrary generation mix in Illustrative Example 2.1. Consequently, the minimized annual cost is \$33,847,450 with an annualized investment cost of \$19,280,650, which means that the annual

Table 2.9 Capacity investment, x_u (MW)

$u = 1$	$u = 2$	$u = 3$
100	30	55

Table 2.10 Operational decisions with generation expansion, $y_{s,t,u}$ (MWh)

Technology	Season	Period $t = 1$	$t = 2$	$t = 3$
$u = 1$	$s = 1$	160	80	40
	$s = 2$	200	400	420
$u = 2$	$s = 1$	120	240	240
	$s = 2$	240	240	0
$u = 3$	$s = 1$	0	280	440
	$s = 2$	440	0	0

Table 2.11 Marginal value of demand with generation expansion, $\lambda_{s,t}$ (\$/MWh)

Season	Period $t = 1$	$t = 2$	$t = 3$
$s = 1$	3660	9150	11,361.5625
$s = 2$	15,752.1875	8266.25	0

Table 2.12 Marginal value of capacity with generation expansion, $\beta_{s,t,u}$ (\$/MWh)

Technology	Season	Period $t = 1$	$t = 2$	$t = 3$
$u = 1$	$s = 1$	3660	9150	11,361.5625
	$s = 2$	15,752.1875	8266.25	0
$u = 2$	$s = 1$	0	5490	7701.5625
	$s = 2$	12,092.1875	4606.25	0
$u = 3$	$s = 1$	0	0	2211.5625
	$s = 2$	6602.1875	0	0

operating cost is \$14,566,800. This is substantially lower than the operating cost of \$48,055,800 in Illustrative Example 2.1 primarily because load shedding is eliminated. Indeed, capacity sizing is such that the generation dispatch in Table 2.10 is sufficient to meet energy demand. In terms of electricity prices, Table 2.11 indicates that coal is the price-setting technology in $s = 1$ and $t = 1$ (since $\lambda_{1,1} = W_1 C^{\text{opr}}_{1,1,2} = 183 \times 20$), whereas gas is the price-setting technology in $s = 1$ and $t = 2$ (since $\lambda_{1,2} = W_1 C^{\text{opr}}_{1,2,3} = 183 \times 50$). Meanwhile, the marginal values of capacity in Table 2.12 may be used to verify (2.19a), e.g., $\sum_{s \in \mathcal{S}} \sum_{t \in \mathcal{T}} \beta_{s,t,1} A_{s,t,1} T_t = 3660 \times 0.20 \times 8 + 9150 \times 0.10 \times 8 + 11361.5625 \times 0.05 \times 8 + 15752.1875 \times 0.25 \times 8 + 8266.25 \times 0.50 \times 8 + 0 \times 0.75 \times 8 = 82290$ for $u = 1$.[13] Thus, the weighted "capacity rents" earned by each technology cover its annualized investment cost, C^{gen}_u. Finally, note that a technology such as gas ($u = 3$) earns just enough revenue to cover its operating cost in instances when it is dispatched at below available capacity, e.g., \$9150/MWh in $s = 1$ and $t = 2$,

[13] In (2.19a) for $u = 1$, $\phi^x_1 = 0$ because $x_1 > 0$.

whereas it earns revenue above its operating cost in instances when it is dispatched at available capacity, e.g., \$11,361.56/MWh in $s = 1$ and $t = 3$.[14]

2.4 Profit Maximization

In Sects. 2.2 and 2.3, we have explored short- and long-run decisions, respectively, in the power sector from a cost-minimization perspective. Due to the deregulation of the power sector in many OECD countries, however, such operational and investment decisions are typically made by profit-maximizing power companies. Thus, instead of meeting demand in a cost-minimizing manner, firms deploy their resources in a manner that is of most benefit to them. If the market is perfectly competitive,[15] then coordination between supply and demand is provided by the market-clearing prices, viz. $\lambda_{s,t}$. These dual variables to the energy-balance constraint, (2.5b) or (2.16b), in the cost-minimization framework ensure that the marginal revenue from incremental generation is such that the optimal mix of resources will be deployed to meet demand. Therefore, under perfect competition, market-clearing prices are exogenous to the participants, and cost-minimizing outcomes can be assured even with profit-maximizing firms because they will be guided by the price signals linked to the market-clearing conditions as in Chap. 4. Hence, in this section, we will focus on a single profit-maximizing firm (since the outcome will be the same if there were several price takers) and treat departures from this admittedly restrictive supposition in Chap. 5.

2.4.1 Short-Run Profit Maximization

Given market-clearing prices, $\lambda_{s,t}$, the short-run profit-maximization problem of a price-taking firm may be formulated as an LP in (2.21a)–(2.21c). We assume that capacities are fixed and ignore certain operational features, such as ramping and storage, which we will revisit later in Sects. 2.5 and 2.6, respectively. Likewise, the load-shedding cost and the market-clearing constraint are ignored here simply to focus on the firm's incentives.

$$\underset{y_{s,t,u}}{\text{Maximize}} \sum_{s\in\mathcal{S}} W_s \sum_{t\in\mathcal{T}} \sum_{u\in\mathcal{U}} \left(\frac{\lambda_{s,t}}{W_s} - C^{\text{opr}}_{s,t,u}\right) y_{s,t,u} \tag{2.21a}$$

[14] By making the annualized investment cost of wind arbitrarily high here, it is possible to recover the result of Illustrative Example 2.2 in which only coal and gas are candidate technologies.

[15] An industry is considered to be perfectly competitive if there is perfect information, consumers believe that the product is identical, transaction costs are low, and there are no barriers to entry (in a long-run framework) [44].

$$\text{s.t. } y_{s,t,u} \leq A_{s,t,u} T_t K_u : \beta_{s,t,u}, \forall s, t, u \tag{2.21b}$$

$$y_{s,t,u} \geq 0 : \phi^y_{s,t,u}, \forall s, t, u \tag{2.21c}$$

The firm's objective function (2.21a) comprises revenues in a given (s, t) combination, $\frac{\lambda_{s,t}}{W_s} y_{s,t,u}$, less the operating costs, $\sum_{u \in \mathcal{U}} C^{\text{opr}}_{s,t,u} y_{s,t,u}$, weighted by the seasons, W_s, and summed over all (s, t). It should be noted from Sect. 2.2.3 that since $\lambda_{s,t}$ is the marginal value of an incremental increase in demand for the entire year, $\frac{\lambda_{s,t}}{W_s}$ is its marginal value in any given (s, t) combination. Meanwhile, (2.21b) is the capacity constraint (just like (2.5c)) and (2.21c) is the non-negativity constraint (just like (2.5e)) with similar interpretations for the dual variables, $\beta_{s,t,u}$ and $\phi^y_{s,t,u}$.

The economic intuition for the solution to the short-run profit-maximization LP (2.21a)–(2.21c) may be developed by examining its KKT conditions. Prior to that, we formulate the corresponding Lagrangian function:[16]

$$\begin{aligned} L = &- \sum_{s \in \mathcal{S}} W_s \sum_{t \in \mathcal{T}} \sum_{u \in \mathcal{U}} \left(\frac{\lambda_{s,t}}{W_s} - C^{\text{opr}}_{s,t,u} \right) y_{s,t,u} \\ &- \sum_{s \in \mathcal{S}} \sum_{t \in \mathcal{T}} \sum_{u \in \mathcal{U}} \beta_{s,t,u} \left(A_{s,t,u} T_t K_u - y_{s,t,u} \right) \\ &- \sum_{s \in \mathcal{S}} \sum_{t \in \mathcal{T}} \sum_{u \in \mathcal{U}} y_{s,t,u} \phi^y_{s,t,u} \end{aligned} \tag{2.22a}$$

Next, we take the KKT conditions as follows:

$$-\lambda_{s,t} + W_s C^{\text{opr}}_{s,t,u} + \beta_{s,t,u} - \phi^y_{s,t,u} = 0, \forall s, t, u \tag{2.23a}$$

$$A_{s,t,u} T_t K_u - y_{s,t,u} \geq 0, \forall s, t, u \tag{2.23b}$$

$$\beta_{s,t,u} \left(A_{s,t,u} T_t K_u - y_{s,t,u} \right) = 0, \forall s, t, u \tag{2.23c}$$

$$\beta_{s,t,u} \geq 0, \forall s, t, u \tag{2.23d}$$

$$y_{s,t,u} \geq 0, \forall s, t, u \tag{2.23e}$$

$$y_{s,t,u} \phi^y_{s,t,u} = 0, \forall s, t, u \tag{2.23f}$$

$$\phi^y_{s,t,u} \geq 0, \forall s, t, u \tag{2.23g}$$

Prominent among these is (2.23a), which states that for a technology u' that is dispatched during (s, t), i.e., $y_{s,t,u'} > 0$ and $\phi^y_{s,t,u'} = 0$, at its available capacity, i.e., $y_{s,t,u'} = A_{s,t,u'} T_t K_{u'}$ and $\beta_{s,t,u'} \geq 0$, the marginal revenue earned equals

[16] In order to facilitate comparison with the Lagrangian function for the cost-minimization problem (2.6a), we express the objective function (2.21a) as the minimization of the negative profit, i.e., $\text{Minimize}_{y_{s,t,u}} - \sum_{s \in \mathcal{S}} W_s \sum_{t \in \mathcal{T}} \sum_{u \in \mathcal{U}} \left(\frac{\lambda_{s,t}}{W_s} - C^{\text{opr}}_{s,t,u} \right) y_{s,t,u}$.

the operating cost plus any capacity rent, i.e., $\lambda_{s,t} = W_s C^{\text{opr}}_{s,t,u'} + \beta_{s,t,u'}$.[17] By contrast, a technology $\hat{u}$ that is dispatched at below its available capacity during (s,t), i.e., $y_{s,t,\hat{u}} > 0$, $\phi^y_{s,t,\hat{u}} = 0$, $y_{s,t,u'} < A_{s,t,\hat{u}} T_t K_{\hat{u}}$, and $\beta_{s,t,\hat{u}} = 0$, earns marginal revenue that is precisely equal to its operating cost, i.e., $\lambda_{s,t} = W_s C^{\text{opr}}_{s,t,\hat{u}}$. Finally, (2.23a) implies that a technology $\overline{u}$ that is not dispatched during (s,t) has $W_s C^{\text{opr}}_{s,t,\overline{u}} = \lambda_{s,t} + \phi^y_{s,t,\overline{u}}$, or $W_s C^{\text{opr}}_{s,t,\overline{u}} \geq \lambda_{s,t}$, i.e., technology $\overline{u}$'s operating costs are too high to justify its dispatch during (s,t). The remaining six KKT conditions, (2.23b)–(2.23g), are similar to those for economic dispatch, i.e., (2.7d), (2.7f), (2.7g), (2.7i), (2.7j), and (2.7l). Note that (2.23b)–(2.23g) takes the firm's myopic perspective of profit maximization and ignores the incentives of other market participants, e.g., consumers who want to minimize their costs of energy procurement, cf. (2.7a), (2.7e), (2.7h), and (2.7k), and the system operator who wants to clear the market, cf. (2.5b).

Comparative statics using the envelope theorem are also similar to those conducted for economic dispatch. For example, $\frac{\partial L}{\partial K_u} = -\sum_{s \in \mathcal{S}} \sum_{t \in \mathcal{T}} A_{s,t,u} T_t \beta_{s,t,u}, \forall u$ reflects the impact on the maximized profit due to a marginal increase in the capacity of technology u, cf. (2.8b). The negative sign may be explained by the fact that we have implicitly rendered (2.21a)–(2.21c) as a problem in which the negative of the profit is to be minimized. Thus, decreasing the minimized objective function here corresponds to increasing the maximized profit.

Illustrative Example 2.6 *Short-run profit-maximizing LP.*

Based on the operating costs, installed capacities, VRES availability, and resulting prices from Illustrative Example 2.1, let us obtain the optimal solution to a firm's short-run profit-maximization problem instance based on (2.21a)–(2.21c). The optimal solution is given in Table 2.13 yielding a maximized profit of \$112,252,200. Wind, coal, and natural-gas plants realize profits of \$7,283,400, \$52,264,800, and \$52,704,000, respectively. Marginal capacity values, $\beta_{s,t,u}$, are identical to those in Table 2.7. However, the optimal generation in Table 2.13 does not match that in Table 2.5, viz. coal generates 240 MWh and 270 MWh in $(s = 1, t = 1)$ and $(s = 2, t = 3)$, respectively, and gas generates 300 MWh and 260 MWh in $(s = 1, t = 2)$ and $(s = 2, t = 2)$, respectively, in Table 2.5 but is not dispatched here in Table 2.13. Although this discrepancy may seem puzzling at first, it does have economic and mathematical explanations.[18] First, the prices, $\lambda_{s,t}$, perceived by the firm are based on the equilibrium condition (2.5b), which is not enforced here. Therefore, the firm behaves as if it can receive the scaled price $\frac{\lambda_{s,t}}{W_s}$ =\$20/MWh in season $s = 1$ and period $t = 1$ without dispatching the coal plant. In fact, (2.23a) includes the possibility that $W_s C^{\text{opr}}_{s,t,\overline{u}} = \lambda_{s,t}$ for a technology $\overline{u}$ not dispatched during (s,t). Yet, in equilibrium, the given prices, $\lambda_{s,t}$, will be

[17] Since we focus on price takers, marginal revenue is simply the market-clearing price, $\lambda_{s,t}$.

[18] Note that coal and gas make zero operating profits in these four instances because they are the marginal technologies.

Table 2.13 Operational decisions for short-run profit maximization, $y_{s,t,u}$ (MWh)

		Period		
Technology	Season	$t = 1$	$t = 2$	$t = 3$
$u = 1$	$s = 1$	40	20	10
	$s = 2$	50	100	150
$u = 2$	$s = 1$	0	280	280
	$s = 2$	280	280	0
$u = 3$	$s = 1$	0	0	320
	$s = 2$	320	0	0

available only in the event of market clearing, which is not enforced here in this (partial-equilibrium) setting. Second, from a mathematical perspective, the optimal solution given in Table 2.13 is not unique. For example, during ($s = 1, t = 1$), a solution comprising 40 MWh of wind, 0 MWh of gas, and any linear combination between 0 MWh and 280 MWh of coal will yield the same profit. Therefore, the cost-minimizing solution in Illustrative Example 2.1 may be supported here with the same market-clearing prices as long as the market or system operator enforces the market-clearing condition (2.5b). More details on market clearing will be provided in Chap. 3. For reference, the marginal impact of an increase in a given technology's capacity is still quantified by (2.8b), i.e., for $u = 1$, $-\sum_{s\in\mathcal{S}}\sum_{t\in\mathcal{T}} A_{s,t,u}T_t\beta_{s,t,u} = -0.20\times 8\times 3660-0.10\times 8\times 9150-0.05\times 8\times 91500-0.25\times 8\times 91500-0.50\times 8\times 9150-0.75\times 8\times 3660 = -291336$. Hence, a *ceteris paribus* increase in the installed capacity of technology $u = 1$ by 1 MW (assuming that this perturbation is within the allowable increase) would decrease the annual minimized negative profit by \$291,336 (or, increase the maximized profit by the same quantity).[19]

The supply stack indicated in Fig. 2.2 is also the firm's short-run supply function as it is constructed by adding up the operating costs of the units. From the preceding discussion of KKT conditions (2.23a)–(2.23g), it is evident that a unit will be dispatched only if the price is high enough at least to cover its operating costs. Thus, Fig. 2.2 can be used to calculate the firm's short-run profit since the market-clearing price is \$50/MWh. In particular, the profits earned by wind, coal, and gas units are $50 \times 12.50 = 625$, $(50 - 20) \times 35 = 1050$, and $(50 - 50) \times 32.50 = 0$, respectively, for a total profit of \$1675. Geometrically, it is the area of the rectangle $\{(0, 0), (0, 50), (80, 50), (80, 0), (0, 0)\}$, which represents the total revenue, minus the area of the shaded region, which represents the total operating

[19] It should be emphasized that changes to installed capacities will in fact affect the market-clearing prices, $\lambda_{s,t}$, even though they are treated as exogenous by a price-taking profit-maximizing firm solving (2.21a)–(2.21c). A fuller understanding of the implications of changing capacities requires executing the appropriate problem instance of the cost-minimization problem (2.5a)–(2.5e) as in Illustrative Example 2.1. Doing so with a *ceteris paribus* increase in the installed capacity of technology $u = 1$ to 200 MW reveals, for example, that market-clearing prices would crash to zero in several instances, thereby nearly halving the profits of a notional price-taking firm. This is the so-called cannibalization effect [25] in which an increase in VRES capacity renders conventional technologies such as coal and natural gas less profitable.

cost. Note that since we ignore the amortized fixed cost, this short-run profit is also known as the producer surplus, i.e., the revenue minus the operating cost.

While we have so far dealt with technologies that exhibit constant marginal costs, it is also plausible to represent them with increasing marginal costs. Such a specification may be warranted to reflect the fact that more efficient units within a class of technology are deployed first. Likewise, the bidding up of fuel prices may lead to increasing marginal costs within a technology class. In the case of linear marginal costs (as posited by Debia et al. [11] for New York), a stylized marginal cost function for technology u may be given as follows:

$$p = C_u^{\text{int}} + C_u^{\text{slp}} y_u \tag{2.24}$$

Here, we suppress time-dependence in order to illustrate the principle of constructing an industry inverse-short-run supply curve by summing up each technology's inverse-short-run supply function. In (2.24), p is the exogenous price (in \$/MWh), C_u^{int} is the intercept parameter (in \$/MWh), C_u^{slp} is the slope parameter (in \$/MWh^2), and y_u is the generation (in MWh). Given the logic of KKT conditions (2.23a)–(2.23g), (2.24) represents the inverse-supply curve for technology u, the short-run marginal cost curve. Consequently, inverting it yields the supply curve for technology u:

$$y_u(p) = \begin{cases} 0 & \text{if } p < C_u^{\text{int}} \\ \frac{p - C_u^{\text{int}}}{C_u^{\text{slp}}} & \text{otherwise} \end{cases} \tag{2.25}$$

Note that the first line of (2.25) reflects the fact that technology u will not be dispatched if it cannot cover its operating (marginal) cost. Based on this specification, the industry supply function is obtained simply by summing all of the individual technology supply functions, i.e., $y(p) = \sum_{u \in \mathcal{U}} y_u(p)$, while taking care to respect the domain of each technology's supply function.

Illustrative Example 2.7 *Short-run supply function for an industry with linear marginal costs.*

We illustrate how to construct the short-run industry supply function with heterogenous technologies that have linear marginal costs. Suppose that the three technologies are again wind ($u = 1$), coal ($u = 2$), and gas ($u = 3$) that exhibit marginal costs as in (2.24). Data for the intercept and slope parameters are given in Table 2.14. On that basis, the technologies' marginal cost functions are:

$$p = 0.10 y_1 \tag{2.26a}$$

$$p = 20 + 0.20 y_2 \tag{2.26b}$$

$$p = 50 + 0.50 y_3 \tag{2.26c}$$

Table 2.14 Data for linear marginal costs

	Technology		
Parameter	$u = 1$	$u = 2$	$u = 3$
C_u^{int}	0	20	50
C_u^{slp}	0.10	0.20	0.50

From (2.25), we invert (2.26a)–(2.26c) to obtain each technology's short-run supply function:

$$y_1(p) = \begin{cases} 0 & \text{if } p < 0 \\ 10p & \text{otherwise} \end{cases} \tag{2.27a}$$

$$y_2(p) = \begin{cases} 0 & \text{if } p < 20 \\ 5p - 100 & \text{otherwise} \end{cases} \tag{2.27b}$$

$$y_3(p) = \begin{cases} 0 & \text{if } p < 50 \\ 2p - 100 & \text{otherwise} \end{cases} \tag{2.27c}$$

Summing up (2.27a)–(2.27c), we obtain the industry short-run supply function:

$$y(p) = \begin{cases} 0 & \text{if } p < 0 \\ 10p & \text{if } 0 \leq p < 20 \\ 15p - 100 & \text{if } 20 \leq p < 50 \\ 17p - 200 & \text{if } p \geq 50 \end{cases} \tag{2.28a}$$

Inverting (2.28a) yields the piecewise linear industry short-run marginal cost:

$$p = \begin{cases} \frac{y}{10} & \text{if } 0 \leq y < 200 \\ \frac{y+100}{15} & \text{if } 200 \leq y < 650 \\ \frac{y+200}{17} & \text{if } y \geq 650 \end{cases} \tag{2.29a}$$

Figure 2.6 illustrates the construction of the piecewise linear short-run industry supply function in bold by summing up each technology's short-run supply function. For a demand of 820 MWh, the market-clearing price is \$60/MWh as $y(p)$ intersects demand at point (820, 60). Thus, \$60/MWh is what each technology receives as compensation, and the dispatch of each technology is obtained via its individual supply function. For example, $y_1(60) = 600$ MWh. Likewise, coal and gas output are 200 MWh and 20 MWh, respectively, for a total industry quantity supplied of 820 MWh, which matches the demand exactly. It is also no coincidence that each technology's marginal cost in equilibrium is \$60/MWh because if it were

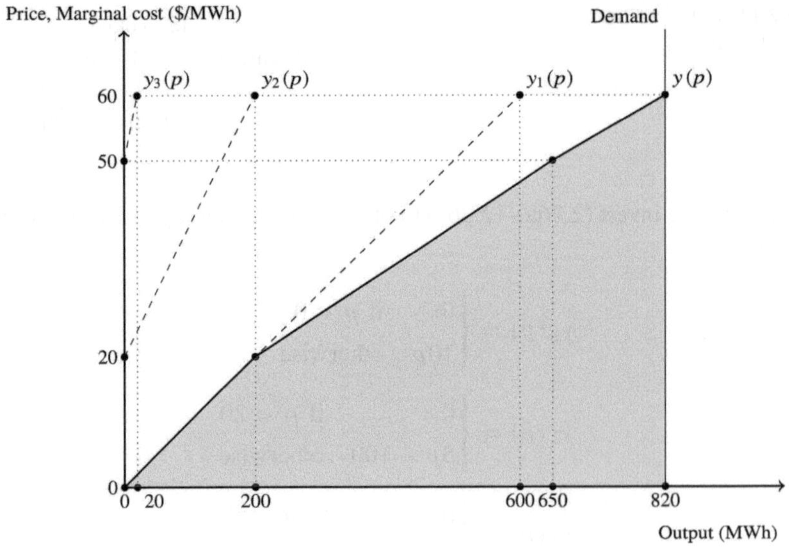

Fig. 2.6 Adding short-run supply functions

not the case, then it would be possible to reduce costs (and increase profit) by infinitesimally reducing output from the technology that had a marginal cost higher than \$60/MWh and simultaneously increasing it infinitesimally from the technology that had a lower marginal cost than \$60/MWh. Finally, from Fig. 2.6, the firm's revenue is $60 \times 820 = \$49{,}200$, while its total operating cost is the area of the shaded region, \$27,100, thereby yielding a profit of \$22,100.[20]

2.4.2 *Long-Run Profit Maximization*

A firm's long-run profit-maximization problem involves both investment and operational decisions. In that sense, the scope of the decision making mirrors that

[20] The area of the shaded region comprises the areas of the triangle $\{(0,0), (200,20), (200,0), (0,0)\}$, the rectangle $\{(200,0), (200,20), (820,20), (820,0), (200,0)\}$, the triangle $\{(200,20), (650,50), (650,20), (200,20)\}$, the rectangle $\{(650,20), (650,50), (820,50), (820,20), (650,20)\}$, and the triangle $\{(650,50), (820,60), (820,50), (650,50)\}$. These work out to \$2000, \$12,400, \$6750, \$5100, and \$850, respectively, for a total cost of \$27,100. Alternatively, it is also possible to calculate the profit for each technology, which works out to $60 \times 600 - \frac{0.10 \times 600 \times 600}{2} = \$18{,}000$, $60 \times 200 - \left(20 \times 200 + \frac{0.20 \times 200 \times 200}{2}\right) = \$4000$, and $60 \times 20 - \left(50 \times 20 + \frac{0.50 \times 20 \times 20}{2}\right) = \$100$ for wind, coal, and gas, respectively.

in Sect. 2.3.3 with a perfectly competitive firm that takes prices as exogenous. Consequently, the problem formulation is similar to that in (2.21a)–(2.21c):

$$\underset{y_{s,t,u},x_u}{\text{Maximize}} \sum_{s\in\mathcal{S}} W_s \sum_{t\in\mathcal{T}} \sum_{u\in\mathcal{U}} \left(\frac{\lambda_{s,t}}{W_s} - C^{\text{opr}}_{s,t,u}\right) y_{s,t,u} - \sum_{u\in\mathcal{U}} C^{\text{gen}}_u x_u \tag{2.30a}$$

$$\text{s.t. } y_{s,t,u} \leq A_{s,t,u} T_t x_u : \beta_{s,t,u}, \forall s, t, u \tag{2.30b}$$

$$x_u \leq \overline{K}_u : \overline{\beta}_u, \forall u \tag{2.30c}$$

$$y_{s,t,u} \geq 0 : \phi^y_{s,t,u}, \forall s, t, u \tag{2.30d}$$

$$x_u \geq 0 : \phi^x_u, \forall u \tag{2.30e}$$

The only change to the firm's objective function (2.30a) from (2.21a) is the incorporation of the amortized investment cost, $\sum_{u\in\mathcal{U}} C^{\text{gen}}_u x_u$. Furthermore, the capacity constraint (2.30b) now assumes greenfield investment such that the maximum availability of any technology u in a given (s, t) combination depends on its capacity adoption, x_u. In order to avoid unboundedness resulting from an arbitrarily large capacity adoption, (2.30c) limits the maximum capacity installation to $\overline{K}_u$ (in MW).[21] Finally, (2.30d) is identical to (2.21c), and (2.30e) is the non-negativity constraint on capacity adoption.

The corresponding Lagrangian function is as follows:

$$\begin{aligned} L = &- \sum_{s\in\mathcal{S}} W_s \sum_{t\in\mathcal{T}} \sum_{u\in\mathcal{U}} \left(\frac{\lambda_{s,t}}{W_s} - C^{\text{opr}}_{s,t,u}\right) y_{s,t,u} + \sum_{u\in\mathcal{U}} C^{\text{gen}}_u x_u \\ &- \sum_{s\in\mathcal{S}} \sum_{t\in\mathcal{T}} \sum_{u\in\mathcal{U}} \beta_{s,t,u} \left(A_{s,t,u} T_t x_u - y_{s,t,u}\right) - \sum_{u\in\mathcal{U}} \overline{\beta}_u \left(\overline{K}_u - x_u\right) \\ &- \sum_{s\in\mathcal{S}} \sum_{t\in\mathcal{T}} \sum_{u\in\mathcal{U}} y_{s,t,u} \phi^y_{s,t,u} - \sum_{u\in\mathcal{U}} x_u \phi^x_u \end{aligned} \tag{2.31a}$$

As with (2.22a), we can examine the KKT conditions in order to obtain economic insights about the long-run decisions. Vis-à-vis (2.23a)–(2.23g), the only KKT conditions that change are (2.23b) and (2.23c) as follows:

$$A_{s,t,u} T_t x_u - y_{s,t,u} \geq 0, \forall s, t, u \tag{2.32a}$$

$$\beta_{s,t,u} \left(A_{s,t,u} T_t x_u - y_{s,t,u}\right) = 0, \forall s, t, u \tag{2.32b}$$

[21] Note that this constraint does not appear in the long-run cost-minimization problem because (2.16a)–(2.16f) includes the market-clearing constraint limiting the dispatch by the demand.

Furthermore, KKT conditions related to x_u are added:

$$C_u^{\text{gen}} - \sum_{s\in\mathcal{S}}\sum_{t\in\mathcal{T}} A_{s,t,u}T_t\beta_{s,t,u} + \overline{\beta}_u - \phi_u^x = 0, \ \forall u \tag{2.33a}$$

$$x_u \geq 0, \ \forall u \tag{2.33b}$$

$$x_u\phi_u^x = 0, \ \forall u \tag{2.33c}$$

$$\phi_u^x \geq 0, \ \forall u \tag{2.33d}$$

$$\overline{K}_u - x_u \geq 0, \ \forall u \tag{2.33e}$$

$$\overline{\beta}_u\left(\overline{K}_u - x_u\right) = 0, \ \forall u \tag{2.33f}$$

$$\overline{\beta}_u \geq 0, \ \forall u \tag{2.33g}$$

Thus, the full set of KKT conditions for the long-run profit-maximization problem is (2.23a), (2.32a)–(2.32b), (2.23d)–(2.23g), and (2.33a)–(2.33g). Note that (2.33a) has the same interpretation as (2.19a) from long-run cost minimization, viz. that if technology u' is adopted, then its earned revenue must cover its annualized investment cost plus annual operating cost, cf. (2.20). The only difference is the inclusion of the dual variable $\overline{\beta}_{u'}$, which is zero if the upper capacity limit is not reached. By contrast, if $x_{u'} = \overline{K}_{u'}$, then $\overline{\beta}_{u'} > 0$, thereby leading to a slightly modified (2.20):

$$\sum_{s\in\mathcal{S}}\sum_{t\in\mathcal{T}} W_s C_{s,t,u'}^{\text{opr}} A_{s,t,u'}T_t + C_{u'}^{\text{gen}} + \overline{\beta}_{u'} = \sum_{s\in\mathcal{S}}\sum_{t\in\mathcal{T}} A_{s,t,u'}T_t\lambda_{s,t} \tag{2.34}$$

This means that a technology u' that is adopted at its capacity limit and dispatched at its available capacity throughout the entire year earns precisely enough revenues to cover its annualized investment cost, annual operating cost, and opportunity cost of the limit on capacity expansion. The latter may be verified via comparative statics on the Lagrangian function (2.31a) with respect to $\overline{K}_u$:

$$\frac{\partial L}{\partial \overline{K}_u} = -\overline{\beta}_u, \ \forall u \tag{2.35}$$

Recall that since (2.31a) effectively minimizes the negative of the profit, (2.35) states that the maximized profit increases at rate $\overline{\beta}_u$.

Illustrative Example 2.8 *Long-run profit-maximizing LP.*

We implement a problem instance of (2.30a)–(2.30e) with data from Illustrative Example 2.6. The only differences are that we define the maximum capacity installation, $\overline{K}_u$, to be 100 MW for all technologies and use the prices, $\lambda_{s,t}$, generated in Table 2.11 instead of the demand data, $D_{s,t}$. Note that the prices in Illustrative Example 2.6 were such that each technology covered its annualized

Table 2.15 Operational decisions with long-run profit-maximizing generation expansion, $y_{s,t,u}$ (MWh)

Technology	Season	Period		
		$t = 1$	$t = 2$	$t = 3$
$u = 1$	$s = 1$	160	80	40
	$s = 2$	200	400	600
$u = 2$	$s = 1$	0	800	800
	$s = 2$	800	800	0
$u = 3$	$s = 1$	0	0	800
	$s = 2$	800	0	0

Table 2.16 Marginal value of capacity with generation expansion under long-run profit maximization, $\beta_{s,t,u}$ (\$/MWh)

Technology	Season	Period		
		$t = 1$	$t = 2$	$t = 3$
$u = 1$	$s = 1$	3660	9150	11,361.5625
	$s = 2$	15,752.1875	8266.25	3660
$u = 2$	$s = 1$	0	5490	7701.5625
	$s = 2$	12,092.1875	4606.25	0
$u = 3$	$s = 1$	0	0	2211.5625
	$s = 2$	6602.1875	0	0

investment cost and annual operating cost. Using those prices here would render zero profits for all technologies and lead a profit-maximizing firm to be indifferent between investing at the maximum capacity limit, $\overline{K}_u$, and not investing at all. In order to bypass these economically trivial outcomes, we modify the price faced by the profit-maximizing firm in $(s, t) = (2, 3)$ to be \$3660/MWh, i.e., $\frac{\lambda_{s,t}}{W_s} =$ \$20/MWh as if coal were the price-setting technology. Consequently, the optimal technology adoption is 100 MW each of wind, coal, and gas with the resulting dispatch decisions given in Table 2.15. The total profit is \$2,196,000, but only wind is profitable, i.e., coal and gas earn zero profit.[22] A comparison of Table 2.15 with its analog for cost minimization in Table 2.10 indicates unrealistic generating patterns for the technologies as if the market could absorb all of their output. However, the capacity rents, $\beta_{s,t,u}$, in Table 2.16 are identical to those in Table 2.12 for cost minimization (apart from $\beta_{2,3,1}$) because they must cover the annualized investment cost, C_u^{gen}, cf. (2.33a). The reason why $\beta_{2,3,1}$ is \$3660/MWh here instead of zero is that it reflects the positive profit earned by wind in that (s, t) combination. Thus, using (2.33a) for wind yields that $\overline{\beta}_1$ must equal this "extra" profit, i.e., $A_{2,3,1}T_3\beta_{2,3,1} = 0.75 \times 8 \times 3660 =$ \$21,960/MW. Moreover, since the annual revenue earned by each MW of wind installed is $\sum_{s\in\mathcal{S}}\sum_{t\in\mathcal{T}} A_{s,t,1}T_t\lambda_{s,t} =$ \$104,250, condition (2.34) may be verified for wind because its left-hand side equals precisely $\sum_{s\in\mathcal{S}}\sum_{t\in\mathcal{T}} W_s C_{s,t,1}^{\text{opr}} A_{s,t,1}T_t + C_1^{\text{gen}} + \overline{\beta}_1 = 0 + 82290 + 21960 =$ \$104,250. Finally, comparative statics with respect to the maximum installed capacity, $\overline{K}_u$, as

[22] This means that another optimal solution is simply zero capacity of coal and gas.

stated in (2.35) for wind may also be verified because the maximized profit increases at rate \$21,960 for a *ceteris paribus* infinitesimal increase in $\overline{K}_1$.

2.5 Variable Renewable Energy Sources

We have emphasized the time-varying output of VRES in Sects. 2.2.3 and 2.3.3 when dealing with short- and long-run decisions in the power sector, respectively. In particular, ignoring the chronology of resource availability could distort the generation mix and result in suboptimal dispatch. Furthermore, in Sect. 2.4.1, we pointed out that increased VRES capacity with zero operating cost could depress electricity prices, which would discourage investment in flexible generation, e.g., gas-fired plants, to complement VRES. Still, we overlooked another important hallmark of power-system operations that becomes more prominent in the presence of VRES: ramping capabilities of conventional generation units.

A real-world consequence of this feature is captured by the so-called duck curve in California. Over the past decade, support for VRES as part of the state's climate objectives has bolstered the capacity of clean but possibly uncontrollable generation. For example, solar generation in California increased from 912 GWh in 2010 to 27,265 GWh in 2018, which represents almost 14% of in-state electricity production [6, 7]. Given the nature of solar availability, the resulting net-load profile, i.e., the difference between forecasted energy demand and VRES output, in Figs. 2.7 and 2.8 has the characteristic shape of the duck curve with increasingly steep ramping requirements from conventional generation units in the evening. In particular, the ramping in the "neck" of the curve beginning at 5 P.M. and going to 8 P.M. due to the sun's setting poses a challenge that requires additional flexibility in order to maintain supply-demand balance. Moreover, the ramping requirement during these

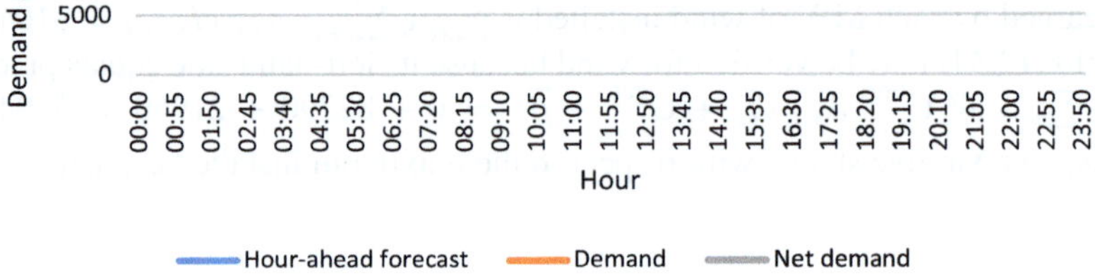

Fig. 2.7 California demand and net demand for April 30, 2018

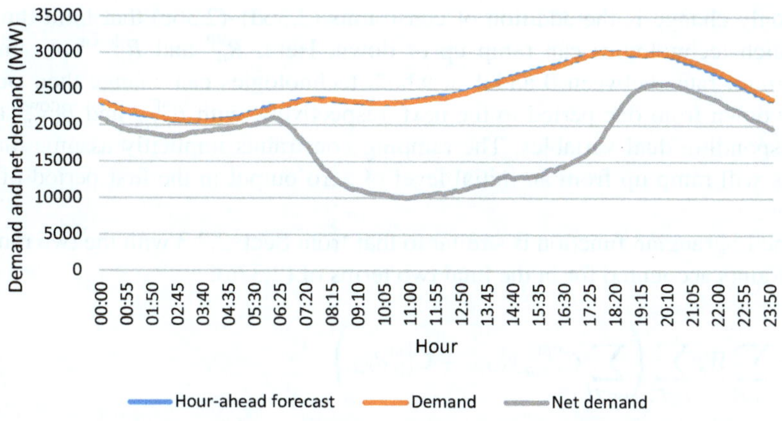

Fig. 2.8 California demand and net demand for April 30, 2021

three evening hours has generally increased from 9190 MW in 2018 to 11,182 MW in 2021 [8]. Such flexibility may be availed through demand-side management (see Chap. 1), energy storage (see Sect. 2.6), increased transmission interconnections (see Chap. 3), and fast-ramping generators. Somewhat paradoxically, the very nature of the duck curve may undermine the profitability of flexible generators like gas-fired power plants (that tend to have high operating costs) because VRES depresses prices, especially due to overgeneration during the middle of the day. Nevertheless, updated market designs that acknowledge this quandary and reward complementary generation technologies may mitigate the worst consequences of the duck curve. For example, improved market-clearing mechanisms [27], support payments to flexible plants [33], ancillary services for ramping [21], and capacity payments [3, 20, 42] have been proposed in the literature.

In order to understand the impact of ramping constraints in the presence of VRES, we modify the economic dispatch model (2.5a)–(2.5e) from Sect. 2.2.3 accordingly:

$$\underset{d_{s,t},y_{s,t,u}}{\text{Minimize}} \sum_{s\in\mathcal{S}} W_s \sum_{t\in\mathcal{T}} \left(\sum_{u\in\mathcal{U}} C^{\text{opr}}_{s,t,u} y_{s,t,u} + C^{\text{lsh}}_{s,t} d_{s,t} \right) \tag{2.36a}$$

$$\text{s.t.} \sum_{u\in\mathcal{U}} y_{s,t,u} + d_{s,t} - D_{s,t} = 0 : \lambda_{s,t}, \forall s, t \tag{2.36b}$$

$$y_{s,t,u} \leq A_{s,t,u} T_t K_u : \beta_{s,t,u}, \forall s, t, u \tag{2.36c}$$

$$y_{s,t,u} - y_{s,t-1,u} \leq R^{\text{up}}_u T_t K_u : \beta^{\text{up}}_{s,t,u}, \forall s, t, u \tag{2.36d}$$

$$-y_{s,t,u} + y_{s,t-1,u} \leq R^{\text{down}}_u T_t K_u : \beta^{\text{down}}_{s,t,u}, \forall s, t, u \tag{2.36e}$$

$$d_{s,t} \geq 0 : \phi^d_{s,t}, \forall s, t \tag{2.36f}$$

$$y_{s,t,u} \geq 0 : \phi^y_{s,t,u}, \forall s, t, u \tag{2.36g}$$

The only change is the addition of constraints (2.36d)–(2.36e) that limit the rates at which technologies can ramp up or down. Here, R_u^{up} and R_u^{down} are unitless maximum rates between 0 and 1 at which technologies can change their outputs up or down from one period to the next, respectively, with $\beta_{s,t,u}^{\text{up}}$ and $\beta_{s,t,u}^{\text{down}}$ as the corresponding dual variables. The ramping constraints implicitly assume that the plants will ramp up from an initial level of zero output in the first period of each season.

The Lagrangian function is similar to that from Sect. 2.2.3 with the two ramping constraints accounted for in the final two terms of (2.37a):

$$\begin{aligned}
L = &\sum_{s\in\mathcal{S}} W_s \sum_{t\in\mathcal{T}} \left(\sum_{u\in\mathcal{U}} C_{s,t,u}^{\text{opr}} y_{s,t,u} + C_{s,t}^{\text{lsh}} d_{s,t} \right) \\
&- \sum_{s\in\mathcal{S}} \sum_{t\in\mathcal{T}} \lambda_{s,t} \left(\sum_{u\in\mathcal{U}} y_{s,t,u} + d_{s,t} - D_{s,t} \right) \\
&- \sum_{s\in\mathcal{S}} \sum_{t\in\mathcal{T}} \sum_{u\in\mathcal{U}} \beta_{s,t,u} \left(A_{s,t,u} T_t K_u - y_{s,t,u} \right) - \sum_{s\in\mathcal{S}} \sum_{t\in\mathcal{T}} d_{s,t} \phi_{s,t}^{d} \\
&- \sum_{s\in\mathcal{S}} \sum_{t\in\mathcal{T}} \sum_{u\in\mathcal{U}} y_{s,t,u} \phi_{s,t,u}^{y} - \sum_{s\in\mathcal{S}} \sum_{t\in\mathcal{T}} \sum_{u\in\mathcal{U}} \beta_{s,t,u}^{\text{up}} \left(R_u^{\text{up}} T_t K_u - y_{s,t,u} + y_{s,t-1,u} \right) \\
&- \sum_{s\in\mathcal{S}} \sum_{t\in\mathcal{T}} \sum_{u\in\mathcal{U}} \beta_{s,t,u}^{\text{down}} \left(R_u^{\text{down}} T_t K_u + y_{s,t,u} - y_{s,t-1,u} \right) \qquad (2.37a)
\end{aligned}$$

Consequently, the KKT conditions for (2.36a)–(2.36g) reflect those in (2.7a)–(2.7l) with changes due to the ramping constraints. Thus, they comprise (2.7a), (2.7c)–(2.7l) and the following:

$$\begin{aligned}
&W_s C_{s,t,u}^{\text{opr}} - \lambda_{s,t} + \beta_{s,t,u} + \left(\beta_{s,t,u}^{\text{up}} - \beta_{s,t,u}^{\text{down}} \right) + \left(\beta_{s,t+1,u}^{\text{down}} - \beta_{s,t+1,u}^{\text{up}} \right) \\
&\quad - \phi_{s,t,u}^{y} = 0, \ \forall s, t, u \qquad (2.38a)
\end{aligned}$$

$$R_u^{\text{up}} T_t K_u - y_{s,t,u} + y_{s,t-1,u} \geq 0, \ \forall s, t, u \qquad (2.38b)$$

$$R_u^{\text{down}} T_t K_u + y_{s,t,u} - y_{s,t-1,u} \geq 0, \ \forall s, t, u \qquad (2.38c)$$

$$\beta_{s,t,u}^{\text{up}} \left(R_u^{\text{up}} T_t K_u - y_{s,t,u} + y_{s,t-1,u} \right) = 0, \ \forall s, t, u \qquad (2.38d)$$

$$\beta_{s,t,u}^{\text{down}} \left(R_u^{\text{down}} T_t K_u + y_{s,t,u} - y_{s,t-1,u} \right) = 0, \ \forall s, t, u \qquad (2.38e)$$

$$\beta_{s,t,u}^{\text{up}} \geq 0, \ \forall s, t, u \qquad (2.38f)$$

$$\beta_{s,t,u}^{\text{down}} \geq 0, \ \forall s, t, u \qquad (2.38g)$$

In particular, (2.38a) modifies (2.7b) by including the shadow price of ramping into the market-clearing price. Otherwise, KKT conditions (2.38b)–(2.38c) are merely the ramping constraints, (2.38d)–(2.38e) are complementarity conditions, and (2.38f)–(2.38g) are non-negativity constraints for the ramping constraints' dual variables. Finally, similar to (2.8b), the envelope theorem may be applied to determine the *ceteris paribus* impact of a marginal increase in the ramping capability on the minimized cost:

$$\frac{\partial L}{\partial R_u^{\mathrm{up}}} = -\sum_{s \in \mathcal{S}} \sum_{t \in \mathcal{T}} \beta_{s,t,u}^{\mathrm{up}} T_t K_u, \ \forall u \tag{2.39a}$$

$$\frac{\partial L}{\partial R_u^{\mathrm{down}}} = -\sum_{s \in \mathcal{S}} \sum_{t \in \mathcal{T}} \beta_{s,t,u}^{\mathrm{down}} T_t K_u, \ \forall u \tag{2.39b}$$

Illustrative Example 2.9 *Cost-minimizing LP for economic dispatch with ramping constraints.*

We implement the ramp-constrained economic dispatch (2.36a)–(2.36g) using the data from Illustrative Example 2.1. The only additions are the ramping constraints (2.36d)–(2.36e) for which R_u^{up} and R_u^{down} need to be defined for each technology. We set the ramp-up and ramp-down rates to be 1.0, 0.3, and 0.6 for wind, coal, and gas, respectively, which are loosely based on data from [13]. Thus, the maximum periodic change in output for coal and gas is $0.3 \times 8 \times 35 = 84$ MWh and $0.6 \times 8 \times 40 = 192$ MWh. Note that ramp rates for wind are somewhat superfluous as its maximum output is limited by exogenous availability factors, $A_{s,t,u}$. With the ramping constraints, the minimized cost almost doubles to \$92,920,080 from \$48,055,800 as conventional plants like coal and gas are unable to "follow" the temporal fluctuations in VRES. Consequently, more load shedding is required in certain periods. For example, in $(s, t) = (1, 2)$, the solution without ramping constraints required 280 MWh of coal and 300 MWh of gas. Although the gas plant can ramp up to 300 MWh in two periods starting from zero, reaching 280 MWh of output in two periods is impossible for coal. Since coal can make it only to 168 MWh, gas is dispatched at capacity to yield 320 MWh, which means that a shortfall of 92 MWh in demand results as evidenced by Tables 2.17 and 2.18. Therefore, the market-clearing price in $(s, t) = (1, 2)$ is \$500/MWh (Table 2.19) as opposed to \$50/MWh because gas is no longer the price-setting technology. Moreover, the marginal value of capacity becomes \$91,500/MWh for wind and \$9150/MWh less for gas while vanishing altogether for coal (Table 2.20). From (2.39a) and Table 2.21, the marginal impact of an increase in the up-ramping capability of coal may be calculated as $-181170 \times 8 \times 35 - 175680 \times 8 \times 35 - 87840 \times 8 \times 35 - 175680 \times 8 \times 35 - 87840 \times 8 \times 35 - 0 \times 8 \times 35 = -198298800$.

Table 2.17 Load-shedding decisions with ramping constraints, $d_{s,t}$ (MWh)

	Period		
Season	$t = 1$	$t = 2$	$t = 3$
$s = 1$	0	92	138
$s = 2$	554	52	0

Table 2.18 Operational decisions with ramping constraints, $y_{s,t,u}$ (MWh)

Technology	Season	Period $t=1$	$t=2$	$t=3$
$u=1$	$s=1$	40	20	10
	$s=2$	50	100	150
$u=2$	$s=1$	84	168	252
	$s=2$	84	168	142
$u=3$	$s=1$	156	320	320
	$s=2$	192	320	128

Table 2.19 Marginal value of demand with ramping constraints, $\lambda_{s,t}$ (\$/MWh)

Season	Period $t=1$	$t=2$	$t=3$
$s=1$	9150	91,500	91,500
$s=2$	91,500	91,500	3660

Table 2.20 Marginal value of capacity with ramping constraints, $\beta_{s,t,u}$ (\$/MWh)

Technology	Season	Period $t=1$	$t=2$	$t=3$
$u=1$	$s=1$	9150	91,500	91,500
	$s=2$	91,500	91,500	3660
$u=2$	$s=1$	0	0	0
	$s=2$	0	0	0
$u=3$	$s=1$	0	82,350	82,350
	$s=2$	0	76,860	0

Table 2.21 Marginal value of up-ramping capacity, $\beta^{\mathrm{up}}_{s,t,u}$ (\$/MWh)

Technology	Season	Period $t=1$	$t=2$	$t=3$
$u=1$	$s=1$	0	0	0
	$s=2$	0	0	0
$u=2$	$s=1$	181,170	175,680	87,840
	$s=2$	175,680	87,840	0
$u=3$	$s=1$	0	0	0
	$s=2$	82,350	0	0

This result can be interpreted as the rate at which the minimized cost will change, i.e., a *ceteris paribus* increase of 0.01 in R_u^{up} for coal will decrease minimized cost by \$1,982,988 (Table 2.21).[23]

[23] Related to the point made about the "cannibalization effect" of higher VRES capacity on producers' profit in Illustrative Example 2.6, it is worth noting that such an effect persists and distorts incentives under ramping constraints as well. For example, if wind capacity were increased to 200 MW, then the profit of the gas plant would be more than halved, i.e., from about \$94 million to under \$44 million. Therefore, an increase in VRES capacity requires more flexible generation, but these resources are precisely the ones to become less attractive to a profit-maximizing firm as prices crash during certain periods.

2.6 Energy Storage

Given the aforementioned challenges with VRES integration stemming from variable output and ramping constraints, it is natural to posit that energy storage could be a possible solution to mitigating spatio-temporal imbalances. Indeed, pumped-hydro storage has long been used to conduct such arbitrage, i.e., to move energy from periods of relative abundance to relative scarcity. In doing so, both the storage operator and society benefit as arbitrage profits are earned while costly peaking generation is avoided [18]. However, suitable sites for pumped-hydro storage are limited by geography, and attention in the past decade has turned to battery storage, e.g., lithium-ion devices, that could be deployed at large scale, i.e., at capacities of greater than 1 MW. Due to cost reductions, e.g., 61% between 2015 and 2017 alone, large-scale battery installations in the U.S. have increased from 59 MW in 2010 to 869 MW in 2018 [16]. The majority of these installations have been of the lithium-ion type because of its high round-trip efficiency and have been adopted by independent power producers as well as regulated entities. Indeed, storage has a variety of applications, such as arbitrage, demand-side management, transmission/distribution deferral, ancillary services for frequency regulation, voltage support, and spinning reserve, which makes it attractive to manifold industry participants.

In spite of its desirability, energy storage can pose a quandary for the power sector precisely because of its numerous modes of operation. While it makes intuitive sense that storage will be welfare enhancing and provide arbitrage profits for owners, the nature of asset ownership in the power sector often puts these objectives in conflict. In an analytical partial-equilibrium model of a stylized perfectly competitive power sector, Sioshansi [37] demonstrates that storage owned by a standalone merchant enhances social welfare vis-à-vis consumer or producer ownership. The explanation for this result is that the merchant is a profit-maximizing operator who merely exercises temporal arbitrage. By contrast, consumers (producers) overuse (underuse) storage capacity in order to engender (to prevent) excessive price-smoothing effects. Extending the analysis to allow for Nash-Cournot equilibria, Sioshansi [39] further shows that storage can be welfare diminishing (compared to a no-storage case) in the presence of strategic generating firms. Moreover, he finds that welfare losses that arise with strategic generating firms can be greater if storage operations are perfectly competitive. Exploring conflicting objectives between profit-maximizing storage operators and social welfare, [12] generalize the findings about strategic behavior by hydropower producers [5, 10] to a generic storage device with efficiency losses. Specifically, a storage-enabled renewable producer behaving à la Cournot in a two-period model uses the device to generate more power in the off-peak period than a perfectly competitive producer does. This strategic decision stems from the producer's desire to boost the peak-period price (and its profit) by "dumping" energy in the off-peak period. Interestingly, [12] prove that such a distortion could arise even under perfect competition as the device's efficiency exogenously increases. Intuitively, a *ceteris paribus* increase in device efficiency enhances the producer's ability to move energy from the off-peak to the peak period, which enhances welfare but dampens the peak price. At a critical level of efficiency, the producer's maximized profit actually starts to decrease as efficiency increases. As a countervailing measure, it aims to prevent the degradation to its profit by increasing off-peak output. Thus, even under perfect competition, private and public incentives involving storage could clash. Likewise, storage may not always facilitate environmental objectives as charging that takes place in off-peak periods is often done via baseload technologies, i.e., coal if VRES is not plentiful, which could increase carbon emissions vis-à-vis not having storage [35, 38, 45]. Investment decisions involving storage adoption in a market-based environment also yield such conflicting objectives [36, 46].

Clearly, analysis of energy storage requires a multi-faceted approach. However, in this section, we will abstract from real-world details such as ownership issues, price-responsive demand, market power, emissions, and spatial arbitrage in order to focus on how storage affects generation and prices. We will first use a stylized two-period model without capacity constraints or VRES that illustrates simple temporal arbitrage before proceeding to a more realistic model with capacity constraints and VRES that captures how storage can both integrate VRES by reducing ramping and affect the profit of conventional generators.

The stylized model assumes a generic generator with linear marginal costs as in (2.24), where $C^{\text{int}} \geq 0$ (in \$/MWh) and $C^{\text{slp}} \geq 0$ (in \$/MWh^2) are the intercept and slope parameters, respectively. Period 1 is the off-peak period with exogenous demand $D_1 \geq 0$ (in MWh), whereas period 2 is the peak period with exogenous demand $D_2 > D_1$ (in MWh). The objective is to select generation in each period, y_1 and y_2 (both in MWh), along with storage discharged in period 2, z (in MWh), in order to minimize total generation cost (2.40a):

$$\underset{y_1,y_2,z}{\text{Minimize}}\ C^{\text{int}}\left(y_1+y_2\right)+\frac{1}{2}C^{\text{slp}}\left(y_1^2+y_2^2\right) \tag{2.40a}$$

$$\text{s.t. } y_1 - Fz - D_1 = 0 : \lambda_1 \tag{2.40b}$$

$$y_2 + z - D_2 = 0 : \lambda_2 \tag{2.40c}$$

The objective function (2.40a) is quadratic in the generation variables and is constrained by energy balance in each period. We abstract from non-negativity constraints on y_1, y_2, and z in order to focus on interior solutions. Here, $F \geq 1$ denotes the inverse of storage efficiency, i.e., a device that is 50% efficient has $F = 2$, which means that if z is to be discharged from storage in period 2, then Fz needs to be charged into storage in period 1. Thus, in (2.40b), storage charging induces an increase in period-1 generation, whereas storage discharging in (2.40c) reduces period-2 generation. It should be noted that an inefficient storage device necessarily means that energy is destroyed. However, its socially optimal use means that energy is moved from a period (or location) in which it is less valued to one in which it is more valued.

Since (2.40a)–(2.40c) is a linearly constrained quadratic program (QP), it will have a global optimal solution if its objective function is convex.[24] Thus, it is sufficient to examine the KKT conditions of (2.40a)–(2.40c):

$$C^{\text{int}} + C^{\text{slp}} y_1 - \lambda_1 = 0 \tag{2.41a}$$

$$C^{\text{int}} + C^{\text{slp}} y_2 - \lambda_2 = 0 \tag{2.41b}$$

$$F\lambda_1 - \lambda_2 = 0 \tag{2.41c}$$

$$y_1 - Fz - D_1 = 0 \tag{2.41d}$$

$$y_2 + z - D_2 = 0 \tag{2.41e}$$

The stationarity conditions (2.41a)–(2.41b) indicate that the price in each period, λ_1 or λ_2 (both in \$/MWh), equals the marginal cost of generation, whereas (2.41c) states that the device's inefficiency determines the price ratio.

Assuming interior solutions, i.e., $y_1 > 0$, $y_2 > 0$, and $z > 0$, we can analytically solve the system of five equations (2.41a)–(2.41e) for the five unknowns, y_1^*, y_2^*, z^*, λ_1^*, and λ_2^*. Given the emphasis on storage, we note that the optimal discharge from storage in period 2 is:

$$z^* = \frac{C^{\text{slp}}(D_2 - FD_1) - C^{\text{int}}(F-1)}{C^{\text{slp}}\left(F^2+1\right)} \tag{2.42}$$

In order for the solution to make economic sense, we require the numerator of (2.42) to be positive, i.e., the device should not be "too inefficient" and the difference in periodic consumption should be high enough to warrant moving energy.[25] For a perfectly efficient storage device with $F = 1$, (2.42) collapses to $z^* = \frac{D_2 - D_1}{2}$, which effectively means that generation in each period equalizes to $\frac{D_1+D_2}{2}$, thereby also leading to equal prices, $C^{\text{int}} + C^{\text{slp}}\left(\frac{D_1+D_2}{2}\right)$. Figure 2.9 depicts the impact of storage on equilibrium for a more general case of $F > 1$, where the top (bottom) panel denotes how generation and prices shift during the off-peak (peak) period. In particular, charging in the off-peak (peak) period induces more (less) generation and an increase (a decrease) in the equilibrium price, i.e., the price-smoothing effect. Although net generation increases, there is a benefit to society as the increase in cost of generation in the off-peak period (denoted by the shaded gray region in the top panel) is less than the decrease in cost of generation in the peak period (denoted by the shaded gray region in the bottom panel).[26] Consequently, generator profit will

---

[24] This may be verified by noting that the Hessian matrix of the objective function (2.40a) is positive definite [28].

[25] From (2.42), $z^* > 0$ requires $C^{\text{int}} < \frac{C^{\text{slp}}(D_2 - FD_1)}{F-1}$.

[26] Using the definition of z^* in (2.42), we note that the change in the minimized cost for period 1 from having storage as opposed to no storage is $z^*\left[F\left(C^{\text{int}} + C^{\text{slp}} D_1\right) + \frac{1}{2}F^2 C^{\text{slp}} z^*\right]$.

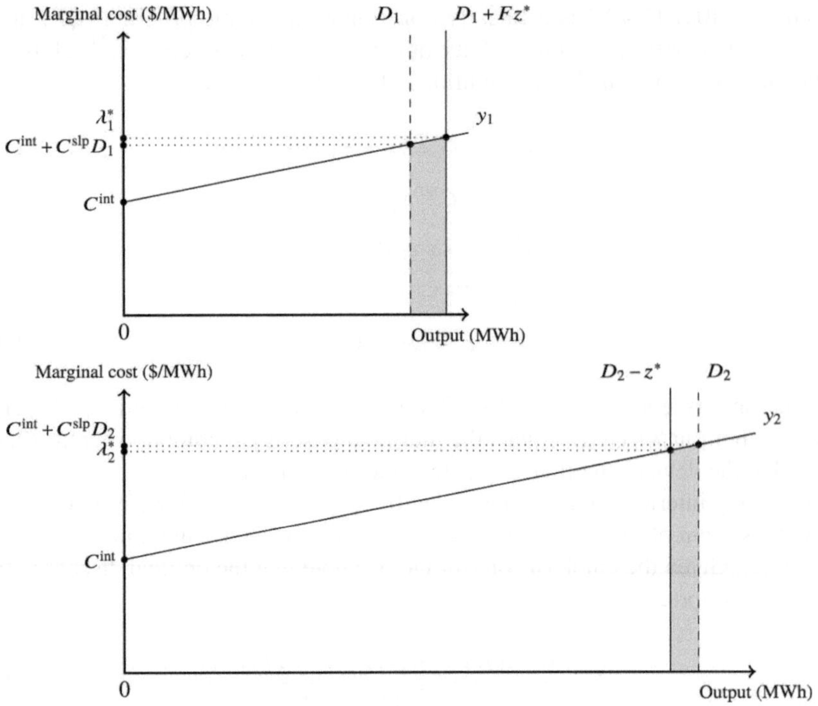

Fig. 2.9 Impact of energy storage on equilibrium prices

decrease if the demand in the second period is relatively large, i.e., $D_2 - FD_1 > \frac{-C^{int}(F-1)}{C^{slp}}$, which is always the case if $z^* > 0$.[27] Meanwhile, the profit from storage operations in this setting will always be zero.[28] Of course, in a more realistic setting, there will be constraints on generation and storage capacity, which will result in positive short-run profits.

Likewise, the change in period-2 minimized cost from having storage is $z^* \left[-\left(C^{int} + C^{slp} D_2\right) + \frac{1}{2} C^{slp} z^* \right]$. Thus, the total change in minimized cost from having storage is $z^* \left[\frac{1}{2} C^{slp} \left(F^2 + 1\right) z^* + (F - 1)\, C^{int} + (FD_1 - D_2)\, C^{slp} \right]$, which is negative as long as $D_2 - FD_1 > \frac{C^{int}(F-1)}{C^{slp}}$. This is the same as the condition for $z^* > 0$, i.e., storage is used only if the minimized cost is reduced.

[27] To see this, note that the change in generator profit due to storage use $z^* > 0$ is $\frac{1}{2} C^{slp} z^* \left[2 (FD_1 - D_2) + z^* \left(F^2 + 1\right)\right]$, which is negative as along as $D_2 - FD_1 > -\frac{C^{int}(F-1)}{C^{slp}}$. Since $z^* > 0$ requires $D_2 - FD_1 > \frac{C^{int}(F-1)}{C^{slp}}$, we have the result that storage use reduces generator profit.

[28] To see this, note that storage profit is $\lambda_2^* z^* - F\lambda_1^* z^* = \left(\lambda_2^* - F\lambda_1^*\right) z^*$. Furthermore, from (2.41c), it is the case that $F\lambda_1^* = \lambda_2^*$.

In a more realistic setting, we allow for VRES and conventional generation capacities as in (2.5a)–(2.5e). We also include constraints on storage operations as follows:

$$\underset{d_{s,t},y_{s,t,u},z^{\text{in}}_{s,t},z^{\text{out}}_{s,t},z^{\text{sto}}_{s,t}}{\text{Minimize}} \sum_{s\in\mathcal{S}} W_s \sum_{t\in\mathcal{T}} \left(\sum_{u\in\mathcal{U}} C^{\text{opr}}_{s,t,u} y_{s,t,u} + C^{\text{lsh}}_{s,t} d_{s,t} \right) \quad (2.43a)$$

$$\text{s.t.} \sum_{u\in\mathcal{U}} y_{s,t,u} + d_{s,t} + z^{\text{out}}_{s,t} - z^{\text{in}}_{s,t} - D_{s,t} = 0 : \lambda_{s,t}, \forall s,t \quad (2.43b)$$

$$z^{\text{in}}_{s,t} \le R^{\text{in}} T_t B : \theta^{\text{in}}_{s,t}, \forall s,t \quad (2.43c)$$

$$z^{\text{out}}_{s,t} \le R^{\text{out}} T_t B : \theta^{\text{out}}_{s,t}, \forall s,t \quad (2.43d)$$

$$z^{\text{sto}}_{s,t} \le T_t B : \overline{\theta}^{\text{sto}}_{s,t}, \forall s,t \quad (2.43e)$$

$$z^{\text{sto}}_{s,t} \ge R^{\text{sto}} T_t B : \underline{\theta}^{\text{sto}}_{s,t}, \forall s,t \quad (2.43f)$$

$$E^{\text{in}} z^{\text{in}}_{s,t} - z^{\text{out}}_{s,t} + \left(1 - E^{\text{sto}}\right)^{T_t} z^{\text{sto}}_{s,t-1} - z^{\text{sto}}_{s,t} = 0 : \theta_{s,t}, \forall s,t \quad (2.43g)$$

$$z^{\text{in}}_{s,t} \ge 0 : \phi^{\text{zin}}_{s,t}, \forall s,t \quad (2.43h)$$

$$z^{\text{out}}_{s,t} \ge 0 : \phi^{\text{zout}}_{s,t}, \forall s,t \quad (2.43i)$$

$$z^{\text{sto}}_{s,t} \ge 0 : \phi^{\text{zsto}}_{s,t}, \forall s,t \quad (2.43j)$$

$$(2.5c) - (2.5e)$$

Here, (2.43a) is the same objective function as (2.5a), i.e., to minimize operating costs. However, there are three new decision variables related to storage operations: $z^{\text{in}}_{s,t}$, $z^{\text{out}}_{s,t}$, and $z^{\text{sto}}_{s,t}$. All three are measured in MWh and indicate storage charging, storage discharging, and the storage level for every given season-period combination, (s,t), respectively. The energy-balance constraint (2.43b) is duly modified from (2.5b) to reflect net discharge from storage, $z^{\text{out}}_{s,t} - z^{\text{in}}_{s,t}$, in (s,t). The rate at which storage can be charged or discharged is limited by unitless paramcters between 0 and 1, R^{in} or R^{out} in (2.43c)–(2.43d). They are linked to the installed battery capacity, B (in MW), which also constrains the battery's maximum and minimum storage levels in (2.43e) and (2.43f), respectively.[29] The minimum state of charge, R^{sto}, in (2.43f) reflects the fact that storage levels are technically constrained from dropping below a threshold. The principal storage-balance equation is (2.43g),

[29] Actually, battery capacity may be expressed in terms of either power or energy capacity. The former refers to the maximum amount of power output available at any instant in time and is measured in MW. By contrast, the latter is the total amount of energy that can be stored and is measured in MWh.

Table 2.22 Storage decisions, $z^{\text{in}}_{s,t}$, $z^{\text{out}}_{s,t}$, and $z^{\text{sto}}_{s,t}$ (MWh)

		Period		
Decision	Season	$t = 1$	$t = 2$	$t = 3$
$z^{\text{in}}_{s,t}$	$s = 1$	149.47	0	0
	$s = 2$	33.68	0	0
$z^{\text{out}}_{s,t}$	$s = 1$	0	0	110
	$s = 2$	0	0	0
$z^{\text{sto}}_{s,t}$	$s = 1$	142	142	32
	$s = 2$	32	32	32

which states that the storage level in (s, t) is equal to the storage level (net of efficiency loss, $1 - E^{\text{sto}}$) in the previous period plus any charges (while accounting for the efficiency of input charging, E^{in}) minus any discharges in (s, t).[30] Non-negativity of these three storage decision variables is expressed by (2.43h)–(2.43j). Finally, constraints (2.5c)–(2.5e) from economic dispatch in Sect. 2.2.3 round out the LP for economic dispatch with energy storage.

Illustrative Example 2.10 *Cost-minimizing LP for economic dispatch with storage.*

We use the same data from Illustrative Example 2.1 to implement a problem instance of (2.43a)–(2.43j) and (2.5c)–(2.5e). The storage device is assumed to have to have a capacity of $B = 40$ MW with a minimum state of charge of $R^{\text{sto}} = 0.1$ and no self-discharge, i.e., $E^{\text{sto}} = 0$. Instead, the device's inefficiency is reflected solely by the input efficiency, $E^{\text{in}} = 0.95$. The maximum charging and discharging rates are $R^{\text{in}} = R^{\text{out}} = 0.5$, which reflect lithium-ion batteries [46]. Due to the availability of the battery, charging occurs during $(s, t) = (1, 1)$ to enable discharging during $(s, t) = (1, 3)$, i.e., arbitrage from a low-demand period to a high-demand one (Table 2.22). This decision also enables load shedding to be eliminated in $(s, t) = (1, 3)$ from 110 MWh, cf. Table 2.4. As a result, the minimized cost is \$42,220,989.47, which is about a 12% reduction due to storage. Furthermore, storage facilitates a reduction in expected ramping of conventional plants by almost 22%, where expected ramping for unit u is defined as $\sum_{s \in \mathcal{S}} W_s \sum_{t \in \mathcal{T}} \left| y_{s,t,u} - y_{s,t-1,u} \right|$. The price-smoothing effect of storage is also apparent as the price increases in $(s, t) = (1, 1)$ due to the dispatch of gas and decreases in $(s, t) = (1, 3)$ due to the avoided load shedding (Tables 2.23 and 2.24). Thus, storage has desirable properties from the perspective of both cost minimization and VRES integration. However, storage could also pose challenges for producers if the price decrease in peak periods more than offsets the price increase off-peak periods. Here, the profit of conventional generators decreases by over 40% due to the presence of storage with coal and gas taking the biggest hits.

[30] The use of representative seasons necessitates inter-seasonal storage constraints similar to (2.43g) that account for net storage input during each season scaled up by the duration of each season (typically the number of weeks in the season) [41].

Table 2.23 Generation decisions with storage, $y_{s,t,u}$ (MWh)

Technology	Season	Period $t=1$	$t=2$	$t=3$
$u=1$	$s=1$	40	20	10
	$s=2$	50	100	150
$u=2$	$s=1$	280	280	280
	$s=2$	280	280	270
$u=3$	$s=1$	109.47	300	320
	$s=2$	320	260	0

Table 2.24 Marginal value of demand with storage, $\lambda_{s,t}$ ($/MWh)

Season	Period $t=1$	$t=2$	$t=3$
$s=1$	9150	9150	9631.58
$s=2$	91,500	9150	3660

Even storage is unprofitable in this problem instance, although this is due to the fact that the minimum state of charge (2.43f) requires charging in $(s,t) = (2,1)$ when the price is high. Depending on the ownership structure, it may be possible to reduce storage capacity to make its operations profitable, albeit at the disadvantage of lower cost savings for society.

2.7 Summary

In this chapter, we have discussed the supply side of the power sector with emphasis on how VRES makes it distinct from conventional economics models. Specifically, we noted that concerns about climate change over the past decade have prompted government policies to lower the costs of solar and wind power. Their intermittent output means that both operational and investment models have to account for the chronology of demand and VRES availability instead of using seasonal averages or screening curves. We show how to collect relevant data on technologies' operating and investment costs such that they could be used to devise short- and long-run cost-minimization models. The connection of the latter with screening curves is also demonstrated. The perspective of a profit-maximizing firm in a perfectly competitive industry is next accommodated before exploring how high VRES penetration could create challenges for the power system's ramping capability. Finally, energy storage is incorporated into an economic dispatch problem in order to illustrate its benefits and complications.

As we have alluded to earlier, we have glossed over some details. First, demand is treated as being price inelastic, which may also be an outdated assumption given the burgeoning smart-grid technologies. However, we made this assumption in order to focus on the supply side and will examine supply-demand interactions more comprehensively in Chaps. 3–4. Second, although we mentioned clustering procedures to extract representative periods that preserve the chronology, we did not go into details. Instead, we refer the reader to the extant literature such as [32] for a fuller explanation and necessary code. Third, we avoided discussion of unit commitment and locational marginal pricing, which are issues that increased VRES penetration may make more prominent. Chapter 4 covers these topics in more detail. Fourth, on a related note, market-design issues that affect VRES and conventional generation capacity, such as environmental policy and conflicting objectives, are taken up in Chaps. 6 and 7, respectively. Finally, given the deregulated nature of the electricity industry, it is natural that incumbent firms will exploit their scale and barriers to entry to exert market power, an issue that we have also bypassed in this chapter and will instead focus on in Chap. 5.

2.8 End-of-Chapter Exercises

2.1 Use the discussion in Sect. 2.1 as a starting point to find relevant policy measures in your jurisdiction that have promoted the use of VRES.

2.2 Follow the procedure described in Sect. 2.2.1 to determine the supply stack for typical seasons in your jurisdiction. Use the collected data and clustered seasons to implement a problem instance of the economic dispatch LP (2.5a)–(2.5e).

2.3 Follow the procedure described in Sect. 2.3.1 to calculate levelized costs for candidate technologies in your jurisdiction. Use the collected data and clustered seasons to implement a problem instance of the investment LP (2.16a)–(2.16f). How do the results compare to those from using the traditional screening-curve approach of Sect. 2.3.2?

2.4 The stylized short-run profit-maximization problem similar to that in Sect. 2.4.1 may equivalently be rendered as:

$$\underset{y_u}{\text{Maximize}} \sum_{u \in \mathcal{U}} \left(\lambda y_u - C_u^{\text{int}} y_u - \frac{1}{2} C_u^{\text{slp}} y_u^2 \right) \tag{2.44}$$

Assuming interior solutions, i.e., $y_u > 0, \ \forall u \in \mathcal{U}$, the KKT condition yields $\lambda = C_u^{\text{int}} + C_u^{\text{slp}} y_u, \ \forall u \in \mathcal{U}$. In other words, each technology's marginal cost equals the price. On this basis, the stylized long-run profit-maximization problem may be formulated as:

$$\underset{y_u, x_u}{\text{Maximize}} \sum_{u \in \mathcal{U}} \left(\lambda y_u - C_u^{\text{int}} y_u - \frac{1}{2} C_u^{\text{slp}} y_u^2 - C_u^{\text{gen}} x_u \right) \tag{2.45a}$$

$$\text{s.t. } y_u \leq x_u : \beta_u, \ \forall u \tag{2.45b}$$

Assuming interior solutions, show that each technology's marginal cost plus the investment cost, C_u^{gen}, equals the price.

2.5 Using appropriate data sources, construct a version of the "duck curve" for your jurisdiction as in Fig. 2.8. Based on the collected data, implement a problem instance of the ramp-constrained economic dispatch LP (2.36a)–(2.36g).

2.6 Investigate the impact of energy storage in relieving ramp constraints by incorporating the ramping restrictions (2.36d)–(2.36e) into the LP (2.43a)–(2.43j) and (2.5c)–(2.5e). You may use the data from Illustrative Examples 2.9 and 2.10. For what range of capacity is energy storage beneficial for society?

2.9 GAMS Codes

Here, we present GAMS codes for solving selected examples numerically. The following code solves Illustrative Example 2.1 to determine the cost-minimizing economic dispatch.

```
* Cost-minimizing LP for economic dispatch

Sets
S seasons /s1*s2/
T periods /t1*t3/
U technologies /u1*u3/;

Parameters

TT(T)       Length of each period in hours
/ t1        8
  t2        8
  t3        8/

W(S)        Weight of each season
/ s1        183
  s2        183/

K(U)        Installed capacity of each technology
/ u1        25
  u2        35
  u3        40
/
;

Table

A(S,T,U)    Maximum availability factor for each technology by
    season and by period
            u1      u2      u3
s1.t1       0.20    1       1
s1.t2       0.10    1       1
```

```
s1.t3    0.05    1    1
s2.t1    0.25    1    1
s2.t2    0.50    1    1
s2.t3    0.75    1    1
;

Table

DD(S,T)    Demand by season and by period
         t1      t2      t3
s1       280     600     720
s2       880     640     420
;

Table

C_lsh(S,T)    Load-shedding cost by season and by period
         t1      t2      t3
s1       500     500     500
s2       500     500     500
;

Table

C_opr(S,T,U)    Operating cost for each technology by season and by period
         u1      u2      u3
s1.t1    0       20      50
s1.t2    0       20      50
s1.t3    0       20      50
s2.t1    0       20      50
s2.t2    0       20      50
s2.t3    0       20      50
;

Variables
OF         Objective function value
d(S,T)     Load shed by season and by period
y(S,T,U)   Dispatch for each technology by season and by period
;

Equations
ObjectiveFunction    Objective function
EnergyBalance        Energy balance by season and by period
CapacityLimit        Capacity limit for each technology by season and by period
NNd                  Non-negativity for load shedding by season and by period
NNy                  Non-negativity for each technology by season and by period
;

ObjectiveFunction.. OF=E=SUM(S, W(S)*SUM(T, d(S,T)*C_lsh(S,T)+SUM(U, y(S,T,U)*C_opr(S,T,U))));
```

```
EnergyBalance(S,T).. SUM(U, y(S,T,U))+d(S,T)-DD(S,T)=E=0;
CapacityLimit(S,T,U).. A(S,T,U)*TT(T)*K(U)-y(S,T,U)=G=0;
NNd(S,T).. d(S,T)=G=0;
NNy(S,T,U).. y(S,T,U)=G=0;

MODEL ED /ALL/;

SOLVE ED USING lp MINIMIZING OF;
```

The following code solves Illustrative Example 2.5 to determine the cost-minimizing generation expansion.

```
* Cost-minimizing LP for generation expansion

Sets
S seasons /s1*s2/
T periods /t1*t3/
U technologies /u1*u3/;

Parameters

C_gen(U)   Annualized investment cost of each technology
/ u1       82290
  u2       239120
  u3       70510/

TT(T)      Length of each period in hours
/ t1       8
  t2       8
  t3       8/

W(S)       Weight of each season
/ s1       183
  s2       183/
;

Table

A(S,T,U)    Maximum availability factor for each technology by season and by period
           u1       u2      u3
s1.t1      0.20     1       1
s1.t2      0.10     1       1
s1.t3      0.05     1       1
s2.t1      0.25     1       1
s2.t2      0.50     1       1
s2.t3      0.75     1       1
;

Table

DD(S,T)    Demand by season and by period
           t1       t2      t3
s1         280      600     720
s2         880      640     420
```

```
;

Table

C_lsh(S,T)    Load-shedding cost by season and by period
             t1       t2      t3
s1           500      500     500
s2           500      500     500
;

Table

C_opr(S,T,U)    Operating cost for each technology by season and by period
             u1       u2      u3
s1.t1        0        20      50
s1.t2        0        20      50
s1.t3        0        20      50
s2.t1        0        20      50
s2.t2        0        20      50
s2.t3        0        20      50
;

Variables
OF          Objective function value
d(S,T)      Load shed by season and by period
y(S,T,U)    Dispatch for each technology by season and by period
x(U)        Capacity adoption for each technology
;

Equations
ObjectiveFunction       Objective function
EnergyBalance           Energy balance by season and by period
CapacityLimit           Capacity limit for each technology by season and by period
NNd                     Non-negativity for load shedding by season and by period
NNy                     Non-negativity for each technology by season and by period
NNx                     Non-negativity for technology adoption
;

ObjectiveFunction.. OF=E=SUM(S, W(S)*SUM(T, d(S,T)*C_lsh(S,T)+SUM(U, y(S,T,U)*C_opr(S,T,U))))+SUM(U, x(U)*C_gen(U));
EnergyBalance(S,T).. SUM(U, y(S,T,U))+d(S,T)-DD(S,T)=E=0;
CapacityLimit(S,T,U).. A(S,T,U)*TT(T)*x(U)-y(S,T,U)=G=0;
NNd(S,T).. d(S,T)=G=0;
NNy(S,T,U).. y(S,T,U)=G=0;
NNx(U).. x(U)=G=0;

MODEL GEP /ALL/;

SOLVE GEP USING lp MINIMIZING OF;
```

The following code solves Illustrative Example 2.6 to implement the short-run profit-maximization problem of a firm.

```
* Profit-maximizing LP for economic dispatch

Sets
S seasons /s1*s2/
T periods /t1*t3/
U technologies /u1*u3/;

Parameters

TT(T)       Length of each period in hours
/ t1        8
  t2        8
  t3        8/

W(S)        Weight of each season
/ s1        183
  s2        183/

K(U)        Installed capacity of each technology
/ u1        25
  u2        35
  u3        40
/
;

Table

A(S,T,U)     Maximum availability factor for each technology by season and by period
            u1       u2     u3
s1.t1       0.20     1      1
s1.t2       0.10     1      1
s1.t3       0.05     1      1
s2.t1       0.25     1      1
s2.t2       0.50     1      1
s2.t3       0.75     1      1
;

Table

C_opr(S,T,U)     Operating cost for each technology by season and by period
            u1       u2     u3
s1.t1       0        20     50
s1.t2       0        20     50
s1.t3       0        20     50
s2.t1       0        20     50
s2.t2       0        20     50
s2.t3       0        20     50
;
```

```
Table

Lambda(S,T)    Price by season and by period
          t1      t2      t3
s1        3660    9150    91500
s2        91500   9150    3660
;

Variables
OF          Objective function value
y(S,T,U)    Dispatch for each technology by season and by period
;

Equations
ObjectiveFunction    Objective function
CapacityLimit        Capacity limit for each technology by season and by period
NNy                  Non-negativity for each technology by season and by period
;

ObjectiveFunction.. OF=E=-SUM(S, W(S)*SUM(T, SUM(U, (Lambda(S,T)/W(S)-C_opr(S,T,U))*y(S,T,U))));
CapacityLimit(S,T,U).. A(S,T,U)*TT(T)*K(U)-y(S,T,U)=G=0;
NNy(S,T,U).. y(S,T,U)=G=0;

MODEL SRPM /ALL/;

SOLVE SRPM USING lp MINIMIZING OF;
```

The following code solves Illustrative Example 2.8 to implement the long-run profit-maximization problem of a firm.

```
* Profit-maximizing LP for generation expansion

Sets
S seasons /s1*s2/
T periods /t1*t3/
U technologies /u1*u3/;

Parameters

TT(T)       Length of each period in hours
/ t1        8
  t2        8
  t3        8/

W(S)        Weight of each season
/ s1        183
  s2        183/

C_gen(U)    Annualized investment cost of each technology
/ u1        82290
```

```
  u2       239120
  u3       70510/

KK(U)      Maximum installed capacity for each technology
/ u1       100
  u2       100
  u3       100/
;

Table

A(S,T,U)    Maximum availability factor for each technology by
     season and by period
          u1       u2      u3
s1.t1    0.20      1       1
s1.t2    0.10      1       1
s1.t3    0.05      1       1
s2.t1    0.25      1       1
s2.t2    0.50      1       1
s2.t3    0.75      1       1
;

Table

C_opr(S,T,U)    Operating cost for each technology by season and
     by period
          u1        u2      u3
s1.t1    0          20      50
s1.t2    0          20      50
s1.t3    0          20      50
s2.t1    0          20      50
s2.t2    0          20      50
s2.t3    0          20      50
;

Table

Lambda(S,T)    Price by season and by period
          t1          t2         t3
s1        3660        9150       11361.56250
s2        15752.18750 8266.25    3660
;

Variables
OF         Objective function value
y(S,T,U)   Dispatch for each technology by season and by period
x(U)       Capacity adoption for each technology
;

Equations
ObjectiveFunction    Objective function
CapacityLimit        Capacity limit for each technology by season
     and by period
MaximumCapacity      Maximum capacity for each technology
```

```
NNy                         Non-negativity for each technology by season and by period
NNx                         Non-negativity for technology adoption
;

ObjectiveFunction.. OF=E=-SUM(S, W(S)*SUM(T, SUM(U, (Lambda(S,T)/W(S)-C_opr(S,T,U))*y(S,T,U))))+SUM(U, x(U)*C_gen(U));
CapacityLimit(S,T,U).. A(S,T,U)*TT(T)*x(U)-y(S,T,U)=G=0;
MaximumCapacity(U).. KK(U)-x(U)=G=0;
NNy(S,T,U).. y(S,T,U)=G=0;
NNx(U).. x(U)=G=0;

MODEL LRPM /ALL/;

SOLVE LRPM USING lp MINIMIZING OF;
```

The following code solves Illustrative Example 2.9 to determine the ramp-constrained cost-minimizing economic dispatch.

```
* Cost-minimizing LP for economic dispatch with ramping constraints

Sets
S seasons /s1*s2/
T periods /t1*t3/
U technologies /u1*u3/;

Parameters

TT(T)      Length of each period in hours
/ t1       8
  t2       8
  t3       8/

W(S)       Weight of each season
/ s1       183
  s2       183/

K(U)       Installed capacity of each technology
/ u1       25
  u2       35
  u3       40
/

R(U)       Ramping limit of each technology
/ u1       1
  u2       0.3
  u3       0.6
/
;

Table
```

```
A(S,T,U)   Maximum availability factor for each technology by season and by period
           u1       u2      u3
s1.t1      0.20     1       1
s1.t2      0.10     1       1
s1.t3      0.05     1       1
s2.t1      0.25     1       1
s2.t2      0.50     1       1
s2.t3      0.75     1       1
;

Table

DD(S,T)   Demand by season and by period
           t1       t2      t3
s1         280      600     720
s2         880      640     420
;


Table

C_lsh(S,T)   Load-shedding cost by season and by period
           t1       t2      t3
s1         500      500     500
s2         500      500     500
;

Table

C_opr(S,T,U)   Operating cost for each technology by season and by period
           u1       u2      u3
s1.t1      0        20      50
s1.t2      0        20      50
s1.t3      0        20      50
s2.t1      0        20      50
s2.t2      0        20      50
s2.t3      0        20      50
;

Variables
OF          Objective function value
d(S,T)      Load shed by season and by period
y(S,T,U)    Dispatch for each technology by season and by period
;

Equations
ObjectiveFunction    Objective function
EnergyBalance        Energy balance by season and by period
CapacityLimit        Capacity limit for each technology by season and by period
RampUpLimit          Up-ramping limit for each technology by season and by period
```

```
RampDownLimit        Down-ramping limit for each technology by season and by period
NNd                  Non-negativity for load shedding by season and by period
NNy                  Non-negativity for each technology by season and by period
;

ObjectiveFunction.. OF=E=SUM(S, W(S)*SUM(T, d(S,T)*C_lsh(S,T)+SUM(U, y(S,T,U)*C_opr(S,T,U))));
EnergyBalance(S,T).. SUM(U, y(S,T,U))+d(S,T)-DD(S,T)=E=0;
CapacityLimit(S,T,U).. A(S,T,U)*TT(T)*K(U)-y(S,T,U)=G=0;
RampUpLimit(S,T,U).. R(U)*TT(T)*K(U)-y(S,T,U)+y(S,T-1,U)=G=0;
RampDownLimit(S,T,U).. R(U)*TT(T)*K(U)+y(S,T,U)-y(S,T-1,U)=G=0;
NNd(S,T).. d(S,T)=G=0;
NNy(S,T,U).. y(S,T,U)=G=0;

MODEL EDR /ALL/;

SOLVE EDR USING lp MINIMIZING OF;
```

The following code solves Illustrative Example 2.10 to determine the cost-minimizing economic dispatch with storage.

```
* Cost-minimizing LP for economic dispatch with storage

Sets
S seasons /s1*s2/
T periods /t1*t3/
U technologies /u1*u3/;

Parameters

TT(T)      Length of each period in hours
/ t1       8
  t2       8
  t3       8/

W(S)       Weight of each season
/ s1       183
  s2       183/

K(U)       Installed capacity of each technology
/ u1       25
  u2       35
  u3       40
/

;

Scalars

Rin      Rate at which storage can be charged /0.5/
```

```
Rout      Rate at which storage can be discharged /0.5/
Rmin      Minimum state of charge /0.1/
Ein       Storage input efficiency /0.95/
Esto      Periodic storage discharge /0.0/
B         Installed storage capacity /40/
;


Table

A(S,T,U)   Maximum availability factor for each technology by
    season and by period
          u1      u2     u3
s1.t1     0.20    1      1
s1.t2     0.10    1      1
s1.t3     0.05    1      1
s2.t1     0.25    1      1
s2.t2     0.50    1      1
s2.t3     0.75    1      1
;

Table

DD(S,T)    Demand by season and by period
          t1      t2     t3
s1        280     600    720
s2        880     640    420
;


Table

C_lsh(S,T)    Load-shedding cost by season and by period
          t1      t2     t3
s1        500     500    500
s2        500     500    500
;

Table

C_opr(S,T,U)   Operating cost for each technology by season and
    by period
          u1      u2     u3
s1.t1     0       20     50
s1.t2     0       20     50
s1.t3     0       20     50
s2.t1     0       20     50
s2.t2     0       20     50
s2.t3     0       20     50
;

Variables
OF         Objective function value
d(S,T)     Load shed by season and by period
```

```
y(S,T,U)   Dispatch for each technology by season and by period
zin(S,T)   Storage charge by season and by period
zout(S,T)  Storage discharge by season and by period
zsto(S,T)  Storage level by season and by period
;

Equations
ObjectiveFunction    Objective function
EnergyBalance        Energy balance by season and by period
CapacityLimit        Capacity limit for each technology by season and by period
StorageCharge        Limit for storage charge by season and by period
StorageDischarge     Limit for storage discharge by season and by period
StorageULimit        Upper limit for storage level by season and by period
StorageLLimit        Lower limit for storage level by season and by period
StorageBalance       Storage balance by season and by period
NNd                  Non-negativity for load shedding by season and by period
NNy                  Non-negativity for each technology by season and by period
NNzin                Non-negativity for storage charge by season and by period
NNzout               Non-negativity for storage discharge by season and by period
NNzsto               Non-negativity for storage level by season and by period
;

ObjectiveFunction.. OF=E=SUM(S, W(S)*SUM(T, d(S,T)*C_lsh(S,T)+SUM(U, y(S,T,U)*C_opr(S,T,U))));
EnergyBalance(S,T).. SUM(U, y(S,T,U))+d(S,T)+zout(S,T)-zin(S,T)-DD(S,T)=E=0;
CapacityLimit(S,T,U).. A(S,T,U)*TT(T)*K(U)-y(S,T,U)=G=0;
StorageBalance(S,T).. Ein*zin(S,T)-zout(S,T)+power(1-Esto,TT(T))*zsto(S,T-1)-zsto(S,T)=E=0;
StorageULimit(S,T).. TT(T)*B-zsto(S,T)=G=0;
StorageLLimit(S,T).. zsto(S,T)-Rmin*TT(T)*B=G=0;
StorageCharge(S,T).. Rin*TT(T)*B-zin(S,T)=G=0;
StorageDischarge(S,T).. Rout*TT(T)*B-zout(S,T)=G=0;
NNd(S,T).. d(S,T)=G=0;
NNy(S,T,U).. y(S,T,U)=G=0;
NNzin(S,T).. zin(S,T)=G=0;
NNzout(S,T).. zout(S,T)=G=0;
NNzsto(S,T).. zsto(S,T)=G=0;

MODEL EDS /ALL/;

SOLVE EDS USING lp MINIMIZING OF;
```

References

1. A.G. Energiebilanzen e.V.: Stromerzeugung nach Energieträgern (Strommix) von 1990 bis 2019 (in TWh) Deutschland insgesamt (2019). https://ag-energiebilanzen.de/28-0-Zusatzinformationen.html
2. Batlle, C., Rodilla, P.: An enhanced screening curves method for considering thermal cycling operation costs in generation expansion planning. IEEE Trans. Power Syst. **28**, 3683–3691 (2013)
3. Bothwell, C., Hobbs, B.F.: Crediting wind and solar renewables in electricity capacity markets: the effects of alternative definitions upon market efficiency. Energy J. **38**, 173–188 (2017)
4. British Columbia: British Columbia's Carbon Tax (2021). https://www2.gov.bc.ca/gov/content/environment/climate-change/clean-economy/carbon-tax
5. Bushnell, J.: A mixed complementarity model of hydrothermal electricity competition in the western United States. Oper. Res. **51**, 80–93 (2003)
6. California Energy Commission: 2018 Total System Electric Generation (2018). https://www.energy.ca.gov/data-reports/energy-almanac/california-electricity-data/2018-total-system-electric-generation
7. California Independent System Operator: What the Duck Curve Tells Us About Managing a Green Grid (2016). https://www.caiso.com/Documents/FlexibleResourcesHelpRenewables_FastFacts.pdf1
8. California Independent System Operator: Current and Forecasted Demand (2021). http://www.caiso.com/TodaysOutlook/Pages/default.aspx
9. Conejo, A.J., Baringo, L., Kazempour, S.J., Siddiqui, A.S.: Investment in Electricity Generation and Transmission: Decision Making under Uncertainty. Springer, Cham (2016)
10. Crampes, C., Moreaux, M.: Water resource and power generation. Int. J. Ind. Org. **19**, 975–997 (2001)
11. Debia, S., Benatia, D., Pineau, P.-O.: Evaluating an interconnection project: Do strategic interactions matter? Energy J. **39**, 99–120 (2018)
12. Debia, S., Pineau, P.-O., Siddiqui, A.S.: Strategic use of storage: the impact of carbon policy, resource availability, and technology efficiency on a renewable-thermal power system. Energy Econ. **80**, 100–122 (2019)
13. Debia, S., Pineau, P.-O., Siddiqui, A.S.: Strategic storage use in a hydro-thermal power system with carbon constraints. Energy Econ. **98**, 105261 (2021)
14. Energy Information Administration: How Much Carbon Dioxide is Produced When Different Fuels are Burned? (2019). https://www.eia.gov/tools/faqs/faq.php?id=73&t=11
15. Energy Information Administration: What is the Efficiency of Different Types of Power Plants? (2019). https://www.eia.gov/tools/faqs/faq.php?id=107&t=3
16. Energy Information Administration: Battery Storage in the United States: An Update on Market Trends (2020). https://www.eia.gov/analysis/studies/electricity/batterystorage/pdf/battery_storage.pdf
17. Energy Information Administration: Capital Cost and Performance Characteristic Estimates for Utility Scale Electric Power Generating Technologies (2020). https://www.eia.gov/analysis/studies/powerplants/capitalcost/pdf/capital_cost_AEO2020.pdf
18. Electric Power Research Institute: Assessment of Energy Storage Systems Suitable for Use by Electric Utilities. Technical Report EPRI-EM-264, Palo Alto, CA (1976)
19. EU Emissions Trading System (2020). https://ec.europa.eu/clima/policies/ets
20. Fabra, N.: A primer on capacity mechanisms. Energy Econ. **75**, 323–335 (2018)
21. Godoy-González, D., Gil, E., Gutiérrez-Alcaraz, G.: Ramping ancillary service for cost-based electricity markets with high penetration of variable renewable energy. Energy Econ. **85**, 104556 (2020)
22. Hobbs, B.F.: Optimization methods for electric utility resource planning. Eur. J. Oper. Res. **83**, 1–20 (1995)

23. Hyman, L.S.: Restructuring electricity policy and financial models. Energy Econ. **32**, 751–757 (2010)
24. Joskow, P., Tirole, J.: Merchant transmission investment. J. Ind. Econ. **53**, 233–264 (2005)
25. López Prol, J., Steininger, K.W., Zilberman, D.: The cannibalization effect of wind and solar in the California wholesale electricity market. Energy Econ. **85**, 104552 (2020)
26. Maurovich-Horvat, L., Boomsma, T.K., Siddiqui, A.S.: Transmission and wind investment in a deregulated electricity industry. IEEE Trans. Power Syst. **30**, 1633–1643 (2015)
27. Morales, J.M., Zugno, M., Pineda, S., Pinson, P.: Electricity market clearing with improved scheduling of stochastic production. Eur. J. Oper. Res. **235**, 765–774 (2014)
28. Nash, S.G., Sofer, A.: Linear and Nonlinear Programming. Springer, McGraw-Hill College, New York (1995)
29. National Renewable Energy Laboratory: 2019 Annual Technology Baseline (2019). https://atb.nrel.gov/electricity/2019/data.html
30. New York Independent System Operator: 2014 Load & Capacity Data (2014). https://www.nyiso.com/documents/20142/2226467/2014-Load-Capacity-Data-Report-Gold-Book.pdf/7f25165f-b808-34dd-269e-093fdebca735
31. Regional Greenhouse Gas Initiative (2020). https://www.rggi.org/
32. Reichenberg, L., Siddiqui, A.S., Wogrin, S.: Policy implications of downscaling the time dimension in power system planning models to represent variability in renewable output. Energy **159**, 870–877 (2018)
33. Rintamäki, T., Siddiqui, A.S., Salo, A.: How much is enough? Optimal support payments in a renewable-rich power system. Energy **117**, 300–313 (2016)
34. Rintamäki, T., Siddiqui, A.S., Salo, A.: Does renewable energy generation decrease the volatility of electricity prices? An analysis of Denmark and Germany. Energy Econ. **62**, 272–282 (2017)
35. Schill, W.-P., Kemfert, C.: Modeling strategic electricity storage: the case of pumped hydro storage in Germany. Energy J. **32**, 59–87 (2011)
36. Siddiqui, A.S., Sioshansi, R., Conejo, A.J.: Merchant storage investment in a restructured electricity industry. Energy J. **40**, 129–163 (2019)
37. Sioshansi, R.: Welfare impacts of electricity storage and the implications of ownership structure. Energy J. **31**, 173–198 (2010)
38. Sioshansi, R.: Emissions impacts of wind and energy storage in a market environment. Environ. Sci. Tech. **45**, 10728–10735 (2011)
39. Sioshansi, R.: When energy storage reduces social welfare. Energy Econ. **41**, 106–116 (2014)
40. Stoft, S.: Power System Economics: Designing Markets for Electricity. Wiley-IEEE Press, Piscataway (2002)
41. Tejada-Arango, D.A., Domeshek, M., Wogrin, S., Centeno, E.: Enhanced representative days and system states modeling for energy storage investment analysis. IEEE Trans. Power Syst. **33**, 6534–6544 (2018)
42. Traber, T.: Capacity remuneration mechanisms for reliability in the integrated European electricity market: effects on welfare and distribution through 2023. Util. Policy **46**, 1–14 (2017)
43. Ueckerdt, F., Hirth, L., Luderer, G., Edenhofer, O.: System LCOE: What are the costs of variable renewables? Energy **63**, 61–75 (2013)
44. Varian, H.R.: Microeconomic Analysis. W.W. Norton & Company, New York (1992)
45. Virasjoki, V., Rocha, P., Siddiqui, A.S., Salo, A.: Market impacts of energy storage in a transmission-constrained power system. IEEE Trans. Power Syst. **31**, 4108–4117 (2016)
46. Virasjoki, V., Siddiqui, A.S., Oliveira, F., Salo, A.: Utility-scale energy storage in an imperfectly competitive power sector. Energy Econ. **88**, 104716 (2020)
47. von Hirschhausen, C.: The German "Energiewende": an introduction. Econ. Energy Environ. Policy **3**, 1–12 (2014)
48. Wilson, R.B.: Architecture of power markets. Econometrica **70**, 1299–1340 (2002)
49. Zhang, T., Baldick, R., Deetjen, T.: Optimized generation capacity expansion using a further improved screening curve method. Electr. Power Syst. Res. **124**, 47–54 (2015)

Chapter 3
Market Clearing

3.1 Introduction

Short-term electricity markets include the day-ahead market, intra-day markets, and real-time markets [6]. This is the case, for instance, in Texas' ERCOT,[1] in the U.S. East Coast's PJM,[2] or in Spain and Portugal's OMIE.[3] The long-term or futures market allows for forward contracts, options, and others and typically spans from one week to several years. Since the focus of this chapter is energy markets, we do not analyze reserve, regulation, or capacity markets

The day-ahead market [1, 11] clears around noon on the day before the one considered. This is the most important market in most jurisdictions, since most of the money involved changes hands through this market.

Real-time markets (also called adjustment markets) clear about one hour before actual energy delivery and allow producers and consumers to make final adjustments in their productions and consumptions, respectively.

Intra-day markets clear every few hours between the clearing of the day-ahead market and the clearing of real-time markets and allow producers and consumers to fix offer and bidding mistakes, respectively, in the day-ahead market.

Futures markets [6] allow for long-term arrangements via forward contracts, options, and others and enable risk control over profits and payments by producers and consumers, respectively.

[1] http://www.ercot.com/.

[2] http://www.pjm.com/.

[3] https://www.omie.es/en/mercado-de-electricidad.

M. Tanaka et al., *Economics of Power Systems*, International Series
in Operations Research & Management Science 327,
https://doi.org/10.1007/978-3-030-92871-1_3

3.2 Day-Ahead Market

The day-ahead market [1, 11] clears through a market-clearing algorithm or auction. If such an auction does not involve non-convexities (minimum production outputs or star-up costs, for example), then it renders meaningful marginal prices that guarantee market adequacy (the total amount paid by consumers is higher than or equal to the total amount to be paid to producers) and cost recovery by producers. We analyze such auctions in this chapter. On the other hand, the effect of non-convexities is analyzed in Chap. 4, which is devoted to pricing.

We consider below several auctions used in different jurisdictions to clear the day-ahead market, namely:

1. Single-node single-period auction (Sect. 3.2.1)
2. Single-node multiple-period auction (Sect. 3.2.2)
3. Network-constrained single-period auction (Sect. 3.2.3)
4. Network-constrained multiple-period auction (Sect. 3.2.4)
5. Stochastic auction (Sect. 3.2.5)

3.2.1 Single-Node Single-Period Auction

This section analyzes a single-node single-period auction, which is the simplest auction. To illustrate how a single-node single-period auction works, we consider the simple example illustrated in Fig. 3.1.

This example involves three producers with marginal costs of \$1, \$2, and \$3 per energy unit and capacities of 10, 10, and 10 power units, respectively (left-hand side of Fig. 3.1). It also involves three consumers with marginal utilities of \$6, \$5, and \$4 per energy unit and maximum demands of 8, 14, and 5 power units, respectively (right-hand side of Fig. 3.1).

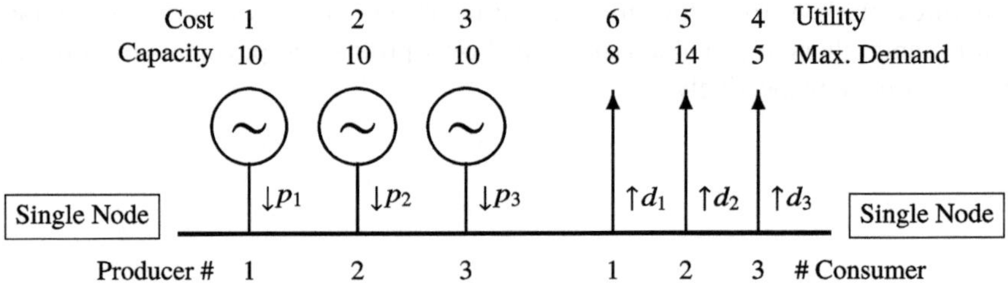

Fig. 3.1 Single-node single-period auction example

For this simple example, the single-node single-period auction has the form:

$$\max_{\substack{d_1,d_2,d_3\\p_1,p_2,p_3}} \quad z = 6\cdot d_1 + 5\cdot d_2 + 4\cdot d_3 - 1\cdot p_1 - 2\cdot p_2 - 3\cdot p_3 \tag{3.1a}$$

$$\text{s. t.} \quad p_1 + p_2 + p_3 = d_1 + d_2 + d_3 \,:\, \lambda \tag{3.1b}$$

$$0 \le p_1 \le 10, \quad 0 \le p_2 \le 10, \quad 0 \le p_3 \le 10 \tag{3.1c}$$

$$0 \le d_1 \le 8, \quad 0 \le d_2 \le 14, \quad 0 \le d_3 \le 5 \tag{3.1d}$$

where the optimization variables are defined below:

d_1, d_2, and d_3 are the consumptions of consumers 1, 2, and 3, respectively, and
p_1, p_2, and p_3 are the productions of producers 1, 2, and 3, respectively.

Additionally,

z is the social welfare (objective function), and
λ is the market-clearing price, which is the dual variable of the single balance constraint.

Objective function (3.1a), to be maximized, is the social welfare, constraint (3.1b) is the power-balance equation, constraints (3.1c) are production bounds, and constraints (3.1d) are consumption bounds.

The solution to this problem, easily obtained by inspection or using the GAMS [7] code provided in Sect. 3.7 of this chapter, is $\begin{cases} p_1^* = 10,\, p_2^* = 10,\, p_3^* = 7, \\ d_1^* = 8,\, d_2^* = 14,\, d_3^* = 5, \\ \lambda^* = 3, \\ z^* = 87 \end{cases}$

This solution is illustrated in Fig. 3.2. The piecewise-constant decreasing curve in the upper part of this figure corresponds to the consumers (demand curve), and the piecewise-constant increasing curve in the bottom part of this figure corresponds to producers (supply curve). All the demand is supplied and thus $d^* = 27$. The clearing price is $\lambda^* = 3$.

If the marginal utility of consumer 3 drops from \$4 to \$2.5 per energy unit, then the clearing solution is $\begin{cases} p_1^* = 10,\, p_2^* = 10,\, p_3^* = 2, \\ d_1^* = 8,\, d_2^* = 14,\, d_3^* = 0, \\ \lambda^* = 3, \\ z^* = 82 \end{cases}$

This second solution is illustrated in Fig. 3.3. We note that only demands 1 and 2 are supplied, while demand 3 is not supplied at all. The total demand supplied is $d^* = 22$ and the clearing price is $\lambda^* = 3$.

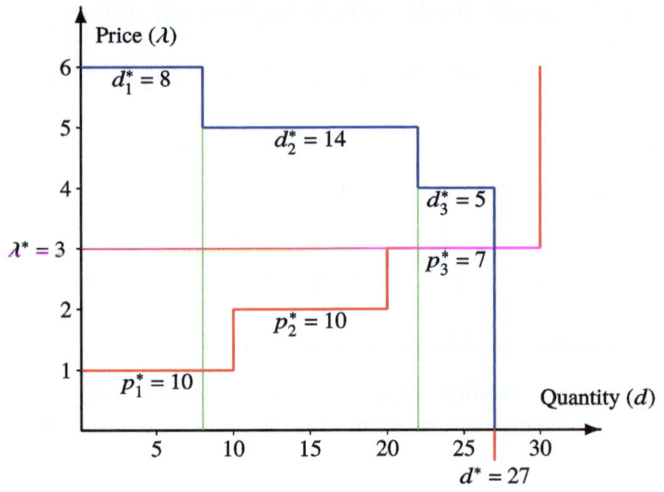

Fig. 3.2 Single-node single-period market clearing

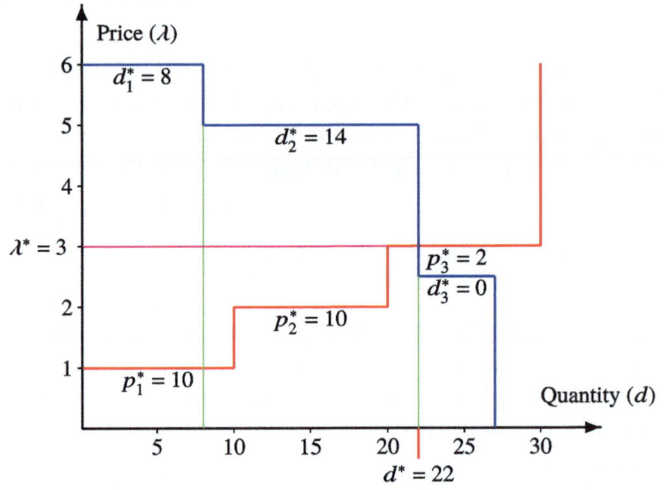

Fig. 3.3 Single-node single-period market clearing (consumer 3 with reduced utility)

A general-enough formulation of a single-node single-period auction is

$$\max_{d_i,\forall i;\, p_j,\forall j} \quad z = \sum_{i\in\Omega^{\mathrm{C}}} b_i \cdot d_i - \sum_{j\in\Omega^{\mathrm{P}}} o_j \cdot p_j \tag{3.2a}$$

$$\text{s. t.} \quad \sum_{j\in\Omega^{\mathrm{P}}} p_j = \sum_{i\in\Omega^{\mathrm{C}}} d_i \; : \; \lambda \tag{3.2b}$$

$$0 \leq d_i \leq d_i^{\max}, \forall i \in \Omega^{\mathrm{C}} \tag{3.2c}$$

$$0 \leq p_j \leq p_j^{\max}, \forall j \in \Omega^{\mathrm{P}} \tag{3.2d}$$

where the optimization variables are defined below:

d_i is the consumption of consumer i in power units,
p_j the production of producer j in power units,
z the social welfare in \$, and
λ the clearing price in \$/energy unit.

The constants are defined below as well:

b_i is the price bid (marginal utility) of consumer i in \$/energy unit,
o_j the price offer (marginal cost) of producer j in \$/energy unit,
$d_i^{\max}$ the maximum demand of consumer i in power units, and
$p_j^{\max}$ the production capacity of producer j in power units.

Sets Ω^{C} and Ω^{P} contain indices of consumers and producers, respectively.

Objective function (3.2a), to be maximized, is the social welfare, constraint (3.2b) is the power-balance equation, and constraints (3.2c) and (3.2d) are consumption and production bounds, respectively.

3.2.2 Single-Node Multi-Period Auction

We expand the simple example in Sect. 3.2.1 to consider 2 periods, not just 1. Figure 3.4 illustrates this revisited example. In this figure, maximum demands and utilities of the consumers for the two periods are provided (right-hand side of Fig. 3.4). Additionally, initial productions and ramping limits for producers are indicated (left-hand side of Fig. 3.4).

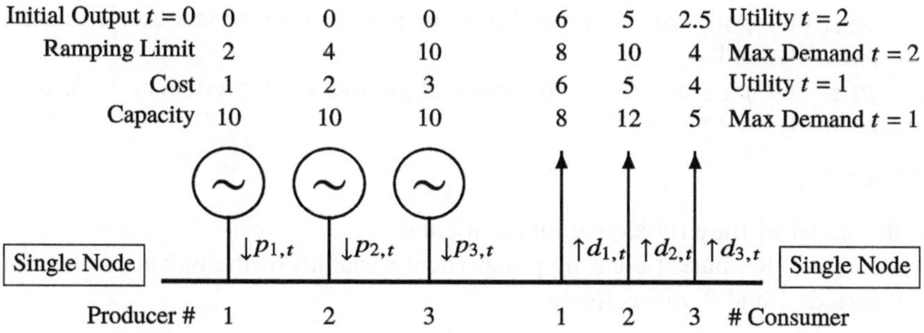

Fig. 3.4 Single-node two-period auction example

For this single-node two-period example, the auction has the form:

$$\max_{\substack{d_{1,1},d_{2,1},d_{3,1}\\ d_{1,2},d_{2,2},d_{3,2}\\ p_{1,1},p_{2,1},p_{3,1}\\ p_{1,2},p_{2,2},p_{3,2}}} \quad z = 6 \cdot d_{1,1} + 5 \cdot d_{2,1} + 4 \cdot d_{3,1} - 1 \cdot p_{1,1} - 2 \cdot p_{2,1} - 3 \cdot p_{3,1} + 6 \cdot d_{1,2} + 5 \cdot d_{2,2} + 2.5 \cdot d_{3,2} - 1 \cdot p_{1,2} - 2 \cdot p_{2,2} - 3 \cdot p_{3,2} \tag{3.3a}$$

$$\text{s. t.} \quad p_{1,1} + p_{2,1} + p_{3,1} = d_{1,1} + d_{2,1} + d_{3,1} \, : \, \lambda_1 \tag{3.3b}$$

$$p_{1,2} + p_{2,2} + p_{3,2} = d_{1,2} + d_{2,2} + d_{3,2} \, : \, \lambda_2 \tag{3.3c}$$

$$0 \leq p_{1,1} \leq 10, \quad 0 \leq p_{2,1} \leq 10, \quad 0 \leq p_{3,1} \leq 10 \tag{3.3d}$$

$$0 \leq p_{1,2} \leq 10, \quad 0 \leq p_{2,2} \leq 10, \quad 0 \leq p_{3,2} \leq 10 \tag{3.3e}$$

$$p_{1,1} - p_{1,0} \leq 2, \quad p_{1,2} - p_{1,1} \leq 2 \tag{3.3f}$$

$$p_{2,1} - p_{2,0} \leq 4, \quad p_{2,2} - p_{2,1} \leq 4 \tag{3.3g}$$

$$p_{3,1} - p_{3,0} \leq 10, \quad p_{3,2} - p_{3,1} \leq 10 \tag{3.3h}$$

$$p_{1,0} - p_{1,1} \leq 2, \quad p_{1,1} - p_{1,2} \leq 2 \tag{3.3i}$$

$$p_{2,0} - p_{2,1} \leq 4, \quad p_{2,1} - p_{2,2} \leq 4 \tag{3.3j}$$

$$p_{3,0} - p_{3,1} \leq 10, \quad p_{3,1} - p_{3,2} \leq 10 \tag{3.3k}$$

$$0 \leq d_{1,1} \leq 8, \quad 0 \leq d_{2,1} \leq 12, \quad 0 \leq d_{3,1} \leq 5 \tag{3.3l}$$

$$0 \leq d_{1,2} \leq 8, \quad 0 \leq d_{2,2} \leq 10, \quad 0 \leq d_{3,2} \leq 4 \tag{3.3m}$$

where the optimization variables are defined below:

$d_{1,1}$, $d_{2,1}$, and $d_{3,1}$ are the consumptions in period 1 of consumers 1, 2, and 3, respectively,
$d_{1,2}$, $d_{2,2}$, and $d_{3,2}$ the consumptions in period 2 of consumers 1, 2, and 3, respectively,
$p_{1,1}$, $p_{2,1}$, and $p_{3,1}$ are the productions in period 1 of producers 1, 2, and 3, respectively, and
$p_{1,2}$, $p_{2,2}$, and $p_{3,2}$ are the productions in period 2 of producers 1, 2, and 3, respectively.

Additionally,

z is the social welfare (objective function), and
λ_1 and λ_2 are the market-clearing prices (dual variables of the balance constraints) in periods 1 and 2, respectively.

Objective function (3.3a), to be maximized, is the social welfare, constraints (3.3b) and (3.3c) are power balances in periods 1 and 2, respectively, constraints (3.3d) and (3.3e) are production bounds in periods 1 and 2, respectively, constraints (3.3f), (3.3g), and (3.3h) are up-ramping limits (from initial status to period 1 and from period 1 to 2) for producers 1, 2, and 3, respectively, constraints (3.3i), (3.3j), and (3.3k) are down-ramping limits (from initial status to period 1 and from period 1 to 2) for producers 1, 2, and 3, respectively, and constraints (3.3l) and (3.3m) are consumption bounds in periods 1 and 2, respectively.

The solution to this problem, easily obtained by inspection or using a GAMS [7] model, is

$$\begin{cases} p_{1,1}^* = 2,\, p_{2,1}^* = 4,\, p_{3,1}^* = 10, \\ d_{1,1}^* = 8,\, d_{2,1}^* = 8,\, d_{3,1}^* = 0, \\ p_{1,2}^* = 4,\, p_{2,2}^* = 8,\, p_{3,2}^* = 6, \\ d_{1,2}^* = 8,\, d_{2,2}^* = 10,\, d_{3,2}^* = 0, \\ \lambda_1^* = 5,\, \lambda_2^* = 3, \\ z^* = 108 \end{cases}$$

This solution is illustrated in Figs. 3.5 (period 1) and 3.6 (period 2). On the one hand, in period 1, demand 1 is fully supplied, demand 2 is supplied up to 8 energy units, and demand 3 is not supplied at all. This limited energy supply is due to active ramping limits. The clearing price is $\lambda_1^* = \$5/\text{energy unit}$. On the other hand, in period 2, demands 1 and 2 are fully supplied, but demand 3 is not supplied. Ramping limits are still active in period 2, but the level of energy supplied is not affected by the ramping bounds. The clearing price is $\lambda_1^* = \$3/\text{energy unit}$.

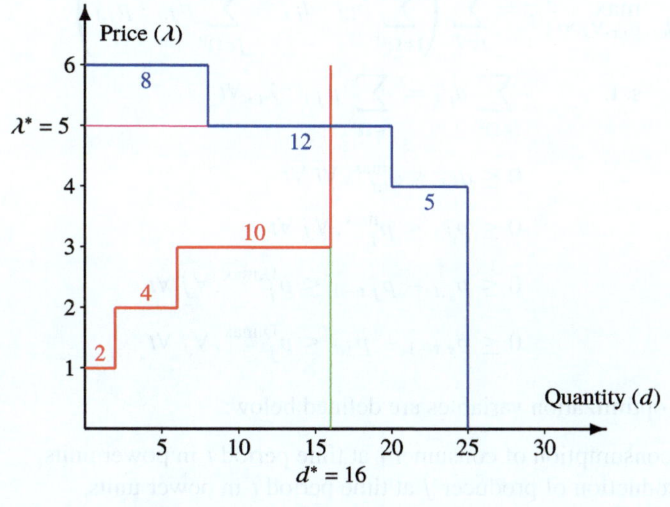

Fig. 3.5 Single-node two-period market clearing: period 1 (values below/above blocks indicate block sizes)

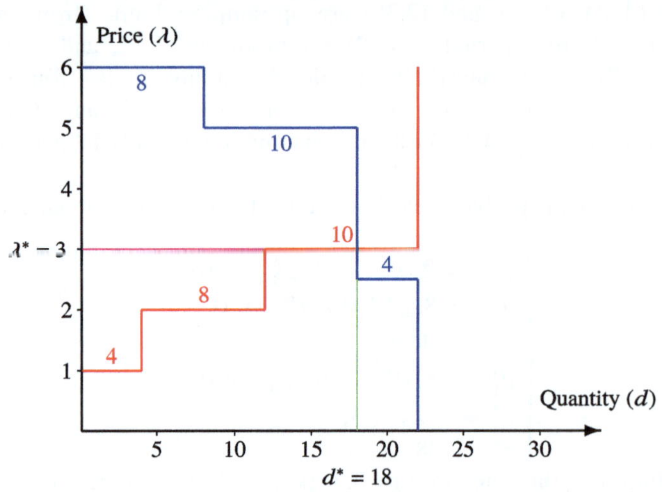

Fig. 3.6 Single-node two-period market clearing: period 2 (values below/above blocks indicate block sizes)

A general-enough formulation of a single-node multi-period auction is provided below:

$$\max_{d_{i,t}, p_{j,t}, \forall j, \forall t} \quad z = \sum_{t \in \mathcal{T}} \left(\sum_{i \in \Omega^{\mathrm{C}}} b_{i,t} \cdot d_{i,t} - \sum_{j \in \Omega^{\mathrm{P}}} o_{j,t} \cdot p_{j,t} \right) \tag{3.4a}$$

$$\text{s. t.} \quad \sum_{i \in \Omega^{\mathrm{C}}} d_{i,t} = \sum_{j \in \Omega^{\mathrm{P}}} p_{j,t} : \lambda_t, \forall t \tag{3.4b}$$

$$0 \leq d_{i,t} \leq d_{i,t}^{\max}, \forall i \; \forall t \tag{3.4c}$$

$$0 \leq p_{j,t} \leq p_j^{\max}, \forall j \; \forall t \tag{3.4d}$$

$$0 \leq p_{j,t} - p_{j,t-1} \leq p_j^{\mathrm{U,max}}, \forall j \; \forall t \tag{3.4e}$$

$$0 \leq p_{j,t-1} - p_{j,t} \leq p_j^{\mathrm{D,max}}, \forall j \; \forall t \tag{3.4f}$$

where the optimization variables are defined below:

$d_{i,t}$ is the consumption of consumer i at time period t in power units,
$p_{j,t}$ the production of producer j at time period t in power units,
z the social welfare in \$, and
λ_t the clearing (locational marginal) price at time period t in \$/energy unit.

The constants are defined below as well:

$b_{i,t}$ is the price bid (marginal utility) of consumer i at time period t in \$/energy unit,
$o_{j,t}$ the price offer (marginal cost) of producer j at time period t in \$/energy unit,
$d_{i,t}^{\max}$ the maximum demand of consumer i at time period t in power units,
$p_j^{\max}$ the production capacity of producer j in power units,
$p_j^{\mathrm{U,max}}$ the ramping-up limit of producer j in power units per time period,
$p_j^{\mathrm{D,max}}$ the ramping-down limit of producer j in power units per time period, and
p_j^0 the actual production of producer j at the beginning of the planning horizon in power units.

Additionally, Ω^{C} is the set of consumer indices and Ω^{P} the set of producer indices.

Objective function (3.4a), to be maximized, is the social welfare, constraints (3.4b) are power-balance equations, constraints (3.4c) and (3.4d) consumption and production bounds, respectively, and constraints (3.4e) and (3.4f) ramping-up and ramping-down limits, respectively, for producers.

3.2.3 Network-Constrained Single-Period Auction

To illustrate a network-constrained single-period auction, we consider the simple example depicted in Fig. 3.7. In this figure, for each producer, we indicate marginal cost and production capacity, for each consumer maximum demand and marginal utility, and for each line its corresponding flow.

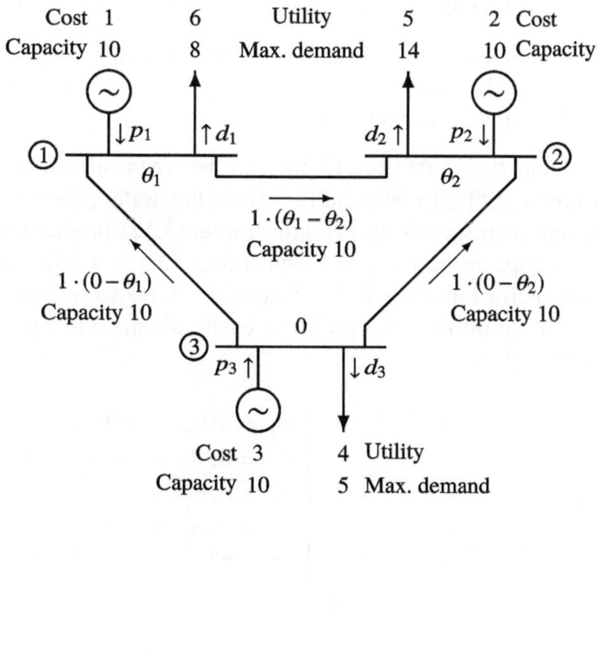

Fig. 3.7 Network-constrained single-period auction

Considering for simplicity that the susceptance (characteristic constant) of each line is 1, the network-constrained single-period auction for this example has the form:

$$\max_{\substack{d_1,d_2,d_3\\p_1,p_2,p_3\\\theta_1,\theta_2}} \quad z = 6 \cdot d_1 + 5 \cdot d_2 + 4 \cdot d_3 - 1 \cdot p_1 - 2 \cdot p_2 - 3 \cdot p_3 \tag{3.5a}$$

$$\text{s. t.} \quad d_1 - p_1 = (0 - \theta_1) + (\theta_2 - \theta_1) : \lambda_1 \tag{3.5b}$$

$$d_2 - p_2 = (\theta_1 - \theta_2) + (0 - \theta_2) : \lambda_2 \tag{3.5c}$$

$$d_3 - p_3 = (\theta_1 - 0) + (\theta_2 - 0) : \lambda_3 \tag{3.5d}$$

$$0 \leq p_1 \leq 10, \quad 0 \leq p_2 \leq 10, \quad 0 \leq p_3 \leq 10 \tag{3.5e}$$

$$0 \leq d_1 \leq 8, \quad 0 \leq d_2 \leq 14, \quad 0 \leq d_3 \leq 5 \tag{3.5f}$$

$$-10 \leq (\theta_1 - \theta_2) \leq 10 \tag{3.5g}$$

$$-10 \leq (\theta_1 - 0) \leq 10 \tag{3.5h}$$

$$-10 \leq (\theta_2 - 0) \leq 10 \tag{3.5i}$$

where the optimization variables are defined below:

d_1, d_2, and d_3 are the consumptions of consumers 1, 2, and 3, respectively,
p_1, p_2, and p_3 are the productions of producers 1, 2, and 3, respectively, and
θ_1 and θ_2 are the angles (state variable) of nodes 1 and 2, respectively [4].

We note that the angle of node 3 is fixed to zero ($\theta_3 = 0$) as a reference. Additionally,

z is the social welfare (objective function), and
λ_1, λ_2, and λ_3 are the market clearing prices (or locational marginal prices) at nodes 1, 2, and 3, respectively.

Objective function (3.5a), to be maximized, is the social welfare, constraints (3.5b), (3.5c), and (3.5d) are the nodal power-balance equations at nodes 1, 2, and 3, respectively [4], constraints (3.5e) production bounds, constraints (3.5f) consumption bounds, and constraints (3.5g), (3.5h), and (3.5i) transmission line bounds for lines $1-2$, $1-3$, and $2-3$, respectively.

The solution to this problem, easily obtained using the GAMS [7] code provided in Sect. 3.7, is

$$\begin{cases} p_1^* = 10, p_2^* = 10, p_3^* = 7, \\ d_1^* = 8, d_2^* = 14, d_3^* = 5, \\ \theta_1^* = 0, \theta_2^* = -2, \\ \lambda_1^* = 3, \lambda_2^* = 3, \lambda_3^* = 3, \\ z^* = 87 \end{cases}$$

This solution is identical to that of the example in Sect. 3.2.1. This is because no transmission line is congested (the capacity of each line is 10 power units) and the transmission system plays no role in the solution. In fact, transmission lines $1-3$ is not used, just transmission lines $1-2$ and $2-3$ are.

If the capacity of the cheapest producer (producer 1) is increased from 10 to 12 power units, then the corresponding solution is

$$\begin{cases} p_1^* = 12, p_2^* = 10, p_3^* = 5, \\ d_1^* = 8, d_2^* = 14, d_3^* = 5, \\ \theta_1^* = 1.333, \theta_2^* = -1.333, \\ \lambda_1^* = 3, \lambda_2^* = 3, \lambda_3^* = 3, \\ z^* = 91 \end{cases}$$

In this case, all transmission lines are used. The flows of lines $1-2$, $1-3$, and $3-2$ are 2.667, 1.333, and 1.333, respectively. No line, however, is congested and, thus, locational marginal prices are all equal: $\lambda_1^* = \lambda_2^* = \lambda_3^* = 3$. We note that the social welfare increases as a result of the capacity increase of the cheapest producer.

If in addition to increasing the capacity of the cheapest producer from 10 to 12, the capacities of transmission lines $1-2$ and $2-3$ are both reduced from 10 to 1 power units, then the corresponding solution is

$$\begin{cases} p_1^* = 11, p_2^* = 10, p_3^* = 2, \\ d_1^* = 8, d_2^* = 10, d_3^* = 5, \\ \theta_1^* = 2, \theta_2^* = 1, \\ \lambda_1^* = 1, \lambda_2^* = 5, \lambda_3^* = 3, \\ z^* = 81 \end{cases}$$

In this case, transmission lines $1-2$ and $2-3$ are congested. The flows of lines $1-2$, $1-3$, and $2-3$ are 1, 2, and 1, respectively. Since some lines are congested, locational marginal prices are different: $\lambda_1^* = 1$, $\lambda_2^* = 5$, $\lambda_3^* = 3$. We note that the social welfare decreases as a result of the capacity reduction of lines $1-2$ and $1-3$.

A general-enough formulation of a network-constrained auction is provided below. For the sake of simplicity, we use a single index for node, producer, and consumer, indicating that at most one producer and/or one consumer is located at each node.

$$\max_{d_i, p_i, \theta_i, \forall i} \quad z = \sum_{i \in \Omega} b_i \cdot d_i - \sum_{i \in \Omega} o_i \cdot p_i \tag{3.6a}$$

$$\text{s. t.} \quad p_i - d_i = \sum_{j \in \Omega_i} B_{i,j} \cdot (\theta_i - \theta_j) : \lambda_i, \forall i \tag{3.6b}$$

$$0 \leq d_i \leq d_i^{\max}, \forall i \in \Omega \tag{3.6c}$$

$$0 \le p_i \le p_i^{\max}, \forall i \in \Omega \tag{3.6d}$$

$$B_{i,j}(\theta_i - \theta_j) \le p_{i,j}^{\max}, \forall i, \forall j \in \Omega_i \tag{3.6e}$$

where the optimization variables are defined below:

d_i is the consumption of consumer i in power units,
p_i the production of producer i in power units,
θ_i the angle (state variable) of node i in radians,
z the social welfare in \$, and
λ_i the clearing (locational marginal) price at node i in \$/energy unit.

The constants are defined below as well:

b_i is the price bid (marginal utility) of consumer i in \$/energy unit,
o_i the price offer (marginal cost) of producer i in \$/energy unit,
$B_{i,j}$ the susceptance of line ij in per unit,
$d_i^{\max}$ the maximum demand of consumer i in power units,
$p_i^{\max}$ the production capacity of producer i in power units, and
$p_{i,j}^{\max}$ the transmission capacity of line $i - j$ in power units.

Additionally, Ω is the set of indices of all nodes/producers/consumers and Ω_i the set of indices of nodes directly connected to node i.

Objective function (3.6a), to be maximized, is the social welfare, constraints (3.6b) are power-balance equations, and constraints (3.6c), (3.6d), and (3.6e) are consumption, production, and transmission bounds, respectively.

3.2.4 Network-Constrained Multi-Period Auction

We expand in this section the network-constrained single-period auction in Sect. 3.2.3 to two periods. Such a network-constrained two-period auction has the form:

$$\max_{\substack{d_{1,1},d_{2,1},d_{3,1}\\ d_{1,2},d_{2,2},d_{3,2}\\ p_{1,1},p_{2,1},p_{3,1}\\ p_{1,2},p_{2,2},p_{3,2}\\ \theta_{1,1},\theta_{2,1},\theta_{1,2},\theta_{2,2}}} \quad z = 6 \cdot d_{1,1} + 5 \cdot d_{2,1} + 4 \cdot d_{3,1} - 1 \cdot p_{1,1} - 2 \cdot p_{2,1} - 3 \cdot p_{3,1} + 6 \cdot d_{1,2} + 5 \cdot d_{2,2} + 2.5 \cdot d_{3,2} - 1 \cdot p_{1,2} - 2 \cdot p_{2,2} - 3 \cdot p_{3,2} \tag{3.7a}$$

$$\text{s. t.} \quad d_{1,1} - p_{1,1} = (0 - \theta_{1,1}) + (\theta_{2,1} - \theta_{1,1}) : \ \lambda_{1,1} \tag{3.7b}$$

$$d_{2,1} - p_{2,1} = (\theta_{1,1} - \theta_{2,1}) + (0 - \theta_{2,1}) : \ \lambda_{2,1} \tag{3.7c}$$

$$d_{3,1} - p_{3,1} = (\theta_{1,1} - 0) + (\theta_{2,1} - 0) : \ \lambda_{3,1} \tag{3.7d}$$

$$0 \leq p_{1,1} \leq 10, \quad 0 \leq p_{2,1} \leq 10, \quad 0 \leq p_{3,1} \leq 10 \tag{3.7e}$$

$$0 \leq d_{1,1} \leq 8, \quad 0 \leq d_{2,1} \leq 12, \quad 0 \leq d_{3,1} \leq 5 \tag{3.7f}$$

$$-10 \leq (\theta_{1,1} - \theta_{2,1}) \leq 10 \tag{3.7g}$$

$$-10 \leq (\theta_{1,1} - 0) \leq 10 \tag{3.7h}$$

$$-10 \leq (\theta_{2,1} - 0) \leq 10 \tag{3.7i}$$

$$d_{1,2} - p_{1,2} = (0 - \theta_{1,2}) + (\theta_{2,2} - \theta_{1,2}) : \lambda_{1,2} \tag{3.7j}$$

$$d_{2,2} - p_{2,2} = (\theta_{1,2} - \theta_{2,2}) + (0 - \theta_{2,2}) : \lambda_{2,2} \tag{3.7k}$$

$$d_{3,2} - p_{3,2} = (\theta_{1,2} - 0) + (\theta_{2,2} - 0) : \lambda_{3,2} \tag{3.7l}$$

$$0 \leq p_{1,2} \leq 10, \quad 0 \leq p_{2,2} \leq 10, \quad 0 \leq p_{3,2} \leq 10 \tag{3.7m}$$

$$0 \leq d_{1,2} \leq 8, \quad 0 \leq d_{2,2} \leq 10, \quad 0 \leq d_{3,2} \leq 4 \tag{3.7n}$$

$$-10 \leq (\theta_{1,2} - \theta_{2,2}) \leq 10 \tag{3.7o}$$

$$-10 \leq (\theta_{1,2} - 0) \leq 10 \tag{3.7p}$$

$$-10 \leq (\theta_{2,2} - 0) \leq 10 \tag{3.7q}$$

$$p_{1,1} - p_{1,0} \leq 2, \quad p_{1,2} - p_{1,1} \leq 2 \tag{3.7r}$$

$$p_{2,1} - p_{2,0} \leq 4, \quad p_{2,2} - p_{2,1} \leq 4 \tag{3.7s}$$

$$p_{3,1} - p_{3,0} \leq 10, \quad p_{3,2} - p_{3,1} \leq 10 \tag{3.7t}$$

$$p_{1,0} - p_{1,1} \leq 2, \quad p_{1,1} - p_{1,2} \leq 2 \tag{3.7u}$$

$$p_{2,0} - p_{2,1} \leq 4, \quad p_{2,1} - p_{2,2} \leq 4 \tag{3.7v}$$

$$p_{3,0} - p_{3,1} \leq 10, \quad p_{3,1} - p_{3,2} \leq 10 \tag{3.7w}$$

where the optimization variables are defined below:

$d_{1,1}$, $d_{2,1}$, and $d_{3,1}$ are the consumptions in period 1 of consumers 1, 2, and 3, respectively,
$d_{1,2}$, $d_{2,2}$, and $d_{3,2}$ the consumptions in period 2 of consumers 1, 2, and 3, respectively,
$p_{1,1}$, $p_{2,1}$, and $p_{3,1}$ the productions in period 1 of producers 1, 2, and 3, respectively,
$p_{1,2}$, $p_{2,2}$, and $p_{3,2}$ the productions in period 2 of producers 1, 2, and 3, respectively,
$\theta_{1,1}$ and $\theta_{2,1}$ the angles (state variables) of nodes 1 and 2, respectively, in period 1, and
$\theta_{1,2}$ and $\theta_{2,2}$ the angles of nodes 1 and 2, respectively, in period 2.

Additionally,

z is the social welfare (objective function),
$\lambda_{1,1}$, $\lambda_{2,1}$, and $\lambda_{3,1}$ the market-clearing prices (dual variables of the balance equations) of nodes 1, 2, and 3, respectively, in period 1, and
$\lambda_{1,2}$, $\lambda_{2,2}$, and $\lambda_{3,2}$ the market-clearing prices (dual variables of the balance equations) of nodes 1, 2, and 3, respectively, in period 2.

Objective function (3.7a), to be maximized, is the social welfare.

Constraints (3.7b), (3.7c), and (3.7d) are power-balance equations at nodes 1, 2, and 3, respectively, in period 1, constraints (3.7e) production bounds in periods 1, constraints (3.7f) consumption bounds in periods 1, constraints (3.7g), (3.7h), and (3.7i) transmission bounds for lines $1-2$, $1-3$, and $2-3$, respectively, in period 1.

Constraints (3.7j), (3.7k), and (3.7l) are power-balance equations at nodes 1, 2, and 3, respectively, in period 2, constraints (3.7m) production bounds in periods 2, constraints (3.7n) consumption bounds in periods 2, constraints (3.7o), (3.7p), and (3.7q) transmission bounds for lines $1-2$, $1-3$, and $2-3$, respectively, in period 2.

Constraints (3.7r), (3.7s), and (3.7t) are ramping-up limits (from initial status to period 1 and from period 1 to 2) for producers 1, 2, and 3, respectively, and constraints (3.7u), (3.7v), and (3.7w) are ramping-down limits (from initial status to period 1 and from period 1 to 2) for producers 1, 2, and 3, respectively.

The solution to this problem, easily obtained using GAMS [7], is

$$\begin{cases} p_{1,1}^* = 2,\ p_{2,1}^* = 4,\ p_{3,1}^* = 10, \\ d_{1,1}^* = 8,\ d_{2,1}^* = 8,\ d_{3,1}^* = 0, \\ p_{1,2}^* = 4,\ p_{2,2}^* = 8,\ p_{3,2}^* = 6, \\ d_{1,2}^* = 8,\ d_{2,2}^* = 10,\ d_{3,2}^* = 0, \\ \lambda_{1,1}^* = 5,\ \lambda_{2,1}^* = 5,\ \lambda_{3,1}^* = 5, \\ \lambda_{1,2}^* = 3,\ \lambda_{2,2}^* = 3,\ \lambda_{3,2}^* = 3, \\ z^* = 108 \end{cases}$$

This solution coincides with that of the example in Sect. 3.2.2 (single-node multi-period auction) since no line is congested (the capacity of each line is 10 power units).

If the capacities of lines $1-2$ and $2-3$ are both set to 1, then the corresponding solution is

$$\begin{cases} p_{1,1}^* = 2,\ p_{2,1}^* = 4,\ p_{3,1}^* = 8, \\ d_{1,1}^* = 5,\ d_{2,1}^* = 5,\ d_{3,1}^* = 5, \\ p_{1,2}^* = 4,\ p_{2,2}^* = 8,\ p_{3,2}^* = 3, \\ d_{1,2}^* = 7,\ d_{2,2}^* = 8,\ d_{3,2}^* = 0, \\ \lambda_{1,1}^* = 6,\ \lambda_{2,1}^* = 5,\ \lambda_{3,1}^* = 3, \\ \lambda_{1,2}^* = 6,\ \lambda_{2,2}^* = 5,\ \lambda_{3,2}^* = 3, \\ z^* = 89 \end{cases}$$

In this case, lines $1-2$ and $2-3$ are congested in both time periods and clearing prices differ per node.

A general-enough formulation of a network-constrained multi-period auction is provided below. For the sake of simplicity, a single index i is used to refer to nodes, producers and consumers, which implies that one producer and/or one consumer is considered per node.

$$\max_{d_{i,t},p_{i,t},\theta_{i,t},\forall i,\forall t} \quad z=\sum_{t\in\mathcal{T}}\left(\sum_{i\in\Omega} b_{i,t}\cdot d_{i,t}-\sum_{i\in\Omega} o_{i,t}\cdot p_{i,t}\right) \tag{3.8a}$$

$$\text{s. t.} \quad p_{i,t}-d_{i,t}=\sum_{j\in\Omega_i} B_{i,j}\cdot(\theta_{i,t}-\theta_{j,t}) : \lambda_{i,t}, \forall i\ \forall t \tag{3.8b}$$

$$0\le d_{i,t}\le d_{i,t}^{\max}, \forall i\ \forall t \tag{3.8c}$$

$$0\le p_{i,t}\le p_i^{\max}, \forall i\ \forall t \tag{3.8d}$$

$$0\le p_{i,t}-p_{i,t-1}\le p_i^{\mathrm{U,max}}, \forall i\ \forall t \tag{3.8e}$$

$$0\le p_{i,t-1}-p_{i,t}\le p_i^{\mathrm{D,max}}, \forall i\ \forall t \tag{3.8f}$$

$$B_{i,j}(\theta_i-\theta_j)\le p_{i,j}^{\max}, \forall i, \forall j\in\Omega_i \tag{3.8g}$$

where the optimization variables are defined below:

$d_{i,t}$ is the consumption of consumer i at time period t in power units,
$p_{i,t}$ the production of producer i at time period t in power units,
$\theta_{i,t}$ the angle (state variable) at node i at time period t in radians,
z the social welfare in \$, and
$\lambda_{i,t}$ the clearing (locational marginal) price at node i and time period t in \$/energy unit.

The constants are defined below as well:

$b_{i,t}$ is the price bid (marginal utility) of consumer i at time period t in \$/energy unit,
$o_{i,t}$ the price offer (marginal cost) of producer i at time period t in \$/energy unit,
$d_{i,t}^{\max}$ the maximum demand of consumer i at time period t in power units,
$p_i^{\max}$ the production capacity of producer i in power units,
$p_i^{\mathrm{U,max}}$ the ramping-up limit of producer i in power units per time period,
$p_i^{\mathrm{D,max}}$ the ramping-down limit of producer i in power units per time period,
p_i^0 the actual production of producer i at the beginning of the planning horizon in power units,
$B_{i,j}$ the susceptance of line ij in per unit, and
$p_{i,j}^{\max}$ the capacity of line $i-j$ in power units.

Additionally, Ω is the set of indices of all nodes/producers/consumers and Ω_i the set of indices of nodes connected to node i.

Objective function (3.8a), to be maximized, is the social welfare, constraints (3.8b) are power-balance equations, constraints (3.8c) and (3.8d) consumption and production bounds, respectively, constraints (3.8e) and (3.8f) ramping-up and ramping-down limits, respectively, for producers, and constraints (3.8f) transmission-capacity limits.

3.2.5 Stochastic Auction

Stochastic auctions [2, 9, 10] are relevant in power systems with highly uncertain supply and/or highly uncertain demand. This is the case of systems with high penetration of weather-dependent production sources, such as wind or solar generating units.

We refer the reader to Sect. 4.5 of Chap. 4, the pricing chapter, for a detailed discussion of stochastic auctions.

3.3 Intra-Day Market

Intra-day markets are similar to the day-ahead market but spanning a shorter time horizon. They clear between the clearing of the day-ahead market of day "d" and that of day "d+1." Each intra-day market typically spans the hours between its clearing and the clearing of the day-ahead market of day "d+1."

Auction formats for the day-ahead market directly apply to intra-day markets.

3.4 Futures Market

Futures markets provide long-term contracting arrangements that enable risk management [3, 5, 8, 12].

Futures market products included forward contracts, options, and others. We briefly describe below forward contracts and options.

A forward contract allows a producer to sell electricity at a given price throughout a given future period. Such an arrangement shields the producer from the price volatility of the short-term markets, i.e., the day-ahead, the intra-day, and the real-time markets. Needless to say, if the average short-term price throughout the validity horizon of the forward contract is higher than the contract price, then the producer would have been better off if it had not signed the contract. And, conversely, if the average short-term price is lower than the contract price, then the producer would have been better off if it had signed the contract. Regarding these forward contracts, we note that a similar reasoning applies to consumers.

An option gives a producer the discretion to utilize a forward contract spanning a future time period. The decision on whether or not to realize the forward contract takes place at an intermediate time between signing the option and realizing the corresponding forward contract. For a fee, an option allows a producer to delay the decision of whether or not to sign a forward contract. This delayed decision reduces the uncertainty faced by the producer, which will eventually allow it to make a better decision. Regarding these options, we note that a similar reasoning applies to consumers.

3.5 Summary

Using a tutorial approach, this chapter describes auctions, i.e., market-clearing algorithms to clear electricity markets. It focuses on the day-ahead market, the most important market in terms of volume of trade and money exchange, and describes:

1. Single-node single-period auctions
2. Single-node multi-period auctions
3. Network-constrained single-period auctions
4. Network-constrained multi-period auctions

Stochastic auctions and the impact of non-convexities (e.g., start-up costs and minimum production levels) in auctions are analyzed in Chap. 4, which focuses on prices.

3.6 End-of-Chapter Exercises

3.1 Expand the example in Sect. 3.2.1 to consider 4 producers (and 3 consumers).

3.2 Expand the example in Sect. 3.2.1 to consider 2 offer blocks per producer and 2 bid blocks per consumer.

3.3 Simplify the example in Sect. 3.2.1 considering all consumers inelastic (that is, consumers with very high (infinite) marginal utilities).

3.4 Expand the example in Sect. 3.2.2 considering 3 time periods.

3.5 Simplify the example in Sect. 3.2.2 by considering all consumers as inelastic (that is, consumers with very high (infinite) marginal utilities).

3.6 Expand the example in Sect. 3.2.3 considering 4 nodes. Analyze cases with congested lines.

3.7 Expand the example in Sect. 3.2.3 considering unserved energy per node.

3.8 Expand the example in Sect. 3.2.4 considering 4 nodes and 3 time periods.

3.7 GAMS Codes

A GAMS [7] input file to solve the single-node single-period auction in Sect. 3.2.1 is provided below:

```
variable z
positive variables d1,d2,d3,p1,p2,p3;
equations of,be,db1,db2,db3,pb1,pb2,pb3;
of..  z =e= 6*d1+5*d2+4*d3-1*p1-2*p2-3*p3;
be..  d1+d2+d3-p1-p2-p3 =e= 0;
db1.. d1 =l=  8;
db2.. d2 =l= 14;
db3.. d3 =l=  5;
pb1.. p1 =l= 10;
pb2.. p2 =l= 10;
pb3.. p3 =l= 10;
model snsp_auction /all/;
solve snsp_auction using lp maximizing z;
display z.l,d1.l,d2.l,d3.l,p1.l,p2.l,p3.l,be.m;
```

Note that this GAMS [7] code reproduces almost verbatim the mathematical formulation of model (3.1).

The relevant part of the corresponding GAMS [7] output file is

```
----      14 VARIABLE z.L                =         87.000
             VARIABLE d1.L               =          8.000
             VARIABLE d2.L               =         14.000
             VARIABLE d3.L               =          5.000
             VARIABLE p1.L               =         10.000
             VARIABLE p2.L               =         10.000
             VARIABLE p3.L               =          7.000
             EQUATION be.M               =          3.000
```

A GAMS [7] input file to solve the network-constrained single-period auction in Sect. 3.2.3 is provided below:

```
variable z;
positive variables d1,d2,d3;
positive variables p1,p2,p3;
free variables theta1,theta2;
*
parameters c1   /01/, c2   /02/, c3   /03/;
parameters u1   /06/, u2   /05/, u3   /04/;
parameters p1up /12/, p2up /10/, p3up /10/;
parameters d1up /08/, d2up /14/, d3up /05/;
*
parameters t12up /1/, t13up /10/, t23up /1/;
*
p1.up = p1up; p2.up = p2up; p3.up = p3up;
d1.up = d1up; d2.up = d2up; d3.up = d3up;
*
equations of,ba1,ba2,ba3;
```

```
equations bt12,bt21,bt13,bt31,bt23,bt32;
*
of.. z=e=u1*d1+u2*d2+u3*d3-c1*p1-c2*p2-c3*p3;
ba1.. d1-p1=e=(0-theta1)+(theta2-theta1);
ba2.. d2-p2=e=(theta1-theta2)+(0-theta2);
ba3.. d3-p3=e=(theta1-0)+(theta2-0);
*
bt12.. (theta1-theta2)=l=t12up;
bt21.. (theta2-theta1)=l=t12up;
bt13.. (theta1-0)=l=t13up;
bt31.. (0-theta1)=l=t13up;
bt23.. (theta2-0)=l=t23up;
bt32.. (0-theta2)=l=t23up;
*
model ncspa /all/;
solve ncspa using lp maximizing z;
*
display z.l,theta1.l,theta2.l;
display p1.l,p2.l,p3.l;
display d1.l,d2.l,d3.l;
display ba1.m,ba2.m,ba3.m;
```

Note that this GAMS [7] code reproduces almost verbatim the mathematical formulation of model (3.5).

The relevant part of the corresponding GAMS [7] output file is

```
----      34 VARIABLE z.L              =        81.000
             VARIABLE theta1.L         =         2.000
             VARIABLE theta2.L         =         1.000
----      35 VARIABLE p1.L             =        11.000
             VARIABLE p2.L             =        10.000
             VARIABLE p3.L             =         2.000
----      36 VARIABLE d1.L             =         8.000
             VARIABLE d2.L             =        10.000
             VARIABLE d3.L             =         5.000
----      37 EQUATION ba1.M            =         1.000
             EQUATION ba2.M            =         5.000
             EQUATION ba3.M            =         3.000
```

References

1. Arroyo, J.M., Conejo, A.J.: Multiperiod auction for a pool-based electricity market. IEEE Trans. Power Syst. **17**, 1225–1231 (2002)
2. Bouffard, F., Galiana, F.D., Conejo, A.J.: Market-clearing with stochastic security–part I: formulation. IEEE Trans. Power Syst. **20**, 1818–1826 (2005)
3. Carrion, M., Arroyo, J.M., Conejo, A.J.: A bilevel stochastic programming approach for retailer futures market trading. IEEE Trans. Power Syst. **24**, 1446–1456 (2009)
4. Conejo, A.J., Baringo, L.: Power System Operations. Springer, New York (2018)

5. Conejo, A.J., Garcia-Bertrand, R., Carrion, M., Caballero, A., de Andres, A.: Optimal involvement in futures markets of a power producer. IEEE Trans. Power Syst. **23**, 703–711 (2008)
6. Conejo, A.J., Carrion, M., Morales, J.M.: Decision Making Under Uncertainty in Electricity Markets. Springer, New York (2010)
7. GAMS Development Corporation: GAMS–a user's guide (2020). http://www.gams.com
8. Kazempour, S.J., Conejo, A.J., Ruiz, C.: Strategic generation investment considering futures and spot markets. IEEE Trans. Power Syst. **27**, 1467–1476 (2012)
9. Morales, J.M., Conejo, A.J., Perez-Ruiz, J.: Economic valuation of reserves in power systems with high penetration of wind power. IEEE Trans. Power Syst. **24**, 900–910 (2009)
10. Morales, J.M., Conejo, A.J., Madsen, H., Pinson, P., Zugno, M.: Integrating Renewables in Electricity Markets. Springer, New York (2014)
11. Motto, A.L., Galiana, F.D., Conejo, A.J., Arroyo, J.M.: Network-constrained multiperiod auction for a pool-based electricity market. IEEE Trans. Power Syst. **17**, 646–653 (2002)
12. Pineda, S., Conejo, A.J., Carrion, M.: Impact of unit failure on forward contracting. IEEE Trans. Power Syst. **23**, 1768–1775 (2008)

Chapter 4
Marginal Pricing

4.1 Introduction

Prices, not only quantities, are most important in markets, as they enable actual economic transactions. This chapter pertains to pricing in power markets and focuses specifically on energy marginal pricing, not capacity markets or capacity payments.

We consider first the cost-recovery property of marginal pricing under perfect competition, a key property that justifies such a pricing mechanism.

We analyze then marginal pricing from a short-term perspective and review the concepts of producer surplus, consumer surplus, network surplus (also referred to as congestion rent or congestion surplus), and social welfare.

We consider next prices from non-convex, stochastic, and multi-period market-clearing algorithms.

Recognizing that power markets are generally imperfect and to ensure sufficient investment in production capacity, capacity payments (being paid just for making capacity available to the market) are used in some markets. Alternatively, capacity markets might be arranged to reward the building of generation capacity following certain policy criteria. Capacity payments and capacity markets are beyond the scope of this chapter.

4.2 Marginal Pricing and Investment-Cost Recovery

The single most important economic reason for using marginal prices is that, under perfect competition, they ensure investment cost recovery [6]. This is analyzed below.

M. Tanaka et al., *Economics of Power Systems*, International Series in Operations Research & Management Science 327,
https://doi.org/10.1007/978-3-030-92871-1_4

4.2.1 Optimal Control and Perfect Knowledge

We consider first that the power system is operated by an optimal controller with perfect knowledge of the technical and economic data of all producers. We assume as well that the demand is inelastic. That is, any consumer is happy to pay whatever price is needed to satisfy its demand for electricity.

For simplicity, we work with three production technologies, namely, peak, medium, and base. The optimal capacities to be built by the optimal controller (and builder) of peak, medium, and base technologies in MW are denoted as p_p, p_m, and p_b, respectively, being their annualized building costs in \$/MW, b_p, b_m, and b_b, respectively, and their variable (marginal) costs in \$/MWh, c_p, c_m, and c_b, respectively. Additionally, the unserved capacity in MW is denoted as p_u, being the unserved energy cost (the cost incurred by the consumer for not having electricity available) in \$/MWh, c_u.

We consider as well that the optimal controller uses a merit-order rule for dispatching the production technologies. Figure 4.1 illustrates the optimal dispatch carried out by the controller (with perfect knowledge of the economic and technical data of the three technologies). Specifically, Fig. 4.1 shows the load-duration curve of the power system. Such a load-duration curve provides the number of hours (x-axis) in per unit (on a base of $365 \times 24 = 8760$ hours) that the power demand is above a power level in MW (y-axis).

From Fig. 4.1, the production hours per technology in per unit (on a base of $365 \times 24 = 8760$ hours) are:

$h_b = 1$ corresponding to the base technology,
h_m corresponding to the medium technology,
h_p corresponding to the peak technology, and
h_u corresponding to the unserved energy,

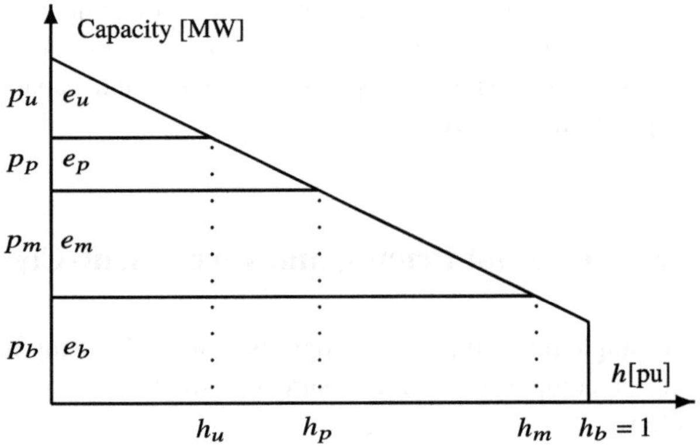

Fig. 4.1 Optimal dispatch on the load-duration curve by an optimal controller

and the energy produced (area slice under the load-duration curve) by the base, medium, and peak technologies is e_b, e_m, and e_p, respectively. Finally, e_u is the unserved energy (Fig. 4.1).

Assuming a merit-order dispatch rule and perfect knowledge, the problem to be solved by the optimal controller to determine the optimal capacity to be built per technology (p_p, p_m, and p_b) is

$$\min_{p_p, p_m, p_b} \quad C(\cdot) = \overbrace{b_b p_b + b_m p_m + b_p p_p}^{C_{\mathrm{I}}(\cdot)} + \overbrace{c_b e_b + c_m e_m + c_p p_m + c_u e_u}^{C_{\mathrm{O}}(\cdot)} \tag{4.1}$$

where $C(\cdot)$ is the total cost, $C_{\mathrm{I}}(\cdot)$ is the annualized investment cost, and $C_{\mathrm{O}}(\cdot)$ is the annual operation cost.

The optimality condition of problem (4.1) is given by

$$\nabla_{p_p, p_m, p_b} C(p_p, p_m, p_b) = 0 \tag{4.2}$$

that is, the gradient of (4.1) has to be zero.

In the following, we analyze (4.2) per technology. Starting with the peak technology, the corresponding optimality condition is

$$b_p + \frac{\partial}{\partial p_p} \left(\underbrace{c_b e_b + c_m e_m + c_p e_p + c_u e_u}_{C_{\mathrm{O}}(\cdot)} \right) = 0 \tag{4.3}$$

To compute the derivative $\frac{\partial}{\partial p_p} C_{\mathrm{O}}(\cdot)$, we rely on Fig. 4.2. From this figure, we observe that the marginal increment in operation cost as a result of a marginal increment Δp_p in the capacity of the peak technology is

$$\Delta C_{\mathrm{O}}(\cdot) = -\Delta p_p h_u \cdot (c_u - c_p) \tag{4.4}$$

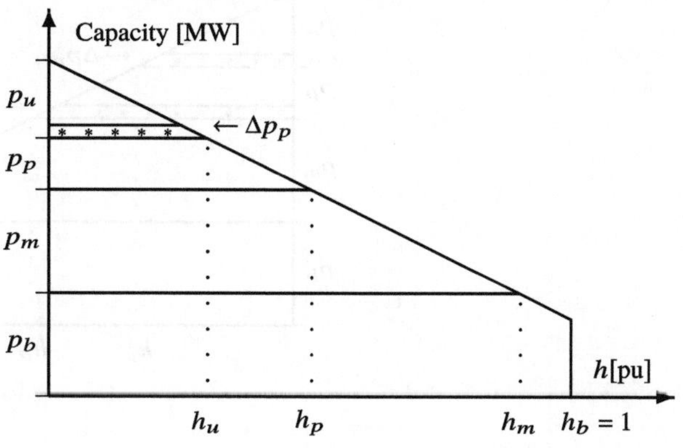

Fig. 4.2 Computation of $\frac{\partial}{\partial p_p} C_{\mathrm{O}}(\cdot)$

where $\Delta p_p h_u$ is the unserved energy covered by the incremental capacity Δp_p in the peak technology (area slice with asterisks in Fig. 4.2) and $(c_u - c_p)$ the difference between the unserved energy variable cost and the variable cost of the peak technology.

Considering marginal changes in (4.4) renders

$$\frac{\partial}{\partial p_p} C_O(\cdot) = -h_u \cdot (c_u - c_p) \tag{4.5}$$

Thus, condition (4.3) becomes

$$b_p - h_u \cdot (c_u - c_p) = 0 \tag{4.6}$$

We consider next the medium technology. The corresponding optimality condition from (4.2) is

$$b_m + \frac{\partial}{\partial p_m} C_O(\cdot) = 0 \tag{4.7}$$

To compute the derivative in (4.7), we consider Fig. 4.3. From this figure, we observe that the marginal increment in operation cost as a result of a marginal increment Δp_m in the medium technology (two area slices with asterisks) is

$$\Delta C_O(\cdot) = -\Delta p_m h_p \cdot (c_p - c_m) - \Delta p_m h_u \cdot (c_u - c_p). \tag{4.8}$$

Therefore,

$$\frac{\partial}{\partial p_m} C_O(\cdot) = -h_p \cdot (c_p - c_m) - h_u \cdot (c_u - c_p) \tag{4.9}$$

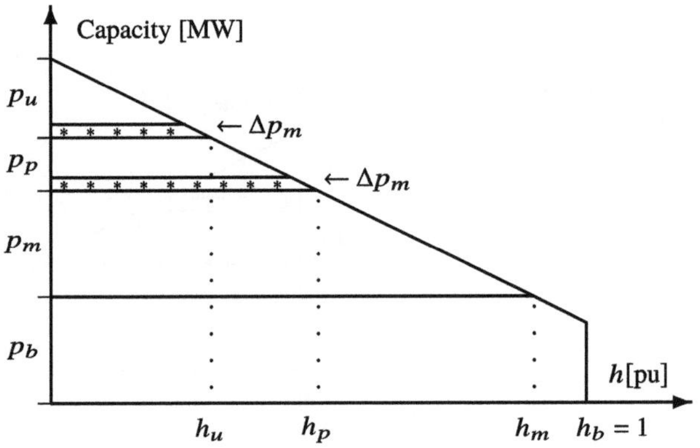

Fig. 4.3 Computation of $\frac{\partial}{\partial p_m} C_O(\cdot)$

and optimality condition (4.7) becomes

$$b_m - h_p \cdot (c_p - c_m) - h_u \cdot (c_u - c_p) = 0 \tag{4.10}$$

Analogously, we derive the optimality condition for the base technology, which is

$$b_b - h_m \cdot (c_m - c_b) - h_p \cdot (c_p - c_m) - h_u \cdot (c_u - c_p) = 0 \tag{4.11}$$

Considering together the optimality condition for the peak, medium, and base technologies, (4.6), (4.10), and (4.11), respectively, we obtain

$$b_p - h_u \cdot (c_u - c_p) = 0 \tag{4.12a}$$

$$b_m - h_p \cdot (c_p - c_m) = b_p \tag{4.12b}$$

$$b_b - h_m \cdot (c_m - c_b) = b_m \tag{4.12c}$$

or

$$b_p + h_u c_p = h_u c_u \tag{4.13a}$$

$$b_m + h_p c_m = b_p + h_p c_p \tag{4.13b}$$

$$b_b + h_m c_b = b_m + h_m c_m \tag{4.13c}$$

which is equivalent to optimality conditions (4.2).

Results (4.13) are illustrated in Fig. 4.4. The lower part of this figure corresponds to the optimal merit-order dispatch of the three power technologies by the optimal controller already illustrated in Fig. 4.1. On the other hand, the upper part of this figure provides the total cost. The annualized building (investment) costs for the base, medium, and peak technologies are represented on the y-axis. Operation costs (variable cost times production hours) are represented by the three straight lines with intercepts different from zero. The straight line starting at the origin provides the unserved energy cost.

Specifically, we note that in Fig. 4.4:

Point P_1 corresponds to condition (4.13a): $b_p + h_u c_p = h_u c_u$.
Point P_2 corresponds to condition (4.13b): $b_m + h_p c_m = b_p + h_p c_p$.
Point P_3 corresponds to condition (4.13c): $b_b + h_m c_b = b_m + h_m c_m$.

Therefore, Fig. 4.4 fully represents (4.13) and provides a complete description of the optimal investment and operation actions of the optimal controller.

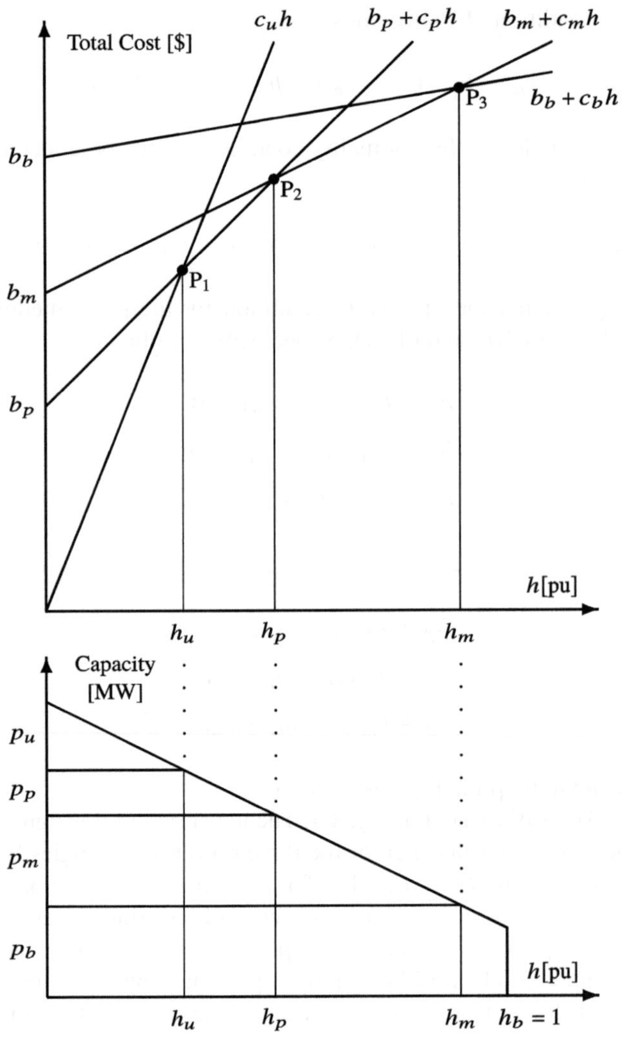

Fig. 4.4 Perfect competition: optimal investment and operation

4.2.2 Perfect Competition

In this subsection, instead of an optimal controller, we consider a perfectly competitive market [1] made of many small producers per each one of the three technologies considered in Sect. 4.2.1 and no economies of scale.

We note that in such a market, the long-term profit per technology should be zero, otherwise producers will either enter or leave the market, which will happen until the market stabilizes under the condition of zero profit.

We consider the three technologies one at a time. Regarding the peak technology, the only period in which such a technology achieves a positive profit is the unserved energy period, where the marginal price (the unserved energy variable cost) is above the variable cost of the peak technology. Taking this into account, and considering the lower part of Fig. 4.4 (or Fig. 4.1), we obtain

$$R_p = p_p h_u c_u \tag{4.14}$$

$$C_p = b_p p_p + p_p h_u c_p \tag{4.15}$$

$$\Pi_p = p_p h_u c_u - b_p p_p - p_p h_u c_p \tag{4.16}$$

where R_p, C_p, and Π_p are the revenue, the cost, and the profit, respectively, of the peak technology.

The revenue, R_p, is computed as the capacity, p_p, times the working hours under the unserved energy condition, h_u, times the unserved energy variable cost, c_u (marginal cost of the unserved energy period).

The cost C_p includes the annualized investment cost and the annual operation cost. The annualized investment cost is the capacity built, p_p, times the annualized building cost, b_p, and the operation cost is the capacity built, p_p, times the working hours under the unserved energy condition, h_u, times the variable cost, c_p.

The profit Π_p is the revenue minus the cost.

Since the profit needs to be zero for the market to operate in steady state, we obtain

$$p_p h_u c_u - b_p p_p - p_p h_u c_p = 0 \tag{4.17}$$

or

$$b_p + h_u c_p = h_u c_u \tag{4.18}$$

which is condition (4.13a), derived under the optimal controller framework.

We consider next the medium technology and note that the profit will be positive during unserved energy hours (where the marginal cost is the unserved energy cost) and peak hours (where the marginal cost is the variable cost of the peak technology). Thus,

$$R_m = p_m h_u c_u + p_m (h_p - h_u) c_p \tag{4.19}$$

$$C_m = b_m p_m + p_m h_p c_m \tag{4.20}$$

$$\Pi_m = p_m h_u c_u + p_m (h_p - h_u) c_p - b_m p_m - p_m h_p c_m \tag{4.21}$$

We note that revenue, cost, and profit above are computed as in the peak-technology case.

Since the profit for the medium technology needs to be zero (for steady-state market conditions), we obtain

$$p_m h_u c_u + p_m (h_p - h_u) c_p - b_m p_m - p_m h_p c_m = 0 \quad (4.22)$$

and using (4.18)

$$b_p + c_p h_p = b_m + c_m h_p \quad (4.23)$$

which is condition (4.13b), derived under the optimal controller framework.

Similarly, imposing zero profit for the base technology,

$$p_b h_u c_u + p_b (h_p - h_u) c_p + p_b (h_m - h_p) c_m - p_b b_b - p_b h_m c_b = 0 \quad (4.24)$$

we obtain

$$b_b + c_b h_m = b_m + c_m h_m \quad (4.25)$$

which is condition (4.13c), derived under the optimal controller framework.

From the study above, two important conclusions are in order:

1. The investment and operation outcomes are identical:
   (a) If the system is operated by an optimal controller with perfect knowledge of the technical and economic data of the producers.
   (b) If a perfectly competitive market is implemented.
2. Investment costs are recovered under marginal pricing, which directly results from the non-profit conditions given by Eqs. (4.24), (4.22), and (4.17), derived from both perspectives, optimal control and perfect competition.

Similar conclusions are reported in [6].

4.3 Marginal Pricing and Short-Term Efficiency

In this section, we consider first prices pertaining to an un-congested market-clearing example and then a congested one, and, finally, we provide a general formulation for a single-period market-clearing algorithm and its associated marginal pricing.

4.3.1 Un-congested Clearing

We consider a market that operates on a simple power system involving two nodes and one line, as depicted in Fig. 4.5.

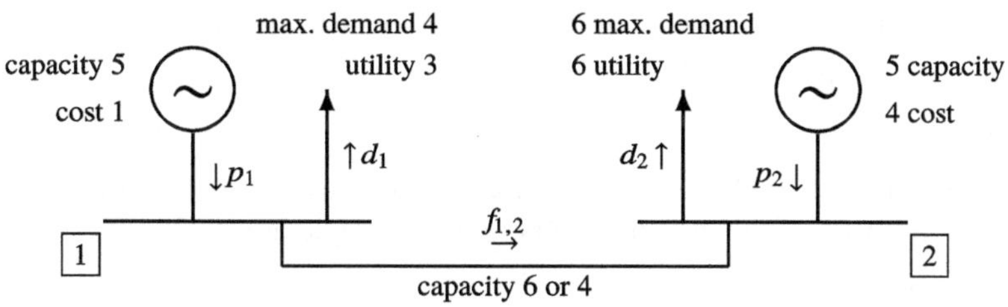

Fig. 4.5 Two-node one-line power system

Producer 1 with a capacity of 5 power units and a variable cost of \$1 per energy unit is located at node 1. Consumer 1 with a maximum demand of 4 power units and a variable utility of \$3 per energy unit is also located at node 1. Similarly, producer 2, located at node 2, has a capacity of 5 power units and a variable cost of \$4 per energy unit. Consumer 2, also located at node 2, has a maximum demand of 6 power units and a variable utility of \$6 per energy unit.

The transmission line connecting nodes 1 and 2 has a capacity of 5 power units. The market-clearing problem to be solved by the market operator is

$$\max_{d_1,d_2,p_1,p_2\geq 0;\, f_{1,2}} \quad z = 3 \cdot d_1 + 6 \cdot d_2 - 1 \cdot p_1 - 4 \cdot p_2 \tag{4.26a}$$

$$\text{s. t.} \quad p_1 - d_1 = f_{1,2} : \lambda_1 \tag{4.26b}$$

$$p_2 - d_2 = -f_{1,2} : \lambda_2 \tag{4.26c}$$

$$p_1 \leq 5; \quad p_2 \leq 5 \tag{4.26d}$$

$$d_1 \leq 4; \quad d_2 \leq 6 \tag{4.26e}$$

$$-6 \leq f_{1,2} \leq 6 \tag{4.26f}$$

where the optimization variables are:

d_1 is the consumption of consumer 1,
d_2 the consumption of consumer 2,
p_1 the production of producer 1,
p_2 the production of producer 2,
λ_1 (dual variable) the clearing price at node 1, and
λ_2 (dual variable) the clearing price at node 2.

Objective function (4.26a) is the social welfare (to be explained at the end of this section). Constraints (4.26b) and (4.26c) are power-balance equations at nodes 1 and 2, respectively. Constraints (4.26d) and (4.26e) are production and consumption upper bounds, respectively. Finally, constraint (4.26d) imposes transmission-capacity bounds.

The solution to this problem, easily obtained by inspection, is:

$p_1^* = 5,\ p_2^* = 1,\ d_1^* = 0,\ d_2^* = 6,\ f_{1,2}^* = 5.$
$\lambda_1^* = 4,\ \lambda_2^* = 4.$

The revenue of a producer is the product of the market price and the production level. The revenues of the two producers in this example are:

$R_1 = \lambda_1^* \cdot p_1^* = 5 \cdot 4 = 20.,$
$R_2 = \lambda_2^* \cdot p_2^* = 1 \cdot 4 = 4.$
Total revenue $R^{\text{total}} = R_1 + R_2 = 24.$

The payment of a consumer is the product of the market price and the consumption level. The payments of the two consumers in this example are:

$P_1 = \lambda_1^* \cdot d_1^* = 4 \cdot 6 = 24.$
$P_2 = \lambda_2^* \cdot d_1^* = 4 \cdot 0 = 0.$
Total payment $P^{\text{total}} = P_1 + P_2 = 24.$

We observe that $R^{\text{total}} = P^{\text{total}}$, which indicates that the market is *revenue adequate*; that is, the market operator collects from consumers the full amount to be paid to producers.

On the one hand, the profit of a producer is the production level multiplied by the difference between the price and the variable cost of the producer. On the other hand, the profit of a consumer is the consumption level multiplied by the difference between the variable utility of the consumer and the price. The profits of producers and consumers in this example are:

$\Pi_1^{\text{P}} = (\lambda_1^* - c_1) \cdot p_1^* = (4 - 1) \cdot 5 = 15.$
$\Pi_2^{\text{P}} = (\lambda_2^* - c_2) \cdot p_2^* = (4 - 4) \cdot 1 = 0.$
$\Pi_1^{\text{C}} = (u_1 - \lambda_1^*) \cdot d_1^* = (3 - 4) \cdot 0 = 0.$
$\Pi_2^{\text{C}} = (u_2 - \lambda_2^*) \cdot d_2^* = (6 - 4) \cdot 6 = 12.$

We observe that the profit of each of the two producers is non-negative. In such a case, we say that the market complies with the *cost recovery* property in terms of operation.

Omitting fixed costs, the producer surplus, which is the profit of all producers, is:

$\text{PS} = \Pi_1^{\text{P}} + \Pi_2^{\text{P}} = 15 + 0 = 15.$

The consumer surplus, which is the profit of all consumers, is:

$\text{CS} = \Pi_1^{\text{C}} + \Pi_2^{\text{C}} = 0 + 12 = 12.$

Finally, the social welfare, which in this case is the producer surplus plus consumer surplus, is:

$\text{SW} = \text{PS} + \text{CS} = 15 + 12 = 27.$

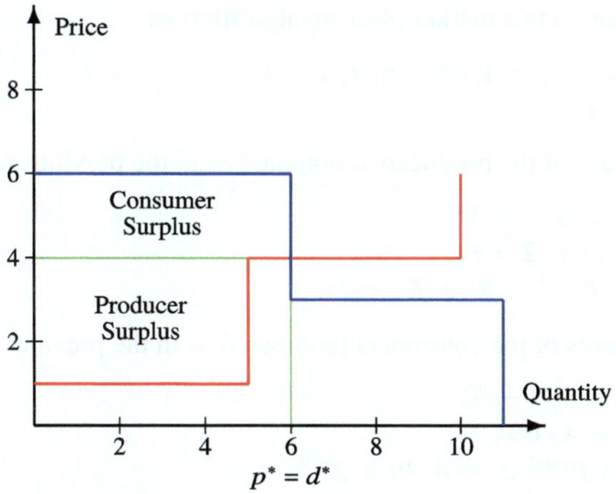

Fig. 4.6 Un-congested market clearing

Figure 4.6 illustrates the clearing of the market for the considered example. The red monotonously increasing stepwise curve is the supply curve, while the blue monotonously decreasing stepwise curve is the demand curve. The clearing price and the quantity produced and consumed are given by the crossing of these two curves and identified in the figure by the two thin green lines. Additionally, we note that the upper box in this figure corresponds to the consumer surplus, while the lower one corresponds to the producer surplus.

The difference between the area under the demand curve and the area under the supply curve is therefore the social welfare. This is in fact how objective function (4.26) is defined.

4.3.2 Congested Clearing

We examine next the same example considered in the previous section but assuming that the capacity of the transmission line is 4, not 6, which leads to a congested operation condition. The corresponding market-clearing algorithm is

$$\max_{d_1,d_2,p_1,p_2\geq 0;\, f_{1,2}} \quad z = 3\cdot d_1 + 6\cdot d_2 - 1\cdot p_1 - 4\cdot p_2 \tag{4.27a}$$

$$\text{s. t.} \quad p_1 - d_1 = f_{1,2} : \lambda_1 \tag{4.27b}$$

$$p_2 - d_2 = -f_{1,2} : \lambda_2 \tag{4.27c}$$

$$p_1 \leq 5; \quad p_2 \leq 5 \tag{4.27d}$$

$$d_1 \leq 4; \quad d_2 \leq 6 \tag{4.27e}$$

$$-4 \leq f_{1,2} \leq 4 \tag{4.27f}$$

The solution to this market-clearing algorithm is:

$p_1^* = 5,\ p_2^* = 2,\ d_1^* = 1,\ d_2^* = 6,\ f_{1,2}^* = 4.$
$\lambda_1^* = 3,\ \lambda_2^* = 4.$

The revenues of the producers (computed as in the previous section) are:

$R_1 = \lambda_1^* \cdot p_1^* = 3 \cdot 5 = 15.$
$R_2 = \lambda_2^* \cdot p_2^* = 4 \cdot 2 = 8.$
Total revenue $R^{\text{total}} = R_1 + R_2 = 23.$

The payments of the consumers (computed as in the previous section) are:

$P_1 = \lambda_1^* \cdot d_1^* = 3 \cdot 1 = 3.$
$P_2 = \lambda_2^* \cdot d_2^* = 4 \cdot 6 = 24.$
Total payment $P^{\text{total}} = P_1 + P_2 = 27.$

We observe that $P^{\text{total}} > R^{\text{total}}$, which indicates that the market is *revenue adequate*; that is, the amount collected from consumers is higher than the amount to be paid to producers.

The profits of producers and consumers (computed as in the previous section) are:

$\Pi_1^{\text{P}} = (\lambda_1^* - c_1) \cdot p_1^* = (3 - 1) \cdot 5 = 10.$
$\Pi_2^{\text{P}} = (\lambda_2^* - c_2) \cdot p_2^* = (4 - 4) \cdot 2 = 0.$
$\Pi_1^{\text{C}} = (u_1 - \lambda_1^*) \cdot d_1^* = (3 - 3) \cdot 1 = 0.$
$\Pi_2^{\text{C}} = (u_2 - \lambda_2^*) \cdot d_2^* = (6 - 4) \cdot 6 = 12.$

As in the un-congested case, we observe that the profit of each of the two producers is non-negative, and, therefore, the market complies with the *cost recovery* property in terms of operations.

The surplus or *profit* of the network (typically used to reinforce the network and therefore allocated to the transmission system operator/owner) is the difference of prices across the line multiplied by the line flow. Thus,

$\Pi^{\text{N}} = (\lambda_2^* - \lambda_1^*) \cdot f_{1,2}^* = (4 - 3) \cdot 4 = 4.$

The producer, consumer, and network surpluses are:

$\text{PS} = \Pi_1^{\text{P}} + \Pi_2^{\text{P}} = 10 + 0 = 10.$

This corresponds to the area of the green-and-red box at the bottom of the left-hand side plot of Fig. 4.7.

$\text{CS} = \Pi_1^{\text{C}} + \Pi_2^{\text{C}} = 0 + 12 = 12.$

This corresponds to the area of the blue-green-and-red box at the top of the right-hand side plot of Fig. 4.7.

$\text{NS} = \Pi^{\text{N}} = 4.$

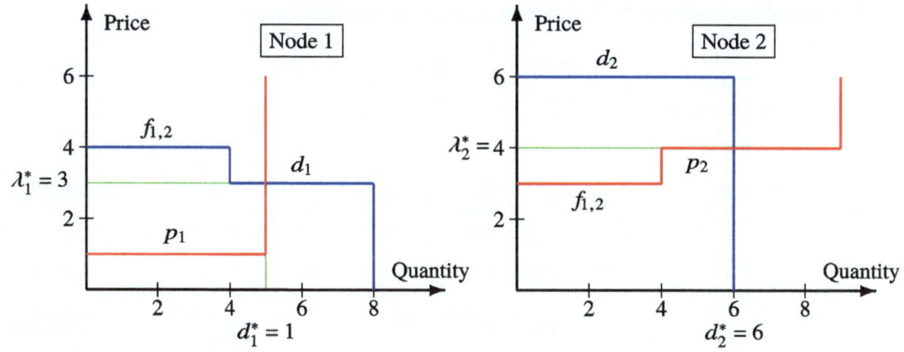

Fig. 4.7 Constrained market clearing

This corresponds to the area of the blue-and-green box at the top of the left-hand side plot of Fig. 4.7 or to the area of the green-and-red box at the bottom of the right-hand side plot of Fig. 4.7.

Finally, the social welfare, which in a congested case is equal to producer surplus plus consumer surplus plus network surplus, is:

$$\text{SW} = \text{PS} + \text{CS} = 10 + 12 + 4 = 26.$$

We observe that the social welfare in this congested case (26) is smaller than that in the un-congested case (27).

Figure 4.7 illustrates this congested market clearing. Regarding node 1, the line behaves as a consumer (i.e., it consumes energy), and, therefore, the supply and demand at that node are those indicated on the left-hand side of Fig. 4.7. The price and cleared quantity are \$3 per energy unit and 5 power units, respectively. Regarding node 2, the line behaves as a producer (i.e., it provides energy), and, therefore, the supply and demand at that node are those indicated on the right-hand side subplot of Fig. 4.7. The price and cleared quantity are \$4 per energy unit and 6 power unit, respectively.

We observe a "market splitting" between nodes 1 and 2. That is, the congestion of the line originates two markets with different cleared quantities and clearing prices.

Since for a given time period, the marginal clearing prices are (or can be) different across nodes, they are denominated *locational* marginal prices, LMPs.

4.3.3 General Formulation

For the sake of simplicity, in the formulation below, we consider that there are at most 1 producer and 1 consumer per node, and, thus, we use a single index i to refer to nodes, producers, and consumers.

A general-enough market-clearing algorithm has the form:

$$\max_{\substack{d_i \ge 0, p_i \ge 0, \theta_i, \forall i; \\ f_{i,j} \forall i, \forall j \in \Omega_i}} \quad z = \sum_i u_i \, d_i - \sum_i c_i \, p_i \tag{4.28a}$$

$$\text{s. t.} \quad p_i - d_i - \sum_{j \in \Omega_i} f_{i,j} = 0 : \; \lambda_i \quad \forall i \tag{4.28b}$$

$$0 \le d_i \le d_i^{\max} \quad \forall i \tag{4.28c}$$

$$0 \le p_i \le p_i^{\max} \quad \forall i \tag{4.28d}$$

$$-f_{i,j}^{\max} \le f_{i,j} \le f_{i,j}^{\max} \quad \forall i, \forall j \in \Omega_i \tag{4.28e}$$

$$f_{i,j} = -f_{j,i} \quad \forall i, \forall j \in \Omega_i \tag{4.28f}$$

$$f_{i,j} = B_{i,j} \cdot (\theta_i - \theta_j) \quad \forall i, \forall j \in \Omega_i \tag{4.28g}$$

$$\theta_k = 0, \text{being } k \text{ an arbitrary node} \tag{4.28h}$$

The optimization variables are described below:

d_i is the consumption of consumer i,
p_i the production of producer i,
$f_{i,j}$ the power flow through line ij from i to j,
θ_i the voltage angle of node i (network state variable), and
λ_i (dual variable) the market-clearing price (locational marginal price) at node i.

The constants are described below:

u_i is the variable utility of consumer i,
c_i the variable cost of producer i,
$d_i^{\max}$ the maximum demand of consumer i,
$p_i^{\max}$ the production capacity of producer i,
$f_{i,j}^{\max}$ the transmission capacity of line ij, and
$B_{i,j}$ the susceptance of line ij.

Finally, Ω_i is the set of nodes directly connected to node i.

Objective function (4.28a) is the social welfare. Constraint (4.28b) is the power-balance equation at node i. Constraints (4.28c) and (4.28d) are consumption and production bounds, respectively. Constraint (4.28e) enforces transmission-capacity bounds. Since the network is assumed to be lossless, constraint (4.28f) enforces that the flow in direction ij is the opposite to that in direction ji. Constraint (4.28g) expresses the flow through line ij as the susceptance of the line times the difference of voltage angles (which are the state variables of the network). Finally, constraint (4.28h) fixes an arbitrary node as the reference one.

The revenue, R_i, of producer i is

$$R_i = \lambda_i^* \cdot p_i^* \tag{4.29}$$

while the payment, P_i, of consumer i is

$$P_i = \lambda_i^* \cdot d_i^* \tag{4.30}$$

The profit, Π_i^{P}, of producer i is

$$\Pi_i^{\mathrm{P}} = (\lambda_i^* - c_i) \cdot p_i^* \tag{4.31}$$

and the producer surplus, PS, is

$$\mathrm{PS} = \sum_i \Pi_i^{\mathrm{P}} \tag{4.32}$$

The profit Π_i^{C} of consumer i is

$$\Pi_i^{\mathrm{C}} = (u_i - \lambda_i^*) \cdot d_i^* \tag{4.33}$$

and the consumer surplus, CS, is

$$\mathrm{CS} = \sum_i \Pi_i^{\mathrm{C}} \tag{4.34}$$

The network surplus, NS, is

$$\mathrm{NS} = \sum_i \sum_{j \in \Omega_i} (\lambda_j^* - \lambda_i^*) \cdot \max\{0, f_{i,j}^*\} \tag{4.35}$$

Finally, the social welfare, SW, is

$$\mathrm{SW} = \mathrm{CS} + \mathrm{PS} + \mathrm{NW} \tag{4.36}$$

4.4 Non-convexities and Marginal Pricing

In this section, we analyze first prices pertaining to a simple illustrative example of a non-convex market-clearing algorithm and then provide a general-enough formulation.

4.4.1 Non-convexities: Illustrative Example

We consider the simple system illustrated in Fig. 4.8 where a power market is in place. For simplicity, we consider that the transmission capacity is large enough to prevent congestion (indicated in Fig. 4.8 by ∞).

Additionally, we consider that the variable utility of each demand is large enough (\$10 per energy unit) for each of them to be fully supplied (i.e., $d_1 = 4$ and $d_2 = 6$).

Producer 1 (left-hand side of Fig. 4.8) has minimum and maximum production capacities of 1 and 6 power units, respectively, a variable cost of \$1 per energy unit, and a start-up cost of \$6 per start-up. Likewise, producer 2 (right-hand side of Fig. 4.8) has minimum and maximum production capacities of 1 and 6 power units, respectively, a variable cost of \$4 per energy unit, and a start-up cost of \$2 per start up.

The *scheduling problem* (to determine the on/off status of production units) to be solved by the market operator is

$$\max_{\substack{d_1,d_2,p_1,p_2\geq 0\\ x_1,x_2\in\{0,1\}}} \quad z = 10 \cdot d_1 + 10 \cdot d_2 - (1 \cdot p_1 + 6 \cdot x_1 + 4 \cdot p_2 + 2 \cdot x_2) \tag{4.37a}$$

$$\text{s. t.} \quad d_1 + d_2 - p_1 - p_2 = 0 \tag{4.37b}$$

$$d_1 \leq 4 \tag{4.37c}$$

$$d_2 \leq 6 \tag{4.37d}$$

$$1 \cdot x_1 \leq p_1 \leq 6 \cdot x_1 \tag{4.37e}$$

$$1 \cdot x_2 \leq p_2 \leq 6 \cdot x_2 \tag{4.37f}$$

where the optimization variables are described below:

d_1 is the consumption of consumer 1,
d_2 the consumption of consumer 2,
p_1 the production of producer 1,

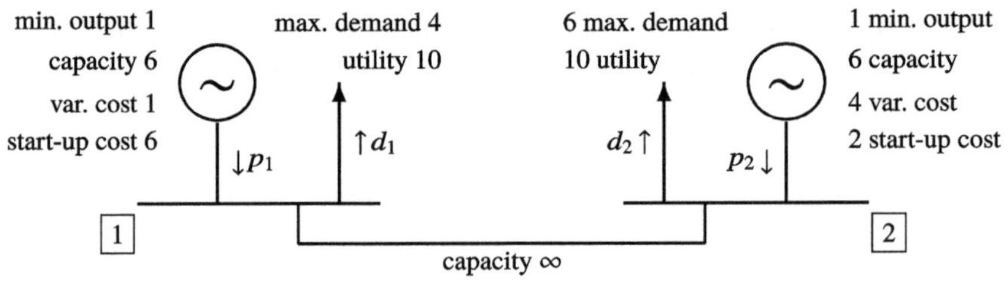

Fig. 4.8 Clearing with non-convexities

p_2 the production of producer 2,
x_1 a binary variable indicating if producer 1 is either on-line (1) or not (0), and
x_2 a binary variable indicating if producer 2 is either on-line (1) or not (0).

Objective function (4.37a) is the social welfare (including start-up costs in this case). Constraint (4.37b) is the single power-balance equation (no transmission congestion). Constraints (4.37c) and (4.37d) are consumption bounds for consumers 1 and 2, respectively. Constraints (4.37e) and (4.37f) are production bounds for producers 1 and 2, respectively.

This is a scheduling problem because it is used to decide on the on/off status of the production units.

Once the above scheduling problem (4.37) has been solved and optimal values for the scheduling variables have been found, x_1^* and x_2^*, the *production and pricing problem* to be solved by the market operator is

$$\max_{d_1,d_2,p_1,p_2\geq 0} \quad z = 10 \cdot d_1 + 10 \cdot d_2 - \left(1 \cdot p_1 + 6 \cdot x_1^* + 4 \cdot p_2 + 2 \cdot x_2^*\right) \tag{4.38a}$$

$$\text{s. t.} \quad d_1 + d_2 - p_1 - p_2 = 0 : \quad \lambda \tag{4.38b}$$

$$d_1 \leq 4 \tag{4.38c}$$

$$d_2 \leq 6 \tag{4.38d}$$

$$1 \cdot x_1^* \leq p_1 \leq 6 \cdot x_1^* \tag{4.38e}$$

$$1 \cdot x_2^* \leq p_2 \leq 6 \cdot x_2^* \tag{4.38f}$$

where

λ (dual variable) is the clearing price.

The solution to problems (4.37) and (4.38), easily obtained by inspection, is:

$d_1^* = 4$, $p_2^* = 6$, $p_1^* = 6$, $p_2^* = 4$, $x_1^* = 1$, $x_2^* = 1$.
$\lambda^* = 4$.

The profits of the consumers are:

$\Pi_1^{\mathrm{C}} = (u_1 - \lambda^*) \cdot 4 = (10 - 4) \cdot 4 = 24$
$\Pi_2^{\mathrm{C}} = (u_2 - \lambda^*) \cdot 6 = (10 - 4) \cdot 6 = 36$

where u_1 and u_2 are the marginal utilities of consumers 1 and 2, respectively.

The total consumer profit is $\Pi^{\mathrm{C}} = \Pi_1^{\mathrm{C}} + \Pi_1^{\mathrm{C}} = 60$.

The profits of the producers are

$\Pi_1^{\mathrm{P}} = (\lambda^* - c_1) \cdot p_1^* - c_1^{\mathrm{SU}} \cdot x_1^* = (4 - 1) \cdot 6 - 6 \cdot 1 = 12$
$\Pi_2^{\mathrm{P}} = (\lambda^* - c_2) \cdot p_2^* - c_2^{\mathrm{SU}} \cdot x_2^* = (4 - 4) \cdot 4 - 2 \cdot 1 = -2$

where

c_1 and c_2 are the variable cost of producers 1 and 2, respectively, and
c_1^{SU} and c_2^{SU} the start-up cost of producers 1 and 2, respectively.

The total producer profit is $\Pi^{\mathrm{P}} = \Pi_1^{\mathrm{P}} + \Pi_1^{\mathrm{P}} = 10$ and the social welfare SW = $\Pi^{\mathrm{C}} + \Pi^{\mathrm{P}} = 60 + 10 = 70$.

We observe that producer 2 does not recover its cost. This is a consequence of the non-convexity of the scheduling problem (4.37).

A remedial action could be giving an uplift, R_2^{UL}, to generator 2, so that it exactly recovers its cost (it is made "whole" in the industry language), i.e.,

$$R_2^{\mathrm{UL}} = 2$$

The final profits of the producers are then:

$\Pi_1^{\mathrm{PF}} = (\lambda^* - c_1) \cdot p_1^* - c_1^{\mathrm{SU}} \cdot x_1^* = (4 - 1) \cdot 6 - 6 \cdot 1 = 12$ (unaltered).
$\Pi_2^{\mathrm{PF}} = (\lambda^* - c_2) \cdot p_2^* - c_2^{\mathrm{SU}} \cdot x_2^* + R_2^{\mathrm{UL}} = (4 - 4) \cdot 4 - 2 \cdot 1 + 2 = 0.$

The final total producer profit is $\Pi^{\mathrm{PF}} = \Pi_1^{\mathrm{PF}} + \Pi_1^{\mathrm{PF}} = 12$.

This uplift needs to be allocated and paid by the consumers, for instance, proportionally to their respective consumptions. In this case, the corresponding payments by the consumers, P_1^{UL} and P_2^{UL} are, respectively,

$$P_1^{\mathrm{UL}} = R_2^{\mathrm{UL}} \frac{d_1^*}{d_1^* + d_2^*} = 2 \frac{4}{4+6} = 0.8.$$
$$P_2^{\mathrm{UL}} = R_2^{\mathrm{UL}} \frac{d_2^*}{d_1^* + d_2^*} = 2 \frac{6}{4+6} = 1.2.$$

The final profits of the consumers are:

$\Pi_1^{\mathrm{CF}} = (u_1 - \lambda) \cdot d_1^* - P_1^{\mathrm{UL}} = (10 - 4) \cdot 4 - 0.8 = 23.2.$
$\Pi_2^{\mathrm{CF}} = (u_2 - \lambda) \cdot d_2^* - P_2^{\mathrm{UL}} = (10 - 4) \cdot 6 - 1.2 = 34.8.$

The final total consumer profit is $\Pi^{\mathrm{CF}} = \Pi_1^{\mathrm{CF}} + \Pi_1^{\mathrm{CF}} = 58$. The final SW is thus

$$\mathrm{SW}^{\mathrm{F}} = \Pi_1^{\mathrm{PF}} + \Pi_2^{\mathrm{PF}} + \Pi_1^{\mathrm{CF}} + \Pi_2^{\mathrm{CF}} = 12 + 0 + 23.2 + 34.8 = 70$$

We note that the social welfare does not change as a result of the uplift, but a profit transfer from consumers to producers occurs, in this case, from both consumers to producer 2.

4.4.2 Non-convexities: General Formulation

A general-enough single-period scheduling algorithm has the form:

$$\max_{\substack{d_i \geq 0, p_i \geq 0, \theta_i \forall i; \\ x_i, y_i, z_i \in \{0,1\} \forall i}} \quad z = \sum_i u_i \, d_i - \sum_i c_i \, p_i - \sum_i c_i^{\text{SU}} \, y_i \tag{4.39a}$$

$$\text{s. t.} \quad p_i - d_i - \sum_{j \in \Omega_i} B_{i,j} \cdot (\theta_i - \theta_j) = 0 \quad \forall i \tag{4.39b}$$

$$0 \leq d_i \leq d_i^{\max} \quad \forall i \tag{4.39c}$$

$$x_i \, p_i^{\min} \leq p_i \leq x_i \, p_i^{\max} \quad \forall i \tag{4.39d}$$

$$y_i - z_i = x_i - x_i^0 \quad \forall i \tag{4.39e}$$

$$y_i + z_i \leq 1 \quad \forall i \tag{4.39f}$$

$$-f_{i,j}^{\max} \leq B_{i,j} \cdot (\theta_i - \theta_j) \leq f_{i,j}^{\max} \quad \forall i, \forall j \in \Omega_i \tag{4.39g}$$

$$\theta_k = 0, \text{ being } k \text{ an arbitrary node} \tag{4.39h}$$

The optimization variables are defined below:

d_i is the consumption of consumer i,
p_i the production of producer i,
x_i a binary variable indicating if producer i is on-line (1) or not (0),
y_i a binary variable indicating is producer i is started-up at the beginning of the considered period (1) or not (0),
z_i a binary variable indicating is producer i is shut-down at the beginning of the considered period (1) or not (0), and
θ_i the voltage angle of node i (network state variable).

The constants are described below:

u_i is the variable utility of consumer i,
$d_i^{\max}$ the maximum demand of consumer i,
c_i the variable cost of producer i,
c_i^{SU} the start-up cost of producer i,
$p_i^{\max}$ the production capacity of producer i,
$p_i^{\min}$ the minimum power output of producer i,
x_i^0 a binary constant indicating whether producer i is on-line (1) in the period prior to the one under consideration or not (0),
$f_{i,j}^{\max}$ the transmission capacity of line ij, and
$B_{i,j}$ the susceptance (proportionality constant) of line ij.

Finally, Ω_i is the set of nodes directly connected to node i.

Objective function (4.39a) is the social welfare. Constraint (4.39b) is the power-balance equation at node i. Constraints (4.39c) and (4.39d) are consumption and production bounds, respectively. Constraints (4.39e) and (4.39f) are logical constraints describing the possibility of starting up or shutting down units that are shut down or operating, respectively, in the considered time period [2]. Constraint (4.39g) enforces transmission-capacity bounds. Finally, constraint (4.39g) fixed an arbitrary node as the reference one.

Once problem (4.39) has been solved and the scheduling variables have been fixed to their optimal values x_i^*, y_i^*, and z_i^*, $\forall i$, the corresponding production and pricing problem has the form:

$$\max_{d_i \geq 0, p_i \geq 0, \theta_i \forall i} \quad z = \sum_i u_i \, d_i - \sum_i c_i \, p_i - \sum_i c_i^{\mathrm{SU}} \, y_i^* \tag{4.40a}$$

$$\text{s. t.} \quad p_i - d_i - \sum_{j \in \Omega_i} B_{i,j} \cdot (\theta_i - \theta_j) = 0 : \; \lambda_i \quad \forall i \tag{4.40b}$$

$$0 \leq d_i \leq d_i^{\max} \quad \forall i \tag{4.40c}$$

$$x_i^* \, p_i^{\min} \leq p_i \leq x_i^* \, p_i^{\max} \quad \forall i \tag{4.40d}$$

$$- f_{i,j}^{\max} \leq B_{i,j} \cdot (\theta_i - \theta_j) \leq f_{i,j}^{\max} \quad \forall i, \forall j \in \Omega_i \tag{4.40e}$$

$$\theta_k = 0, \text{ being } k \text{ an arbitrary node} \tag{4.40f}$$

Once problem (4.40) has been solved and d_i^* and p_i^*, $\forall i$, identified, the profit Π_i^{P} of producer i is

$$\Pi_i^{\mathrm{P}} = (\lambda_i^* - c_i) \cdot p_i^* + R_i^{\mathrm{UL}} \tag{4.41}$$

where R_i^{UL} is the uplift revenue potentially needed by producer i to cover its losses. Such an uplift might be needed because the scheduling problem (4.39) is non-convex.

The producer surplus, PS, is

$$\mathrm{PS} = \sum_i \Pi_i^{\mathrm{P}} \tag{4.42}$$

The profit, Π_i^{C}, of consumer i is

$$\Pi_i^{\mathrm{C}} = (u_i - \lambda_i^*) \cdot d_i^* - P_i^{\mathrm{UL}} \tag{4.43}$$

where P_i^{UL} is the uplift payment by consumer i to cover producer losses.

This uplift may be calculated as (proportional allocation to consumption level)

$$P_i^{\mathrm{UL}} = \sum_i R_i^{\mathrm{UL}} \left(\frac{d_i^*}{\sum_i d_i^*} \right)$$

The consumer surplus, CS, is

$$\mathrm{CS} = \sum_i \Pi_i^{\mathrm{C}} \tag{4.44}$$

The uplift balance is

$$\sum_i R_i^{\mathrm{UL}} = \sum_i P_i^{\mathrm{UL}}$$

The network surplus, NS, is

$$\mathrm{NS} = \sum_i \sum_{j \in \Omega_i} (\lambda_j^* - \lambda_i^*) \cdot \max\{0, f_{i,j}^*\} \tag{4.45}$$

Finally, the social welfare, SW, is

$$\mathrm{SW} = \mathrm{CS} + \mathrm{PS} + \mathrm{NW} \tag{4.46}$$

From the above analysis, it is apparent that non-convexities make marginal prices rather useless, and "heuristic" remedial actions are needed. Such remedial actions, typically uplifts, are necessarily controversial, as they are discriminatory (they are not given to all producers, but to selected ones) and to some extent arbitrary.

4.5 Uncertainty: Two-Stage Marginal Pricing

In this section, we first analyze a simple illustrative example of pricing on a two-stage market-clearing algorithm. The first stage of this algorithm allows identifying optimal scheduling decisions (decisions that are typically made one day ahead of actual operation). The second stage of the algorithm *simulates* actual operation considering different uncertainty realizations (scenarios), which allows identifying optimal operation decisions for each scenario considered. Then, we provide a general-enough formulation of a two-stage market-clearing algorithm.

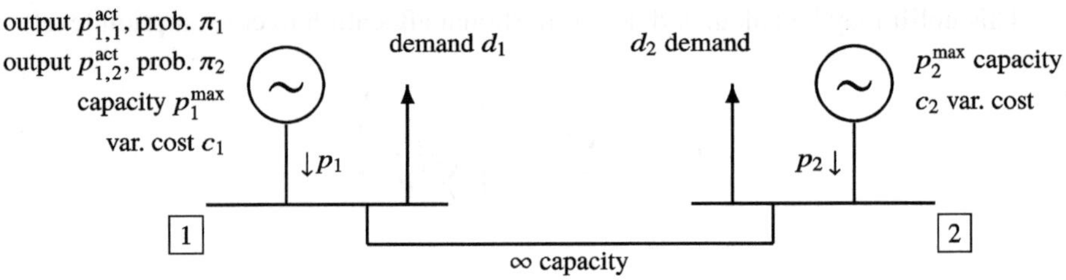

Fig. 4.9 Stochastic two-stage market clearing

4.5.1 *Uncertainty: Illustrative Example*

We consider the power system in Fig. 4.9 that operates under a stochastic two-stage electricity market framework.

Producer 1 is stochastic (e.g., a wind or a solar power producer), and its power output is either $p^{act}_{1,1}$ with probability π_1 or $p^{act}_{1,2}$ with probability π_2. That is, we consider solely 2 scenarios to describe the stochastic output of this producer. Its variable cost is assumed to be c_1 (typically, a small value).

On the other hand, producer 2 is deterministic and its variable cost is c_2. This producer is the source of reserve for the system, and we consider that it offers to the market all available up-/down-reserve. That is, regarding up-reserve, it offers to increase power from actual production to capacity, and, regarding down-reserve, it offers to decrease power from actual production to zero. Its variable cost for deploying up-reserve is $c^U_2 > c_2$, while for deploying down-reserve is $c^D_2 < c_2$.

Both demands are inelastic (i.e., the marginal utility of each of them is large enough to accept any clearing price) with a total value of $d_1 + d_2 = d$.

For simplicity, the transmission capacity is assumed unlimited, and, thus, no network constraint is enforced.

The two-stage stochastic market-clearing algorithm to clear this market has the form:

$$\min_{\substack{p_1, p_2 \geq 0 \\ s_{1,1}, s_{1,2} \geq 0 \\ r^U_{2,1}, r^D_{2,1}, r^U_{2,2}, r^D_{2,2} \geq 0}} \quad c_1 p_1 + c_2 p_2 + \pi_1 \left(c^U_2 r^U_{2,1} - c^D_2 r^D_{2,1}\right) + \pi_2 \left(c^U_2 r^U_{2,1} - c^D_2 r^D_{2,1}\right) \tag{4.47a}$$

$$\text{s. t.} \quad p_1 + p_2 = d : \quad \lambda \tag{4.47b}$$

$$p_1 \leq p^{max}_1 \tag{4.47c}$$

$$p_2 \leq p^{max}_2 \tag{4.47d}$$

$$(r^U_{2,1} - r^D_{2,1}) + (p^{act}_{1,1} - p_1 - s_{1,1}) = 0 : \quad \gamma_1 \tag{4.47e}$$

$$0 \leq p_2 + (r_{2,1}^{\mathrm{U}} - r_{2,1}^{\mathrm{D}}) \leq p_2^{\max} \tag{4.47f}$$

$$s_{1,1} \leq p_{1,1}^{\mathrm{act}} \tag{4.47g}$$

$$(r_{2,2}^{\mathrm{U}} - r_{2,2}^{\mathrm{D}}) + (p_{1,2}^{\mathrm{act}} - p_1 - s_{1,2}) = 0 : \quad \gamma_2 \tag{4.47h}$$

$$0 \leq p_2 + (r_{2,2}^{\mathrm{U}} - r_{2,2}^{\mathrm{D}}) \leq p_2^{\max} \tag{4.47i}$$

$$s_{1,2} \leq p_{1,2}^{\mathrm{act}} \tag{4.47j}$$

where the optimization variables of this problem are defined below:

p_1 is the scheduled power output or producer 1,
p_2 the scheduled power output or producer 2,
$s_{1,1}$ the power spillage (power that is available but not used due to system constraints) of producer 1 in scenario 1,
$s_{1,2}$ the power spillage of producer 1 in scenario 2,
$r_{2,1}^{\mathrm{U}}$ the deployed up-reserve of producer 2 in scenario 1,
$r_{2,1}^{\mathrm{D}}$ the deployed down-reserve of producer 2 in scenario 1,
$r_{2,2}^{\mathrm{U}}$ the deployed up-reserve of producer 2 in scenario 2, and
$r_{2,2}^{\mathrm{D}}$ the deployed down-reserve of producer 2 in scenario 2,

and the real-time prices are

$$\lambda_1 = \frac{\gamma_1}{\pi_1}, \qquad \lambda_2 = \frac{\gamma_2}{\pi_2} \tag{4.48}$$

We note that marginal prices λ_1 and λ_2 are obtained by adjusting the dual variables of the incremental scenario-based power-balance equations, (4.47e) and (4.47h), respectively, with their respective probabilities.

The objective function (4.47a) is the expected production cost, including the production cost pertaining to the planned production, $c_1 p_1 + c_2 p_2$, and cost adjustments per scenario $\pi_1(c_2^{\mathrm{U}} r_{2,1}^{\mathrm{U}} - c_2^{\mathrm{D}} r_{2,1}^{\mathrm{d}})$ for scenario 1 and $\pi_2(c_2^{\mathrm{U}} r_{2,1}^{\mathrm{U}} - c_2^{\mathrm{D}} r_{2,1}^{\mathrm{d}})$ for scenario 2.

Constraint (4.47b) is the power-balance constraint at the operation planning stage whose dual variable is the scheduling market-clearing price. Constraints (4.47c) and (4.47d) are power output bounds at the operation planning stage for units 1 and 2, respectively.

Constraint (4.47e) is the incremental power-balance constraint at real-time operation under the first scenario conditions. This constraint is written in incremental form to avoid redundancy and, thus, to derive correct prices (dual variables). The dual variable of this constraint is the market-clearing price at the real-time stage under the first scenario conditions multiplied by the scenario probability (see objective function (4.47a)). Constraint (4.47f) imposes (down and up) power bounds to the operation of producer 2 under the first scenario conditions. Constraint (4.47g) enforces that the power spilled by producer 1 should be below its capacity under the first scenario conditions.

Table 4.1 Stochastic pricing: data (left table) and outcome (right table)

Case	1	2	3
d	10	10	10
c_1	0	0	1
$p_{1,1}^{\text{act}}$	2	2	2
π_1	0.4	0.4	0.4
$p_{1,2}^{\text{act}}$	8	1,2	8
π_2	0.6	0.6	0.6
c_2	4	4	4
c_2^{U}	4.5	4.5	4.5
c_2^{D}	3	3	3

Case	1	2	3
p_1^*	8	10	2
p_2^*	2	0	8
λ^*	4	1.8	4
λ_1^*	4.5	4.5	3
λ_2^*	$3.\hat{6}$[a]	0	3
$r_{2,1}^{\text{U}*}$	6	8	0
$r_{2,1}^{\text{D}*}$	0	0	0
$r_{2,2}^{\text{U}*}$	0	0	0
$r_{2,2}^{\text{D}*}$	0	0	6
$s_{1,1}^*$	0	0	0
$s_{1,2}^*$	0	2	0

[a] $3.\hat{6} = 11/3$

Similarly, constraint (4.47h) is the incremental power-balance constraint at real-time operation under the second scenario conditions. The dual variable of this constraint is the market-clearing price at the real-time stage under the second scenario conditions multiplied by the scenario probability (see objective function (4.47a)). Constraint (4.47i) imposes (down and up) power bounds to the operation of producer 2 under the second scenario conditions. Constraint (4.47j) enforces that the power spilled by producer 1 should be below its capacity under the second scenario conditions.

Table 4.1 provides data (left-hand side subtable) and results (right-hand side subtable) for three cases.

Case 1 (data in column 2 of the left-hand side subtable in Table 4.1) results in a scheduling price of $\lambda = 4$ and real-time prices of $\lambda_1 = 4.5$ and $\lambda_2 = 11/3$ for scenarios 1 and 2, respectively. The optimal planned productions for producers 1 and 2 are $p_1 = 8$ and $p_2 = 2$, respectively. If the first scenario realizes an actual production of producer 1 of $p_{1,1}^{\text{act}} = 2$, then an up-reserve deployment by producer 2 of $r_{2,1}^{\text{U}} = 6$ is needed to meet the demand $d = 10$. If, on the other hand, the second scenario realizes, then no reserve deployment is needed. Additionally, no energy is spilled in either of the two scenarios.

Case 2 (data in column 3 of the left-hand side subtable in Table 4.1) differs from case 1 in that the actual production of producer 1 in scenario 2 increases from 8 to 12 (boxed value in column 3 of the left-hand side subtable of Table 4.1), which is larger than the total demand. This case results in a first-stage price of $\lambda = 1.8$ and real-time prices of $\lambda_1 = 4.5$ and $\lambda_2 = 0$ for scenarios 1 and 2, respectively. The optimal planned productions of producers 1 and 2 are $p_1 = 10$ and $p_2 = 0$, respectively. If the first scenario realizes an actual production of producer 1 of $p_{1,1}^{\text{act}} = 2$, then an up-reserve deployment by producer 2 of $r_{2,1}^{\text{U}} = 8$ is needed to meet the demand $d = 10$. If, on the other hand, the second scenario realizes, then no reserve deployment is needed. Additionally, if scenario 2 realizes, then producer 1 needs to spill an amount of energy of $s_{1,2} = 2$.

Case 3 (data in column 4 of the left-hand side subtable in Table 4.1) differs from case 1 in that the variable cost of producer 1 is 1, not 0 (boxed value in column 3 of the left-hand side subtable of Table 4.1). This case results in a first-stage price of $\lambda = 4$ and real-time prices of $\lambda_1 = 3$ and $\lambda_2 = 3$ for scenarios 1 and 2, respectively. The optimal scheduled productions of producers 1 and 2 are $p_1 = 2$ and $p_2 = 8$, respectively. If the first scenario realizes, then no reserve deployment is needed. If, on the other hand, the second scenario realizes with an actual production of producer 1 of $p_{1,1}^{\text{act}} = 8$, then a down-reserve deployment by producer 2 of $r_{2,2}^{\text{D}} = 6$ is needed to meet the demand $d = 10$. Additionally, no energy is spilled in either of the two scenarios.

Regarding prices, it is relevant to note that the first-stage price is the average of the real-time prices, provided that the variable cost of the stochastic source is 0. That is,

$$\lambda = \pi_1 \lambda_1 + \pi_2 \lambda_2, \text{ if } c_1 = 0 \tag{4.49}$$

which can be verified in Table 4.1, cases 1 and 2.

Specifically, in case 1,

$$4 = 0.4 \cdot 4.5 + 0.6 \cdot \frac{11}{3}$$

and in case 2,

$$1.8 = 0.4 \cdot 4.5 + 0.6 \cdot 0$$

however, this is not the case in case 3 because $c_1 = 1$. Thus,

$$4 \neq 0.4 \cdot 3 + 0.6 \cdot 3$$

We compute below first revenues and then profits.

The revenues of producer 1 per scenario and on average are

$$R_{1,1} = p_1^* \cdot \lambda^* + (p_{1,1}^{\text{act}} - p_1^* - s_{1,1}^*) \cdot \lambda_1^* \tag{4.50}$$

$$R_{1,2} = p_1^* \cdot \lambda^* + (p_{1,2}^{\text{act}} - p_1^* - s_{1,2}^*) \cdot \lambda_2^* \tag{4.51}$$

$$R_1^{\text{E}} = \pi_1 \cdot R_{1,1} + \pi_2 \cdot R_{1,2} \tag{4.52}$$

The revenues of producer 2 per scenario and on average are

$$R_{2,1} = p_2^* \cdot \lambda^* + (r_{2,1}^{\text{U}*} - r_{2,1}^{\text{D}*}) \cdot \lambda_1^* \tag{4.53}$$

$$R_{2,2} = p_2^* \cdot \lambda^* + (r_{2,2}^{\text{U}*} - r_{2,2}^{\text{D}*}) \cdot \lambda_2^* \tag{4.54}$$

$$R_2^{\text{E}} = \pi_1 \cdot R_{2,1} + \pi_2 \cdot R_{2,2} \tag{4.55}$$

The profits of producer 1 per scenario and on average are

$$\Pi_{1,1} = p_1^* \cdot \lambda^* + (p_{1,1}^{\text{act}} - p_1^* - s_{1,1}^*) \cdot \lambda_1^* - c_1 \cdot p_{1,1}^{\text{act}} \tag{4.56}$$

$$\Pi_{1,2} = p_1^* \cdot \lambda^* + (p_{1,2}^{\text{act}} - p_1^* - s_{1,2}^*) \cdot \lambda_2^* - c_1 \cdot p_{1,2}^{\text{act}} \tag{4.57}$$

$$\Pi_1^{\text{E}} = \pi_1 \cdot \Pi_{1,1} + \pi_2 \cdot \Pi_{1,2} \tag{4.58}$$

The profits of producer 2 per scenario and on average are

$$\Pi_{2,1} = p_2^* \cdot \lambda^* + \left(r_{2,1}^{\text{U}*} - r_{2,1}^{\text{D}*}\right) \cdot \lambda_1^* - c_2 \cdot \left(p_2^* + \left(r_{2,1}^{\text{U}*} - r_{2,1}^{\text{D}*}\right)\right) \tag{4.59}$$

$$\Pi_{2,2} = p_2^* \cdot \lambda^* + \left(r_{2,2}^{\text{U}*} - r_{2,2}^{\text{D}*}\right) \cdot \lambda_2^* - c_2 \cdot \left(p_2^* + \left(r_{2,2}^{\text{U}*} - r_{2,2}^{\text{D}*}\right)\right) \tag{4.60}$$

$$\Pi_2^{\text{E}} = \pi_1 \cdot \Pi_{2,1} + \pi_2 \cdot \Pi_{2,2} \tag{4.61}$$

The average profit of the two producers is

$$\Pi^{\text{E}} = \Pi_1^{\text{E}} + \Pi_2^{\text{E}} \tag{4.62}$$

The average revenue of the two producers is

$$R^{\text{E}} = R_1^{\text{E}} + R_2^{\text{E}} \tag{4.63}$$

and the demand payment is

$$P = d \cdot \lambda^* \tag{4.64}$$

Table 4.2 provides data (left-hand side subtable) and profits, revenues, and payments (right-hand side subtable) for three cases.

We observe from Table 4.2 that both producers recover their respective costs on average, but not per scenario. For example, producer 1's profit in case 2 (third column in both tables) is $\Pi_1^{\text{E}} = 3.6$ on average, but $\Pi_{1,1} = -18$ in scenario 1.

The fact that *all producers have non-negative profits on average* is an important property, which is formally shown, for instance, in [4] or [5]. It is known as *cost recovery in expectation*.

From Table 4.2, we observe as well that the total expected revenue obtained by producers is equal to the total expected payment by the demands (right-hand side, the last two rows). This means that the market is *revenue adequate in expectation*, as shown, for instance, in [4] or [5]. In most cases, it is also revenue adequate per scenario, as discussed in [5]. This is the case of the example above in the three cases.

A GAMS [3] code to solve this example is provided in Sect. 4.9.

Table 4.2 Stochastic pricing: data (left table) and revenues, profits, and payments (right table)

Case	1	2	3
d	10	10	10
c_1	0	0	1
$p_{1,1}^{\text{act}}$	2	2	2
π_1	0.4	0.4	0.4
$p_{1,2}^{\text{act}}$	8	12	8
π_2	0.6	0.6	0.6
c_2	4	4	4
c_2^{U}	4.5	4.5	4.5
c_2^{D}	3	3	3

Case	1	2	3
$\Pi_{1,1}$	5	−18	6
$\Pi_{1,2}$	32	18	24
Π_1^{E}	21.2	3.6	16.8
$\Pi_{2,1}$	3	4	0
$\Pi_{2,2}$	0	0	6
Π_2^{E}	1.2	1.6	3.6
$R_{1,1}$	5	−18	8
$R_{1,2}$	32	18	26
R_1^{E}	21.2	3.6	18.8
$R_{2,1}$	35	36	32
$R_{2,2}$	8	0	14
R_2^{E}	18.8	14.4	21.2
R	40	18	40
P	40	18	40

4.5.2 Uncertainty: General Formulation

A general-enough formulation of a two-stage market-clearing algorithm and its corresponding marginal pricing is provided below. For simplicity, a single time period is considered and no transmission constraints are enforced.

$$\min_{\substack{p_k \geq 0, k \in \Omega^{\text{S}} \cup \Omega^{\text{D}} \\ r_{j,s}^{\text{U}}, r_{j,s}^{\text{D}} \geq 0, j \in \Omega^{\text{D}}, \forall s \\ s_{i,s} \geq 0, i \in \Omega^{\text{S}}, \forall s}} \quad \sum_{i \in \Omega^{\text{S}}} c_i p_i + \sum_{j \in \Omega^{\text{D}}} c_j p_j + \sum_s \sum_{j \in \Omega^{\text{D}}} \pi_s \left(c_j^{\text{U}} r_{j,s}^{\text{U}} - c_j^{\text{D}} r_{j,s}^{\text{D}} \right) \tag{4.65a}$$

$$\text{s. t.} \quad \sum_{k \in \Omega^{\text{S}} \cup \Omega^{\text{D}}} p_k = d \; : \; \lambda \tag{4.65b}$$

$$0 \leq p_k \leq p_k^{\max}, \quad \forall k \in \Omega^{\text{S}} \cup \Omega^{\text{D}} \tag{4.65c}$$

$$\sum_{j \in \Omega^{\text{D}}} \left(r_{j,s}^{\text{U}} - r_{j,s}^{\text{D}} \right) + \sum_{i \in \Omega^{\text{S}}} \left(p_{i,s}^{\text{act}} - p_i - s_{i,s} \right) = 0 \; : \; \gamma_s, \; \forall s \tag{4.65d}$$

$$0 \leq p_j + \left(r_{j,s}^{\text{U}} - r_{j,s}^{\text{D}} \right) \leq p_j^{\max}, \; \forall j \in \Omega^{\text{D}}, \forall s \tag{4.65e}$$

$$s_{i,s} \leq p_{i,s}^{\text{act}}, \; \forall i \in \Omega^{\text{S}}, \forall s \tag{4.65f}$$

where the real-time price in scenario s is

$$\lambda_s = \frac{\gamma_s}{\pi_s} \tag{4.66}$$

The optimization variables of problem (4.65) above are provided below:

p_k is the scheduled power output of producer k (both stochastic and deterministic producers),
$r^{\mathrm{U}}_{j,s}$ the deployed up-reserve of deterministic producer j in scenario s,
$r^{\mathrm{D}}_{j,s}$ the deployed down-reserve of deterministic producer j in scenario s,
$s_{i,s}$ the spilled power by stochastic producer i in scenario s,
Ω^{D} the set of deterministic producers, and
Ω^{S} the set of stochastic producers.

Objective function (4.65a) is the expected cost, including the cost at the operation planning stage ($\sum_{i\in\Omega^{\mathrm{S}}} c_i p_i + \sum_{j\in\Omega^{\mathrm{D}}} c_j p_j$) and the expected cost of production adjustments ($\sum_s \sum_{j\in\Omega^{\mathrm{D}}} \pi_s \left(c^{\mathrm{U}}_j r^{\mathrm{U}}_{j,s} - c^{\mathrm{D}}_j r^{\mathrm{D}}_{j,s}\right)$).

Constraint (4.65b) is the power-balance constraint at the operation planning stage. Its dual variable (λ) is the first-stage price.

Constraints (4.65c) are power bounds for all producers (deterministic and stochastic).

Constraint (4.65d) is the incremental power-balance constraint in scenario s. Its dual variable (γ_s) is the probability-adjusted real-time price in scenario s.

The revenue, $R_{i,s}$, of stochastic producer $i \in \Omega^{\mathrm{S}}$ in scenario s is

$$R_{i,s} = p_i^* \lambda^* + \left(p^{\mathrm{act}}_{i,s} - p_i^* - s^*_{i,s}\right) \lambda^*_s \tag{4.67}$$

and its profit $\Pi_{i,s}$ is

$$\Pi_{i,s} = p_i^* \lambda^* + \left(p^{\mathrm{act}}_{i,s} - p_i^* - s^*_{i,s}\right) \lambda^*_s - c_i p^{\mathrm{act}}_{i,s} \tag{4.68}$$

The average revenue, R^{E}_i, and profit, Π^{E}_i, of stochastic producer $i \in \Omega^{\mathrm{S}}$ are, respectively,

$$R^{\mathrm{E}}_i = \sum_{s\in\mathcal{S}} \pi_s R_{i,s} \tag{4.69}$$

$$\Pi^{\mathrm{E}}_i = \sum_{s\in\mathcal{S}} \pi_s \Pi_{i,s} \tag{4.70}$$

where $\mathcal{S}$ is the set of scenarios considered.

The revenue, $R_{j,s}$, of deterministic producer $j \in \Omega^{\mathrm{D}}$ in scenario s is

$$R_{j,s} = p_j^* \lambda^* + \left(r_{j,s}^{\mathrm{U}*} - r_{j,s}^{\mathrm{D}*}\right) \lambda_s^* \tag{4.71}$$

and its profit, $\Pi_{j,s}$ is

$$\Pi_{j,s} = p_j^* \lambda^* + \left(r_{j,s}^{\mathrm{U}*} - r_{j,s}^{\mathrm{D}*}\right) \lambda_s^* - c_j \left(p_j^* + \left(r_{j,s}^{\mathrm{U}*} - r_{j,s}^{\mathrm{D}*}\right)\right) \tag{4.72}$$

The average revenue, R_j^{E}, and profit, Π_j^{E}, of deterministic producer $j \in \Omega^{\mathrm{D}}$ are, respectively,

$$R_j^{\mathrm{E}} = \sum_{s \in \mathcal{S}} \pi_s R_{j,s} \tag{4.73}$$

$$\Pi_j^{\mathrm{E}} = \sum_{s \in \mathcal{S}} \pi_s \Pi_{j,s} \tag{4.74}$$

The *cost recovery on average* property ensures for stochastic and deterministic producers, respectively, that

$$\Pi_i^{\mathrm{E}} \geq 0 \;\; \forall i \in \Omega^{\mathrm{S}} \qquad \text{and} \qquad \Pi_j^{\mathrm{E}} \geq 0 \;\; \forall j \in \Omega^{\mathrm{D}} \tag{4.75}$$

The *revenue adequacy on average* property ensures that

$$d\,\lambda^* \geq \sum_{i \in \Omega^{\mathrm{S}}} R_i^{\mathrm{E}} + \sum_{j \in \Omega^{\mathrm{D}}} R_j^{\mathrm{E}} \tag{4.76}$$

that is, the total payment by the demand is greater than or equal to the average total revenue obtained by all (stochastic and deterministic) producers.

4.6 Multi-Period Marginal Pricing

We analyze in this section multi-period clearing algorithms and the corresponding marginal prices. We focus on the impact on marginal prices of ramping constraints that couple together two consecutive time periods. We consider first an illustrative example followed by a general-enough formulation.

4.6.1 Multi-Period: Illustrative Example

The two-period clearing example with ramping limits considered in this section is illustrated in Fig. 4.10.

The maximum demands for consumer 1 (left-hand side of Fig. 4.10) in periods 1 and 2 are 2 and 4 power units, respectively, and its marginal utilities 2 and 3, respectively. Similarly, the maximum demands for consumer 2 (right-hand side of Fig. 4.10) in periods 1 and 2 are 4 and 6 power units, respectively, and its marginal utilities 4 and 6, respectively.

The up- and down-ramping limits for producer 1 (left-hand side of Fig. 4.10) are r_1^{U} and r_1^{D}, respectively, and for producer 2 (right-hand side of Fig. 4.10) r_2^{U} and r_2^{D}, respectively. Prior to the beginning of the market horizon, the power outputs of producers 1 and 2 are $p_{1,0} = 4$ and $p_{2,0} = 1$ power units, respectively.

Additional data for this example are identical to those in Sect. 4.3.2.

The formulation (closely related to (4.27)) of this two-period clearing algorithm is given below:

$$\max_{\substack{d_{1,1},d_{2,1},p_{1,1},p_{2,1}\geq 0;\, f_{1,2,1}\\ d_{1,2},d_{2,2},p_{1,2},p_{2,2}\geq 0;\, f_{1,2,2}}} \quad z = 2\cdot d_{1,1} + 4\cdot d_{2,1} - 1\cdot p_{1,1} - 4\cdot p_{2,1}$$

$$+ 3\cdot d_{1,2} + 6\cdot d_{2,2} - 1\cdot p_{1,2} - 4\cdot p_{2,2} \tag{4.77a}$$

$$\text{s. t.} \quad p_{1,1} - d_{1,1} = f_{1,2,1} : \lambda_{1,1} \tag{4.77b}$$

$$p_{2,1} - d_{2,1} = -f_{1,2,1} : \lambda_{2,1} \tag{4.77c}$$

$$p_{1,1} \leq 5; \quad p_{2,1} \leq 5 \tag{4.77d}$$

$$d_{1,1} \leq 2; \quad d_{2,1} \leq 4 \tag{4.77e}$$

$$-4 \leq f_{1,2,1} \leq 4 \tag{4.77f}$$

$$p_{1,2} - d_{1,2} = f_{1,2,2} : \lambda_{1,2} \tag{4.77g}$$

$$p_{2,2} - d_{2,2} = -f_{1,2,2} : \lambda_{2,2} \tag{4.77h}$$

$$p_{1,2} \leq 5; \quad p_{2,2} \leq 5 \tag{4.77i}$$

$$d_{1,2} \leq 4; \quad d_{2,2} \leq 6 \tag{4.77j}$$

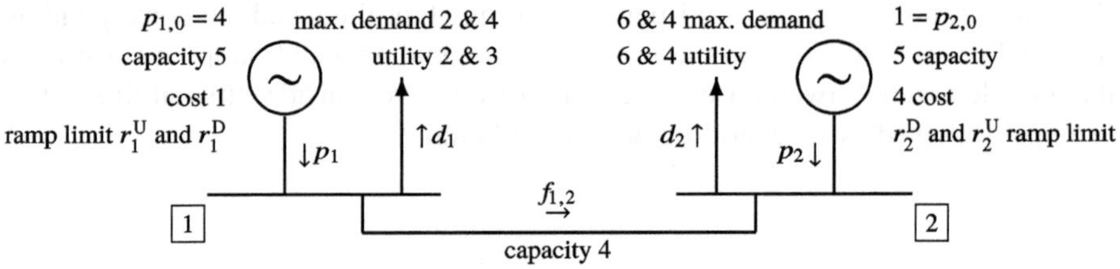

Fig. 4.10 Multi-period clearing: simple example

$$-4 \leq f_{1,2,2} \leq 4 \tag{4.77k}$$

$$p_{1,1} - 4 \leq r_1^{\mathrm{U}} \tag{4.77l}$$

$$4 - p_{1,1} \leq r_1^{\mathrm{D}} \tag{4.77m}$$

$$p_{1,2} - p_{1,1} \leq r_1^{\mathrm{U}} \tag{4.77n}$$

$$p_{1,1} - p_{1,2} \leq r_1^{\mathrm{D}} \tag{4.77o}$$

$$p_{2,1} - 1 \leq r_2^{\mathrm{U}} \tag{4.77p}$$

$$1 - p_{2,1} \leq r_2^{\mathrm{D}} \tag{4.77q}$$

$$p_{2,2} - p_{2,1} \leq r_2^{\mathrm{U}} \tag{4.77r}$$

$$p_{2,1} - p_{2,2} \leq r_2^{\mathrm{D}} \tag{4.77s}$$

where

$d_{1,1}$ and $d_{2,1}$ are the consumptions in period 1 of consumers 1 and 2, respectively,
$d_{1,2}$ and $d_{2,2}$ are the consumptions in period 2 of consumers 1 and 2, respectively,
$p_{1,1}$ and $p_{2,1}$ are the productions in period 1 of producers 1 and 2, respectively,
$p_{1,2}$ and $p_{2,2}$ are the productions in period 2 of producers 1 and 2, respectively, and
$f_{1,2,1}$ and $f_{1,2,2}$ are the flows through line 12 in periods 1 and 2, respectively.

Objective function (4.77a) is the social welfare spanning the two time periods; $2 \cdot d_{1,1} + 4 \cdot d_{2,1} - 1 \cdot p_{1,1} - 4 \cdot p_{2,1}$ corresponds to period 1 and $3 \cdot d_{1,2} + 6 \cdot d_{2,2} - 1 \cdot p_{1,2} - 4 \cdot p_{2,2}$ to period 2.

Constraints (4.77b) and (4.77c) are power balances at nodes 1 and 2, respectively, in period 1, leading to locational marginal prices $\lambda_{1,1}$ and $\lambda_{2,1}$, respectively. Constraints (4.77d) and (4.77e) are production and demand bounds, respectively, in period 1. Constraints (4.77f) enforce the transmission-capacity limit in both directions in period 1.

Constraints (4.77g) and (4.77h) are power balances at nodes 1 and 2, respectively, in period 2, leading to locational marginal prices $\lambda_{1,2}$ and $\lambda_{2,2}$, respectively. Constraints (4.77i) and (4.77j) are production and demand bounds, respectively, in period 2. Constraints (4.77k) enforce the transmission-capacity limit in both directions in period 2.

Constraints (4.77l)–(4.77m) and (4.77n)–(4.77o) are production up- and down-ramping limits for producer 1, from periods 0 to 1 and 1 to 2, respectively. Likewise, constraints (4.77p)–(4.77q) and (4.77r)–(4.77s) are production up- and down-ramping limits for producer 2, from periods 0 to 1 and 1 to 2, respectively.

The outcome of this clearing algorithm is provided in Table 4.3 for two cases, tight ramping limits and relaxed ones. For the case of tight ramping limits ($r_1^{\mathrm{U}} = r_1^{\mathrm{D}} = r_2^{\mathrm{U}} = r_2^{\mathrm{D}} = 1$), from the left-hand side of Table 4.3, we note that the market clears under congested conditions in period 2. The ramping-up constraint of producer 1 from period 1 to period 2 is binding, limiting the capacity of such

Table 4.3 Two-period pricing: outcome

	$r_1^U = r_1^D = r_2^U = r_2^D = 1$		$r_1^U = r_1^D = r_2^U = r_2^D = 5$	
Case	Period 1	Period 2	Period 1	Period 2
z^*	37		39	
$p_{1,1}^*, p_{1,2}^*$	5	5	5	5
$p_{2,1}^*, p_{2,2}^*$	0	1	0	2
$d_{1,1}^*, d_{1,2}^*$	1	1	1	1
$d_{2,1}^*, d_{2,2}^*$	4	5	4	6
$f_{1,2,1}^*, f_{1,2,1}^*$	4	4	4	4
$\lambda_{1,1}^*, \lambda_{1,2}^*$	2	3	2	3
$\lambda_{2,1}^*, \lambda_{2,2}^*$	2	6	4	4

producer to increase power. In this case, clearing prices ($\lambda_{1,1}^* = 2, \lambda_{2,1}^* = 2, \lambda_{1,2}^* = 3, \lambda_{2,2}^* = 6$) are determined by balance constraints and influenced by transmission bounds and ramping limits. The transmission constraint is binding in period 2 and at the limit but not binding (other constraint is binding instead) in period 1. Thus, marginal prices are different across nodes in period 2, but not in period 1.

For the case of relaxed ramping limits ($r_1^U = r_1^D = r_2^U = r_2^D = 5$), from the right-hand side of Table 4.3, we note that the market clears under congested conditions in both periods. There is no binding ramping limit in this case. Clearing prices ($\lambda_{1,1}^* = 2, \lambda_{2,1}^* = 4, \lambda_{1,2}^* = 3, \lambda_{2,2}^* = 4$) are determined by balance constraints and influenced by transmission bounds. Transmission constraints are binding in both periods. Thus, marginal prices are different across nodes in both periods.

Producer revenues (R_1 and R_2), consumer payments (P_1 and P_2), producer profits (Π_1^P and Π_2^P), consumer profits (Π_1^C and Π_2^C), surpluses, and social welfare are reported in Table 4.4.

4.6.2 Multi-Period: General Formulation

A general-enough multi-period market-clearing algorithm has the form:

$$\max_{\substack{d_{i,t}\geq 0, p_{i,t}\geq 0, \theta_{i,t}, \forall i, \forall t;\\ f_{i,j,t} \forall i, \forall j \in \Omega_i, \forall t}} \quad z = \sum_t \left(\sum_i u_{i,t}\, d_{i,t} - \sum_i c_i\, p_{i,t} \right) \tag{4.78a}$$

$$\text{s. t.} \quad p_{i,t} - d_{i,t} - \sum_{j\in\Omega_i} f_{i,j,t} = 0 : \ \lambda_{i,t} \quad \forall i, \forall t \tag{4.78b}$$

$$0 \leq d_{i,t} \leq d_{i,t}^{\max} \quad \forall i, \forall t \tag{4.78c}$$

$$0 \leq p_{i,t} \leq p_i^{\max} \quad \forall i, \forall t \tag{4.78d}$$

Table 4.4 Two-period pricing: revenues, payments, profits, surpluses, and social welfare

Case	$r_1^U = r_1^D = r_2^U = r_2^D = 1$	$r_1^U = r_1^D = r_2^U = r_2^D = 5$
R_1	25	25
R_2	6	8
Total revenue	31	33
P_1	5	5
P_2	38	40
Total payment	43	45
Π_1^P	15	15
Π_2^P	2	0
Total producer profit	17	15
Π_1^C	0	0
Π_2^C	8	12
Total consumer profit	8	12
Network surplus	12	12
Social welfare	37	39

$$0 \leq p_{i,t} - p_{i,t-1} \leq p_i^{U,\max}, \forall i \; \forall t \tag{4.78e}$$

$$0 \leq p_{i,t-1} - p_{i,t} \leq p_i^{D,\max}, \forall i \; \forall t \tag{4.78f}$$

$$- f_{i,j}^{\max} \leq f_{i,j,t} \leq f_{i,j}^{\max} \quad \forall i, \forall j \in \Omega_i, \forall t \tag{4.78g}$$

$$f_{i,j,t} = -f_{jit} \quad \forall i, \forall j \in \Omega_i, \forall t \tag{4.78h}$$

$$f_{i,j,t} = B_{i,j} \cdot (\theta_{i,t} - \theta_{jt}) \quad \forall i, \forall j \in \Omega_i, \forall t \tag{4.78i}$$

$$\theta_{kt} = 0, \forall t, \text{being } k \text{ an arbitrary node} \tag{4.78j}$$

The optimization variables are described below:

$d_{i,t}$ is the consumption of consumer i in period t,
$p_{i,t}$ the production of producer i in period t,
$f_{i,j,t}$ the power flow through line ij from i to j in period t,
$\theta_{i,t}$ the voltage angle of node i (network state variable) in period t, and
$\lambda_{i,t}$ (dual variable) the market-clearing price at node i in period t.

The constants are described below:

$u_{i,t}$ is the variable utility of consumer i in period t,
c_i the variable cost of consumer i,
$d_{i,t}^{\max}$ the maximum demand of consumer i in period t,
$p_i^{\max}$ the capacity of producer i,
$p_i^{U,\max}$ the ramping-up limit of producer i,

$p_i^{\mathrm{D,max}}$ the ramping-down limit of producer i,
p_i^0 the actual production of producer i at the beginning of the planning horizon,
$f_{i,j}^{\max}$ the transmission capacity of line ij, and
$B_{i,j}$ the susceptance of line ij.

Finally, Ω_i is the set of nodes directly connected to node i.

Objective function (4.78a) is the social welfare for the whole study horizon (summation over all time periods). Constraint (4.78b) is the power-balance equation at node i in period t, leading to the locational marginal price $\lambda_{i,t}$. Constraints (4.78c) and (4.78d) are consumption and production bounds, respectively, in period t. Constraints (4.78e) and (4.78f) are ramping-up and ramping-down limits, respectively, for producers. Constraint (4.78g) enforces transmission-capacity bounds in period t. Since the network is assumed to be lossless, constraint (4.78h) enforces that the flow in direction ij is the opposite to that in direction ji in period t. Constraint (4.78i) expresses the flow through line ij in period t as the susceptance of the line times the difference of voltage angles at its sending and receiving ends in period t. Finally, constraint (4.78j) fixes an arbitrary node as the reference one in period t.

4.7 Summary

1. Marginal pricing is the (almost) universal paradigm in electricity markets for two main reasons. Under perfect competition:

   (a) Marginal pricing ensures investment cost recovery (a most desirable long-term property).
   (b) Marginal pricing ensures short-term efficiency, i.e., maximum social welfare.

   Moreover, under perfect competition, revenue adequacy (for the operator) and cost recovery (for producers) are guaranteed.
2. Embedding non-convexities (start-up cost and minimum power output, among others) in market-clearing algorithms destroys the above most desirable properties, and cost recovery cannot be generally guaranteed.
3. Binding network constraints results in locational (spatial) marginal prices and the "splitting" of the market.
4. Inter-temporal constraints, such as the ramping limit of production units, may have a significant impact of marginal-clearing prices.
5. Market-clearing algorithms can be tailored, via stochastic programming, to represent the inherent uncertainty plaguing weather-dependent producers. Under perfect competition, revenue adequacy and cost recovery are then guaranteed in expectation.

4.8 End-of-Chapter Exercises

4.1 Regarding the model in Sect. 4.2.1, calculate

$$\frac{\partial}{\partial p_b} C_O(\cdot)$$

where

$$C_O(\cdot) = c_b e_b + c_m e_m + c_p p_m + c_u e_u$$

That is, calculate the derivative of the operation cost with respect to a small capacity change in the base technology.

4.2 Consider the market-clearing examples in Sect. 4.3 (Fig. 4.5), Sects. 4.3.1, and 4.3.2. Expand them from 2 nodes to 3 nodes, with producers at nodes 1 and 2 and the demand at node 3. Solve congested and un-congested instances, and discuss the prices obtained.

4.3 Expand the non-convex market-clearing example in Sect. 4.4.1 (Fig. 4.8) to include network constraints. Specifically, consider a 3-node example. Solve congested and un-congested instances, and discuss the prices obtained.

4.4 Expand the stochastic market-clearing example in Sect. 4.5.1 (Fig. 4.9) to include network constraints. Specifically, consider a 3-node example. Solve congested and un-congested instances, and discuss the prices obtained.

4.5 Expand the stochastic market-clearing example in Sect. 4.5.1 (Fig. 4.9) to include non-convexities. Specifically, include start-up costs and minimum power output constraints. Discuss the prices obtained.

4.6 Expand the stochastic market-clearing example in Sect. 4.5.1 (Fig. 4.9) to three time periods. Analyze the impact on prices of ramping constraints. Discuss the prices obtained.

4.9 GAMS Codes

An input GAMS [3] file to solve the stochastic market-clearing example in Sect. 4.5.1 is provided below:

```
variable z;
positive variables p1,p2;
positive variables s11,s12;
positive variables r21u,r21d,r22u,r22d;
*
variables prices1,prices2;
variables profit11, profit12, profit1E;
```

```
variables profit21, profit22, profit2E;
*
variables rev11, rev12, rev1E;
variables rev21, rev22, rev2E;
*
variable dpay, revtotal;
*
parameters c1/1/, c2/4/, d/10/;
parameters cap1/20/, cap2/20/;
*
parameters p1r1 / 02/, p1r2 / 08/;
parameters ps1  /0.4/, ps2  /0.6/;
parameter epsu /0.5/, epsd /1.0/;
*
equations of,ba,bd1a,bd2a;
equations bs1,bds1u,bds1d,bs2,bds2u,bds2d;
equations spl1,spl2;
*
of..    z =e= c1*p1+c2*p2 + ps1*((c2+epsu)*r21u - (c2-epsd)*r21d)
                          + ps2*((c2+epsu)*r22u - (c2-epsd)*r22d)
                              ;
*
ba..    p1+p2 =e= d;
bd1a..  p1 =l= cap1;
bd2a..  p2 =l= cap2;
*
bs1..   (r21u-r21d)+(p1r1-p1-s11) =e= 0;
bds1u.. p2+(r21u-r21d) =l= cap2;
bds1d.. p2+(r21u-r21d) =g= 0;
spl1..  s11 =l= p1r1;
*
bs2..   (r22u-r22d)+(p1r2-p1-s12) =e= 0;
bds2u.. p2+(r22u-r22d) =l= cap2;
bds2d.. p2+(r22u-r22d) =g= 0;
spl2..  s12 =l= p1r2;
*
model stoclear /all/;
solve stoclear using lp minimizing z;
*
prices1.l= bs1.m/ps1;
prices2.l= bs2.m/ps2;
*
profit11.l= p1.l*ba.m+(p1r1-p1.l-s11.l)*prices1.l - c1*p1r1;
profit12.l= p1.l*ba.m+(p1r2-p1.l-s12.l)*prices2.l - c1*p1r1;
profit1E.l= ps1*profit11.l + ps2*profit12.l;
*
profit21.l= p2.l*ba.m+(r21u.l-r21d.l)*prices1.l - c2*(p2.l+(r21u.
    l-r21d.l));
profit22.l= p2.l*ba.m+(r22u.l-r22d.l)*prices2.l - c2*(p2.l+(r22u.
    l-r22d.l));
profit2E.l= ps1*profit21.l + ps2*profit22.l;
*
rev11.l= p1.l*ba.m+(p1r1-p1.l-s11.l)*prices1.l;
rev12.l= p1.l*ba.m+(p1r2-p1.l-s12.l)*prices2.l;
```

```
revlE.l= ps1*rev11.l + ps2*rev12.l;
*
rev21.l= p2.l*ba.m+(r21u.l-r21d.l)*prices1.l;
rev22.l= p2.l*ba.m+(r22u.l-r22d.l)*prices2.l;
rev2E.l= ps1*rev21.l + ps2*rev22.l;
*
dpay.l= d*ba.m;
revtotal.l= rev1E.l+rev2E.l;
*
display p1.l,p2.l;
display ba.m,prices1.l,prices2.l;
display r21u.l,r21d.l,r22u.l,r22d.l;
display s11.l,s12.l;
*
display profit11.l,profit12.l,profit1E.l;
display profit21.l,profit22.l,profit2E.l;
*
display rev11.l,rev12.l,rev1E.l;
display rev21.l,rev22.l,rev2E.l;
*
display dpay.l,revtotal.l;
```

Note that this GAMS code reproduces almost verbatim the mathematical formulation of model (4.47).

References

1. Chang, H.J.: Economics. The User's Guide. Bloomsbury Press, New York (2014)
2. Conejo, A.J., Baringo, L.: Power System Operations. Springer, New York (2018)
3. GAMS Development Corporation: GAMS–A User's Guide. http://www.gams.com (2020)
4. Morales, J.M., Conejo, A.J., Liu, K., Zhong, J.: Pricing electricity in pools with wind producers. IEEE Trans. Power Syst. **27**, 1366–1376 (2012)
5. Pritchard, G., Zakeri, G., Philpott, A.: A single-settlement, energy-only electric power market for unpredictable and intermittent participants. Oper. Res. **58**, 1210–1219 (2010)
6. Ventosa, M., Linares, P., Perez-Arriaga, I.J.: Power system economics. In: Perez-Arriaga, I.J. (ed.) Regulation of the Power Sector. Springer, New York (2014)

Chapter 5
Market Power

5.1 Introduction

Deregulated electricity markets in many countries and regions typically exhibit the characteristics of oligopolistic ownership. For instance, [15] found evidence of considerable deviation of prices from marginal costs in the British electricity spot market, while [2] demonstrated market power of strategic generators in the restructured wholesale electricity market of California. Tangerås and Mauritzen [13] investigated market power in a hydro-based wholesale electricity market of the Nordic power exchange, Nord Pool. The manipulation of prices by strategic generators would lead to significant loss of social welfare. These welfare-distorting effects of market power are exacerbated by the fact that electricity demand is relatively inelastic, and it is difficult to store electric power economically [2].

In this chapter, we first examine the characteristics of market power.[1] To understand the concept of market power, we consider two polar cases of a monopoly with a single producer and a monopsony with a single consumer. Next, we investigate an oligopoly market, where several strategic producers can exert market power. After reviewing the Nash equilibrium concept in game theory, we present the framework of a Cournot oligopoly model, where producers determine their outputs simultaneously. Another framework of a Stackelberg oligopoly model with sequential decision makers is also analyzed. Finally, the basic Stackelberg model is extended to a more general framework of a leader-follower oligopoly, in which both producers and consumers can be leading entities, submitting offer/bid prices strategically to the auctioneer.

[1] General models of market power in monopoly and oligopoly are presented in detail in [1, 14]. See also [4, 8] for models of imperfectly competitive power markets.

M. Tanaka et al., *Economics of Power Systems*, International Series in Operations Research & Management Science 327,
https://doi.org/10.1007/978-3-030-92871-1_5

5.2 Concept of Market Power

This section discusses the concept of market power by focusing on a monopoly, in which a single producer manipulates the market. A useful index is introduced to measure the degree of market power. We also discuss another polar case of monopsony, where a single consumer exercises market power.

5.2.1 *Monopoly*

In a perfectly competitive market, a producer is assumed to be a price taker, taking the market price as given. Letting $\hat{p}$ and $C(q)$, respectively, denote the prevailing market price and the cost function, the profit maximization of a producer is written as:

$$\underset{q \geq 0}{\text{Maximize}} \ \hat{p}q - C(q) \tag{5.1}$$

Assuming an interior solution, i.e., $q > 0$, we obtain the following first-order condition:

$$\hat{p} = C'(q) \tag{5.2}$$

Thus, a perfectly competitive producer just equates the given market price and its marginal cost to maximize its profit as discussed in Chap. 2.

In contrast to a price taker, a producer that possesses market power can be seen as a price maker or a price setter. A producer is said to have market power if it can manipulate the market. To understand this, we consider a monopoly, in which a single producer faces the entire demand of the market and freely chooses the price and output of its good. Let $P(q)$ denote the inverse-demand function of the market and substitute $P(q)$ for the constant price, $\hat{p}$, in (5.1). Then, the profit maximization of a monopoly producer is expressed as follows:

$$\underset{q \geq 0}{\text{Maximize}} \ P(q)q - C(q) \tag{5.3}$$

An interior solution yields the following first-order condition for a monopolist:

$$P(q) + P'(q)q = C'(q) \tag{5.4}$$

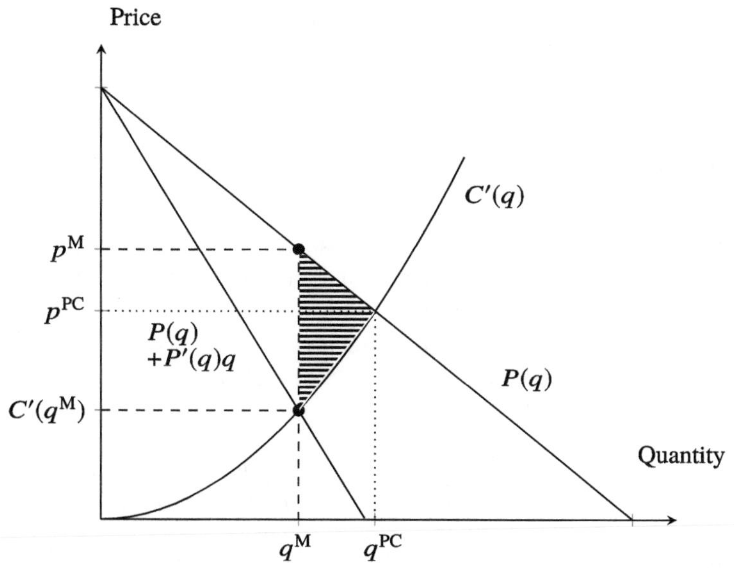

Fig. 5.1 Monopoly

A monopolist equates its marginal revenue expressed in the left-hand side of (5.4) to its marginal cost.[2] Condition (5.4) implies that the monopoly price is greater than the marginal cost since the market-demand curve (inverse-demand function) is typically downward sloping, i.e., $P'(q) < 0$, and, hence, $P'(q)q < 0$.

Figure 5.1 illustrates the results, where $(q^{\mathrm{PC}}, p^{\mathrm{PC}})$ and $(q^{\mathrm{M}}, p^{\mathrm{M}})$ denote the perfectly competitive and monopoly outcomes, respectively. Under monopoly, the price rises, $p^{\mathrm{M}} > p^{\mathrm{PC}}$, while the output decreases, $q^{\mathrm{M}} < q^{\mathrm{PC}}$. The deviation of the monopoly price from the marginal cost, i.e., $p^{\mathrm{M}} > C'(q^{\mathrm{M}})$, implies an inefficient outcome with a loss of social surplus (a deadweight loss) depicted in the hatched area in Fig. 5.1.

Illustrative Example 5.1 *Monopoly.*

We consider a simple example of monopoly, in which the cost function and the inverse-demand function are $C(q) = 10q$ and $P(q) = 30 - 0.2q$, respectively. Then, the profit maximization of a monopoly producer is written as follows:

$$\underset{q \geq 0}{\text{Maximize}} \ (30 - 0.2q)q - 10q \tag{5.5}$$

We can find an interior solution (i.e., $q > 0$) for this problem. Indeed, by equating the marginal revenue and the marginal cost, i.e., $30 - 0.4q = 10$, we attain the

[2] When the monopolist infinitesimally reduces its output, the revenue decreases by $P(q)$ due to lost sales, whereas the revenue increases by $|P'(q)q|$ because of the rise in the price.

monopoly output, $q^{\mathrm{M}} = 50$. The monopoly price is $p^{\mathrm{M}} = P(q^{\mathrm{M}}) = 20$, which is greater than the marginal cost of $C'(q^{\mathrm{M}}) = 10$.

5.2.2 *Lerner Index*

Market power of a producer can be defined as its ability to raise the price of a good above the marginal cost. The degree of market power can be then measured by the price-cost markup, called the Lerner index, which is defined as the difference between price and marginal cost as a fraction of price, i.e., $\frac{P(q)-C'(q)}{P(q)}$. Simple rearrangement of the first-order condition (5.4) yields a useful expression for the Lerner index denoted as LI:

$$\mathrm{LI} = \frac{P(q) - C'(q)}{P(q)} = -\frac{P'(q)q}{P(q)} = -\frac{1}{e} \tag{5.6}$$

where e denotes the price elasticity of demand as defined in Chap. 1. Note also that $\frac{P'(q)q}{P(q)}$ is the "inverse" of the elasticity, e.

Expression (5.6) for the Lerner index suggests that the degree of producer's market power depends on the price elasticity of demand. If the elasticity of a good is relatively high (i.e., the absolute value of elasticity, $|e|$, is large), then the price-cost margin is low, implying less market power. On the contrary, if the elasticity of a good is relatively low (i.e., the absolute value of elasticity, $|e|$, is small), then the price-cost markup is high, implying greater market power. Hence, when the demand of some good is inelastic, i.e., $e > -1$ ($|e| < 1$), market power could be substantial. Indeed, as alluded to in Chap. 1, the demand for electricity is considered inelastic empirically, which raises significant concerns of the exercise of market power by suppliers.

5.2.3 *Monopsony*

Consumers may also exert market power as the major purchasers of some goods. Particularly, such cases are often discussed in the context of input markets such as labor markets [10]. Here, we consider consumers' market power in output markets in line with Sect. 5.2.1.

As demonstrated in Chap. 1, a price-taking consumer maximizes its consumer surplus expressed as the difference between its gross benefit and payment, i.e., $CS(q) = B(q) - \hat{p}q$, given the market price of the good, $\hat{p}$:

$$\underset{q \geq 0}{\text{Maximize}}\ B(q) - \hat{p}q \tag{5.7}$$

We obtain the first-order condition with an assumption of an interior solution as follows:

$$B'(q) = \hat{p} \tag{5.8}$$

Thus, a perfectly competitive consumer equalizes its marginal benefit of consuming the good with the given market price. With the condition for price-taking producers, $\hat{p} = C'(q)$, in (5.2), the marginal benefit of consumption is equated with the marginal cost of production through the market price under perfect competition:

$$B'(q) = C'(q) = \hat{p} \tag{5.9}$$

By contrast, a polar case in which there is a single consumer and, hence, a single purchaser, is called a monopsony, analogous to a monopoly. In this case, a consumer can manipulate the market price facing the entire supply from price-taking producers, represented by $\hat{p} = C'(q)$. Substituting $\hat{p} = C'(q)$ for the constant price, $\hat{p}$, in (5.7), the surplus-maximization problem of a monopsony consumer is then expressed as follows:

$$\underset{q \geq 0}{\text{Maximize}}\ B(q) - C'(q)q \tag{5.10}$$

An interior solution gives the following first-order condition for a monopsony consumer:

$$B'(q) = C'(q) + C''(q)q \tag{5.11}$$

When we assume $C''(q) > 0$, (5.11) implies that the marginal benefit of consumption is greater than the marginal cost of production and, hence, greater than the price under monopsony.[3]

In Fig. 5.2, (q^{PC}, p^{PC}) and (q^{MS}, p^{MS}) denote the perfectly competitive and monopsony outcomes, respectively. Under monopsony, both the price and output decrease, i.e., $p^{MS} < p^{PC}$ and $q^{MS} < q^{PC}$, respectively. The deviation of the monopsony price from the marginal benefit of consumption, i.e., $p^{MS} < B'(q^{MS})$, suggests an inefficient outcome with a loss of social surplus (a deadweight loss) illustrated in the hatched area in Fig. 5.2.

[3] The right-hand side of (5.11) expresses the marginal expense of the monopsony consumer. When the monopsony consumer infinitesimally reduces its consumption, the expense decreases by $C'(q)$ due to reduced consumption of the good and also by $C''(q)q$ because of the fall in the price.

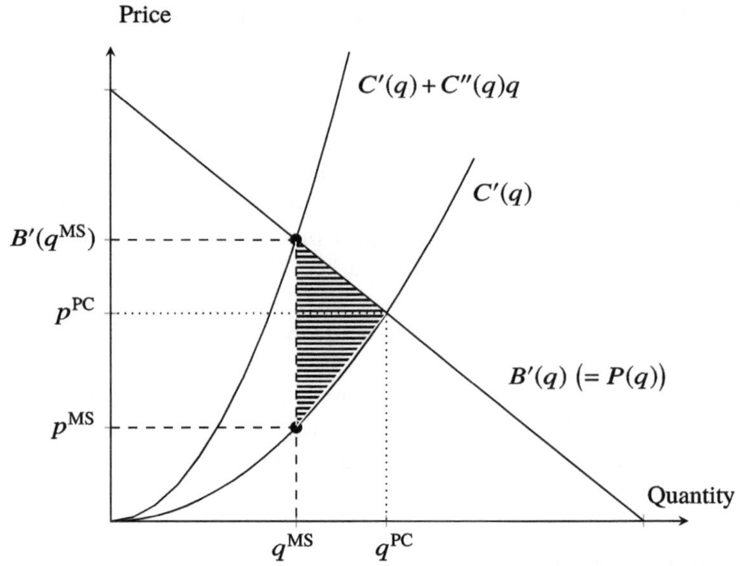

Fig. 5.2 Monopsony

5.3 Oligopoly

This section discusses the basic framework of an oligopoly, in which several producers can manipulate the market. To understand the strategic interactions among producers, we first review the concept of a Nash equilibrium in game theory. We then examine a Cournot oligopoly model, where producers determine their outputs simultaneously. A useful index is introduced to measure the degree of market concentration. We also investigate another framework of a Stackelberg oligopoly model, which considers sequential decision makers.

5.3.1 Game Theory

This subsection summarizes the strategic decision making and the equilibrium concept in basic game theory to better understand oligopolistic markets. A basic game consists of three elements, viz. players, strategies, and payoffs. We here consider a simple game with two producers (players), two actions (strategies), and corresponding profits (payoffs) as in Table 5.1. Each producer decides to take either a moderate advertisement of its product, labeled as action M, or a heavy advertisement, labeled as action H. The cell in the matrix indicates the profits obtained by each producer, where the left and right values correspond to producers 1 and 2, respectively. When both producers choose to take moderate advertising,

Table 5.1 Two-player game

		Producer 2			
		M		*H*	
Producer 1	*M*	120	120	60	160
	H	160	60	100	100

M, each earns a profit of \$120 million. By contrast, when both producers decide to take heavy advertising, H, aggressively criticizing the opponent's product, they end up with a profit of \$100 million each due to possible damage to reputation. Another possibility is that one aggressive producer makes a profit of \$160 million by implementing a heavy advertisement when the opponent is involved in a moderate advertisement, leading to the worst case of \$60 million for the moderate producer.

The important feature of a game is that each player's payoff depends not only on its own strategy but also on another player's strategy. We here examine the strategic decision making process of producer 1. If producer 1 thinks that producer 2 takes moderate advertising, M, then the best response for producer 1 is to choose heavy advertising, H, to gain \$160 million. By a similar reasoning, producer 1's best reaction to producer 2's heavy advertising, H, is again to choose the same action, H, making profits of \$100 million. Therefore, producer 1 chooses heavy advertising, H, in either case. On the other hand, producer 2 also takes heavy advertising, H, by making the same reasoning in this simple symmetric game.

More formally, we can describe the interaction of strategic decision makers using best-response functions. Let $BR_i(\cdot)$ denote the best-response function of producer $i = 1, 2$, where the argument of the function is the opponent producer's action. The best-response function of producer 1 is expressed as $H = BR_1(M)$ and $H = BR_1(H)$. Symmetrically, $H = BR_2(M)$ and $H = BR_2(H)$ for producer 2. Then, the pair of actions, (H, H), is called a Nash equilibrium in the sense that action H is the best response to each other, i.e., $H = BR_1(H)$ and $H = BR_2(H)$ hold simultaneously. This means that no player has an incentive to deviate from that state. In other words, a pair of actions constitutes a Nash equilibrium if no player can unilaterally change its action in a way that improves its payoff.

5.3.2 *Cournot Oligopoly*

In contrast to a monopoly, a market structure in which more than one producer has market power is called an oligopoly. Particularly, the case in which producers set their quantities strategically is called a Cournot oligopoly. Suppose that there are n oligopolistic producers $i = 1, \ldots, n$ with a cost function, $C_i(x_i)$, supplying total quantity, $q = \sum_i^n x_i$, in the market. The profit-maximization problem of each Cournot oligopolist i who decides its output level, x_i, can be written as follows:

$$\underset{x_i \geq 0}{\text{Maximize}}\ P(q)x_i - C_i(x_i) \tag{5.12}$$

With an assumption of an interior solution, the first-order condition for an oligopolist i can be obtained as:

$$P(q) + P'(q)x_i = C_i'(x_i) \tag{5.13}$$

Analogous to a monopoly, (5.13) implies that the oligopoly price is greater than the marginal cost with $P'(q) < 0$, thereby leading to an inefficient resource allocation.

We now investigate the behavior of strategic producers and resulting Nash equilibrium in the context of Cournot oligopoly. Consider a duopoly consisting of two firms $i = 1, 2$ with an output level, x_i. For simplicity, we assume that the producers are symmetric in that they have an identical cost function, $C_i(x_i) = cx_i$, with a constant marginal cost, $C_i'(x_i) = c$. The linear inverse-demand function of the market is given by $P(q) = a - bq$ with $q = x_1 + x_2$. $a > c$ is also assumed so that the marginal cost, c, is lower than the vertical intercept of demand, a.

We focus on Cournot producer 1, who determines x_1 strategically to maximize its profit given its belief about the rival's output, x_2:

$$\underset{x_1 \geq 0}{\text{Maximize}} \ (a - bq)x_1 - cx_1 \tag{5.14}$$

Note that a Cournot oligopolist is not a price taker because it faces the market demand, $a - b(x_1 + x_2)$, often called residual demand given the opponent's output. The problem (5.14) exhibits the feature of a game in the sense that the profit of producer 1 depends not only on its own decision but also on the rival's output, similar to the simple two-player game in the previous subsection. Indeed, from the first-order condition for an interior solution, i.e., $a - 2bx_1 - bx_2 = c$, we can obtain the best-response function for producer 1 as follows:

$$x_1 = BR_1(x_2) = \frac{a - c - bx_2}{2b} \tag{5.15}$$

Producer 1's best-response function (5.15) represents the profit-maximizing and, hence, best reaction to every possible decision of the rival producer 2. Similarly, the best-response function of producer 2 can be easily derived because of the symmetric structure of the problem:

$$x_2 = BR_2(x_1) = \frac{a - c - bx_1}{2b} \tag{5.16}$$

Then, we obtain a pair of outputs, (x_1^{CO}, x_2^{CO}), by solving the two best-response equations, $x_1 = BR_1(x_2)$ and $x_2 = BR_2(x_1)$, simultaneously:

$$x_1^{CO} = x_2^{CO} = \frac{a - c}{3b} \tag{5.17}$$

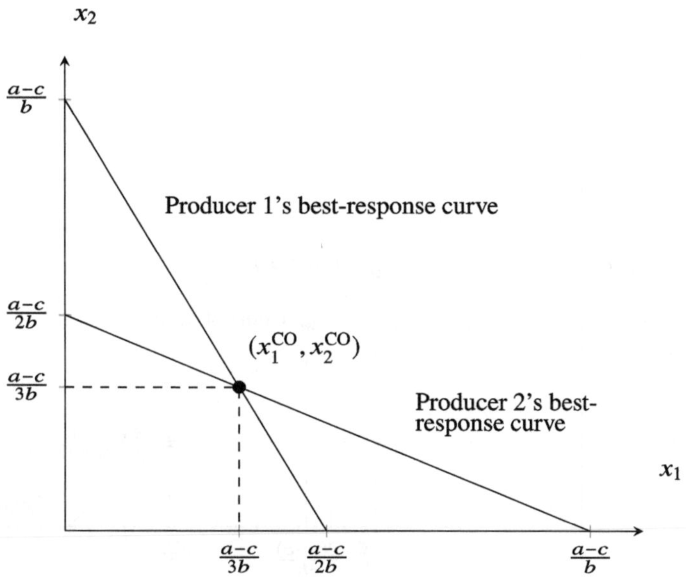

Fig. 5.3 Best-response curves and Nash-Cournot equilibrium

The pair (x_1^{CO}, x_2^{CO}) is a Nash equilibrium, or often called a Nash-Cournot equilibrium, as the outputs are the best responses to each other, i.e., $x_1^{CO} = BR_1(x_2^{CO})$ and $x_2^{CO} = BR_2(x_1^{CO})$ hold simultaneously. Figure 5.3 illustrates the Nash-Cournot equilibrium at the intersection of two best-response curves. Furthermore, simple calculation yields the total outputs, q^{CO}, and the market price, p^{CO}, for the Nash-Cournot equilibrium:

$$q^{CO} = \frac{2(a-c)}{3b}, \quad p^{CO} = P(q^{CO}) = \frac{a+2c}{3} \tag{5.18}$$

The equilibrium outcome under Cournot oligopoly is less efficient than that under perfect competition due to exercise of market power. We can easily check this fact by comparing the equilibria of two different market structures. Let q^{PC} denote the total equilibrium output in a perfectly competitive market. The perfectly competitive price, p^{PC}, is equal to the marginal cost, i.e., $p^{PC} = P(q^{PC}) = c$, which is lower than $p^{CO} = \frac{a+2c}{3}$. Solving $P(q^{PC}) = c$ gives the total output under perfect competition, i.e., $q^{PC} = \frac{a-c}{b}$, which is greater than $q^{CO} = \frac{2(a-c)}{3b}$.

On the other hand, the equilibrium outcome under Cournot oligopoly is more efficient than that under monopoly. By equating the marginal revenue and the marginal cost, i.e., $a - 2bq = c$, we obtain the monopoly output, $q^M = \frac{a-c}{2b}$, which is less than $q^{CO} = \frac{2(a-c)}{3b}$. The monopoly price is $p^M = P(q^M) = \frac{a+c}{2}$, which is higher than $p^{CO} = \frac{a+2c}{3}$.

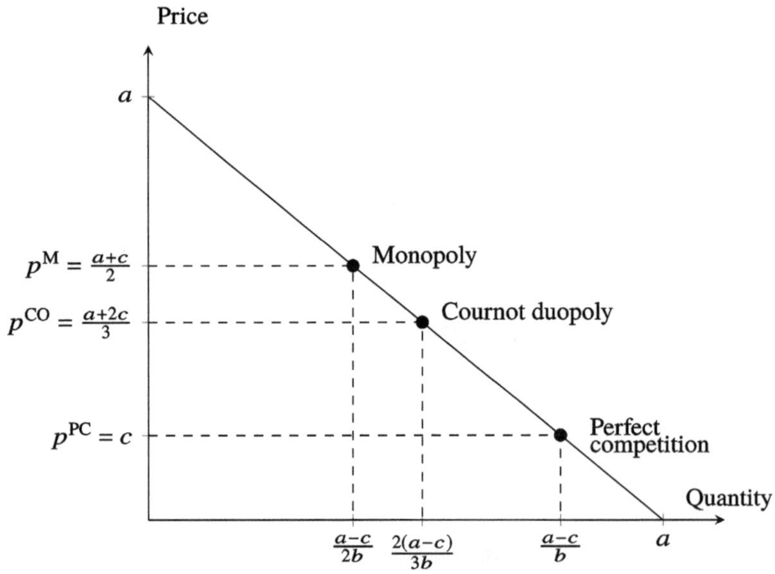

Fig. 5.4 Comparison of outcomes for different market structures

Figure 5.4 compares the equilibrium outcomes of monopoly, Cournot oligopoly, and perfect competition. We confirm that $p^{M} > p^{CO} > p^{PC} = c$. This implies that the equilibrium price in a Cournot oligopoly market deviates upward from the marginal cost, demonstrating the distortional effect of market power, but better than the case of monopoly.

The analysis of a Cournot duopoly can be extended to n strategic producers. To keep the analysis simple, we retain the same setup of a symmetric oligopoly with an identical cost function, $C_i(x_i) = cx_i$, for producers $i = 1, \ldots, n$.[4] The linear inverse-demand function of the market is again given by $P(q) = a - bq$ with $q = \sum_i^n x_i$ and $a > c$. The aggregate output of producers except for i is expressed as $x_{-i} = q - x_i$.

As an extension of a duopoly case, the first-order condition for the profit maximization of producer i can be expressed as $a - 2bx_i - bx_{-i} = c$, assuming an interior solution. Thus, we can obtain the best-response function for producer i similar to that of the duopoly case as follows:

$$x_i = BR_i(x_{-i}) = \frac{a - c - bx_{-i}}{2b} \tag{5.19}$$

[4] See, for example, [1] for the discussion of a Cournot oligopoly with n asymmetric and heterogenous producers.

Let x_i^{CO} denote the equilibrium output of a symmetric producer. Because of the symmetry of producers, we have an identical equilibrium solution, $x_1^{\mathrm{CO}} = x_2^{\mathrm{CO}} = \cdots = x_n^{\mathrm{CO}}$, as already observed in the symmetric duopoly equilibrium in (5.17). The total output in equilibrium can be then represented as $q^{\mathrm{CO}} = nx_i^{\mathrm{CO}}$ and, hence, $x_{-i}^{\mathrm{CO}} = q^{\mathrm{CO}} - x_i^{\mathrm{CO}} = (n-1)x_i^{\mathrm{CO}}$ holds. Consequently, the following equilibrium condition can be derived using (5.19):

$$x_i^{\mathrm{CO}} = \frac{a - c - bx_{-i}^{\mathrm{CO}}}{2b} = \frac{a - c - b(n-1)x_i^{\mathrm{CO}}}{2b} \tag{5.20}$$

Solving (5.20) yields the Nash-Cournot equilibrium for n symmetric producers as follows:

$$x_i^{\mathrm{CO}} = \frac{a - c}{b(n+1)} \tag{5.21}$$

Moreover, simple calculation gives the total output and market price in equilibrium:

$$q^{\mathrm{CO}} = \frac{n(a-c)}{b(n+1)}, \quad p^{\mathrm{CO}} = P(q^{\mathrm{CO}}) = \frac{a + nc}{n+1} \tag{5.22}$$

The equilibrium results of (5.22) can be regarded general enough to understand the outcomes of different market structures. Suppose that there is only a single producer in the market and substitute $n = 1$ into (5.22). Then, we obtain the monopoly outcomes, $q^{\mathrm{M}} = \frac{a-c}{2b}$ and $p^{\mathrm{M}} = \frac{a+c}{2}$, as illustrated in Fig. 5.4. In contrast, suppose that there are a huge number of producers in the market and let the number approach infinity. Then, the results of (5.22) converge to those of perfect competition, i.e., $q^{\mathrm{PC}} = \frac{a-c}{b}$ and $p^{\mathrm{PC}} = c$, as indicated in Fig. 5.4. Intuitively, when the number of producers increases, their influence on the market price and, hence, the degree of market power tend to vanish.

Illustrative Example 5.2 *Symmetric Cournot duopoly.*

We consider a simple example of symmetric Cournot duopoly, in which the cost function and the inverse-demand function are $C_i(x_i) = 10x_i$ for $i = 1, 2$ and $P(q) = 100 - q$ with $q = x_1 + x_2$, respectively. Then, the profit maximization of Cournot producer 1 is described as follows:

$$\underset{x_1 \geq 0}{\text{Maximize}} \ \big(100 - x_1 - x_2\big)x_1 - 10x_1 \tag{5.23}$$

The Karush–Kuhn–Tucker (KKT) condition is simply derived as:

$$0 \leq x_1 \perp 90 - 2x_1 - x_2 \leq 0 \tag{5.24}$$

where $\perp$ denotes complementarity, i.e., $0 \leq a \perp b \geq 0$ is equivalent to $a \geq 0$, $b \geq 0$ and $ab = 0$. Similarly, Cournot producer 2's problem is written as follows:

$$\underset{x_2 \geq 0}{\text{Maximize}} \ (100 - x_1 - x_2)x_2 - 10x_2 \tag{5.25}$$

We also have a similar KKT condition:

$$0 \leq x_2 \perp 90 - x_1 - 2x_2 \leq 0 \tag{5.26}$$

In this example, interior solutions (i.e., $x_1 > 0$ and $x_2 > 0$) to the problems of both producers constitute the Nash-Cournot equilibrium, (x_1^{CO}, x_2^{CO}). This can be easily verified by considering equality constraints for the right-hand side inequalities of (5.24) and (5.26):

$$x_1 = BR_1(x_2) = \frac{90 - x_2}{2} \tag{5.27a}$$

$$x_2 = BR_2(x_1) = \frac{90 - x_1}{2} \tag{5.27b}$$

Solving those best-response equations simultaneously yields $(x_1^{CO}, x_2^{CO}) = (30, 30)$, which are indeed strictly positive. Figure 5.5 illustrates the Nash-Cournot equilibrium of this symmetric Cournot duopoly. Moreover, we attain $q^{CO} = 60$ and $p^{CO} = 40$. Note that the equilibrium price is greater than the marginal cost

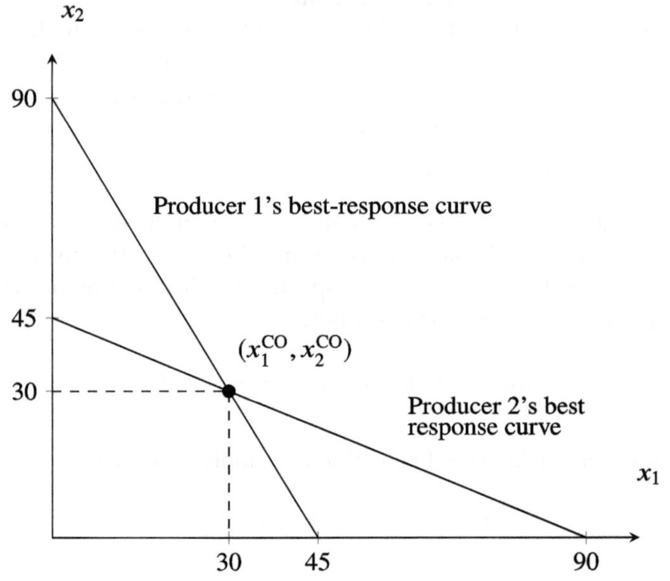

Fig. 5.5 Cournot duopoly

of 10, implying exercise of market power under Cournot duopoly. Consequently, a symmetric Cournot producer earns a profit of 900 each, whereas the profit is 0 with the price equal to the constant marginal cost under perfect competition.

Illustrative Example 5.3 *Asymmetric Cournot duopoly.*

We next examine an example of asymmetric Cournot duopoly, in which the non-identical cost functions are $C_1(x_1) = 6x_1$ and $C_2(x_2) = 12x_2$ for producers 1 and 2, respectively, while the inverse-demand function is $P(q) = 60 - q$ with $q = x_1 + x_2$. We also assume generation capacity limits, 28 and 24, with corresponding dual variables, β_1 and β_2, for producers 1 and 2, respectively. Then, the profit maximization of Cournot producer 1 is formulated as follows:

$$\underset{x_1 \geq 0}{\text{Maximize}} \left(60 - x_1 - x_2\right)x_1 - 6x_1 \quad (5.28a)$$

$$\text{s.t. } x_1 \leq 28 : \beta_1 \quad (5.28b)$$

The KKT conditions are derived as:

$$0 \leq x_1 \perp 54 - 2x_1 - x_2 - \beta_1 \leq 0 \quad (5.29a)$$

$$0 \leq \beta_1 \perp x_1 - 28 \leq 0 \quad (5.29b)$$

On the other hand, Cournot producer 2's problem is similarly described as follows:

$$\underset{x_2 \geq 0}{\text{Maximize}} \left(60 - x_1 - x_2\right)x_2 - 12x_2 \quad (5.30a)$$

$$\text{s.t. } x_2 \leq 24 : \beta_2 \quad (5.30b)$$

The KKT conditions are written as:

$$0 \leq x_2 \perp 48 - x_1 - 2x_2 - \beta_2 \leq 0 \quad (5.31a)$$

$$0 \leq \beta_2 \perp x_2 - 24 \leq 0 \quad (5.31b)$$

In this example, interior solutions (i.e., $0 < x_1 < 28$ and $0 < x_2 < 24$) to the problems of both producers constitute the Nash-Cournot equilibrium, $(x_1^{\text{CO}}, x_2^{\text{CO}})$. We can verify this by considering equality constraints for the right-hand side inequalities of (5.29a) and (5.31a) and by letting $\beta_1 = \beta_2 = 0$:

$$x_1 = BR_1(x_2) = \frac{54 - x_2}{2} \quad (5.32a)$$

$$x_2 = BR_2(x_1) = \frac{48 - x_1}{2} \quad (5.32b)$$

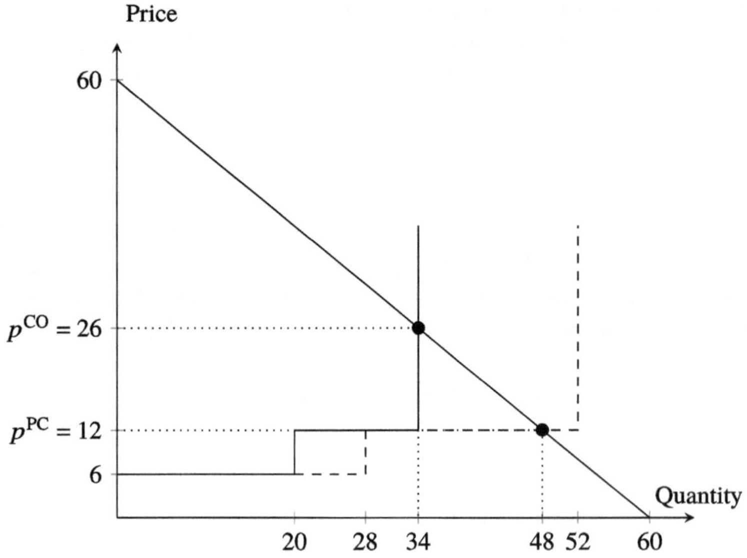

Fig. 5.6 Cournot duopoly and perfect competition

Solving the best-response equations simultaneously, we indeed obtain interior solutions, $(x_1^{CO}, x_2^{CO}) = (20, 14)$. Furthermore, $q^{CO} = 34$ and $p^{CO} = 26$.

Figure 5.6 compares the results of Cournot duopoly and perfect competition. As shown in the dashed line for perfect competition, producer 1 with a lower marginal cost of $C_1'(x_1) = 6$ supplies up to its capacity limit, 28, whereas producer 2 with a higher marginal cost of $C_2'(x_2) = 12$ generates 20, below its capacity limit. This is the result of the usual efficient economic dispatch based on the merit order of generating units. The market price for perfect competition, p^{PC}, is equal to the marginal cost of producer 2, $C_2'(x_2) = 12$, with total quantity of 48. By contrast, under Cournot duopoly as indicated in the solid-line step function, both producers exert market power to strategically withdraw their outputs to $(x_1^{CO}, x_2^{CO}) = (20, 14)$ and $q^{CO} = 34$ in total, raising the market price to $p^{CO} = 26$. As a result, Cournot producers 1 and 2, respectively, make profits of 400 and 196, which are greater than the profits of 168 and 0 under perfect competition.

5.3.3 Herfindahl-Hirschman Index

In contrast to a single producer in a monopoly, several producers may have the ability to manipulate the market in an oligopoly. Hence, it would be useful to evaluate the degree of market concentration based on some indices. One popular measure is the Herfindahl-Hirschman index (HHI) defined as the sum of the squared market shares for n producers in the market. Letting $s_i = \frac{x_i}{q}$ denote the market share of producer i with $q = \sum_i^n x_i$, the HHI is defined as follows:

$$\text{HHI} = \sum_i^n s_i^2 \tag{5.33}$$

The HHI ranges from 0 to 1. In a monopoly with a single producer, the HHI is obviously 1, while the HHI approaches 0 if there are a huge number of producers with a small market share in a perfectly competitive market.

Sometimes, the HHI is multiplied by 10,000 considering a value in percentage terms for the market share and, then, the value of the HHI varies from 0 to 10,000. For instance, the merger guidelines of the U.S. Department of Justice and the Federal Trade Commission view the value of the HHI over 1,800 highly concentrated, raising concerns about competition [3].

The HHI is not only of use in practice but also has a foundation in a Cournot oligopoly model. First, rearranging the first-order condition (5.13) for Cournot producer i yields the oligopoly version of the Lerner index, LI_i, for each producer:

$$\text{LI}_i = \frac{P(q) - C_i'(x_i)}{P(q)} = -\frac{P'(q)q}{P(q)}\frac{x_i}{q} = -\frac{s_i}{e} \tag{5.34}$$

where $\frac{P'(q)q}{P(q)}$ is the inverse of the price elasticity of demand, e. Hence, the price-cost markup of Cournot producer i depends not only on the elasticity but also on its market share. Specifically, the less elastic the market demand and the larger the market share, the greater the price-cost markup.

Next, using the individual Lerner index for each producer, we can further define some average index for n producers in the entire market. Let us take the average of LI_i weighted by the market share, s_i, of each producer based on (5.34):

$$\sum_i^n s_i \text{LI}_i = \frac{P(q) - \sum_i^n s_i C_i'(x_i)}{P(q)} = -\frac{\sum_i^n s_i^2}{e} = -\frac{\text{HHI}}{e} \tag{5.35}$$

The (share-weighted) average Lerner index, $\sum_i^n s_i \text{LI}_i$, represents the average markup in the market, i.e., the difference between price and average marginal cost as a fraction of price. Expression (5.35) implies that the average markup in the market is proportional to the HHI. In other words, the degree of market power in a Cournot oligopoly is captured by the degree of market concentration. Thus, the higher the HHI, the greater the market power under Cournot oligopoly.

5.3.4 Stackelberg Oligopoly

In a Cournot oligopoly model, all the producers decide their outputs simultaneously. In contrast, there may be a leading producer in the market who chooses its output before the other producers determine their outputs. This type of market is called a Stackelberg oligopoly, in which there is a leader and followers with sequential decision making. More specifically, the leader producer with knowledge about its rivals decides its output first, anticipating the subsequent reaction of the follower producers. The follower producers then choose their outputs, given the decision of the leader producer.[5]

We consider a Stackelberg duopoly using the setup of a symmetric Cournot duopoly in the previous subsection. Again, producers have an identical cost function, $C_i(x_i) = cx_i$, $i = 1, 2$ and the linear inverse-demand function of the market is given by $P(q) = a - bq$ with $q = x_1 + x_2$ and $a > c$. We assume that producer 1 is the leader and producer 2 is the follower.

Follower producer 2 chooses its profit-maximizing output, x_2, given producer 1's decision, x_1. As derived in (5.16) in the previous subsection, producer 2's decision can be described by its best-response function assuming an interior solution:

$$x_2 = BR_2(x_1) = \frac{a - c - bx_1}{2b} \tag{5.36}$$

As backward induction (i.e., solving backward in decision sequence), we can formulate the profit-maximization problem of leader producer 1. Leader producer 1 attempts to maximize its profit, anticipating producer 2's subsequent reaction, i.e., best-response function (5.36), as follows:

$$\underset{x_1 \geq 0}{\text{Maximize}} \ \big(a - bx_1 - bx_2\big)x_1 - cx_1 \tag{5.37a}$$

$$\text{s.t.} \ x_2 = \frac{a - c - bx_1}{2b} \tag{5.37b}$$

We can substitute (5.37b) into the objective function (5.37a) to form an unconstrained maximization problem:

$$\underset{x_1 \geq 0}{\text{Maximize}} \ \frac{1}{2}\big(a - c - bx_1\big)x_1 \tag{5.38}$$

[5] A Cournot oligopoly model can be regarded as a one-period static game where all the producers choose their outputs simultaneously. A Stackelberg oligopoly model can be viewed as a multi-period dynamic game where producers determine their outputs sequentially rather than simultaneously.

From the first-order condition, $\frac{1}{2}\left(a - c - 2bx_1\right) = 0$, with the assumption of an interior solution, we obtain the equilibrium outputs, $(x_1^{\mathrm{SO}}, x_2^{\mathrm{SO}})$, of a Stackelberg duopoly as follows:

$$x_1^{\mathrm{SO}} = \frac{a-c}{2b} > x_2^{\mathrm{SO}} = BR_2(x_1^{\mathrm{SO}}) = \frac{a-c}{4b} \tag{5.39}$$

Notably, leader producer 1 supplies more output than the follower producer 2 and, hence, gains more profit even though both producers have identical cost functions. This is because leader producer 1 has the first-mover advantage. Moreover, the total output in equilibrium is $q^{\mathrm{SO}} = \frac{3(a-c)}{4b}$, which is greater than $q^{\mathrm{CO}} = \frac{2(a-c)}{3b}$ under Cournot oligopoly as derived in the previous subsection. Consequently, the equilibrium price, $p^{\mathrm{SO}} = P(q^{\mathrm{SO}}) = \frac{a+3c}{4}$, under Stackelberg oligopoly is lower than that under Cournot oligopoly. Those results are typical in a basic Stackelberg duopoly model.

Illustrative Example 5.4 *Stackelberg duopoly.*

Consider a Stackelberg duopoly, where producer 1 is the leader with a cost function, $C_1(x_1) = 10x_1$, and producer 2 is the follower with $C_2(x_2) = 20x_2$. The inverse-demand function is $P(q) = 60 - 2q$ with $q = x_1 + x_2$. Follower producer 2 maximizes its profit, $\left(60 - 2x_1 - 2x_2\right)x_2 - 20x_2$, and the first-order condition gives its best-response function, $x_2 = BR_2(x_1) = \frac{20-x_1}{2}$, assuming an interior solution. Leader producer 1 maximizes its profit, anticipating producer 2's reaction:

$$\underset{x_1 \geq 0}{\text{Maximize}} \left(60 - 2x_1 - 2x_2\right)x_1 - 10x_1 \tag{5.40a}$$

$$\text{s.t. } x_2 = \frac{20 - x_1}{2} \tag{5.40b}$$

Substituting (5.40b) into the objective function (5.40a) yields an unconstrained maximization problem as follows:

$$\underset{x_1 \geq 0}{\text{Maximize}} \left(30 - x_1\right)x_1 \tag{5.41}$$

Then, it is straightforward to derive the equilibrium outputs, $(x_1^{\mathrm{SO}}, x_2^{\mathrm{SO}})$, of a Stackelberg duopoly as follows:

$$x_1^{\mathrm{SO}} = 15 > x_2^{\mathrm{SO}} = BR_2\left(x_1^{\mathrm{SO}}\right) = 2.5 \tag{5.42}$$

The total output and price in equilibrium are $q^{\mathrm{SO}} = 17.5$ and $p^{\mathrm{SO}} = P(q^{\mathrm{SO}}) = 25$, respectively.

A Stackelberg oligopoly among producers can be extended to a more general framework of a leader-follower oligopoly based on various setups. For example, the follower can be an auctioneer who clears the market. Specifically, it can be an independent system operator (ISO) or similar entities in the context of power markets. Not only a producer but also a consumer can be the leader. There may be even multiple leaders in the market. Those leaders may submit offer or bid prices strategically to the auctioneer. In the next section, we will examine such cases.

5.4 Multiple Leaders

In this section we first review a market-clearing algorithm that collects offers by producers and bids by consumers to identify the quantities to be produced (by producers) and consumed (by consumers) and the market-clearing price. The considered pricing scheme is marginal; that is, the clearing price is the dual variable (shadow price) of the energy-balance constraint. We refer the reader to Chap. 4 for further details.

Generally, the market-clearing algorithm can be manipulated by a strategic producer/consumer pursuing the maximization of its own profit. The strategic producer/consumer intends to do so by modifying its offer/bid price. For convenience, we present the market-clearing algorithm as a primal optimization problem, as a dual optimization problem, and via optimality conditions. Then, we consider the problem to be solved by a producer/consumer to exercise its market power (if it can), which uses the market-clearing algorithm in the form of optimality conditions.

We conclude with a number of observations and GAMS [9] codes for selected models.

5.4.1 *Market Clearing: Primal Problem, Dual Problem, and Optimality Conditions*

We consider a power market including two producers with marginal costs \$2 and \$3 per energy unit, and capacities 10 and 10 power units, respectively, and two consumers with marginal utilities \$5 and \$4 per energy unit and maximum demands of 6 and 6 power units, respectively. For the sake of simplicity, no network constraints are considered. This power market is illustrated in Fig. 5.7.

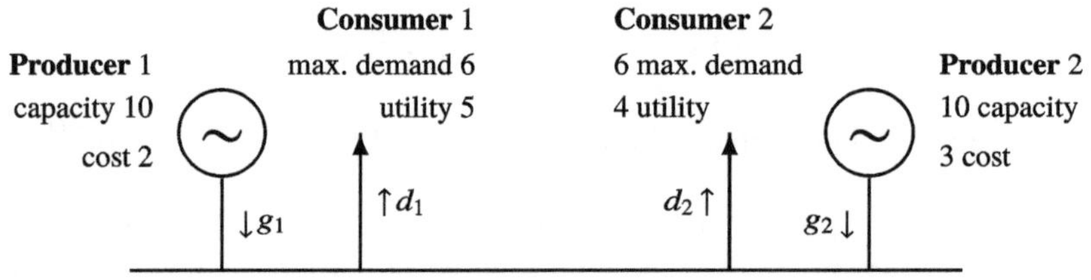

Fig. 5.7 Two-producer two-consumer market

The primal optimization problem [12] representing the clearing of the market [5] is formulated below. It is a linear programming problem easy to solve.

$$\min_{d_1,d_2,g_1,g_2 \geq 0} \quad z_p = -5\, d_1 - 4\, d_2 + 2\, g_1 + 3\, g_2 \tag{5.43a}$$

$$\text{s. t.} \quad g_1 + g_2 - d_1 - d_2 = 0 : \; p \tag{5.43b}$$

$$d_1 \leq 6 : \; \alpha_1 \tag{5.43c}$$

$$d_2 \leq 6 : \; \alpha_2 \tag{5.43d}$$

$$g_1 \leq 10 : \; \beta_1 \tag{5.43e}$$

$$g_2 \leq 10 : \; \beta_2 \tag{5.43f}$$

where the optimization variables are defined below:

d_1 and d_2 are the consumptions of consumers 1, and 2, respectively, and
g_1 and g_2 are the productions of producers 1, and 2, respectively.

Additionally,

z_p is the minus social welfare (objective function to be minimized),
p is the market-clearing price, which is the dual variable of the energy-balance constraint, and
α_1, α_2, β_1, and β_2 are other dual variables.

We minimize the "minus social welfare" instead of maximizing the social welfare to derive optimality conditions in their most common form (that corresponds to a minimization problem).

Objective function (5.43a), to be minimized, is the minus social welfare, constraint (5.43b) is the power-balance equation, constraints (5.43c) and (5.43d) are consumption bounds, and constraints (5.43e) and (5.43f) production bounds.

A GAMS [9] code for this problem and its solution, easily obtained by inspection, are provided in Sect. 5.7 of this chapter. The solution is

$$\begin{cases} d_1^* = 6, d_2^* = 6 \\ g_1^* = 10, g_2^* = 2 \\ p^* = 3 \\ \alpha_1^* = -2, \alpha_2^* = -1 \\ \beta_1^* = -1, \beta_2^* = 0 \\ z_p^* = -28 \end{cases}$$

Consumers 1 and 2 are fully supplied because their marginal utilities, \$5 and \$4 per energy unit, respectively, are higher that the marginal cost of the most expensive producer (\$3 per energy unit), thus, $d_1^* = 6$ and $d_2^* = 6$. The cheapest producer works at capacity, i.e., $g_1^* = 10$, and the other producer supplies the remaining demand ($12 - 10 = 2$), thus $g_2^* = 2$. This second producer is, thus, at margin and

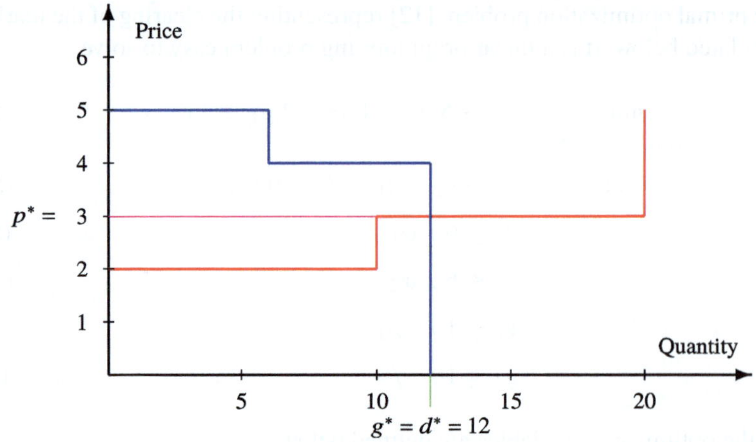

Fig. 5.8 Market clearing using a primal optimization problem

sets the clearing price (dual variable of the balance constraint) to its marginal cost, thus $p^* = 3$.

The dual variables corresponding to the maximum consumptions of consumers 1 and 2 are $\alpha_1^* = -2$ and $\alpha_2^* = -1$, respectively. This is consistent with the fact that both consumers consume at their maximum levels (binding constraints). The dual variables corresponding to the capacities of producers 1 and 2 are $\beta_1^* = -1$ and $\beta_2^* = 0$, respectively. This is consistent with the fact that producer 1 is working at capacity (binding constraint), while producer 2 is not (non-binding constraint). This solution is illustrated in Fig. 5.8.

Additionally, the profits of each of the two producers (revenue minus cost) and of each of the two consumers (utility minus payment) are $\begin{cases} \Pi_1^{\mathrm{C}} = (5-3)\cdot 6 = 12 \\ \Pi_2^{\mathrm{C}} = (4-3)\cdot 6 = 6 \\ \Pi_1^{\mathrm{P}} = (3-2)\cdot 10 = 10 \\ \Pi_2^{\mathrm{P}} = (3-3)\cdot 2 = 0, \end{cases}$

where Π_1^{C} and Π_1^{C} are the profits of consumers 1 and 2, respectively, and Π_1^{P} and Π_1^{P} are the profits of producers 1 and 2, respectively.

The dual optimization problem describing the clearing of the market (and corresponding to primal problem (5.43)) is formulated below. Regarding how to derive a dual problem from a primal one that is linear, the reader is referred to [12].

$$\max_{\substack{p\in\mathbb{R} \\ \alpha_1,\alpha_2,\beta_1,\beta_2\leq 0}} \quad z_d = 6\,\alpha_1 + 6\,\alpha_2 + 10\,\beta_1 + 10\,\beta_2 \tag{5.44a}$$

$$\text{s. t.} \quad -p + \alpha_1 \leq -5 : \; d_1 \tag{5.44b}$$

$$-p + \alpha_2 \leq -4 : \; d_2 \tag{5.44c}$$

$$p + \beta_1 \leq 2 : \; g_1 \tag{5.44d}$$

$$p + \beta_2 \leq 3 : \; g_2 \tag{5.44e}$$

A GAMS [9] code for this linear problem (the dual problem of a linear primal problem is linear) and its output are provided in Sect. 5.7 of this chapter. The solution is

$$\begin{cases} p^* = 3 \\ \alpha_1^* = -2, \alpha_2^* = -1 \\ \beta_1^* = -1, \beta_2^* = 0 \\ d_1^* = 6, d_2^* = 6 \\ g_1^* = 10, g_2^* = 2 \\ z_d^* = -28 \end{cases}$$

We observe that the primal and the dual solutions are identical. Considering the primal problem (5.43) and the dual one (5.44), the optimality-condition optimization problem corresponding to the clearing of the market is:

$$\max_{\substack{d_1, d_2, g_1, g_2 \geq 0 \\ p \in \mathbb{R} \\ \alpha_1, \alpha_2, \beta_1, \beta_2 \leq 0}} \quad z_o = 1 \tag{5.45a}$$

$$\text{s. t.} \quad g_1 + g_2 - d_1 - d_2 = 0 \tag{5.45b}$$

$$d_1 \leq 6 \tag{5.45c}$$

$$d_2 \leq 6 \tag{5.45d}$$

$$g_1 \leq 10 \tag{5.45e}$$

$$g_2 \leq 10 \tag{5.45f}$$

$$-\, p + \alpha_1 \leq -5 \tag{5.45g}$$

$$-\, p + \alpha_2 \leq -4 \tag{5.45h}$$

$$p + \beta_1 \leq 2 \tag{5.45i}$$

$$p + \beta_2 \leq 3 \tag{5.45j}$$

$$-\, 5\, d_1 - 4\, d_2 + 2\, g_1 + 3\, g_2 = 6\, \alpha_1 + 6\, \alpha_2 + 10\, \beta_1 + 10\, \beta_2 \tag{5.45k}$$

The objective function (5.45a) is arbitrarily fixed to 1 (this value is immaterial since we seek to identify a solution that just complies with the optimality conditions). Constraints (5.45b)–(5.45f) are the primal constraints (see problem (5.43)), constraints (5.45g)–(5.45j) are the dual constraints (see problem (5.44)), and constraint (5.45k) is the strong-duality equality. The strong-duality equality states that for the optimal solutions of the primal and dual problems, the objective function values of these two problems are equal [12].

A GAMS [9] code for this problem and its output are provided in Sect. 5.7 of this chapter. The solution is

$$\begin{cases} d_1^* = 6, d_2^* = 6 \\ g_1^* = 10, g_2^* = 2 \\ p^* = 3 \\ \alpha_1^* = -2, \alpha_2^* = -1 \\ \beta_1^* = -1, \beta_2^* = 0 \end{cases}$$

We observe that the primal, the dual, and the optimality-condition solutions are identical. Problem (5.45) is used by strategic producers/consumers to exercise market power, as explained below.

5.4.2 Producer 1 Exercising Market Power

Producer 1 changes optimally its offer price o_1 (to a value equal to or higher than its marginal cost of \$2 per energy unit) with the purpose of maximizing its own profit [6–8, 11]. It seeks do so by altering the clearing of the market (via changing o_1) and, particularly, by raising the market-clearing price p and by altering its own cleared production g_1. To this purpose, producer 1 solves the non-linear optimization problem below:

$$\max_{\substack{o_1 \geq 2 \\ d_1, d_2, g_1, g_2 \geq 0 \\ p \in \mathbb{R} \\ \alpha_1, \alpha_2, \beta_1, \beta_2 \leq 0}} \quad z = (p - 2) \cdot g_1 \tag{5.46a}$$

$$\text{s. t.} \quad g_1 + g_2 - d_1 - d_2 = 0 \tag{5.46b}$$

$$d_1 \leq 6 \tag{5.46c}$$

$$d_2 \leq 6 \tag{5.46d}$$

$$g_1 \leq 10 \tag{5.46e}$$

$$g_2 \leq 10 \tag{5.46f}$$

$$-p + \alpha_1 \leq -5 \tag{5.46g}$$

$$-p + \alpha_2 \leq -4 \tag{5.46h}$$

$$p + \beta_1 \leq o_1 \tag{5.46i}$$

Table 5.2 Market power: market outcomes I

	Competitive	Prod. 1 leads
		$o_1 = 2.45$
d_1	6	6
d_2	6	6
g_1	10	10
g_2	2	2
p	3	3
Π_1^C	12	12
Π_2^C	6	6
Π_1^P	10	10
Π_2^P	0	0
SW	28	28

$$p + \beta_2 \leq 3 \tag{5.46j}$$

$$-5\,d_1 - 4\,d_2 + o_1 \cdot g_1 + 3\,g_2 = 6\,\alpha_1 + 6\,\alpha_2 + 10\,\beta_1 + 10\,\beta_2 \tag{5.46k}$$

where o_1 is the decision variable used by producer 1 to exercise market power. The objective function (5.46a) is the profit of producer 1, and constraints (5.46b)–(5.46k) are the optimality conditions for the clearing of the market (see problem (5.45)).

Problem (5.46) is a mathematical program with equilibrium constraints (MPEC) [8], since it is an optimization problem that is subject to optimality conditions representing the clearing of the market, which are "equilibrium" constraints.

A GAMS [9] code for this non-linear optimization problem and its output are provided in Sect. 5.7 of this chapter. The solution to problem (5.46) is provided in Table 5.2, column "Prod. 1 leads." This table also provides the market-clearing solution if producers/consumers offer/bid at marginal cost/utility (Problem (5.43)), i.e., if they act competitively, column "Competitive."

From Table 5.2, we conclude that producer 1 has no incentive to offer a price higher than \$3 per energy unit (the competitive market-clearing price). Since the clearing price is set by the competitive offer of producer 2 (\$3 per energy unit), producer 1 may offer any price between \$2 and just below \$3 per energy unit (the optimization solver arbitrarily selects $o_1 = 2.45$). If, on the other hand, producer 1 offers above \$3 per energy unit, then its profit decreases (with respect to that corresponding to the case of offering between \$2 and just below \$3 per energy unit) and is, therefore, not willing to do so. We conclude that producer 1 has no market power. This is illustrated in Fig. 5.9.

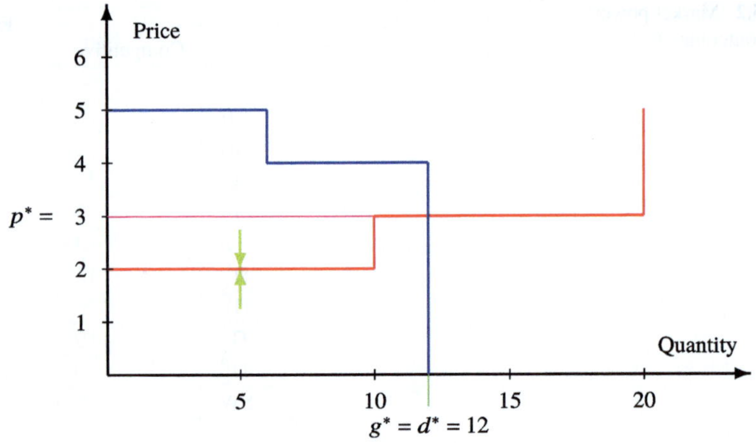

Fig. 5.9 Producer 1 exercising its market power

5.4.3 Producer 2 Exercising Market Power

Producer 2 changes optimally its offer price o_2 (to a value equal to or higher than its marginal cost \$3 per energy unit) with the purpose of increasing its own profit. To this end, producer 2 solves the non-linear optimization problem below:

$$\max_{\substack{o_2 \geq 3 \\ d_1, d_2, g_1, g_2 \geq 0 \\ p \in \mathbb{R} \\ \alpha_1, \alpha_2, \beta_1, \beta_2 \leq 0}} \quad z = (p - 3) \cdot g_2 \tag{5.47a}$$

$$\text{s. t.} \quad g_1 + g_2 - d_1 - d_2 = 0 \tag{5.47b}$$

$$d_1 \leq 6 \tag{5.47c}$$

$$d_2 \leq 6 \tag{5.47d}$$

$$g_1 \leq 10 \tag{5.47e}$$

$$g_2 \leq 10 \tag{5.47f}$$

$$-p + \alpha_1 \leq -5 \tag{5.47g}$$

$$-p + \alpha_2 \leq -4 \tag{5.47h}$$

$$p + \beta_1 \leq 2 \tag{5.47i}$$

$$p + \beta_2 \leq o_2 \tag{5.47j}$$

$$-5\, d_1 - 4\, d_2 + 2\, g_1 + o_2 \cdot g_2 = 6\, \alpha_1 + 6\, \alpha_2 + 10\, \beta_1 + 10\, \beta_2 \tag{5.47k}$$

Table 5.3 Market power: market outcomes II

	Competitive	Prod. 1 leads	Prod. 2 leads
		$o_1 = 2.45$	$o_2 = 4$
d_1	6	6	6
d_2	6	6	6
g_1	10	10	10
g_2	2	2	2
p	3	3	4
Π_1^C	12	12	6
Π_2^C	6	6	0
Π_1^P	10	10	20
Π_2^P	0	0	2
SW	28	28	28

where o_2 is the decision variable used by producer 2 to exercise market power. The objective function (5.47a) is the profit of producer 2, and constraints (5.47b)–(5.47k) are the optimality conditions for the clearing of the market (see problem (5.45)).

The solution to problem (5.46) is provided in Table 5.3, column "Prod. 2 leads." This table provides as well the market-clearing solution if producers/consumers offer/bid at marginal cost/utility (Problem (5.43)), column "Competitive," and the solution if only producer 1 exercises market power, column "Prod. 1 leads."

From Table 5.3, we conclude that producer 2 exercises its market power and is able to raise its profit from \$0 to \$2. Producer 1, doing nothing, dramatically benefits from the action of producer 2 since its profit increases from \$10 to \$20. That is, by exercising market power, producer 2 benefits producer 1 to a higher degree (from \$10 to \$20) that it benefits itself (from \$0 to \$2). This is not rare in practice and may induce producers 1 and 2 to collude. We conclude that producer 2 has market power and exercises it. This is illustrated in Fig. 5.10.

5.4.4 Consumer 1 Exercising Market Power

Consumer 1 changes optimally its bid price u_1 (to a non-negative value lower than its marginal utility of \$5 per energy unit) with the purpose of increasing its own profit. To this end, consumer 1 solves the non-linear optimization problem below:

$$\max_{\substack{0\leq u_1\leq 5\\ d_1,d_2,g_1,g_2\geq 0\\ p\in\mathbb{R}\\ \alpha_1,\alpha_2,\beta_1,\beta_2\leq 0}} \quad z = (5-p)\cdot d_1 \tag{5.48a}$$

$$\text{s. t.} \quad g_1 + g_2 - d_1 - d_2 = 0 \tag{5.48b}$$

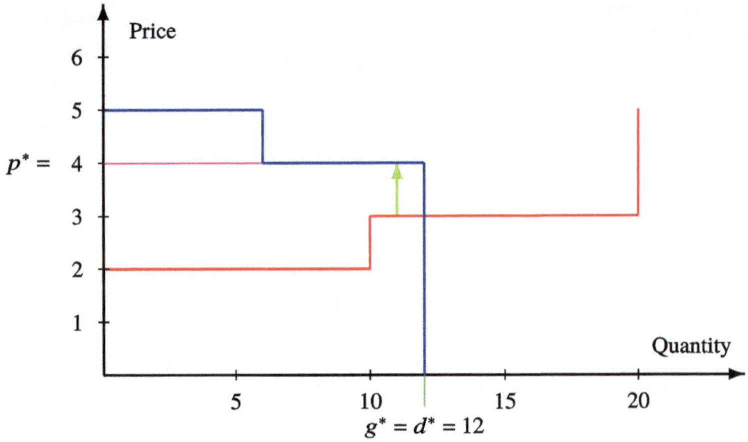

Fig. 5.10 Producer 2 exercising its market power

$$d_1 \leq 6 \tag{5.48c}$$

$$d_2 \leq 6 \tag{5.48d}$$

$$g_1 \leq 10 \tag{5.48e}$$

$$g_2 \leq 10 \tag{5.48f}$$

$$-p + \alpha_1 \leq -u_1 \tag{5.48g}$$

$$-p + \alpha_2 \leq -4 \tag{5.48h}$$

$$p + \beta_1 \leq 2 \tag{5.48i}$$

$$p + \beta_2 \leq 3 \tag{5.48j}$$

$$-u_1 \cdot d_1 - 4\,d_2 + 2\,g_1 + 3\,g_2 = 6\,\alpha_1 + 6\,\alpha_2 + 10\,\beta_1 + 10\,\beta_2 \tag{5.48k}$$

where u_1 is the decision variable used by consumer 1 to exercise market power. The objective function (5.48a) is the profit of consumer 1, and constraints (5.48b)–(5.48k) are the optimality conditions for the clearing of the market (see problem (5.45)).

The solution to problem (5.48) is provided in Table 5.4, column "Cons. 1 leads." This table provides as well the market-clearing solution if producers/consumers offer/bid at marginal cost/utility (problem (5.43)), column "Competitive," the solution if only producer 1 exercises market power, column "Prod. 1 leads," and the solution if only producer 2 exercises market power, column "Prod. 2 leads."

A GAMS [9] code for problem (5.48) and its output are provided in Sect. 5.7 of this chapter.

Table 5.4 Market power: market outcomes III

	Competitive	Prod. 1 leads	Prod. 2 leads	Cons. 1 leads
		$o_1 = 2.45$	$o_2 = 4$	$u_1 = 2$
d_1	6	6	6	4
d_2	6	6	6	6
g_1	10	10	10	10
g_2	2	2	2	0
p	3	3	4	2
Π_1^C	12	12	6	12
Π_2^C	6	6	0	12
Π_1^P	10	10	20	0
Π_2^P	0	0	2	0
SW	28	28	28	24

From Table 5.4, we conclude that consumer 1 exercises its market power and is able to decrease the market-clearing price from \$3 to \$2 per energy unit. This does not change the profit of consumer 1 (with respect to its competitive profit), but increases the profit of consumer 2 from \$6 to \$12. This is so because the decrease in price is compensated by a decrease in consumption (by consumer 1). That is, by exercising market power, consumer 1 does not benefit itself but greatly benefits consumer 2. We conclude that consumer 1 has market power and exercises it, not to its own benefit but to that of its rival consumer (consumer 2). This is illustrated in Fig. 5.11.

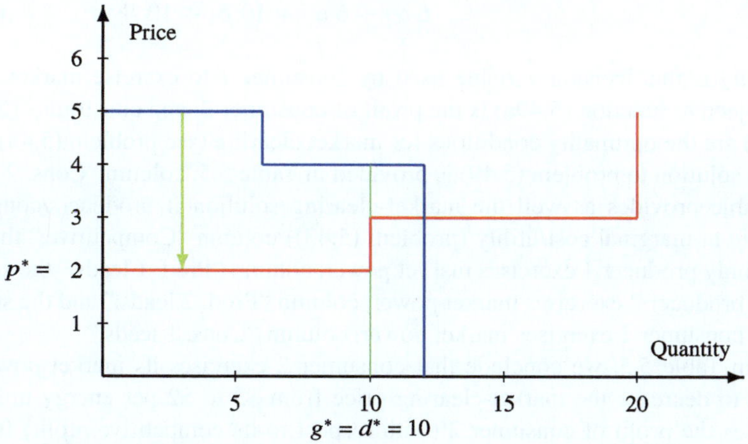

Fig. 5.11 Consumer 1 exercising its market power

5.4.5 Consumer 2 Exercising Market Power

Consumer 2 changes optimally its bid price u_2 (to a non-negative value lower than its marginal utility of \$4 per energy unit) with the purpose of increasing its own profit. To this end, consumer 2 solves the non-linear optimization problem below:

$$\max_{\substack{0\le u_2\le 4\\ d_1,d_2,g_1,g_2\ge 0\\ p\in\mathbb{R}\\ \alpha_1,\alpha_2,\beta_1,\beta_2\le 0}} \quad z = (4-p)\cdot d_2 \tag{5.49a}$$

$$\text{s. t.} \quad g_1 + g_2 - d_1 - d_2 = 0 \tag{5.49b}$$

$$d_1 \le 6 \tag{5.49c}$$

$$d_2 \le 6 \tag{5.49d}$$

$$g_1 \le 10 \tag{5.49e}$$

$$g_2 \le 10 \tag{5.49f}$$

$$-p + \alpha_1 \le -5 \tag{5.49g}$$

$$-p + \alpha_2 \le -u_2 \tag{5.49h}$$

$$p + \beta_1 \le 2 \tag{5.49i}$$

$$p + \beta_2 \le 3 \tag{5.49j}$$

$$-5\,d_1 - u_2\cdot d_2 + 2\,g_1 + 3\,g_2 = 6\,\alpha_1 + 6\,\alpha_2 + 10\,\beta_1 + 10\,\beta_2 \tag{5.49k}$$

where u_2 is the decision variable used by consumer 2 to exercise market power. The objective function (5.49a) is the profit of consumer 2, and constraints (5.49b)–(5.49k) are the optimality conditions for market clearing (see problem (5.45)).

The solution to problem (5.49) is provided in Table 5.5, column "Cons. 2 leads." This table provides as well the market-clearing solution if producers/consumers offer/bid at marginal cost/utility (problem (5.43)) column "Competitive," the solution if only producer 1 exercises market power, column "Prod. 1 leads," the solution if only producer 2 exercises market power, column "Prod. 2 leads," and the solution if only consumer 1 exercises market power, column "Cons. 1 leads."

From Table 5.5, we conclude that consumer 2 exercises its market power and is able to decrease the market-clearing price from \$3 to \$2 per energy unit. This increases the profit of consumer 2 (with respect to its competitive profit) from \$6 to \$8, increasing along the way the profit of consumer 1 from \$12 to \$18. That is, by exercising market power, consumer 2 benefits itself, but benefits consumer 2 to a greater degree. We conclude that consumer 2 has market power and exercises

Table 5.5 Market power: market outcomes IV

	Competitive	Prod. 1 leads	Prod. 2 leads	Cons. 1 leads	Cons. 2 leads
		$o_1 = 2.45$	$o_2 = 4$	$u_1 = 2$	$u_2 = 2$
d_1	6	6	6	4	6
d_2	6	6	6	6	4
g_1	10	10	10	10	10
g_2	2	2	2	0	0
p	3	3	4	2	2
Π_1^C	12	12	6	12	18
Π_2^C	6	6	0	12	8
Π_1^P	10	10	20	0	0
Π_2^P	0	0	2	0	0
SW	28	28	28	24	26

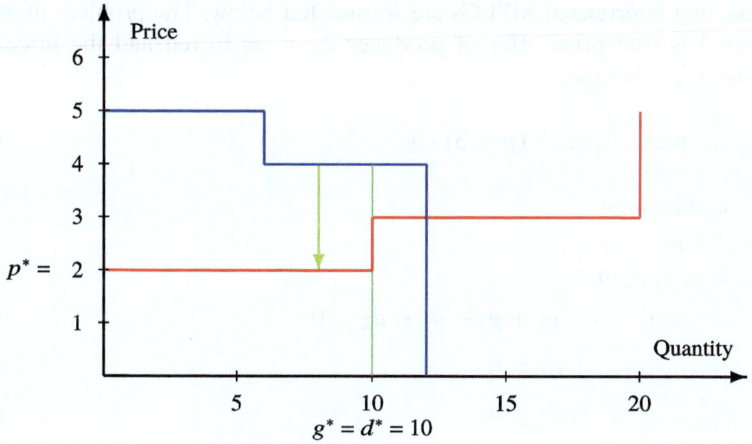

Fig. 5.12 Consumer 2 exercising its market power

it, to its own benefit and to that of its rival consumer (to a greater extent). This is illustrated in Fig. 5.12.

5.4.6 Multiple Agents Exercising Market Power

For the sake of simplicity, we consider that solely producer 2 and consumer 1 are strategic, i.e., they are willing to exercise market power. Therefore, each one of them tries individually to alter the clearing of the market to its own benefit. Producer 2 is willing to raise its offer price above its marginal cost of \$3 per energy unit, but not to decrease it. Similarly, consumer 1 is willing to decrease its non-negative bid price below its marginal utility of \$5 per energy unit.

On the other hand, producer 1 and consumer 2 are not strategic. Producer 1 offers at its marginal cost of \$2 per energy unit in all circumstances, and, similarly, consumer 2 bids at its marginal utility of \$4 per energy unit in all circumstances.

Considering all the assumptions above, we need to jointly solve the profit-maximization problems of producer 2 and consumer 1.

We note that the profit-maximization problem of strategic producer 2 depends on the strategic bid u_1 of strategic consumer 1, and, conversely, the profit-maximization problem of strategic consumer 1 depends on the strategic offer o_2 of strategic producer 2. Therefore, these problems are interrelated, have to be solved simultaneously, and constitute an equilibrium problem [8]. This equilibrium problem is in fact an equilibrium program with equilibrium constraints (EPEC) [8]. This is so because both the problem of strategic producer 2 and that of strategic consumer 1 are MPECs.

These two interrelated MPECs are formulated below. The problem of strategic producer 2 is (the price offer of producer 2, o_2, is in red and the price bid of consumer 1, u_1, in blue):

$$\max_{\substack{o_2 \geq 3 \\ d_1, d_2, g_1, g_2 \geq 0 \\ p \in \mathbb{R} \\ \alpha_1, \alpha_2, \beta_1, \beta_2 \leq 0}} \quad z = (p - 3) \cdot g_2 \tag{5.50a}$$

$$\text{s. t.} \quad g_1 + g_2 - d_1 - d_2 = 0 \tag{5.50b}$$

$$d_1 \leq 6 \tag{5.50c}$$

$$d_2 \leq 6 \tag{5.50d}$$

$$g_1 \leq 10 \tag{5.50e}$$

$$g_2 \leq 10 \tag{5.50f}$$

$$-p + \alpha_1 \leq -u_1 \tag{5.50g}$$

$$-p + \alpha_2 \leq -4 \tag{5.50h}$$

$$p + \beta_1 \leq 2 \tag{5.50i}$$

$$p + \beta_2 \leq o_2 \tag{5.50j}$$

$$-u_1 \cdot d_1 - 4\, d_2 + 2\, g_1 + o_2 \cdot g_2 = 6\, \alpha_1 + 6\, \alpha_2 + 10\, \beta_1 + 10\, \beta_2 \tag{5.50k}$$

The problem of strategic consumer 1 is (the price bid of consumer 1, u_1, is in red and the price offer of producer 2, o_2, in blue):

$$\max_{\substack{0 \le u_1 \le 5 \\ d_1, d_2, g_1, g_2 \ge 0 \\ p \in \mathbb{R} \\ \alpha_1, \alpha_2, \beta_1, \beta_2 \le 0}} \quad z = (5 - p) \cdot d_1 \tag{5.51a}$$

$$\text{s. t.} \quad g_1 + g_2 - d_1 - d_2 = 0 \tag{5.51b}$$

$$d_1 \le 6 \tag{5.51c}$$

$$d_2 \le 6 \tag{5.51d}$$

$$g_1 \le 10 \tag{5.51e}$$

$$g_2 \le 10 \tag{5.51f}$$

$$-p + \alpha_1 \le -u_1 \tag{5.51g}$$

$$-p + \alpha_2 \le -4 \tag{5.51h}$$

$$p + \beta_1 \le 2 \tag{5.51i}$$

$$p + \beta_2 \le o_2 \tag{5.51j}$$

$$-u_1 \cdot d_1 - 4\, d_2 + 2\, g_1 + o_2 \cdot g_2 = 6\, \alpha_1 + 6\, \alpha_2 + 10\, \beta_1 + 10\, \beta_2 \tag{5.51k}$$

We jointly solve problems (5.50) and (5.51) using the *diagonalization* algorithm [8] described below:

0. Initialization: We initialize the strategic offer price of producer 2, o_2, to an initial value, and solve MPEC (5.51) of strategic consumer 1 to obtain its strategic bid price u_1 (row 0 of Table 5.6).

Table 5.6 Equilibrium: diagonalization

Iteration #	Problem of strategic	Cons. 1 profit ($)	Cons. 2 profit ($)	Prod. 1 profit ($)	Prod. 2 profit ($)	Optimal bid or offer
0	Consumer 1 with $o_2 = 4$ (solving MPEC (5.51))	12	12	0	0	$u_1 = 2$
1	Producer 2 with $u_1 = 2$ (solving MPEC (5.50))	12	12	0	0	$o_2 = 3$
2	Consumer 1 with $o_2 = 3$ (solving MPEC (5.51))	12	12	0	0	$u_1 = 2$
3	Producer 2 with $u_1 = 2$ (solving MPEC (5.50))	12	12	0	0	$o_2 = 3$

1. Strategic producer problem: We fix the strategic bid price of consumer 1, u_1, to the previously obtained value, and solve MPEC (5.50) of strategic producer 2 to obtain its strategic offer price o_2.
2. Strategic consumer problem: We fix the strategic offer price of producer 2, o_2, to the previously obtained value, and solve MPEC (5.51) of strategic consumer 1 to obtain its strategic bid price u_1.
3. Convergence: Steps 1 and 2 are repeated until the values of u_1 and o_2 stabilize, i.e., until convergence is attained (rows 2 and 3 of Table 5.6).

The diagonalization algorithm above may have started as well with an initial strategic offer price of consumer 1, u_1, and the subsequent solution of MPEC (5.50) of producer 2.

The solution obtained using the diagonalization algorithm is provided in Table 5.6. After 3 iterations, the stationary bid price of consumer 1 is $u_1 = 2$ and the stationary offer price of producer 2 is $o_2 = 3$.

Regarding numerical simulations, to ensure that the bid of strategic consumer 1 ($u_1 = 2$) is accepted, we may wish to perturb the marginal offer of competitive producer 1 to $2 - \epsilon$, slightly below its marginal cost of 2. This is illustrated in Fig. 5.12.

We note that EPECs can be solved with algorithms other than the diagonalization one described above. The reader is referred to [8] and [11] for further details.

Next, we further verify that the stationary point found ($u_1 = 2$ and $o_2 = 3$) is indeed a Nash equilibrium via perturbation analysis. The perturbation checking below is just a local heuristic, which verifies a Nash equilibrium only locally.

Regarding the offer price of consumer 1, feasible perturbations are possible in both directions, increasing and decreasing. Regarding the bid price of producer 2, the only feasible perturbation is in the increasing direction since producer 2 does not offer below its marginal production cost. On the other hand, since consumer 2 is not strategic and always bids at its marginal utility ($4 per energy unit), no perturbation is feasible. Likewise, since producer 1 is not strategic and always offers at its marginal cost ($2 per energy unit), no perturbation is feasible. The perturbation considered is $\epsilon = 0.001$.

To carry out this verification, we perturb the stationary offer price of producer 2, $o_2 = 3$ (one direction) and solve market-clearing problem (5.43). Next we perturb the stationary bid price of consumer 1, $u_1 = 2$ (two directions) and solve twice market-clearing problem (5.43).

Table 5.7 illustrates the perturbation analysis that verifies that the stationary point found is, indeed, a Nash equilibrium. Rows 1, 2, 3 and 4 correspond to consumer 1, consumer 2, producer 1 and producer 2, respectively. The columns provides profits (of consumer 1, consumer 2, producer 1 and producer 2) for four cases (1) no perturbation, (2) positive perturbation in the offer of producer 2, (3) positive perturbation in the bid of consumer 1, and (4) negative perturbation in the bid of consumer 1.

We observe that consumer 1 is unable to improve its profit by unilateral positive/negative feasible perturbations (row "Consumer 1" of Table 5.7) with

Table 5.7 Equilibrium: verification

	Profit ($)			
	No perturbation	$o_2 + \epsilon$	$u_1 + \epsilon$	$u_1 - \epsilon$
	–	3.001	2.001	1.999
Consumer 1	12	12	11.996	0
Consumer 2	12	12	11.994	12
Producer 1	0	0	0.010	0
Producer 2	0	0	0	0

Table 5.8 Perturbations: market outcomes

	Perturbation			
	No perturbation	$o_2 + \epsilon$	$u_1 + \epsilon$	$u_1 - \epsilon$
	–	3.001	2.001	1.999
Price ($/energy unit)	2	2	2.001	2
Consumption 1 (energy units)	4	4	4	0
Consumption 2 (energy units)	6	6	6	6
Production 1 (energy units)	10	10	10	6
Production 2 (energy units)	0	0	0	0
Profit consumer 1 ($)	12	12	11.994	0
Profit consumer 2 ($)	12	12	11.994	12
Profit producer 1 ($)	0	0	0.010	0
Profit producer 2 ($)	0	0	0	0

respect to the case "No perturbation" (first numerical column). Likewise, producer 2 is unable to improve its profits by an unilateral positive feasible perturbation (row "Producer 2" of Table 5.7) with respect to the case "No perturbation" (first numerical column). We verify that $u_1 = 2$ and $o_2 = 3$ constitute a Nash equilibrium.

Regarding Table 5.7, we note that a consumption bid with identical price than a production offer is supplied in its entirety, provided that enough supply capacity is available. This is so regardless of the fact that the *declared* social welfare (as seen by the market operator) does not change if the consumption bid is either supplied in its entirety or not supplied at all.

Table 5.8 complements Table 5.7 providing additional market outcomes (the results of market-clearing problem (5.43)).

5.5 Summary

In this chapter, we have discussed the issues of market power:

1. A monopolist raises its price above the marginal cost of production, resulting in a loss of social surplus.

2. The Lerner index measures the degree of market power. The less elastic the market demand, the greater the Lerner index and, hence, market power.
3. A monopsonist lowers its price below the marginal benefit of consumption, resulting in a loss of social surplus.
4. In a Cournot oligopoly model with simultaneous decision makers, producers exert market power to strategically withdraw their outputs and raise the market price.
5. The Herfindahl-Hirschman index (HHI) measures the degree of market concentration. The degree of market power in a Cournot oligopoly is captured by the HHI. The higher the HHI, the greater the market power under Cournot oligopoly.
6. In a Stackelberg oligopoly model with sequential decision makers, the leader producer has the first-mover advantage, gaining more profits than the follower producers.

From the analysis of the multiple-leader case, the observations below are in order:

1. Producers/consumers typically intend to exercise market power by modifying their respective offer/bid prices.
2. By exercising market power, a producer/consumer may benefit its competitors (producers/consumers) to a larger extent than it benefits itself.
3. If several producers/consumers exercise market power, then the resulting equilibrium solution (provided that it exists) may benefit all of them, some of them, or none of them.
4. Operators/regulators are advised to implement market-surveillance procedures to prevent producers/consumers to exercise their potential market power. Market-surveillance tools allow operators/regulators to monitor on an hourly basis the functioning of the market under surveillance and to check suspicious market outcomes that may indicate uncompetitive behavior by producers/consumers.

5.6 End-of-Chapter Exercises

5.1 Consider a monopoly with the cost function and the inverse-demand function, $C(q) = 5q$ and $P(q) = 53 - q$, respectively. Calculate the monopoly output, price, and profit. Calculate the deadweight loss. Derive the Lerner index and the price elasticity of demand. Then, confirm that expression (5.6) holds true.

5.2 Based on the analysis of Fig. 5.4, derive the profits of producers and the deadweight loss under monopoly, Cournot oligopoly, and perfect competition. Then, compare those results among three different market structures.

5.3 Consider a Cournot duopoly with two asymmetric producers 1 and 2. The non-identical cost functions are $C_1(x_1) = 4x_1$ and $C_2(x_2) = 20x_2$ for producers 1 and 2, respectively, while the inverse-demand function is $P(q) = 60 - q$ with $q = x_1 + x_2$. Calculate the Nash-Cournot equilibrium outputs and price. Calculate the Herfindahl-Hirschman index (HHI). Then, confirm that expression (5.35) holds true.

5.4 Calculate the HHI of the power sector in your country.

5.5 Using the same cost functions and the inverse-demand function in the end-of-chapter exercise 5.3, consider a Stackelberg duopoly with leader producer 1 and follower producer 2. Calculate the equilibrium outputs and price and compare them with the results of the Cournot duopoly in the end-of-chapter exercise 5.3. Also compare the profits of producers between the Stackelberg and Cournot duopoly.

5.6 Expand the example in Sect. 5.4.1 to include two nodes and one power line. Producer 1 and consumer 1 are located at node 1, while producer 2 and consumer 2 are located at node 2. Formulate the clearing of this market using (1) a primal optimization problem, (2) a dual optimization problem, and (3) a optimality-condition optimization problem.

5.7 Considering the market clearing in the End-of-Chapter Exercise 5.6 above and the profit-maximization problem of producer 2 in Sect. 5.4.3, analyze how different transmission limits alter the market power of producer 2.

5.8 Considering the market clearing in the End-of-Chapter Exercise 5.6 above and the profit-maximization problem of consumer 1 in Sect. 5.4.4, analyze how different transmission limits alter the market power of consumer 1.

5.9 Expand the EPEC in Sect. 5.4.6 to include the two producers and the two consumers as strategic agents.

5.7 GAMS Codes

GAMS [9] codes for selected examples are provided below.

A GAMS [9] input file to solve the market-clearing problem described in Sect. 5.43 is provided below:

```
variable zp;
positive variables d1,d2,p1,p2;
positive variables pp1,pp2,pd1,pd2;
parameters o1 /2/, o2 /3/, u1 /5/, u2 /4/;
parameters lp1 /10/, lp2 /10/, ld1 /6/, ld2 /6/;
equations of,be,bp1,bp2,bd1,bd2;
of..  zp =e= -u1*d1-u2*d2+o1*p1+o2*p2;
be..  p1+p2-d1-d2 =e= 0;
bp1.. p1 =l= lp1;
bp2.. p2 =l= lp2;
bd1.. d1 =l= ld1;
bd2.. d2 =l= ld2;
model mcalprimal /all/;
solve mcalprimal using lp minimizing zp;
pp1.l=(be.m-o1)*p1.l;
pp2.l=(be.m-o2)*p2.l;
pd1.l=(u1-be.m)*d1.l;
pd2.l=(u2-be.m)*d2.l;
```

```
display zp.l;
display d1.l,d2.l,p1.l,p2.l;
display be.m;
display bd1.m,bd2.m,bp1.m,bp2.m;
display pd1.l,pd2.l,pp1.l,pp2.l;
```

Note that this GAMS code reproduces almost verbatim the mathematical formulation of model (5.43).

The relevant part of the corresponding GAMS output file is:

```
----     19 VARIABLE zp.L                  =       -28.000

----     20 VARIABLE d1.L                  =         6.000
            VARIABLE d2.L                  =         6.000
            VARIABLE p1.L                  =        10.000
            VARIABLE p2.L                  =         2.000

----     21 EQUATION be.M                  =         3.000

----     22 EQUATION bd1.M                 =        -2.000
            EQUATION bd2.M                 =        -1.000
            EQUATION bp1.M                 =        -1.000
            EQUATION bp2.M                 =         0.000

----     23 VARIABLE pd1.L                 =        12.000
            VARIABLE pd2.L                 =         6.000
            VARIABLE pp1.L                 =        10.000
            VARIABLE pp2.L                 =         0.000
```

A GAMS [9] input file to solve the market-clearing problem formulated in Sect. 5.44 is provided below.

```
variable zd;
variable lambda;
negative variables alpha1,alpha2,beta1,beta2;
parameters o1 /2/, o2 /3/, u1 /5/, u2 /4/;
parameters lp1 /10/, lp2 /10/, ld1 /6/, ld2 /6/;
equations ofd,c1,c2,c3,c4;
ofd.. zd =e= ld1*alpha1+ld2*alpha2+lp1*beta1+lp2*beta2;
c1..  -lambda+alpha1 =l= -u1;
c2..  -lambda+alpha2 =l= -u2;
c3..   lambda+beta1  =l=  o1;
c4..   lambda+beta2  =l=  o2;
model mca1dual /all/;
solve mca1dual usin lp maximizing zd;
display zd.l;
display lambda.l,alpha1.l,alpha2.l,beta1.l,beta2.l;
display c1.m,c2.m,c3.m,c4.m;
```

The relevant part of the corresponding GAMS output file is:

```
----     14 VARIABLE zd.L                =     -28.000

----     15 VARIABLE lambda.L            =       3.000
            VARIABLE alpha1.L            =      -2.000
            VARIABLE alpha2.L            =      -1.000
            VARIABLE beta1.L             =      -1.000
            VARIABLE beta2.L             =       0.000

----     16 EQUATION c1.M                =       6.000
            EQUATION c2.M                =       6.000
            EQUATION c3.M                =      10.000
            EQUATION c4.M                =       2.000
```

A GAMS [9] input file to solve the market-clearing problem described in Sect. 5.45 is provided below:

```
parameters o1 /2/, o2 /3/, u1 /5/, u2 /4/;
parameters lp1 /10/, lp2 /10/, ld1 /6/, ld2 /6/;
variable zo;
positive variables d1,d2,p1,p2;
variable lambda;
negative variables alpha1,alpha2,beta1,beta2;
equations ofo,c1,c2,c3,c4;
ofo.. zo =e= 1;
c1..  -lambda+alpha1 =l= -u1;
c2..  -lambda+alpha2 =l= -u2;
c3..   lambda+beta1  =l=  o1;
c4..   lambda+beta2  =l=  o2;
equations be,bp1,bp2,bd1,bd2;
be..  p1+p2-d1-d2 =e= 0;
bp1.. p1 =l= lp1;
bp2.. p2 =l= lp2;
bd1.. d1 =l= ld1;
bd2.. d2 =l= ld2;
equation sde;
sde.. ld1*alpha1+ld2*alpha2+lp1*beta1+lp2*beta2
=e=
-u1*d1-u2*d2+o1*p1+o2*p2;
model mcaloc /all/;
solve mcaloc usin lp maximizing zo;
display d1.l,d2.l,p1.l,p2.l;
display lambda.l,alpha1.l,alpha2.l,beta1.l,beta2.l;
```

The relevant part of the corresponding GAMS output file is:

```
----     25 VARIABLE d1.L                =       6.000
            VARIABLE d2.L                =       6.000
            VARIABLE p1.L                =      10.000
            VARIABLE p2.L                =       2.000
```

```
----      26 VARIABLE lambda.L                =         3.000
             VARIABLE alpha1.L                =        -2.000
             VARIABLE alpha2.L                =        -1.000
             VARIABLE beta1.L                 =        -1.000
             VARIABLE beta2.L                 =         0.000
```

A GAMS [9] input file to solve the profit-maximization problem of producer 1 described in Sect. 5.4.2 is provided below:

```
option NLP = BARON;
parameters o2 /3/, u1 /5/, u2 /4/;
parameters lp1 /10/, lp2 /10/, ld1 /6/, ld2 /6/;
positive variable o1;
* true o1 is 2
o1.l=3;
variable zp1;
positive variables d1,d2,p1,p2;
p1.l=10;
p2.l=2;
d1.l=6;
d2.l=6;
variable lambda;
negative variables alpha1,alpha2,beta1,beta2;
variables pp1,pp2,pd1,pd2;
equations ofo,c1,c2,c3,c4;
ofo.. zp1 =e= (lambda-2)*p1;
c1..  -lambda+alpha1 =l= -u1;
c2..  -lambda+alpha2 =l= -u2;
c3..   lambda+beta1  =l=  o1;
c4..   lambda+beta2  =l=  o2;
equations be,bp1,bp2,bd1,bd2;
be..  p1+p2-d1-d2 =e= 0;
bp1.. p1 =l= lp1;
bp2.. p2 =l= lp2;
bd1.. d1 =l= ld1;
bd2.. d2 =l= ld2;
equation sde;
sde.. ld1*alpha1+ld2*alpha2+lp1*beta1+lp2*beta2
=e=
-u1*d1-u2*d2+o1*p1+o2*p2;
model p1leads /all/;
solve p1leads using nlp maximizing zp1;
pp1.l=(lambda.l- 2)*p1.l;
pp2.l=(lambda.l-o2)*p2.l;
pd1.l=(u1-lambda.l)*d1.l;
pd2.l=(u2-lambda.l)*d2.l;
display zp1.l;
display o1.l;
display d1.l,d2.l,p1.l,p2.l;
display lambda.l,alpha1.l,alpha2.l,beta1.l,beta2.l;
display pd1.l,pd2.l,pp1.l,pp2.l;
```

The relevant part of the corresponding GAMS output file is:

```
----      38 VARIABLE zp1.L                =        10.000

----      39 VARIABLE o1.L                 =         2.455

----      40 VARIABLE d1.L                 =         6.000
             VARIABLE d2.L                 =         6.000
             VARIABLE p1.L                 =        10.000
             VARIABLE p2.L                 =         2.000

----      41 VARIABLE lambda.L             =         3.000
             VARIABLE alpha1.L             =        -2.000
             VARIABLE alpha2.L             =        -1.000
             VARIABLE beta1.L              =        -0.545
             VARIABLE beta2.L              =         0.000

----      42 VARIABLE pd1.L                =        12.000
             VARIABLE pd2.L                =         6.000
             VARIABLE pp1.L                =        10.000
             VARIABLE pp2.L                =   1.33227E-14
```

A GAMS [9] input file to solve the profit-maximization problem of consumer 1 described in Sect. 5.4.5 is provided below:

```
option NLP = BARON;
parameters o1 /2/, o2 /3/, u2 /4/;
parameters lp1 /10/, lp2 /10/, ld1 /6/, ld2 /6/;
positive variable u1;
* true u1 is 5
u1.up=5;
u1.l=5;
variable zd1;
positive variables d1,d2,p1,p2;
p1.l=10;
p2.l=2;
d1.l=6;
d2.l=6;
variable lambda;
negative variables alpha1,alpha2,beta1,beta2;
variables pp1,pp2,pd1,pd2;
equations ofo,c1,c2,c3,c4;
ofo.. zd1 =e= (5-lambda)*d1;
c1.. -lambda+alpha1 =l= -u1;
c2..  -lambda+alpha2 =l= -u2;
c3..  lambda+beta1  =l=  o1;
c4..   lambda+beta2  =l=  o2;
equations be,bp1,bp2,bd1,bd2;
be..  p1+p2-d1-d2 =e= 0;
bp1.. p1 =l= lp1;
bp2.. p2 =l= lp2;
bd1.. d1 =l= ld1;
bd2.. d2 =l= ld2;
equation sde;
```

```
sde.. ld1*alpha1+ld2*alpha2+lp1*beta1+lp2*beta2
=e=
-u1*d1-u2*d2+o1*p1+o2*p2;
model p1leads /all/;
solve p1leads using nlp maximizing zd1;
pp1.l=(lambda.l-o1)*p1.l;
pp2.l=(lambda.l-o2)*p2.l;
pd1.l=( 5-lambda.l)*d1.l;
pd2.l=(u2-lambda.l)*d2.l;
display zd1.l;
display u1.l;
display d1.l,d2.l,p1.l,p2.l;
display lambda.l,alpha1.l,alpha2.l,beta1.l,beta2.l;
display pd1.l,pd2.l,pp1.l,pp2.l;
```

The relevant part of the corresponding GAMS output file is:

```
----      39 VARIABLE zd1.L                  =        12.000

----      40 VARIABLE u1.L                   =         2.000

----      41 VARIABLE d1.L                   =         4.000
             VARIABLE d2.L                   =         6.000
             VARIABLE p1.L                   =        10.000
             VARIABLE p2.L                   =         0.000

----      42 VARIABLE lambda.L               =         2.000
             VARIABLE alpha1.L               =         0.000
             VARIABLE alpha2.L               =        -2.000
             VARIABLE beta1.L                =         0.000
             VARIABLE beta2.L                =         0.000

----      43 VARIABLE pd1.L                  =        12.000
             VARIABLE pd2.L                  =        12.000
             VARIABLE pp1.L                  =         0.000
             VARIABLE pp2.L                  =         0.000
```

References

1. Belleflamme, P., Peitz, M.: Industrial Organization: Markets and Strategies. Cambridge University Press, Cambridge (2010)
2. Borenstein, S., Bushnell, J.B., Wolak, F.A.: Measuring market inefficiencies in California's restructured wholesale electricity market. Amer. Econ. Rev. **92**, 1376–1405 (2002)
3. Carlton, D.W., Perloff, J.M.: Modern Industrial Organization. Addison Wesley, New York (2000)
4. Chen, Y., Siddiqui, A.S., Tanaka, M.: Analysis of Environmental Policy in the Power Sector. Springer International Publishing, Switzerland (2020)
5. Conejo, A.J., Baringo, L.: Power System Operations. Springer, New York (2018)
6. Conejo, A.J., Chen, S., Constante, G.E,: Operations and long-term expansion planning of natural-gas and power systems: A market perspective. Proc. IEEE **108**, 1541–1557 (2020)

7. Conejo, A.J., Ruiz, C.: Complementarity, not optimization, is the language of markets. IEEE Open Access J. Power Energy. **7**, 344353 (2020)
8. Gabriel, S.A., Conejo, A.J., Fuller, J.D., Hobbs, B.F., Ruiz, C.: Complementarity Modeling in Energy Markets. Springer, New York (2013)
9. GAMS Development Corporation: GAMS–A User's Guide. http://www.gams.com (2021)
10. Nicholson, W., Snyder, C.: Microeconomic Theory: Basic Principles and Extensions. Cengage Learning, Boston (2016)
11. Ruiz, C., Conejo, A.J., Fuller, J.D., Gabriel, S.A., Hobbs, B.F.,: A tutorial review of complementarity models for decision-making in energy markets. EURO J. Decision Processes. **2**, 91–120 (2014)
12. Sioshansi, R., Conejo, A.J.: Optimization in Engineering. Models and Algorithms. Springer, New York (2017)
13. Tangerås, T.P., Mauritzen, J.: Real-time versus day-ahead market power in a hydro-based electricity market. J. Ind. Econ. **66**, 904–941 (2018)
14. Tirole, J.: The Theory of Industrial Organization. MIT Press, Boston (1988)
15. Wolfram, C.D.: Measuring duopoly power in the british electricity spot market. Amer. Econ. Rev. **89**, 805–826 (1999)

Chapter 6
Environmental Externalities

6.1 Introduction

A negative externality, a type of market failure, occurs if the actions of one agent adversely affect the activities of others in ways that are not reflected in market transactions [13, 18]. Environmental pollution from power plants is a typical example of a negative externality, in which power companies would not take account of the damage to others if no regulation is implemented. In other words, power companies would face only their private costs but not the social costs inclusive of those associated with pollution when making production decisions. The electricity sector accounts for 25% of all greenhouse gas (GHG) emissions, particularly 31% of carbon dioxide (CO_2) emissions, in the U.S. during 2019 [6].[1] The combustion of fossil fuels to generate electricity is also the major source of other local air pollutants such as sulfur dioxide (SO_2) and nitrogen oxides (NOx).

This chapter first discusses the basic concept of negative externalities, taking a stylized example of the impact from CO_2 emissions. We demonstrate a welfare-distorting effect of negative externalities. Next, two major economic instruments, environmental taxation and emission-permit schemes, are introduced to overcome such externalities. Another scheme called renewable portfolio standards (RPS) that sets a target for renewable energy generation is also examined instead of directly curbing CO_2 emissions. We then extend those stylized models to more detailed network-constrained models with externalities to incorporate more realistic spatial, technological, and temporal factors present in power systems. The models also consider market power of producers. GAMS codes for solving selected numerical examples of this chapter are presented in Sect. 6.7.

[1] Greenhouse gases include CO_2, methane (CH_4), nitrous oxide (N_2O), and fluorinated gases.

M. Tanaka et al., *Economics of Power Systems*, International Series
in Operations Research & Management Science 327,
https://doi.org/10.1007/978-3-030-92871-1_6

6.2 Negative Externalities

To understand the basic concept of negative externality, we examine a simple case, in which firm $i \in I$ (e.g., a power plant) emits CO_2 when producing its output, y_i. For the sake of simplicity, we here assume that one unit of output leads to one unit of CO_2, i.e., CO_2 emission rate, E_i, is equal to 1. Let $c_i(y_i)$, $b(y)$, and $p(y)$ denote the cost function of firm i, the gross benefit function of consumers, and the inverse-demand function, respectively, where $y = \sum_{i \in I} y_i$. Note that the marginal benefit function is equal to the inverse-demand function, i.e., $b'(y) = p(y)$, as discussed in Chap. 1. The production capacity constraint is omitted for simplicity in this chapter unless otherwise stated.

First, consider a welfare-maximization problem without incorporating the cost of damage from CO_2 emissions:

$$\underset{\mathbf{y} \geq \mathbf{0}}{\text{Maximize}}\ b(y) - \sum_{i \in I} c_i(y_i) \tag{6.1}$$

We call this situation a business-as-usual case, in which only the "private costs" of firms are considered. Corresponding interior solutions (i.e., neither zero nor maximum production), y_i^{BAU} and y^{BAU}, satisfy the following first-order condition with respect to firm i:

$$b'(y) = p(y) = c_i'(y_i) \tag{6.2}$$

This case is equivalent to perfect competition without any consideration for CO_2 emissions, equating prices to the individual private marginal costs, $c_i'(y_i)$.

Next, we introduce the damage cost function, sometimes called external cost function, $d(e)$, resulting from CO_2 emissions, where e represents the total CO_2 emissions, $e = \sum_{i \in I} E_i y_i$. Since we assume $E_i = 1$, $e = y$ in the current case. Let us assume a simple linear damage cost function, $d(e) = Ze = Zy$, where Z is a parameter for cost of damage. With this damage cost function, the welfare-maximization problem is now represented as follows:

$$\underset{\mathbf{y} \geq \mathbf{0}}{\text{Maximize}}\ b(y) - \sum_{i \in I} c_i(y_i) - Zy \tag{6.3}$$

The social welfare takes account of the "social costs" inclusive of the damage cost from CO_2 emissions. Assuming interior solutions (i.e., neither zero nor maximum production), the optimal outputs, y_i^* and y^*, satisfy the following first-order condition with respect to firm i:

$$b'(y) = p(y) = c_i'(y_i) + Z \tag{6.4}$$

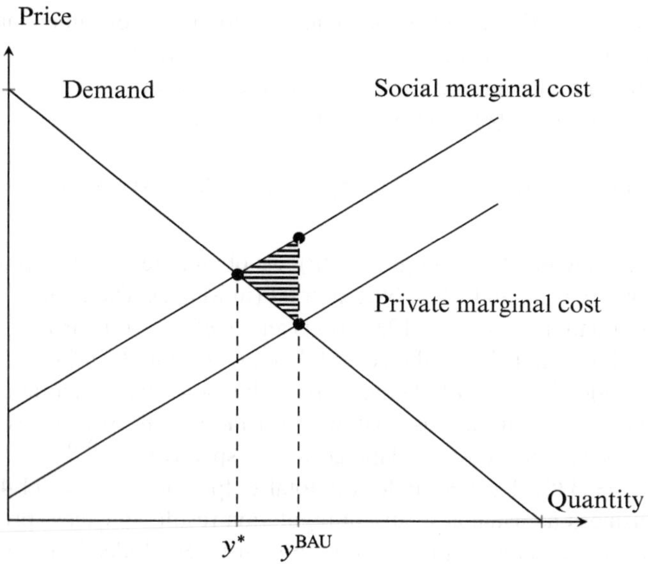

Fig. 6.1 Negative externalities

This is the socially optimal condition, taking into consideration the social marginal costs, $c_i'(y_i) + Z$.

As can be seen in conditions (6.2) and (6.4), the private marginal costs are less than the social marginal costs by Z, which leads to excess production and CO_2 emissions compared to the socially optimal levels. Figure 6.1 illustrates the socially optimal output, y^*, obtained at the intersection of the demand curve and the industry-wide social marginal cost curve. In contrast, the market equilibrium absent any environmental regulation is obtained at the intersection of the demand curve and the industry-wide private marginal cost curve, yielding the excess output, $y^{\text{BAU}} > y^*$. The social marginal cost exceeds the marginal benefit at y^{BAU}. Thus, if no environmental regulation is implemented, the market equilibrium, y^{BAU}, causes a loss of social welfare (a deadweight loss) depicted as the hatched area in Fig. 6.1 as a consequence of negative externalities.

Illustrative Example 6.1 *Central-planning outcome with externalities.*

As a benchmark, we consider a stylized example of a central planner that controls generation and consumption of electricity under externalities. In what follows, the cost and benefit are expressed in dollars ($). Two firms $i = 1, 2$ generate electrical energy with quadratic cost functions, $c_1(y_1) = 0.25y_1^2$ and $c_2(y_2) = y_2^2$, respectively. The total generation outputs are $y = \sum_{i \in \mathcal{I}} y_i$ (in MWh). The total CO_2 emissions are given by $e = \sum_{i \in \mathcal{I}} E_i y_i$ (in t, which means "tonne") with emission rates of $E_1 = 4$ and $E_2 = 2$ (in t/MWh). We assume a quadratic damage cost function, $d(e) = 0.5Ze^2$, with the parameter for the damage cost being $Z = 0.1$ (in

$/t^2$). The gross benefit and inverse-demand functions of consumers are expressed as $b(y) = 100y - 0.5y^2$ and $p(y) = 100 - y$, respectively.

Under central planning, the social welfare inclusive of the cost of damage, i.e., $b(y) - \sum_{i \in \mathcal{I}} c_i(y_i) - d(e)$, is maximized as follows:

$$\underset{y_1, y_2 \geq 0}{\text{Maximize}} \ 100y - 0.5y^2 - 0.25y_1^2 - y_2^2 - 0.05\,(4y_1 + 2y_2)^2 \tag{6.5}$$

Solving this simple quadratic program (QP), we obtain the socially optimal outputs, $y_1^* = 21.9$, $y_2^* = 17.8$, and $y^* = 39.7$ in total (in MWh). The total CO_2 emissions and the cost of damage are $e^* = 123.3$ (in t) and $d(e^*) = 760.0$ (in \$), respectively. The social welfare inclusive of the cost of damage is 1986.3 (in \$).

If we exclude the cost of damage from the objective function in (6.5), we obtain the business-as-usual case without considering the social costs. The total CO_2 emissions and the cost of damage are, respectively, $e^{\mathrm{BAU}} = 257.1$ (in t) and $d(e^{\mathrm{BAU}}) = 3306.1$ (in \$) under the total output of $y^{\mathrm{BAU}} = 71.4$ (in MWh). Thus, the business-as-usual case absent regulation results in excess production and CO_2 emissions compared to the socially optimal levels. Indeed, the social welfare inclusive of the cost of damage is 265.3 (in \$), which is lower than that under central planning.

6.3 Market-Based Mechanisms for Pollution Control

As alluded to in the previous section, markets without any regulatory intervention would fail under externalities. This section discusses market-based instruments for managing externalities. Section 6.3.1 focuses on the two major economic instruments, taxation and permit schemes, which could have the same effects in equilibrium. Then, Sect. 6.3.2 discusses a renewable portfolio standard policy that sets a target for renewable energy generation to mitigate the impact of negative externalities.

6.3.1 Taxation and Permit Schemes

Using the same setup as that in the previous section, we derive condition (6.2) again but from the firm's perspective. Price-taking firm i in a perfectly competitive market without environmental regulation maximizes its profit, taking the market price of the good, $\hat{p}$, as given:

$$\underset{y_i \geq 0}{\text{Maximize}} \ \hat{p} y_i - c_i(y_i) \tag{6.6}$$

Assuming an interior solution, the first-order condition for firm i is expressed as follows:

$$\hat{p} = c_i'(y_i) \tag{6.7}$$

Since $\hat{p} = b'(y) = p(y)$ holds in equilibrium as discussed in Chap. 1, we obtain condition (6.2). Again, this implies that each firm only faces individual private marginal cost if no regulation is in place, resulting in excess production, y_i^{BAU} and y^{BAU}.

An environmental tax, known as a Pigouvian tax, can be used to force the firms to internalize the cost of externality. Let R^{tax} denote a per unit tax on CO_2 emissions. Then, firm i needs to pay $R^{\text{tax}} E_i y_i = R^{\text{tax}} y_i$ with the assumption for emission rate, $E_i = 1$, as in the previous section. Firm i now maximizes its profit, taking the market price, $\hat{p}$, and the Pigouvian tax, R^{tax}, as given:

$$\underset{y_i \geq 0}{\text{Maximize}} \ \hat{p} y_i - c_i(y_i) - R^{\text{tax}} y_i \tag{6.8}$$

An interior solution yields the following first-order condition for firm i:

$$\hat{p} = c_i'(y_i) + R^{\text{tax}} \tag{6.9}$$

The level of a Pigouvian tax is determined by the marginal damage cost or the marginal external cost, $d'(e^*)$, which is evaluated at the socially optimal level of CO_2 emissions, $e^* = \sum_{i \in I} E_i y_i^* = y^*$. Since we assume a linear form of the damage cost function, $d(e) = Ze = Zy$, the optimal level of a Pigouvian tax is simply obtained as $R^{\text{tax}} = d'(e^*) = Z$. Consequently, firm i faces the social marginal costs, $c_i'(y_i) + Z$ under Pigouvian taxation as in condition (6.4), thereby leading to the optimal outputs, y_i^* and y^*.

Alternatively, a scheme of emission permits, also called a cap-and-trade (C&T) program, can be employed to attain the socially optimal outcome. Let ρ^{CT} denote a per unit price for CO_2 emission permits. Firm i has to purchase the emission permits for CO_2 emissions. Hence, each firm pays $\rho^{\text{CT}} E_i y_i = \rho^{\text{CT}} y_i$ under the assumption of $E_i = 1$. Firm i then maximizes its profit, taking as given the market prices of the good and permits, $\hat{p}$ and ρ^{CT}, respectively:

$$\underset{y_i \geq 0}{\text{Maximize}} \ \hat{p} y_i - c_i(y_i) - \rho^{\text{CT}} y_i \tag{6.10}$$

With the assumption of an interior solution, the first-order condition for firm i is written as

$$\hat{p} = c_i'(y_i) + \rho^{\text{CT}} \tag{6.11}$$

The environmental authority controls the total supply of permits denoted by S. If the authority decreases the amount of permits provided in the market, the permit price tends to rise because of increasing scarcity. Generally, the market-clearing condition for the emission permits can be expressed as a complementarity condition as follows [3]:

$$0 \leq \rho^{\mathrm{CT}} \perp S - \sum_{i \in I} y_i \geq 0 \tag{6.12}$$

where $\perp$ denotes complementarity, i.e., $0 \leq a \perp b \geq 0$ is equivalent to $a \geq 0$, $b \geq 0$, and $ab = 0$. In case there is an excess supply of permits, $S > \sum_{i \in I} y_i$, then the permit price, ρ^{CT}, will be zero. Otherwise, the emission-permit price will be positive. When the environmental authority sets the total supply of permits at the socially optimal level of CO_2 emissions, i.e., $S = e^*$, then, the permit price, ρ^{CT}, equals $d'(e^*) = Z$ in equilibrium. As a result, firm i faces the social marginal costs, $c_i'(y_i) + Z$ under the emission-permit scheme, thereby leading to the optimal outputs, y_i^* and y^*.

A policymaker can either utilize Pigouvian taxation or emission permits to achieve the socially optimal outcomes under externalities. We will illustrate this fact in stylized examples.

Illustrative Example 6.2 *Pigouvian taxation.*

We here use the same setup of Illustrative Example 6.1 and introduce a Pigouvian tax. Recall the quadratic damage cost function, $d(e) = 0.5Ze^2$. Then, the level of a Pigouvian tax is set by the marginal damage cost, $d'(e^*) = Ze^*$, evaluated at the socially optimal level of CO_2 emissions, e^*. From Illustrative Example 6.1, $e^* = 123.3$ (in t), and, hence, the environmental authority sets the Pigouvian tax, R^{tax}, at $d'(e^*) = 12.3$ (in \$/t).

In a deregulated electricity industry, price-taking firm i maximizes its profit, $\hat{p}y_i - c_i(y_i) - R^{\mathrm{tax}}E_i y_i$, taking the market price of electricity, $\hat{p}$, and the Pigouvian tax, R^{tax}, as given. The profit-maximization problems of firm 1 and firm 2 are, respectively, represented as follows:

$$\underset{y_1 \geq 0}{\text{Maximize}} \ \hat{p}y_1 - 0.25y_1^2 - 4R^{\mathrm{tax}}y_1 \tag{6.13a}$$

$$\underset{y_2 \geq 0}{\text{Maximize}} \ \hat{p}y_2 - y_2^2 - 2R^{\mathrm{tax}}y_2 \tag{6.13b}$$

where we use $R^{\mathrm{tax}} = 12.3288$ (in \$/t) with four decimal places for calculation. Noting that $\hat{p} = b'(y) = p(y)$ holds in equilibrium, the Karush–Kuhn–Tucker (KKT) conditions are written as follows:

$$0 \leq y_1 \perp 100 - (y_1 + y_2) - 0.5y_1 - 4R^{\mathrm{tax}} \leq 0 \tag{6.14a}$$

$$0 \leq y_2 \perp 100 - (y_1 + y_2) - 2y_2 - 2R^{\mathrm{tax}} \leq 0 \tag{6.14b}$$

Those conditions form a complementarity problem (CP), which can be solved by off-the-shelf solvers. Solving this CP yields the socially optimal outputs, $y_1^* = 21.9$, $y_2^* = 17.8$, and $y^* = 39.7$ in total (in MWh). The total CO_2 emissions and the cost of damage are $e^* = 123.3$ (in t) and $d(e^*) = 760.0$ (in \$), respectively. The social welfare inclusive of the cost of damage is 1986.3 (in \$), as in Illustrative Example 6.1. This example illustrates that Pigouvian taxation can attain the socially optimal outcomes under externalities in a deregulated electricity industry.

Illustrative Example 6.3 *Emission permits.*

We use the same setup as in Illustrative Example 6.1 and examine the emission permits system. The environmental authority determines the total supply of permits, S, at the socially optimal level of CO_2 emissions, $e^* = 123.3$ (in t). The market-clearing condition for the emission permits can be written as follows:

$$0 \leq \rho^{\text{CT}} \perp S - (4y_1 + 2y_2) \geq 0 \tag{6.15}$$

where we use $S = 123.2877$ (in t) with four decimal places.

Price-taking firm i maximizes its profit, $\hat{p}y_i - c_i(y_i) - \rho^{\text{CT}} E_i y_i$, taking the market price of electricity, $\hat{p}$, and the permit price, ρ^{CT}, as given. The profit-maximization problems of firm 1 and firm 2 are, respectively, expressed as follows:

$$\underset{y_1 \geq 0}{\text{Maximize}} \; \hat{p}y_1 - 0.25y_1^2 - 4\rho^{\text{CT}} y_1 \tag{6.16a}$$

$$\underset{y_2 \geq 0}{\text{Maximize}} \; \hat{p}y_2 - y_2^2 - 2\rho^{\text{CT}} y_2 \tag{6.16b}$$

Noting again that $\hat{p} = b'(y) = p(y)$ holds in equilibrium, the KKT conditions are derived as follows:

$$0 \leq y_1 \perp 100 - (y_1 + y_2) - 0.5y_1 - 4\rho^{\text{CT}} \leq 0 \tag{6.17a}$$

$$0 \leq y_2 \perp 100 - (y_1 + y_2) - 2y_2 - 2\rho^{\text{CT}} \leq 0 \tag{6.17b}$$

Conditions (6.15), (6.17a), and (6.17b) form a CP. Solving it yields the permit price of $\rho^{\text{CT}} = 12.3$ (in \$/t), which exactly equals the marginal damage cost, $d'(e^*) = Ze^*$, evaluated at the socially optimal level of CO_2 emissions. As in Illustrative Example 6.2, the socially optimal outputs are obtained, i.e., $y_1^* = 21.9$, $y_2^* = 17.8$, and $y^* = 39.7$ in total (in MWh). The social welfare inclusive of the cost of damage is 1986.3 (in \$). This illustrates that both Pigouvian taxation and emission permits can have the same effects in equilibrium.

The results of Illustrative Examples 6.1–6.3 are summarized in Table 6.1. The social welfare inclusive of the cost of damage is denoted by SW in the table.

Table 6.1 Outcomes of Illustrative Examples 6.1–6.3

	BAU	Social planning	Pigouvian tax	Emission permits
y	71.4	39.7	39.7	39.7
e	257.1	123.3	123.3	123.3
$d(e)$	3306.1	760.0	760.0	760.0
$d'(e)$	25.7	12.3	12.3	12.3
R^{tax}	–	–	12.3	–
ρ^{CT}	–	–	–	12.3
S	–	–	–	123.3
SW	265.3	1986.3	1986.3	1986.3

6.3.2 Renewable Portfolio Standards

The renewable portfolio standard (RPS) policy sets a target for renewable energy (RE) generation instead of explicitly controlling CO_2 emissions. Typically, RPS mandates a certain percentage of total electricity generation to be from RE sources. Producers can usually fulfill the RPS requirement by self-generation of RE and/or purchasing renewable energy certificates (RECs).

We here consider a simple case, where firms are divided into two groups, i.e., $i \in \mathcal{I}^{\text{RE}}$ with RE generation plants and $i \in \mathcal{I}^{\text{NRE}}$ with non-renewable energy (NRE) generation plants. Note that $\mathcal{I}^{\text{RE}} \cup \mathcal{I}^{\text{NRE}} = \mathcal{I}$ and $\mathcal{I}^{\text{RE}} \cap \mathcal{I}^{\text{NRE}} = \emptyset$. Let $Q \in [0, 1]$ and ρ^{REC} denote the RPS requirement and the REC price (e.g., in \$/MWh), respectively.

Firms with NRE generation plants need to purchase the RECs by paying $\rho^{\text{REC}} Q y_i$ to compensate for the unfulfilled RPS requirement. Pricing-taking firm $i \in \mathcal{I}^{\text{NRE}}$ maximizes its profit, taking $\hat{p}$ and ρ^{REC} as given:

$$\underset{y_i \geq 0}{\text{Maximize}}\ \hat{p} y_i - c_i(y_i) - \rho^{\text{REC}} Q y_i \tag{6.18a}$$

$$\text{s.t.}\ \ y_i \leq K_i \,:\, \beta_i \tag{6.18b}$$

where K_i and β_i denote the installed NRE generation capacity and the dual variable for the capacity constraint, respectively. Noting that $\hat{p} = b'(y) = p(y)$ holds in equilibrium, the KKT conditions are written as follows:

$$0 \leq y_i \perp p(y) - c_i'(y_i) - \rho^{\text{REC}} Q - \beta_i \leq 0 \tag{6.19a}$$

$$0 \leq \beta_i \perp y_i - K_i \leq 0 \tag{6.19b}$$

In contrast, firms with RE generation plants gain revenues, $\rho^{\text{REC}}(1 - Q)y_i$, from the sales of their excess RECs.[2] Pricing-taking firm $i \in \mathcal{I}^{\text{RE}}$ maximizes its profit, taking $\hat{p}$ and ρ^{REC} as given:

$$\underset{y_i \geq 0}{\text{Maximize}} \ \hat{p} y_i - c_i(y_i) + \rho^{\text{REC}}(1 - Q)y_i \tag{6.20a}$$

$$\text{s.t.} \ \ y_i \leq K_i : \beta_i \tag{6.20b}$$

where K_i and β_i denote the installed RE generation capacity and the dual variable for the capacity constraint, respectively. With $\hat{p} = b'(y) = p(y)$, the KKT conditions are derived as follows:

$$0 \leq y_i \perp p(y) - c_i'(y_i) + \rho^{\text{REC}}(1 - Q) - \beta_i \leq 0 \tag{6.21a}$$

$$0 \leq \beta_i \perp y_i - K_i \leq 0 \tag{6.21b}$$

The REC price is determined by the market-clearing condition for the certificates as follows [16, 17]:

$$0 \leq \rho^{\text{REC}} \perp \sum_{i \in \mathcal{I}^{\text{RE}}} y_i - Q \sum_{i \in \mathcal{I}} y_i \geq 0 \tag{6.22}$$

The REC price tends to rise when the target for RE generation, Q, increases.

In the RPS scheme, firms with NRE generation are effectively levied a "tax," whereas firms with RE generation virtually obtain a "subsidy." Hence, there is a transfer of wealth from NRE to RE sources. It is worth noting the key difference between RPS policy and Pigouvian taxation. Under Pigouvian taxation, RE generation plants with zero CO_2 emissions pay no tax but gain no subsidy either. By contrast, RPS policy further subsidizes RE generation plants using the revenue levied from NRE generation plants. This implies some efficiency loss under the RPS scheme in the short term.

Illustrative Example 6.4 *RPS.*

We here consider a stylized example of two firms, firm 1 with RE generation plants and firm 2 with NRE generation plants, to illustrate the mechanism of RPS policy. In what follows, the cost and benefit are expressed in dollars ($). We assume a zero short-run operating cost for firm 1 with RE plants, i.e., $c_1(y_1) = 0$, while we assume a quadratic cost function, $c_2(y_2) = y_2^2$, for firm 2 with NRE plants. The total generation outputs are $y = \sum_{i \in \mathcal{I}} y_i$ (in MWh); the installed generation capacities are $K_1 = 15$ and $K_2 = 50$ (in MW); and the emission rates are $E_1 = 0$ and $E_2 = 2$ (in t/MWh), and, hence, the total CO_2 emissions are $e = 2y_2$ (in t). We

[2] If firms own both RE and NRE generation plants, revenues associated with RECs can be expressed as $\rho^{\text{REC}}\left[\text{RE outputs} - Q\ (\text{RE outputs} + \text{NRE outputs})\right]$.

assume a quadratic damage cost function, $d(e) = 0.5Ze^2$, with the parameter for the damage cost, $Z = 0.1$ (in \$/t^2). The gross benefit and inverse-demand functions of consumers are expressed as $b(y) = 100y - 0.5y^2$ and $p(y) = 100 - y$, respectively.

Now, the environmental authority sets the RPS target of $Q = 0.4$. Noting that $\hat{p} = b'(y) = p(y)$ holds in equilibrium, the KKT conditions for those firms and the market-clearing condition for the certificates form a CP as follows:

$$0 \le y_1 \perp 100 - (y_1 + y_2) + (1 - 0.4)\rho^{\text{REC}} - \beta_1 \le 0 \quad (6.23a)$$

$$0 \le \beta_1 \perp y_1 - 15 \le 0 \quad (6.23b)$$

$$0 \le y_2 \perp 100 - (y_1 + y_2) - 2y_2 - 0.4\rho^{\text{REC}} - \beta_2 \le 0 \quad (6.23c)$$

$$0 \le \beta_2 \perp y_2 - 50 \le 0 \quad (6.23d)$$

$$0 \le \rho^{\text{REC}} \perp y_1 - 0.4(y_1 + y_2) \ge 0 \quad (6.23e)$$

Solving this CP yields the equilibrium outcomes using the notation of a bar over a letter. The REC price is $\bar{\rho}^{\text{REC}} = 43.8$ (in \$/MWh). RE plants generate $\bar{y}_1 = 15.0$ up to the capacity, while NRE plants generate $\bar{y}_2 = 22.5$ below the capacity and, hence, $\bar{y} = 37.5$ in total (in MWh). The total CO_2 emissions and the cost of damage are $\bar{e} = 45.0$ (in t) and $d(\bar{e}) = 101.3$ (in \$), respectively. The social welfare inclusive of the cost of damage is derived as $b(\bar{y}) - \sum_{i \in \mathcal{I}} c_i(\bar{y}_i) - d(\bar{e}) = 2439.4$ (in \$).

For comparison, we calculate the outcomes of a central planner as in Illustrative Example 6.1. Under central planning, the social welfare inclusive of the cost of damage is maximized subject to generation capacity constraints. The socially optimal outputs are derived as $y_1^* = 15.0$ up to the capacity for RE plants, $y_2^* = 25.0$ for NRE plants and, hence, $y^* = 40.0$ in total (in MWh). The total CO_2 emissions and the cost of damage are $e^* = 50.0$ (in t) and $d(e^*) = 125.0$ (in \$), respectively. The social welfare inclusive of the cost of damage is calculated as $b(y^*) - \sum_{i \in \mathcal{I}} c_i(y_i^*) - d(e^*) = 2450.0$ (in \$).

Due to the inherent distortional effects of RPS policy, the social welfare is lower under the RPS scheme than that of central planning. Particularly, this is because RPS policy over-suppresses the NRE outputs compared to the socially optimal level (i.e., $\bar{y}_2 = 22.5 < 25.0 = y_2^*$). The RPS scheme cannot achieve the social optimum even if we vary the RPS target, Q (see End-of-Chapter Exercise 6.3).

The results of Illustrative Example 6.4 are summarized in Table 6.2. The social welfare inclusive of the cost of damage is denoted by SW in the table.

6.4 Network-Constrained Models with Externalities

In order to complement the stylized models in Sect. 6.3, we now turn to more detailed representations of how externalities affect incentives in power systems. Thus, this section mirrors the structure of the previous one with exposition of (i)

Table 6.2 Outcomes of Illustrative Example 6.4

	Social planning	RPS
y_1	15.0	15.0
y_2	25.0	22.5
y	40.0	37.5
e	50.0	45.0
$d(e)$	125.0	101.3
$d'(e)$	5.0	4.5
ρ^{REC}	–	43.8
SW	2450.0	2439.4

first-best, (ii) taxation, and (iii) RPS policies for mitigating externalities from CO_2 emissions. The key difference is that the framework presented in this section allows for a more realistic spatial, technological, and temporal context. While these features facilitate a more nuanced assessment of the interplay between policy and industry response, their incorporation necessitates numerical solutions to problem instances of bi-level models. We use standard reformulation techniques to render these bi-level problem instances as either mixed-integer quadratic programs (MIQPs) or mixed-integer quadratically constrained quadratic programs (MIQCQPs) that can be readily tackled by off-the-shelf solvers.

6.4.1 First-Best Policy for CO_2 Emissions

As alluded to in Sect. 6.3, a first-best approach to tackling externalities is simply for them to be internalized into the policymaker's calculus via a so-called damage function. This admittedly unrealistic supposition involves a benevolent central planner that controls all aspects of the power system, viz., generation, consumption, and power flows. Nevertheless, it provides an ideal benchmark in the form of a Pigouvian tax on CO_2 emissions that could be used as a basis for comparison. More important, it allows the investigation of how the power system should behave in direct response to the damage cost parameter. Indeed, this is the standard approach in environmental economics and can be adapted to decentralized industries, e.g., with distinct ownership of assets and the presence of market power, accordingly [2].

Although the framework in this section incorporates demand response (Chap. 1), temporal variation (Chap. 2), spatial variation (Chap. 4), and market power (Chap. 5), it is still based on some simplifying assumptions. First, only operational decisions assuming fixed generation and transmission capacities are considered. While environmental policy invariably affects investment decisions, the analysis of such an interaction was conducted in Chapters 7 and 8 of [3]. Meanwhile, Chap. 7 of this book covers generation and transmission investment under market power. Thus, it is expedient to focus here on how environmental policy drives industry operations. Second, fluctuations in demand and VRES output are captured by representative days [14] instead of as uncertain parameters. This is because we have a medium-term operational assessment of how environmental policy impacts decisions over a given year. If our focus were on short-term risk management, then scenarios for demand and VRES output could be generated from time-series analysis in a multi-stage stochastic programming framework [4]. Third, power flows are modeled via the DC approximation because AC power flow analysis is highly non-linear [12]. Fourth, the cost of damage from emissions is a quadratic function of total emissions, i.e., $\frac{1}{2}Z\left(\sum_{s\in\mathcal{S}} W_s \sum_{t\in\mathcal{T}} \sum_{n\in\mathcal{N}} \sum_{i\in\mathcal{I}} \sum_{u\in\mathcal{U}_{i,n}} E_u y_{i,n,s,t,u}\right)^2$, where $Z \geq 0$ (in $/t^2) is the damage cost parameter and $E_u y_{i,n,s,t,u}$ are the CO_2 emissions (in t) from technology u owned by firm i at node n during period t of season s. Convexity of the damage function is standard in the environmental economics literature [15] and reflects increasing marginal costs of damage from CO_2 emissions.

The notation for the subsequent problem formulation is similar to that used in Chap. 2 as well as that in Chap. 7.

Indices and Sets

$i \in \mathcal{I}$	Firms.
$\ell \in \mathcal{L}$	Transmission lines.
$\mathcal{L}_n^+, \mathcal{L}_n^-$	Transmission lines whose sending/receiving node is n.
$n \in \mathcal{N}$	Nodes.
n_ℓ^+, n_ℓ^-	Sending/receiving node of line ℓ.
$s \in \mathcal{S}$	Seasons.
$t \in \mathcal{T}$	Time periods.
$u \in \mathcal{U}_{i,n}$	Generating units belonging to firm i at node n.

Parameters

$A_{n,s,t,u}$	Maximum availability factor for technology u at node n in season s and period t [–].
B_ℓ	Susceptance of transmission line ℓ [S].
$C_{i,n,u}^{\text{opr}}$	Operating cost of generation unit $u \in \mathcal{U}_{i,n}$ at node n belonging to firm i [$/MWh].
$D_{n,s,t}^{\text{int}}$	Intercept of inverse demand at node n in season s and period t [$/MWh].
$D_{n,s,t}^{\text{slp}}$	Slope of inverse demand at node n in season s and period t [$/MWh^2].
E_u	CO_2 emission rate of generation unit u [t/MWh].
$K_{i,n,u}^{\text{gen}}$	Installed generation capacity of generation unit $u \in \mathcal{U}_{i,n}$ at node n belonging to firm i [MW].
R_u^{up}	Maximum ramping-up rate of generation unit u [–].
R_u^{down}	Maximum ramping-down rate of generation unit u [–].
T_t	Length of period t [h].
W_s	Weight of season s [–].
Z	Parameter for cost of damage from CO_2 emissions [$/t^2].

Continuous Variables

$c_{n,s,t}$ Energy consumption at node n in season s and period t [MWh].
$\hat{f}_{\ell,s,t}$ Realized power flow on line ℓ in season s and period t [MW].
$v_{n,s,t}$ Voltage angle at node n in season s and period t [rad].
$y_{i,n,s,t,u}$ Generation from unit $u \in \mathcal{U}_{i,n}$ at node n belonging to firm i in season s and period t [MWh].

Under central planning, the objective is to maximize social welfare inclusive of the cost of damage from CO_2 emissions subject to operational constraints:

$$\underset{\Omega^{\mathrm{CP}}}{\text{Maximize}} \sum_{s\in\mathcal{S}} W_s \sum_{t\in\mathcal{T}} \sum_{n\in\mathcal{N}} \left[\left(D^{\mathrm{int}}_{n,s,t} c_{n,s,t} - \frac{1}{2} D^{\mathrm{slp}}_{n,s,t} c^2_{n,s,t} \right) - \sum_{i\in\mathcal{I}} \sum_{u\in\mathcal{U}_{i,n}} C^{\mathrm{opr}}_{i,n,u} y_{i,n,s,t,u} \right]$$

$$- \frac{1}{2} Z \left(\sum_{s\in\mathcal{S}} W_s \sum_{t\in\mathcal{T}} \sum_{n\in\mathcal{N}} \sum_{i\in\mathcal{I}} \sum_{u\in\mathcal{U}_{i,n}} E_u y_{i,n,s,t,u} \right)^2 \quad (6.24a)$$

$$\text{s.t. } \hat{f}_{\ell,s,t} = B_\ell \left(v_{n^+_\ell,s,t} - v_{n^-_\ell,s,t} \right), \forall \ell, s, t \quad (6.24b)$$

$$- K^{\mathrm{trn}}_\ell \le \hat{f}_{\ell,s,t} \le K^{\mathrm{trn}}_\ell, \ \forall \ell, s, t \quad (6.24c)$$

$$- \pi \le v_{n,s,t} \le \pi, \ \forall n, s, t \quad (6.24d)$$

$$c_{n,s,t} - \sum_{i\in\mathcal{I}} \sum_{u\in\mathcal{U}_{i,n}} y_{i,n,s,t,u} + T_t \sum_{\ell\in\mathcal{L}^+_n} \hat{f}_{\ell,s,t} - T_t \sum_{\ell\in\mathcal{L}^-_n} \hat{f}_{\ell,s,t} = 0,$$

$$\forall n, s, t \quad (6.24e)$$

$$y_{i,n,s,t,u} \le T_t A_{n,s,t,u} K^{\mathrm{gen}}_{i,n,u}, \ \forall i, n, s, t, u \in \mathcal{U}_{i,n} \quad (6.24f)$$

$$y_{i,n,s,t,u} - y_{i,n,s,t-1,u} \le T_t R^{\mathrm{up}}_u K^{\mathrm{gen}}_{i,n,u}, \ \forall i, n, s, t, u \in \mathcal{U}_{i,n} \quad (6.24g)$$

$$- y_{i,n,s,t,u} + y_{i,n,s,t-1,u} \le T_t R^{\mathrm{down}}_u K^{\mathrm{gen}}_{i,n,u}, \ \forall i, n, s, t, u \in \mathcal{U}_{i,n} \quad (6.24h)$$

$$c_{n,s,t} \ge 0, \ \forall n, s, t \quad (6.24i)$$

$$y_{i,n,s,t,u} \ge 0, \ \forall i, n, s, t, u \in \mathcal{U}_{i,n} \quad (6.24j)$$

$$\hat{f}_{\ell,s,t} \text{ u.r.s.}, \ \forall \ell, s, t \quad (6.24k)$$

$$v_{n,s,t} \text{ u.r.s.}, \ \forall n, s, t \quad (6.24l)$$

where $\Omega^{\mathrm{CP}} \equiv \left\{ c_{n,s,t}, \hat{f}_{\ell,s,t}, v_{n,s,t}, y_{i,n,s,t,u} \right\}$ is the set of optimization variables and "u.r.s." refers to "unrestricted in sign." It should be emphasized that market-based instruments for curbing CO_2 emissions are not necessary because the central planner internalizes their cost and directly adjusts operations. Indeed, social welfare in (6.24a) includes the cost of damage from CO_2 emissions among its components, viz., consumer surplus (CS), producer surplus (PS), merchandising surplus (MS), and damage cost (DC). These are explicitly defined as follows:

- CS is the consumption benefit, $\sum_{s\in\mathcal{S}}\sum_{t\in\mathcal{T}}\sum_{n\in\mathcal{N}} W_s\left(D^{\text{int}}_{n,s,t}c_{n,s,t} - \frac{1}{2}D^{\text{slp}}_{n,s,t}\,c^2_{n,s,t}\right)$, minus its cost, $\sum_{s\in\mathcal{S}}\sum_{t\in\mathcal{T}}\sum_{n\in\mathcal{N}} W_s p_{n,s,t}c_{n,s,t}$, where $p_{n,s,t}$ is the equilibrium price.
- PS is the revenue from sales, $\sum_{s\in\mathcal{S}}\sum_{t\in\mathcal{T}}\sum_{n\in\mathcal{N}}\sum_{i\in\mathcal{I}}\sum_{u\in\mathcal{U}_{i,n}} W_s p_{n,s,t}\, y_{i,n,s,t,u}$, minus the operating costs, $\sum_{s\in\mathcal{S}}\sum_{t\in\mathcal{T}}\sum_{n\in\mathcal{N}}\sum_{i\in\mathcal{I}}\sum_{u\in\mathcal{U}_{i,n}} W_s C^{\text{opr}}_{i,n,u}\, y_{i,n,s,t,u}$, assuming that the sunk cost of generation investment is irrelevant.
- MS is the revenue earned by the ISO from transmitting power from an injecting to a withdrawing node, $\sum_{s\in\mathcal{S}}\sum_{t\in\mathcal{T}}\sum_{n\in\mathcal{N}} W_s T_t p_{n,s,t}\left(\sum_{\ell\in\mathcal{L}_n^-}\hat{f}_{\ell,s,t} - \sum_{\ell\in\mathcal{L}_n^+}\hat{f}_{\ell,s,t}\right)$.
- DC from CO_2 emissions is a convex function of total CO_2 emissions, i.e., $\frac{1}{2}Z\left(\sum_{s\in\mathcal{S}} W_s\sum_{t\in\mathcal{T}}\sum_{n\in\mathcal{N}}\sum_{i\in\mathcal{I}}\sum_{u\in\mathcal{U}_{i,n}} E_u y_{i,n,s,t,u}\right)^2$.

From the energy-balance constraint (6.24e), we have $c_{n,s,t} = \sum_{i\in\mathcal{I}}\sum_{u\in\mathcal{U}_{i,n}} y_{i,n,s,t,u} - T_t\sum_{\ell\in\mathcal{L}_n^+}\hat{f}_{\ell,s,t} + T_t\sum_{\ell\in\mathcal{L}_n^-}\hat{f}_{\ell,s,t}, \forall n,s,t$. Consequently, the cost to consumers in CS, $\sum_{s\in\mathcal{S}}\sum_{t\in\mathcal{T}}\sum_{n\in\mathcal{N}} W_s p_{n,s,t}c_{n,s,t}$, cancels with the revenue to firms in PS, $\sum_{s\in\mathcal{S}}\sum_{t\in\mathcal{T}}\sum_{n\in\mathcal{N}}\sum_{i\in\mathcal{I}}\sum_{u\in\mathcal{U}_{i,n}} W_s p_{n,s,t}\, y_{i,n,s,t,u}$, plus all of the revenue in MS, $\sum_{s\in\mathcal{S}}\sum_{t\in\mathcal{T}}\sum_{n\in\mathcal{N}} W_s T_t p_{n,s,t}\left(\sum_{\ell\in\mathcal{L}_n^-}\hat{f}_{\ell,s,t} - \sum_{\ell\in\mathcal{L}_n^+}\hat{f}_{\ell,s,t}\right)$. Thus, summing CS, PS, MS, and DC yields precisely the social welfare in (6.24a).

The operational constraints under central planning pertain to Kirchhoff's laws that govern power flows and transmission limits (6.24b)–(6.24d), nodal energy balance (6.24e), generation capacity and ramping (6.24f)–(6.24h), and variable restrictions (6.24i)–(6.24l). In particular, (6.24b) states that power flow on a line is proportional to the voltage angle difference between the sending and receiving nodes of that line. Power flows in either the positive or the negative direction are constrained by transmission capacity as specified by (6.24c), while (6.24d) constrains voltage angles. At each node and during each period of each season, (6.24e) states that energy consumed must equal the local generation plus net imports. Constraint (6.24f) limits generation by the available installed capacity, and (6.24g)–(6.24h) limit by how much plants can ramp up or down. Since there are no integer variables or bilinear terms, the optimization problem (6.24a)–(6.24l) is a quadratic program (QP).

For *ex post* analysis, it also useful to keep track of two performance metrics: the marginal cost of damage (MCD) from emissions and the proportion of generation from renewable energy (RE). The MCD captures how an infinitesimal increase in CO_2 emissions, $\sum_{s\in\mathcal{S}} W_s\sum_{t\in\mathcal{T}}\sum_{n\in\mathcal{N}}\sum_{i\in\mathcal{I}}\sum_{u\in\mathcal{U}_{i,n}} E_u y_{i,n,s,t,u}$, affects the cost of damage. In effect, it is simply the derivative of the damage function with respect to CO_2 emissions:

$$Z\left(\sum_{s\in\mathcal{S}} W_s\sum_{t\in\mathcal{T}}\sum_{n\in\mathcal{N}}\sum_{i\in\mathcal{I}}\sum_{u\in\mathcal{U}_{i,n}} E_u y_{i,n,s,t,u}\right) \tag{6.25}$$

Under central planning, the MCD is equivalent to the Pigouvian tax since the cost of damage from CO_2 emissions is internalized. If $\mathcal{U}^{C}_{i,n}$ and $\mathcal{U}^{R}_{i,n}$ define the set of non-renewable energy (NRE), i.e., conventional, and RE technologies, respectively, owned by firm i at node n, then the proportion of generation from RE is

$$\frac{\sum_{s\in\mathcal{S}} W_s \sum_{t\in\mathcal{T}} \sum_{n\in\mathcal{N}} \sum_{i\in\mathcal{I}} \sum_{u\in\mathcal{U}^{R}_{i,n}} y_{i,n,s,t,u}}{\sum_{s\in\mathcal{S}} W_s \sum_{t\in\mathcal{T}} \sum_{n\in\mathcal{N}} \sum_{i\in\mathcal{I}} \sum_{u\in\mathcal{U}_{i,n}} y_{i,n,s,t,u}} \tag{6.26}$$

In (6.26), $\mathcal{U}^{C}_{i,n} \cup \mathcal{U}^{R}_{i,n} = \mathcal{U}_{i,n}$ and $\mathcal{U}^{C}_{i,n} \cap \mathcal{U}^{R}_{i,n} = \emptyset$.

Illustrative Example 6.5 *Welfare-maximizing QP for centrally planned power-system operations with externalities.*

In order to demonstrate the first-best policy for mitigating the cost of damage from CO_2 emissions, we implement the central-planning QP (6.24a)–(6.24l) for the three-node network in Fig. 6.2. Demand data are given in Table 6.3. Note that node $n = 1$ is the load center, while node $n = 3$ has the lowest consumption. We use two seasons, i.e., $W_s = 183$, with three periods within each season that are eight-hours long, i.e., $T_t = 8$. While demand parameters are constant across seasons and periods, VRES owned by firm $i = 2$ at the low-demand nodes, $n = 2$ and $n = 3$, have availability parameters, $A_{n,s,t,u}$ (Tables 6.4 and 6.5). Meanwhile, fossil-fuel technologies, $u = 3$ (coal) and $u = 4$ (gas), at node $n = 1$ belong to firm $i = 1$ (Table 6.6) with operating costs from Illustrative Example 2.1. CO_2 emission rates, E_u, are also provided. Finally, each transmission line has capacity $K^{\text{trn}}_{\ell} = 48.8$ and susceptance $B_{\ell} = 5100$ S.

We investigate the impact of the externality from CO_2 emissions by letting Z vary in the interval [0, 0.02]. The lower limit of this interval corresponds to a situation in which there is no cost of damage from CO_2 emissions, while consumption and

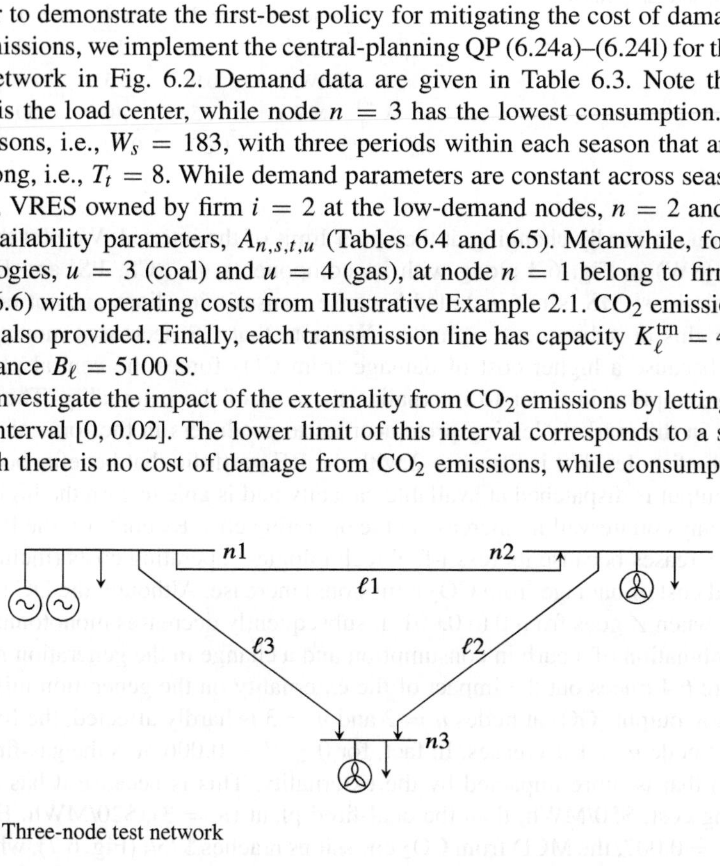

Fig. 6.2 Three-node test network

Table 6.3 Demand parameters for all (s, t)

	Node		
Parameter	$n = 1$	$n = 2$	$n = 3$
$D^{\text{int}}_{n,s,t}$ (\$/MWh)	220	140	120
$D^{\text{slp}}_{n,s,t}$ (\$/MWh^2)	1	1	1

Table 6.4 Availability parameters for VRES technology $u = 1$ at node $n = 2$, $A_{n,s,t,u}$ (–)

Season	Period $t = 1$	$t = 2$	$t = 3$
$s = 1$	0.20	0.10	0.05
$s = 2$	0.25	0.50	0.75

Table 6.5 Availability parameters for VRES technology $u = 2$ at node $n = 3$, $A_{n,s,t,u}$ (–)

Season	Period $t = 1$	$t = 2$	$t = 3$
$s = 1$	0.20	0.40	0.50
$s = 2$	1.00	0.75	0.10

Table 6.6 Generation costs, CO_2 emission rates installed capacities, and ramp rates

Parameter	$i = 1$, $n = 1$, $u = 3$	$i = 1$, $n = 1$, $u = 4$	$i = 2$, $n = 2$, $u = 1$	$i = 2$, $n = 3$, $u = 2$
$C^{\text{opr}}_{i,n,u}$ (\$/MWh)	20	50	0	0
E_u (t/MWh)	0.9	0.5	0	0
$K^{\text{gen}}_{i,n,u}$ (MW)	35	40	50	50
$R^{\text{up}}_u = R^{\text{down}}_u$ (–)	0.30	0.60	1	1

generation are hardly changing at the upper limit of the interval. We plot the social welfare (SW) in Fig. 6.3 along with its components, i.e., CS, PS, and DC from CO_2 emissions. MS is not included because transmission lines are not congested in either this or subsequent examples. We note that CS decreases monotonically with Z because a higher cost of damage from CO_2 forces the central planner to curb consumption in order to internalize the cost of the externality. The ensuing increase in the market-clearing price accrues to producers in the form of a higher PS. At the firm level, it is firm $i = 2$ with the RE portfolio that benefits because its VRES output is dispatched at available capacity and is able to earn the higher price without any countervailing increase in the operating cost. By contrast, the PS of firm $i = 1$ decreases because its fossil-fuel technologies' operating costs (including the marginal cost of damage from CO_2 emissions) increase. Although the DC increases initially when Z goes from 0 to 0.001, it subsequently decreases monotonically due to a combination of a curb in consumption and a change in the generation mix.

Figure 6.4 traces out the impact of the externality on the generation mix. While generation output (GO) at nodes $n = 2$ and $n = 3$ is hardly affected, the fossil-fuel output at node $n = 1$ decreases. In fact, for $0 \leq Z \leq 0.006$, it is the gas-fired plant ($u = 4$) that is more impacted by the externality. This is because it has a higher operating cost, \$50/MWh, than the coal-fired plant ($u = 3$), \$20/MWh. However, when $Z = 0.007$, the MCD from CO_2 emissions reaches \$75/t (Fig. 6.7), which puts the two fossil-fuel technologies' effective operating costs at parity, i.e., \$20/MWh+ 0.9t/MWh × \$75/t = \$50/MWh + 0.5t/MWh × \$75/t = \$87.50/MWh. At this threshold, gas-fired generation makes a comeback and virtually eliminates coal when $Z = 0.012$. This also marks the turning point of the gas-fired technology's brief reprieve. Thus, the net import (NI) at node $n = 1$ increases monotonically,

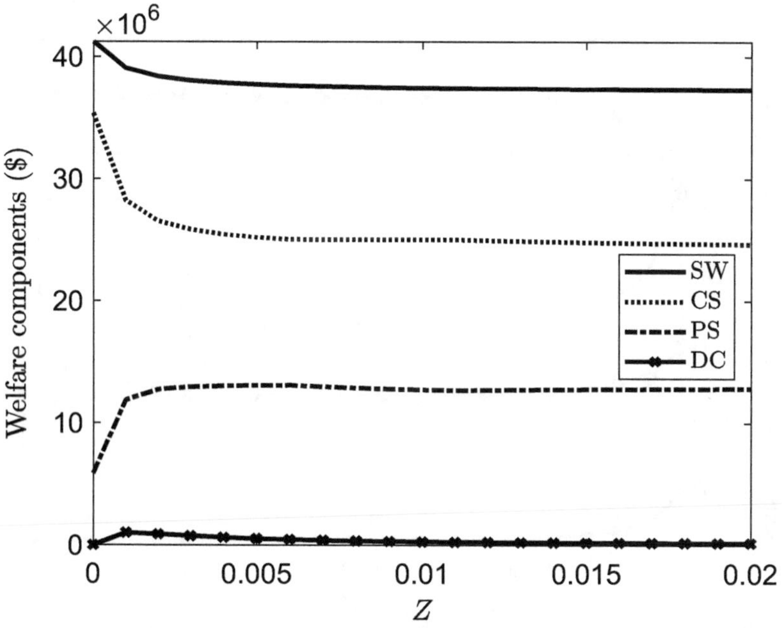

Fig. 6.3 Welfare components under central planning with respect to Z

while that at nodes $n = 2$ and $n = 3$ decreases monotonically. This pattern is also reflected in the higher transmission flow (TF) on lines $\ell = 1$ and $\ell = 3$ in the "negative" direction, i.e., heading toward node $n = 1$ (Fig. 6.5). Finally, CO_2 emissions decrease monotonically with Z (Fig. 6.6) in reflection of the higher MCD in Fig. 6.7.

6.4.2 CO_2 Taxation in a Deregulated Electricity Industry

Unlike the central-planning paradigm of Sect. 6.4.1, in a deregulated electricity industry, a policymaker has no operational control to align public and private incentives. However, a policymaker can indirectly influence industry outcomes by anticipating its decisions when proactively setting market-based instruments such as CO_2 taxes and RPS. We first tackle the problem of optimal CO_2 taxation via a bi-level framework in which the upper level comprises a welfare-maximizing policymaker in anticipation of lower-level profit- or surplus-maximizing operational decisions by firms or an ISO, respectively. Moreover, the policymaker needs to adapt CO_2 taxation to not only the damage cost parameter, Z, but also the exertion of market power by power companies. This framework may also be characterized as a Stackelberg game [16, 18]. In the rest of this chapter, we use the initialisms CP,

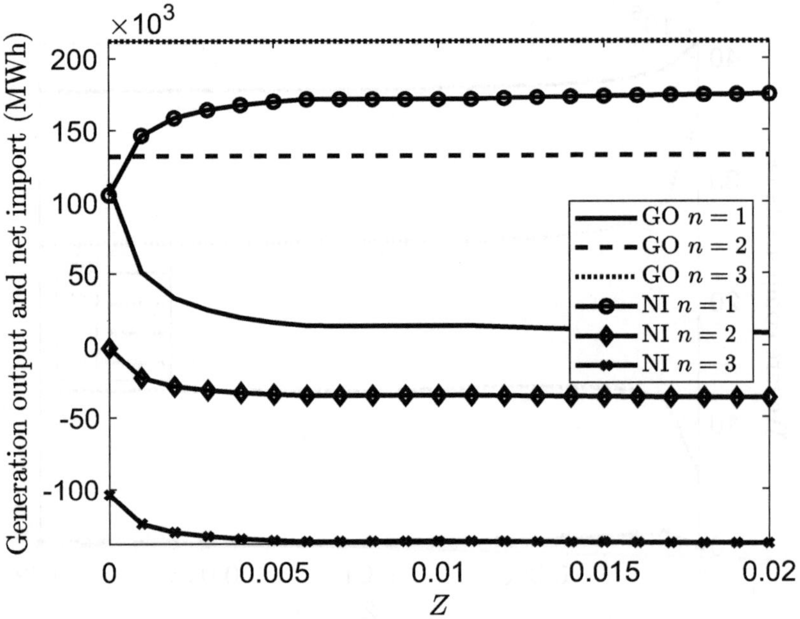

Fig. 6.4 Generation output and net import under central planning with respect to Z

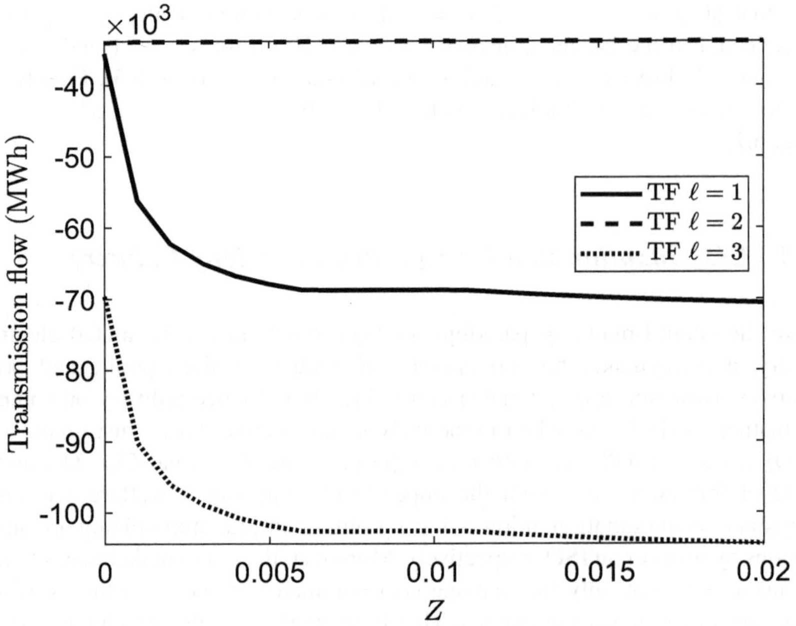

Fig. 6.5 Transmission flow under central planning with respect to Z

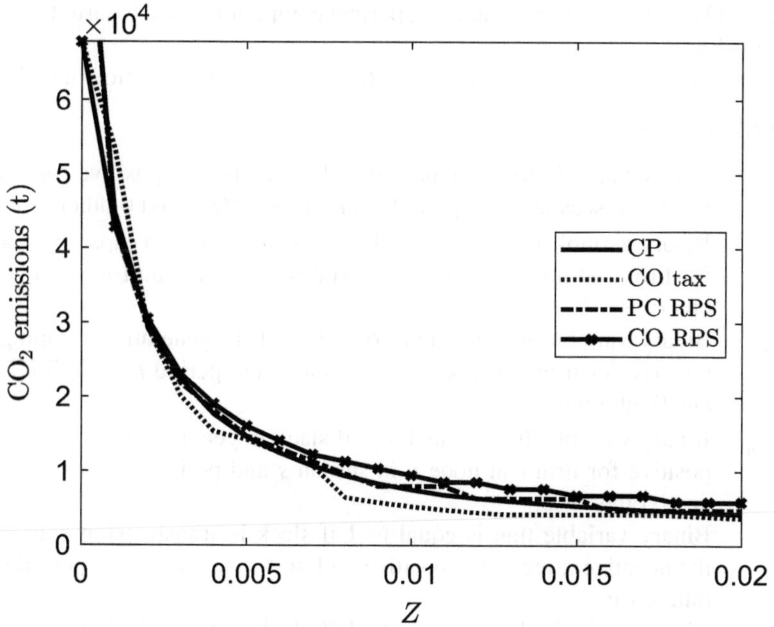

Fig. 6.6 CO_2 emissions with respect to Z

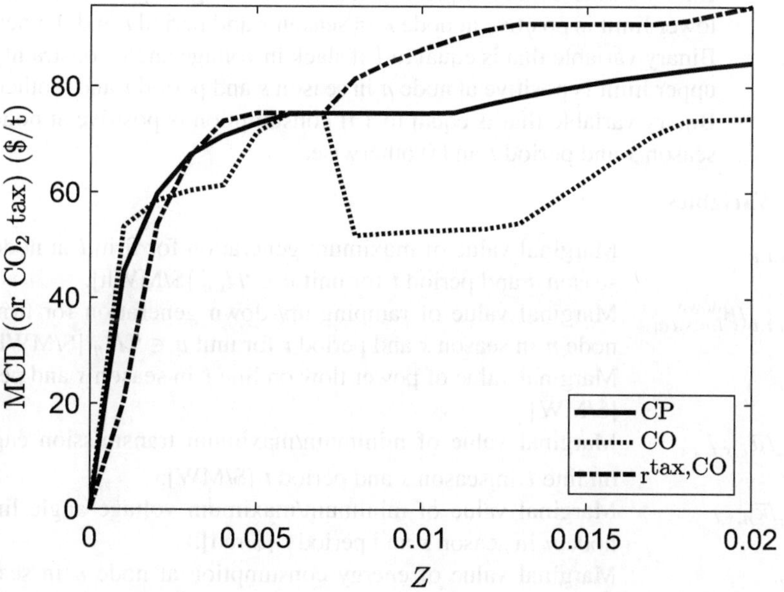

Fig. 6.7 Marginal cost of damage from CO_2 emissions (or CO_2 tax) with respect to Z

PC, and CO to refer to central planning, perfect competition, and Cournot oligopoly, respectively.

The notation follows from that in Sect. 6.4.1 along with the following additions:

Binary Variables

$x^{\mathrm{y}}_{i,n,s,t,u}$ Binary variable that is equal to 1 if generation is positive for firm i at node n in season s and period t for unit $u \in \mathcal{U}_{i,n}$ and 0 otherwise.

$x^{\beta}_{i,n,s,t,u}$ Binary variable that is equal to 1 if slack in generation capacity is positive for firm i at node n in season s and period t for unit $u \in \mathcal{U}_{i,n}$ and 0 otherwise.

$x^{\beta^{\mathrm{up}}}_{i,n,s,t,u}$ Binary variable that is equal to 1 if slack in generation ramping-up is positive for firm i at node n in season s and period t for unit $u \in \mathcal{U}_{i,n}$ and 0 otherwise.

$x^{\beta^{\mathrm{down}}}_{i,n,s,t,u}$ Binary variable that is equal to 1 if slack in generation ramping-down is positive for firm i at node n in season s and period t for unit $u \in \mathcal{U}_{i,n}$ and 0 otherwise.

$x^{\underline{\mu}}_{\ell,s,t}$ Binary variable that is equal to 1 if slack in transmission constraint in the negative direction is positive on line ℓ in season s and period t and 0 otherwise.

$x^{\overline{\mu}}_{\ell,s,t}$ Binary variable that is equal to 1 if slack in transmission constraint in the positive direction is positive on line ℓ in season s and period t and 0 otherwise.

$x^{\underline{\kappa}}_{n,s,t}$ Binary variable that is equal to 1 if slack in voltage angle constraint at the lower limit is positive at node n in season s and period t and 0 otherwise.

$x^{\overline{\kappa}}_{n,s,t}$ Binary variable that is equal to 1 if slack in voltage angle constraint at the upper limit is positive at node n in season s and period t and 0 otherwise.

$x^{\mathrm{c}}_{n,s,t}$ Binary variable that is equal to 1 if consumption is positive at node n in season s and period t and 0 otherwise.

Dual Variables

$\beta_{i,n,s,t,u}$ Marginal value of maximum generation for firm i at node n in season s and period t for unit $u \in \mathcal{U}_{i,n}$ [\$/MWh].

$\beta^{\mathrm{up}}_{i,n,s,t,u}/\beta^{\mathrm{down}}_{i,n,s,t,u}$ Marginal value of ramping-up/-down generation for firm i at node n in season s and period t for unit $u \in \mathcal{U}_{i,n}$ [\$/MWh].

$\mu_{\ell,s,t}$ Marginal value of power flow on line ℓ in season s and period t [\$/MW].

$\underline{\mu}_{\ell,s,t}/\overline{\mu}_{\ell,s,t}$ Marginal value of minimum/maximum transmission capacity on line ℓ in season s and period t [\$/MW].

$\underline{\kappa}_{n,s,t}/\overline{\kappa}_{n,s,t}$ Marginal value of minimum/maximum voltage angle limit at node n in season s and period t [\$/rad].

$\lambda_{n,s,t}$ Marginal value of energy consumption at node n in season s and period t [\$/MWh].

$\phi^{c}_{n,s,t}$ Marginal value of non-negativity of consumption at node n in season s and period t [\$/MWh].

$\phi^{y}_{i,n,s,t,u}$ Marginal value of non-negativity of generation output by firm i at node n in season s and period t for unit $u \in \mathcal{U}_{i,n}$ [$/MWh].

Primal Variable

r^{tax} Optimal tax on CO_2 emissions [$/t].

We begin at the upper level where the policymaker sets the optimal CO_2 tax, r^{tax}, in anticipation of power-sector operations at the lower level while internalizing the cost of damage from emissions:

$$\underset{r^{\text{tax}}}{\text{Maximize}} \ (6.24\text{a})$$

$$\text{s.t. } r^{\text{tax}} \geq 0 \tag{6.27a}$$

Note that while the policymaker has the same objective function as under central planning in Sect. 6.4.1, its sole decision variable is the CO_2 tax. In other words, it has no control over the generation, consumption, or transmission of power. Yet, its choice of the CO_2 tax can force industry to internalize the cost of damage from emissions.

At the lower level, there are two types of decision makers, viz., firms and the ISO. First, each firm $i \in \mathcal{I}$ determines generation from its plants in order to maximize its operational profit:

$$\underset{y_{i,n,s,t,u}}{\text{Maximize}} \sum_{s\in\mathcal{S}} W_s \sum_{n\in\mathcal{N}} \sum_{t\in\mathcal{T}} \sum_{u\in\mathcal{U}_{i,n}} \left(D^{\text{int}}_{n,s,t} - D^{\text{slp}}_{n,s,t} \left(\sum_{i'\in\mathcal{I}} \sum_{u'\in\mathcal{U}_{i',n}} y_{i',n,s,t,u'} \right.\right.$$
$$\left.\left. - T_t \left(\sum_{\ell\in\mathcal{L}^+_n} \hat{f}_{\ell,s,t} - \sum_{\ell\in\mathcal{L}^-_n} \hat{f}_{\ell,s,t} \right)\right) - C^{\text{opr}}_{i,n,u} - r^{\text{tax}} E_u \right) y_{i,n,s,t,u} \tag{6.28a}$$

$$\text{s.t. } y_{i,n,s,t,u} \leq T_t A_{n,s,t,u} K^{\text{gen}}_{i,n,u} \ : \ \beta_{i,n,s,t,u}, \ \forall n, s, t, u \in \mathcal{U}_{i,n} \tag{6.28b}$$

$$y_{i,n,s,t,u} - y_{i,n,s,t-1,u} \leq T_t R^{\text{up}}_u K^{\text{gen}}_{i,n,u} \ : \ \beta^{\text{up}}_{i,n,s,t,u}, \ \forall n, s, t, u \in \mathcal{U}_{i,n} \tag{6.28c}$$

$$- y_{i,n,s,t,u} + y_{i,n,s,t-1,u} \leq T_t R^{\text{down}}_u K^{\text{gen}}_{i,n,u} \ : \ \beta^{\text{down}}_{i,n,s,t,u},$$
$$\forall n, s, t, u \in \mathcal{U}_{i,n} \tag{6.28d}$$

$$y_{i,n,s,t,u} \geq 0 : \ \phi^{y}_{i,n,s,t,u}, \ \forall n, s, t, u \in \mathcal{U}_{i,n} \tag{6.28e}$$

In doing so, each firm behaves as a Nash player in a quantity game by taking the CO_2 tax, r^{tax}, as given along with the generation of all other firms and the ISO's decisions about consumption and power flows. The objective function of firm $i \in \mathcal{I}$ in (6.28a) is simply revenues from sales minus costs from operations and the CO_2

tax. In order to allow for market power à la Cournot, we insert the full inverse-demand function, $D^{\text{int}}_{n,s,t} - D^{\text{slp}}_{n,s,t} c_{n,s,t}$, as perceived by firm $i \in \mathcal{I}$. Furthermore, the consumption, $c_{n,s,t}$, is substituted by the local generation from all firms and net inflows, $\sum_{i' \in \mathcal{I}} \sum_{u' \in \mathcal{U}_{i',n}} y_{i',n,s,t,u'} - T_t \left(\sum_{\ell \in \mathcal{L}^+_n} \hat{f}_{\ell,s,t} - \sum_{\ell \in \mathcal{L}^-_n} \hat{f}_{\ell,s,t} \right)$. This latter substitution is possible because of nodal energy balance, cf. (6.24e). If the firm is perfectly competitive, then it takes the price as given. The firm faces constraints on its available generation capacity (6.28b), ramping-up and ramping-down limits on generation (6.28c)–(6.28d), and non-negativity restrictions on its generation (6.28e). Thus, problem (6.28a)–(6.28e) is a QP. Lower-case Greek letters adjacent to each constraint are the associated dual variables.

Second, the ISO's surplus-maximization problem is

$$\underset{c_{n,s,t}, \hat{f}_{\ell,s,t}, v_{n,s,t}}{\text{Maximize}} \sum_{s \in \mathcal{S}} W_s \sum_{t \in \mathcal{T}} \sum_{n \in \mathcal{N}} \left(D^{\text{int}}_{n,s,t} c_{n,s,t} - \frac{1}{2} D^{\text{slp}}_{n,s,t} c^2_{n,s,t} \right) \tag{6.29a}$$

$$\text{s.t. } \hat{f}_{\ell,s,t} - B_\ell \left(v_{n^+_\ell,s,t} - v_{n^-_\ell,s,t} \right) = 0 : \mu_{\ell,s,t}, \forall \ell, s, t \tag{6.29b}$$

$$\underline{\mu}_{\ell,s,t} : -K^{\text{trn}}_\ell \le \hat{f}_{\ell,s,t} \le K^{\text{trn}}_\ell : \overline{\mu}_{\ell,s,t}, \forall \ell, s, t \tag{6.29c}$$

$$\underline{\kappa}_{n,s,t} : -\pi \le v_{n,s,t} \le \pi : \overline{\kappa}_{n,s,t}, \forall n, s, t \tag{6.29d}$$

$$c_{n,s,t} - \sum_{i \in \mathcal{I}} \sum_{u \in \mathcal{U}_{i,n}} y_{i,n,s,t,u} + T_t \sum_{\ell \in \mathcal{L}^+_n} \hat{f}_{\ell,s,t} - T_t \sum_{\ell \in \mathcal{L}^-_n} \hat{f}_{\ell,s,t} = 0 :$$

$$\lambda_{n,s,t}, \forall n, s, t \tag{6.29e}$$

$$c_{n,s,t} \ge 0 : \phi^c_{n,s,t}, \forall n, s, t \tag{6.29f}$$

$$\hat{f}_{\ell,s,t} \text{ u.r.s.}, \forall \ell, s, t \tag{6.29g}$$

$$v_{n,s,t} \text{ u.r.s.}, \forall n, s, t \tag{6.29h}$$

The ISO takes the generation of all firms as given, i.e., again the Nash assumption. In its objective function (6.29a), the ISO maximizes social surplus from consumption. Note that neither the ISO nor any firm directly encounters the cost of damage from CO_2 emissions. The ISO controls consumption, power flows, and voltage angles. Thus, its problem is constrained by the DC load-flow representation of Kirchhoff's laws (6.29b), transmission capacities (6.29c), limits on voltage angles (6.29d), nodal energy balance (6.29e), and restrictions on decision variables (6.29f)–(6.29h). The ISO's problem (6.29a)–(6.29h) is also a QP.

Overall, the problems of the firms and the ISO at the lower level constitute an equilibrium problem, which may be solved by taking the first-order necessary conditions, or Karush–Kuhn–Tucker (KKT) conditions, for each problem. Since each problem is a QP and, thus, convex, these KKT conditions are also sufficient for optimality and comprise a mixed-complementarity problem (MCP). A solution to such an MCP constitutes a Nash-Cournot equilibrium, i.e., a solution from which no player will unilaterally deviate [8]. Thus, we replace each lower-level problem by its KKT conditions.

The KKT conditions corresponding to the lower-level optimization problem of firm i (6.28a)–(6.28e) are

$$W_s C^{\text{opr}}_{i,n,u} + W_s E_u r^{\text{tax}} + W_s D^{\text{slp}}_{n,s,t} \sum_{\hat{u} \in \mathcal{U}_{i,n}} y_{i,n,s,t,\hat{u}} + \beta_{i,n,s,t,u} + \beta^{\text{up}}_{i,n,s,t,u}$$

$$- W_s \left(D^{\text{int}}_{n,s,t} - D^{\text{slp}}_{n,s,t} \left(\sum_{i' \in \mathcal{I}} \sum_{u' \in \mathcal{U}_{i',n}} y_{i',n,s,t,u'} - T_t \left(\sum_{\ell \in \mathcal{L}_n^+} \hat{f}_{\ell,s,t} - \sum_{\ell \in \mathcal{L}_n^-} \hat{f}_{\ell,s,t} \right) \right) \right)$$

$$- \beta^{\text{down}}_{i,n,s,t,u} - \beta^{\text{up}}_{i,n,s,t+1,u} + \beta^{\text{down}}_{i,n,s,t+1,u} - \phi^{y}_{i,n,s,t,u} = 0, \forall n, s, t, u \in \mathcal{U}_{i,n} \quad (6.30a)$$

$$0 \leq \phi^{y}_{i,n,s,t,u} \perp y_{i,n,s,t,u} \geq 0, \forall n, s, t, u \in \mathcal{U}_{i,n} \quad (6.30b)$$

$$0 \leq \beta_{i,n,s,t,u} \perp T_t A_{n,s,t,u} K^{\text{gen}}_{i,n,u} - y_{i,n,s,t,u} \geq 0,$$

$$\forall n, s, t, u \in \mathcal{U}_{i,n} \quad (6.30c)$$

$$0 \leq \beta^{\text{up}}_{i,n,s,t,u} \perp T_t R^{\text{up}}_u K^{\text{gen}}_{i,n,u} - y_{i,n,s,t,u} + y_{i,n,s,t-1,u} \geq 0,$$

$$\forall n, s, t, u \in \mathcal{U}_{i,n} \quad (6.30d)$$

$$0 \leq \beta^{\text{down}}_{i,n,s,t,u} \perp T_t R^{\text{down}}_u K^{\text{gen}}_{i,n,u} + y_{i,n,s,t,u} - y_{i,n,s,t-1,u} \geq 0,$$

$$\forall n, s, t, u \in \mathcal{U}_{i,n} \quad (6.30e)$$

The "perp" symbol, $\perp$, denotes complementarity, i.e., $0 \leq a \perp b \geq 0$ is equivalent to $a \geq 0,\ b \geq 0,\ ab = 0$. For example, (6.30b) states that if $y_{i,n,s,t,u} > 0$, then $\phi^{y}_{i,n,s,t,u} = 0$. Correspondingly, the KKT condition (6.30a) states that the marginal revenue from generation, $W_s \left(D^{\text{int}}_{n,s,t} - D^{\text{slp}}_{n,s,t} c_{n,s,t} \right) - W_s D^{\text{slp}}_{n,s,t} \sum_{\hat{u} \in \mathcal{U}_{i,n}} y_{i,n,s,t,\hat{u}}$, equals the operating cost, $W_s C^{\text{opr}}_{i,n,u}$, CO_2 tax expenditure, $W_s E_u r^{\text{tax}}$, and shadow prices on generation and ramping capacities. Note that if the firm is a price taker, then the $-W_s D^{\text{slp}}_{n,s,t} \sum_{\hat{u} \in \mathcal{U}_{i,n}} y_{i,n,s,t,\hat{u}}$ term is dropped from marginal revenue. The other KKT conditions (6.30c)–(6.30e) pair up dual variables with the constraints (6.28b)–(6.28d) in the profit-maximization problem.

In a similar vein, the KKT conditions for the ISO's optimization problem (6.29a)–(6.29h) are

$$- W_s \left(D^{\text{int}}_{n,s,t} - D^{\text{slp}}_{n,s,t} c_{n,s,t} \right) + \lambda_{n,s,t} - \phi^{c}_{n,s,t} = 0, \forall n, s, t \quad (6.31a)$$

$$\mu_{\ell,s,t} + \overline{\mu}_{\ell,s,t} - \underline{\mu}_{\ell,s,t} + T_t \lambda_{n_\ell^+,s,t} - T_t \lambda_{n_\ell^-,s,t} = 0, \forall \ell, s, t \quad (6.31b)$$

$$- \sum_{\ell \in \mathcal{L}_n^+} B_\ell \mu_{\ell,s,t} + \sum_{\ell \in \mathcal{L}_n^-} B_\ell \mu_{\ell,s,t} + \overline{\kappa}_{n,s,t} - \underline{\kappa}_{n,s,t} = 0, \forall n, s, t \quad (6.31c)$$

$$\mu_{\ell,s,t} \text{ u.r.s.}, \hat{f}_{\ell,s,t} - B_\ell \left(v_{n_\ell^+,s,t} - v_{n_\ell^-,s,t} \right) = 0, \forall \ell, s, t \quad (6.31d)$$

$$0 \le \underline{\mu}_{\ell,s,t} \perp \hat{f}_{\ell,s,t} + K_{\ell}^{\text{trn}} \ge 0, \ \forall \ell, s, t \tag{6.31e}$$

$$0 \le \overline{\mu}_{\ell,s,t} \perp -\hat{f}_{\ell,s,t} + K_{\ell}^{\text{trn}} \ge 0, \ \forall \ell, s, t \tag{6.31f}$$

$$0 \le \underline{\kappa}_{n,s,t} \perp \upsilon_{n,s,t} + \pi \ge 0, \ \forall n, s, t \tag{6.31g}$$

$$0 \le \overline{\kappa}_{n,s,t} \perp -\upsilon_{n,s,t} + \pi \ge 0, \ \forall n, s, t \tag{6.31h}$$

$$\lambda_{n,s,t} \text{ u.r.s., } c_{n,s,t} - \sum_{i \in \mathcal{I}} \sum_{u \in \mathcal{U}_{i,n}} y_{i,n,s,t,u} + T_t \sum_{\ell \in \mathcal{L}_n^+} \hat{f}_{\ell,s,t} - T_t \sum_{\ell \in \mathcal{L}_n^-} \hat{f}_{\ell,s,t} = 0, \ \forall n, s, t \tag{6.31i}$$

$$0 \le \phi_{n,s,t}^{c} \perp c_{n,s,t} \ge 0, \ \forall n, s, t \tag{6.31j}$$

Here, (6.31d)–(6.31j) rehash constraints (6.29b)–(6.29f) from the ISO's optimization problem, while (6.31a)–(6.31c) correspond to KKT conditions with respect to decision variables $c_{n,s,t}$, $\hat{f}_{\ell,s,t}$, and $\upsilon_{n,s,t}$, respectively. In particular, (6.31j) states that if $c_{n,s,t} > 0$, then $\phi_{n,s,t}^{c} = 0$. Therefore, in (6.31a), we have the result that $\lambda_{n,s,t} = W_s \left(D_{n,s,t}^{\text{int}} - D_{n,s,t}^{\text{slp}} c_{n,s,t} \right)$.

Using these KKT conditions to replace the lower-level problems, the bi-level model to set an optimal CO_2 tax in a deregulated electricity industry may be reformulated as the following mathematical program with equilibrium constraints (MPEC):

$$\begin{aligned} \underset{r^{\text{tax}} \cup \Omega^{\text{LL}} \cup \Omega^{\text{DV}}}{\text{Maximize}} \quad & (6.24\text{a}) \\ \text{s.t.} \quad & (6.27\text{a}) \\ & (6.30\text{a})-(6.30\text{e}), \ \forall i \in \mathcal{I} \\ & (6.31\text{a})-(6.31\text{j}) \end{aligned}$$

where $\Omega^{\text{LL}} \equiv \{c_{n,s,t}, \hat{f}_{\ell,s,t}, \upsilon_{n,s,t}, y_{i,n,s,t,u}\}$ and $\Omega^{\text{DV}} \equiv \{\beta_{i,n,s,t,u}, \beta_{i,n,s,t,u}^{\text{up}}, \beta_{i,n,s,t,u}^{\text{down}}, \phi_{i,n,s,t,u}^{y}, \underline{\mu}_{\ell,s,t}, \overline{\mu}_{\ell,s,t}, \underline{\kappa}_{n,s,t}, \overline{\kappa}_{n,s,t}, \phi_{n,s,t}^{c}, \lambda_{n,s,t}, \mu_{\ell,s,t}\}$.

This MPEC, however, is non-linear due to the complementarity conditions arising from (6.30b)–(6.30e), $\forall i \in \mathcal{I}$, and (6.31e)–(6.31h) plus (6.31j). Following the approach of [7], disjunctive constraints resolve these non-linear expressions for the firms as follows:

$$0 \le y_{i,n,s,t,u} \le M^{\text{y}} x_{i,n,s,t,u}^{\text{y}}, \ \forall i, n, s, t, u \in \mathcal{U}_{i,n} \tag{6.32a}$$

$$0 \le \phi_{i,n,s,t,u}^{\text{y}} \le M^{\text{y}} \left(1 - x_{i,n,s,t,u}^{\text{y}} \right), \ \forall i, n, s, t, u \in \mathcal{U}_{i,n} \tag{6.32b}$$

$$0 \le T_t A_{n,s,t,u} K_{i,n,u}^{\text{gen}} - y_{i,n,s,t,u} \le M^{\beta} x_{i,n,s,t,u}^{\beta},$$

$$\forall i, n, s, t, u \in \mathcal{U}_{i,n} \tag{6.32c}$$

$$0 \leq \beta_{i,n,s,t,u} \leq M^{\beta}\left(1 - x^{\beta}_{i,n,s,t,u}\right), \; \forall i, n, s, t, u \in \mathcal{U}_{i,n} \tag{6.32d}$$

$$0 \leq T_t R^{\text{up}}_u K^{\text{gen}}_{i,n,u} - y_{i,n,s,t,u} + y_{i,n,s,t-1,u}$$

$$\leq M^{\beta^{\text{up}}} x^{\beta^{\text{up}}}_{i,n,s,t,u}, \; \forall i, n, s, t, u \in \mathcal{U}_{i,n} \tag{6.32e}$$

$$0 \leq \beta^{\text{up}}_{i,n,s,t,u} \leq M^{\beta^{\text{up}}}\left(1 - x^{\beta^{\text{up}}}_{i,n,s,t,u}\right), \; \forall i, n, s, t, u \in \mathcal{U}_{i,n} \tag{6.32f}$$

$$0 \leq T_t R^{\text{down}}_u K^{\text{gen}}_{i,n,u} + y_{i,n,s,t,u} - y_{i,n,s,t-1,u}$$

$$\leq M^{\beta^{\text{down}}} x^{\beta^{\text{down}}}_{i,n,s,t,u}, \; \forall i, n, s, t, u \in \mathcal{U}_{i,n} \tag{6.32g}$$

$$0 \leq \beta^{\text{down}}_{i,n,s,t,u} \leq M^{\beta^{\text{down}}}\left(1 - x^{\beta^{\text{down}}}_{i,n,s,t,u}\right), \; \forall i, n, s, t, u \in \mathcal{U}_{i,n} \tag{6.32h}$$

$$x^{\text{y}}_{i,n,s,t,u} \in \{0, 1\}, \; x^{\beta}_{i,n,s,t,u} \in \{0, 1\}, \; x^{\beta^{\text{up}}}_{i,n,s,t,u} \in \{0, 1\},$$

$$x^{\beta^{\text{down}}}_{i,n,s,t,u} \in \{0, 1\}, \; \forall i, n, s, t, u \in \mathcal{U}_{i,n} \tag{6.32i}$$

Likewise, the ISO's complementarity conditions may be linearized as

$$0 \leq \hat{f}_{\ell,s,t} + K^{\text{trn}}_{\ell} \leq M^{\underline{\mu}} x^{\underline{\mu}}_{\ell,s,t}, \; \forall \ell, s, t \tag{6.33a}$$

$$0 \leq \underline{\mu}_{\ell,s,t} \leq M^{\underline{\mu}}\left(1 - x^{\underline{\mu}}_{\ell,s,t}\right), \; \forall \ell, s, t \tag{6.33b}$$

$$0 \leq -\hat{f}_{\ell,s,t} + K^{\text{trn}}_{\ell} \leq M^{\overline{\mu}} x^{\overline{\mu}}_{\ell,s,t}, \; \forall \ell, s, t \tag{6.33c}$$

$$0 \leq \overline{\mu}_{\ell,s,t} \leq M^{\overline{\mu}}\left(1 - x^{\overline{\mu}}_{\ell,s,t}\right), \; \forall \ell, s, t \tag{6.33d}$$

$$0 \leq v_{n,s,t} + \pi \leq M^{\underline{\kappa}} x^{\underline{\kappa}}_{n,s,t}, \; \forall n, s, t \tag{6.33e}$$

$$0 \leq \underline{\kappa}_{n,s,t} \leq M^{\underline{\kappa}}\left(1 - x^{\underline{\kappa}}_{n,s,t}\right), \; \forall n, s, t \tag{6.33f}$$

$$0 \leq -v_{n,s,t} + \pi \leq M^{\overline{\kappa}} x^{\overline{\kappa}}_{n,s,t}, \; \forall n, s, t \tag{6.33g}$$

$$0 \leq \overline{\kappa}_{n,s,t} \leq M^{\overline{\kappa}}\left(1 - x^{\overline{\kappa}}_{n,s,t}\right), \; \forall n, s, t \tag{6.33h}$$

$$0 \leq c_{n,s,t} \leq M^{\text{c}} x^{\text{c}}_{n,s,t}, \; \forall n, s, t \tag{6.33i}$$

$$0 \leq \phi^{\text{c}}_{n,s,t} \leq M^{\text{c}}\left(1 - x^{\text{c}}_{n,s,t}\right), \; \forall n, s, t \tag{6.33j}$$

$$x^{\underline{\mu}}_{\ell,s,t} \in \{0, 1\}, \; x^{\overline{\mu}}_{\ell,s,t} \in \{0, 1\}, \; \forall \ell, s, t \tag{6.33k}$$

$$x^{\underline{\kappa}}_{n,s,t} \in \{0, 1\}, \; x^{\overline{\kappa}}_{n,s,t} \in \{0, 1\}, \; x^{\text{c}}_{n,s,t} \in \{0, 1\}, \; \forall n, s, t \tag{6.33l}$$

Hence, the MPEC for optimal CO_2 taxation in a deregulated electricity industry becomes the following MIQP:

$$\underset{r^{\text{tax}} \cup \Omega^{\text{LL}} \cup \Omega^{\text{DV}} \cup \Omega^{\text{BV}}}{\text{Maximize}} \quad (6.24\text{a})$$

$$\text{s.t.} \quad (6.27\text{a})$$

$$(6.30\text{a}), \; \forall i \in \mathcal{I}$$

$$(6.31\text{a})\text{–}(6.31\text{d}), \; (6.31\text{i})$$

$$(6.32\text{a})\text{–}(6.32\text{i})$$

$$(6.33\text{a})\text{–}(6.33\text{l})$$

where $\Omega^{\text{BV}} \equiv \{x^{\text{y}}_{i,n,s,t,u}, x^{\beta}_{i,n,s,t,u}, x^{\beta^{\text{up}}}_{i,n,s,t,u}, x^{\beta^{\text{down}}}_{i,n,s,t,u}, x^{\underline{\mu}}_{\ell,s,t}, x^{\overline{\mu}}_{\ell,s,t}, x^{\underline{\kappa}}_{n,s,t}, x^{\overline{\kappa}}_{n,s,t}, x^{\text{c}}_{n,s,t}\}$ refers to the binary variables used in the disjunctive constraints.

Illustrative Example 6.6 *Welfare-maximizing MIQP for optimal CO_2 taxation under Cournot oligopoly.*

We use the same data from Illustrative Example 6.5 here and vary Z over the interval $[0, 0.02]$. In the case of perfect competition, we remove the term $W_s D^{\text{slp}}_{n,s,t} \sum_{\hat{u} \in \mathcal{U}_{i,n}} y_{i,n,s,t,\hat{u}}$ from firm i's KKT condition (6.30a). Since perfect competition with CO_2 taxation set by a welfare-maximizing policymaker leads to full internalization of the cost of the externality, there is no difference between this model and the first-best central-planning one in Illustrative Example 6.5. The optimal CO_2 tax when industry is perfectly competitive is simply the MCD under central planning as indicated in Fig. 6.7. A discrepancy in how PS is calculated may arise because of the CO_2 tax imposed on firms but collected in the form of government revenue (GR). However, all other welfare components and operational metrics, e.g., consumption, generation, and CO_2 emissions, are identical.

By contrast, if power companies at the lower level behave à la Cournot, then a significantly different CO_2 tax is optimal. From Fig. 6.7, r^{tax} for an oligopoly is lower than the MCD under central planning when Z is relatively low only to increase thereafter. Furthermore, r^{tax} for an oligopoly is initially lower than its *own* MCD as well. This outcome has to do with the fact that a policymaker in this bi-level setting has to contend with two types of distortions: CO_2 emissions and exertion of market power by firms. If it were to set r^{tax} at the MCD, then it could possibly increase the leverage of firms in increasing the market-clearing price. From Fig. 6.8, the impact of market power vis-à-vis the welfare components in Fig. 6.3 is evident in that it decreases CS and increases PS. Indeed, all generation is withheld under a Cournot oligopoly, cf. Figs. 6.4 and 6.9. In fact, gas-fired generation is not dispatched at all initially, and CO_2 emissions even briefly increase above those from central planning (Fig. 6.6). As Z increases from 0, a positive CO_2 tax curbs coal generation, and the resulting increase in the market-clearing price entices RE output. When $Z = 0.005$, the CO_2 tax equals \$75/t and leads to cost parity between

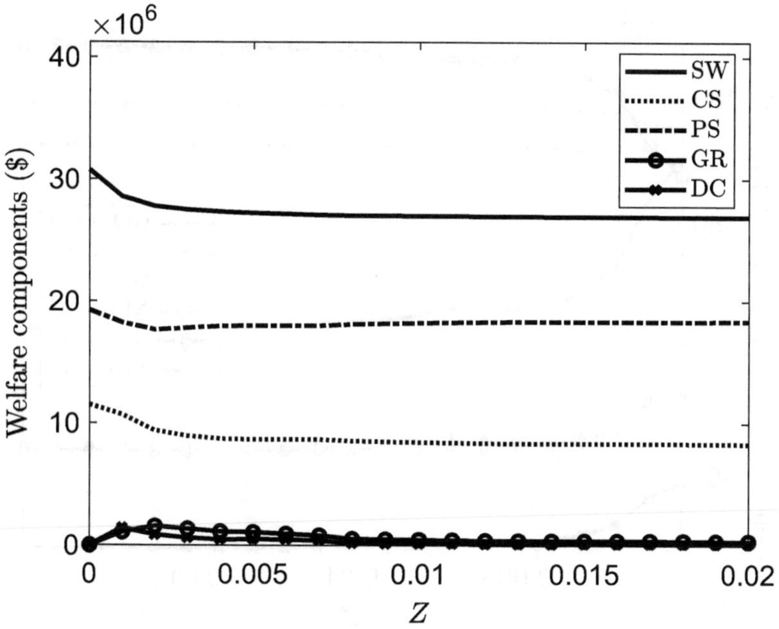

Fig. 6.8 Welfare components under Cournot oligopoly and a CO_2 tax with respect to Z

the two fossil-fuel technologies, thereby incentivizing the first appearance of the gas-fired technology. When $Z = 0.007$, coal is eliminated from the generation mix, while gas-fired generation increases until $Z = 0.008$. After this point, gas-fired generation decreases monotonically, whereas RE output increases monotonically. Thus, a plausible explanation for why the CO_2 tax under a Cournot oligopoly is relatively low initially is that the policymaker wishes to mitigate the impact of market power and relies on the low-cost coal technology in spite of its high CO_2 emissions. Once it is able to entice gas generation to replace coal, the policymaker uses a relatively high CO_2 tax to lower CO_2 emissions. While such a policy may reduce CS further, its impact is mitigated by the fact that it also induces more RE generation. Finally, the patterns of NI and TF in Figs. 6.9 and 6.10 are similar to those in Figs. 6.4 and 6.5.

6.4.3 Renewable Portfolio Standard in a Deregulated Electricity Industry

Instead of a direct curb on CO_2 emissions via taxation, RPS sets a target for RE generation. This target is usually specified in terms of a percentage of total generation, e.g., 50%, and is implemented as an equilibrium constraint on industry.

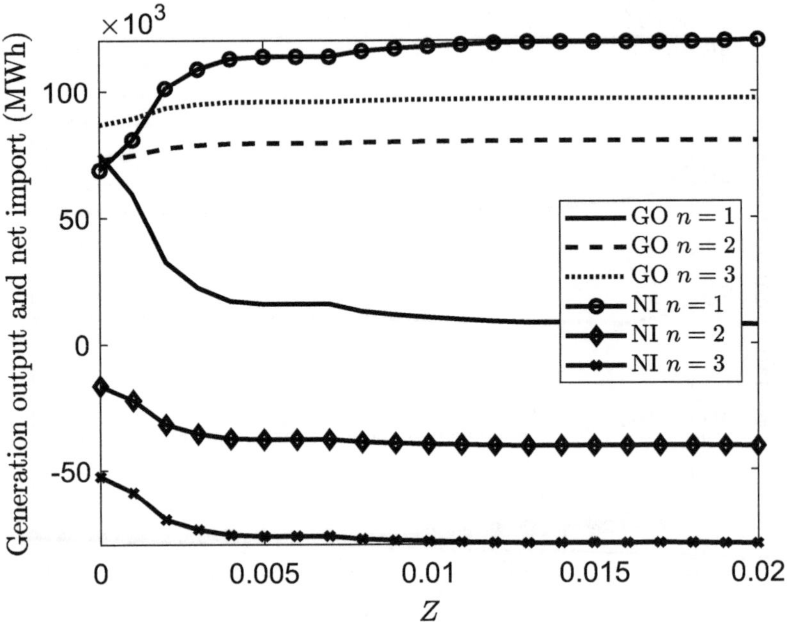

Fig. 6.9 Generation output and net import under Cournot oligopoly and a CO_2 tax with respect to Z

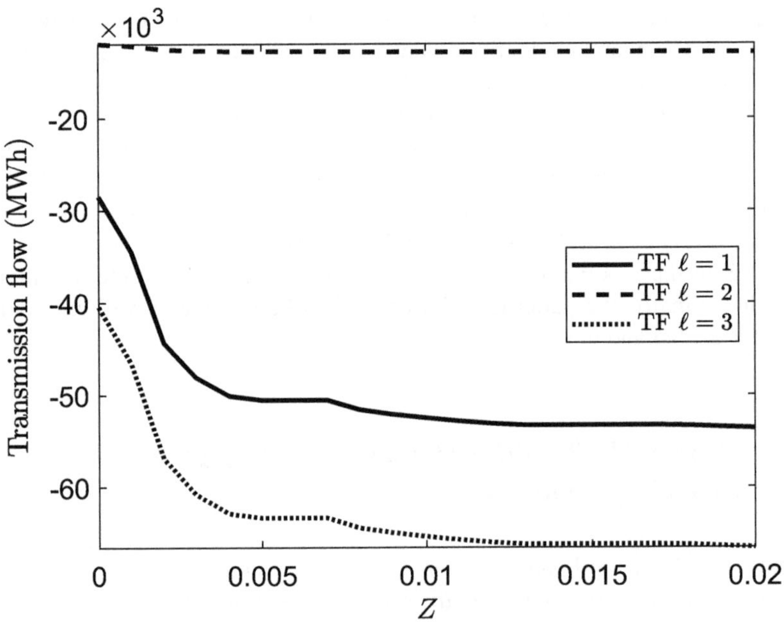

Fig. 6.10 Transmission flow under Cournot oligopoly and a CO_2 tax with respect to Z

The shadow price on this constraint, i.e., the price of renewable energy certificates (RECs), is taken as given by firms and becomes either an extra revenue (for RE) or an extra cost (for NRE) term. In the long run, RPS aims to incentivize further RE adoption and to discourage NRE generation without severely impacting consumption. Furthermore, in contrast to CO_2 taxation, RPS does not generate any government revenues because the REC revenue for RE is financed by the REC cost incurred by NRE. Otherwise, the framework for analysis is similar to the bi-level model from Sect. 6.4.2, viz., a welfare-maximizing policymaker at the upper level sets the RPS target, while industry at the lower level makes its generation and consumption decisions while internalizing the REC price.

The notation follows from that in Sects. 6.4.1 and 6.4.2 along with the following additions:

Indices and Sets

$j \in \mathcal{J}$ Discrete RPS level.
$\mathcal{U}^{\mathrm{C}}_{i,n}$ Conventional, i.e., NRE, plants for firm i at node n.
$\mathcal{U}^{\mathrm{R}}_{i,n}$ RE plants for firm i at node n.

Note that $\mathcal{U}^{\mathrm{C}}_{i,n} \cup \mathcal{U}^{\mathrm{R}}_{i,n} = \mathcal{U}_{i,n}$ and $\mathcal{U}^{\mathrm{C}}_{i,n} \cap \mathcal{U}^{\mathrm{R}}_{i,n} = \emptyset$.

Parameters

$\overline{M}^{\mathrm{y}}$ Large positive constant used to linearize the RPS constraint [–].
$\underline{M}^{\mathrm{y}}$ Large positive constant used to linearize the RPS constraint [–].
$\overline{M}^{\rho}$ Large positive constant used to linearize REC revenue [–].
$\underline{M}^{\rho}$ Large positive constant used to linearize REC revenue [–].
Q_j RPS percentage in level j [–].

Binary Variable

x_j Binary variable that is equal to 1 if discrete RPS level $j \in \mathcal{J}$ is selected and 0 otherwise.

Continuous Variables

e_j Auxiliary variable used to linearize REC revenue for level j [\$/MWh].
g_j Auxiliary variable used to linearize RE target for level j [MWh].
r_j REC revenue for level j [\$/MWh].
w_j RE target for level j [MWh].

Dual Variables

ρ REC price [\$/MWh].

Although the RPS target is a continuous variable in [0, 1], we discretize it in order to linearize the bi-level problem. In particular, we use RPS levels $Q_j \in [0, 1], \forall j \in \mathcal{J}$ with corresponding binary variables $x_j \in \{0, 1\}$. Thus, if RPS level j^* is selected, then $x_{j^*} = 1$ and $x_{j'} = 0, \forall j' \neq j^*$. Furthermore, the RPS target for industry is Q_{j^*}. Given this discretization, the policymaker sets the optimal RPS target, x_j, at the upper level in anticipation of power-sector operations at the lower level while internalizing the cost of damage from emissions:

$$\underset{x_j}{\text{Maximize}}\ (6.24a)$$

$$\text{s.t. } x_j \in \{0, 1\},\ \forall j \in \mathcal{J} \tag{6.34a}$$

$$\sum_{j \in \mathcal{J}} x_j = 1 \tag{6.34b}$$

The objective function (6.24a) is again the maximization of social welfare inclusive of the damage from CO_2 emissions. Since the policymaker cannot directly control industry operations, its only decision variable is the selection of the RPS target via x_j. Toward that end, constraints (6.34a) and (6.34b) specify the binary restriction on x_j and constrain exactly one RPS level to be selected, which could be a target of zero.

At the lower level, each firm $i \in \mathcal{I}$ maximizes its profit by deciding its generation output, while the ISO maximize social surplus by selecting nodal consumption and requisite power flows. Thus, their problems are similar to (6.28a)–(6.28e), $\forall i \in \mathcal{I}$, and (6.29a)–(6.29h), thereby comprising an equilibrium problem. However, there are two crucial differences here from the lower level in Sect. 6.4.2:

1. Industry faces the exogenous RPS equilibrium constraint:

$$\sum_{s \in \mathcal{S}} W_s \sum_{i \in \mathcal{I}} \sum_{t \in \mathcal{T}} \sum_{n \in \mathcal{N}} \sum_{u \in \mathcal{U}_{i,n}^R} y_{i,n,s,t,u} \geq \sum_{j \in \mathcal{J}} Q_j x_j \sum_{s \in \mathcal{S}} W_s \sum_{i \in \mathcal{I}} \sum_{t \in \mathcal{T}} \sum_{n \in \mathcal{N}} \sum_{u \in \mathcal{U}_{i,n}} y_{i,n,s,t,u}$$

   Its corresponding dual variable, ρ, is the REC price.
2. Instead of taking a CO_2 tax as given, each firm $i \in \mathcal{I}$ takes as exogenous the revenue or cost from RECs. Thus, (6.28a) is adjusted by first deleting the term related to CO_2 taxation, $-\sum_{s \in \mathcal{S}} W_s \sum_{t \in \mathcal{T}} \sum_{n \in \mathcal{N}} \sum_{u \in \mathcal{U}_{i,n}} r^{\text{tax}} E_u y_{i,n,s,t,u}$. Next, the net revenue from RECs is added to (6.28a) as

$$\rho \sum_{s \in \mathcal{S}} W_s \sum_{t \in \mathcal{T}} \sum_{n \in \mathcal{N}} \left(\sum_{u \in \mathcal{U}_{i,n}^R} y_{i,n,s,t,u} - \sum_{j \in \mathcal{J}} Q_j x_j \sum_{u \in \mathcal{U}_{i,n}} y_{i,n,s,t,u} \right)$$

At this stage, we could resolve this lower-level equilibrium problem as an MCP via the KKT conditions of each agent's problem plus the equilibrium constraint. Such a resolution would enable reformulation of the bi-level problem as an MPEC as in Sect. 6.4.2. Rather than using the MPEC approach, we opt to recast the bi-level problem as a mathematical program with primal and dual constraints (MPPDCs). An advantage of the MPPDC approach is that it does not require binary variables to linearize the complementarity conditions from the lower level. Instead, it replaces the lower-level problem by (i) its primal constraints, (ii) its dual constraints, and (iii) the strong-duality equality [8]. Prior to doing so, however, we first need to convert the lower-level equilibrium problem into a single-agent optimization problem. Following [9] and [10], we are able to do so because of the linearity of the supply and demand functions as well as transportation costs that are proportional to the distance covered. Consequently, the exercise of market power by firms can be captured via an extended-cost term, $-\frac{1}{2}\sum_{s\in\mathcal{S}} W_s \sum_{t\in\mathcal{T}} \sum_{n\in\mathcal{N}} D^{\text{slp}}_{n,s,t} \sum_{i\in\mathcal{I}} \left(\sum_{u\in\mathcal{U}_{i,n}} y_{i,n,s,t,u}\right)^2$, which ensures that the KKT condition (and dual constraint) corresponding to $y_{i,n,s,t,u}$ reflects the plant's marginal revenue. Therefore, lower-level QP comprising the firms' profit-maximization and the ISO's surplus-maximization problems is

$$\underset{\overline{\Omega}^{\text{LL}}}{\text{Maximize}} \sum_{s\in\mathcal{S}} W_s \sum_{t\in\mathcal{T}} \sum_{n\in\mathcal{N}} \left[D^{\text{int}}_{n,s,t} c_{n,s,t} - \frac{1}{2} D^{\text{slp}}_{n,s,t} c^2_{n,s,t} - \sum_{i\in\mathcal{I}} \sum_{u\in\mathcal{U}_{i,n}} C^{\text{opr}}_{i,n,u} y_{i,n,s,t,u} \right.$$
$$\left. -\frac{1}{2} D^{\text{slp}}_{n,s,t} \sum_{i\in\mathcal{I}} \left(\sum_{u\in\mathcal{U}_{i,n}} y_{i,n,s,t,u} \right)^2 \right] \tag{6.35a}$$

$$\text{s.t. } (6.28\text{b})–(6.28\text{e}),\ \forall i \in \mathcal{I}$$
$$(6.29\text{b})–(6.29\text{h})$$
$$\sum_{s\in\mathcal{S}} W_s \sum_{i\in\mathcal{I}} \sum_{t\in\mathcal{T}} \sum_{n\in\mathcal{N}} \sum_{u\in\mathcal{U}^R_{i,n}} y_{i,n,s,t,u}$$
$$-\sum_{j\in\mathcal{J}} Q_j x_j \sum_{s\in\mathcal{S}} W_s \sum_{i\in\mathcal{I}} \sum_{t\in\mathcal{T}} \sum_{n\in\mathcal{N}} \sum_{u\in\mathcal{U}_{i,n}} y_{i,n,s,t,u} \geq 0 : \rho \tag{6.35b}$$

where $\overline{\Omega}^{\text{LL}} \equiv \{c_{n,s,t}, \hat{f}_{\ell,s,t}, v_{n,s,t}, y_{i,n,s,t,u}\}$.

Given x_j, the lower-level problem comprising (6.35a), (6.28b)–(6.28e), $\forall i \in \mathcal{I}$, (6.29b)–(6.29h), and (6.35b) is a QP and, thus, a convex problem. Consequently, it may be replaced by its primal constraints, its dual constraints, and the strong-duality equality. The primal constraints are simply (6.28b)–(6.28e), $\forall i \in \mathcal{I}$, (6.29b)–(6.29h), and (6.35b), while the dual constraints are related to the QP's KKT conditions:

$$W_s C^{\text{opr}}_{i,n,u} + \beta_{i,n,s,t,u} + \beta^{\text{up}}_{i,n,s,t,u} - \beta^{\text{down}}_{i,n,s,t,u} - \beta^{\text{up}}_{i,n,s,t+1,u} + \beta^{\text{down}}_{i,n,s,t+1,u}$$
$$- \lambda_{n,s,t} + W_s D^{\text{slp}}_{n,s,t} \sum_{u'\in\mathcal{U}_{i,n}} y_{i,n,s,t,u'} - \phi^{y}_{i,n,s,t,u} + W_s \left(\sum_{j\in\mathcal{J}} Q_j x_j - 1 \right) \rho = 0,$$
$$\forall i, n, s, t, u \in \mathcal{U}^{\text{R}}_{i,n} \tag{6.36a}$$

$$W_s C^{\text{opr}}_{i,n,u} + \beta_{i,n,s,t,u} + \beta^{\text{up}}_{i,n,s,t,u} - \beta^{\text{down}}_{i,n,s,t,u} - \beta^{\text{up}}_{i,n,s,t+1,u} + \beta^{\text{down}}_{i,n,s,t+1,u}$$

$$- \lambda_{n,s,t} + W_s D^{\text{slp}}_{n,s,t} \sum_{u' \in \mathcal{U}_{i,n}} y_{i,n,s,t,u'} - \phi^{y}_{i,n,s,t,u} + W_s \sum_{j \in \mathcal{J}} Q_j x_j \rho = 0,$$

$$\forall i, n, s, t, u \in \mathcal{U}^{\text{C}}_{i,n} \tag{6.36b}$$

$$- W_s \left(D^{\text{int}}_{n,s,t} - D^{\text{slp}}_{n,s,t} c_{n,s,t} \right) + \lambda_{n,s,t} - \phi^{c}_{n,s,t} = 0, \ \forall n, s, t \tag{6.36c}$$

$$\mu_{\ell,s,t} + \overline{\mu}_{\ell,s,t} - \underline{\mu}_{\ell,s,t} + T_t \lambda_{n^+_\ell,s,t} - T_t \lambda_{n^-_\ell,s,t} = 0, \ \forall \ell, s, t \tag{6.36d}$$

$$- \sum_{\ell \in \mathcal{L}^+_n} B_\ell \mu_{\ell,s,t} + \sum_{\ell \in \mathcal{L}^-_n} B_\ell \mu_{\ell,s,t} + \overline{\kappa}_{n,s,t} - \underline{\kappa}_{n,s,t} = 0, \forall n, s, t \tag{6.36e}$$

$$\beta_{i,n,s,t,u} \geq 0, \ \beta^{\text{up}}_{i,n,s,t,u} \geq 0, \ \beta^{\text{down}}_{i,n,s,t,u} \geq 0, \ \phi^{y}_{i,n,s,t,u} \geq 0, \ \forall i, n, s, t, u \in \mathcal{U}_{i,n} \tag{6.36f}$$

$$\underline{\mu}_{\ell,s,t} \geq 0, \overline{\mu}_{\ell,s,t} \geq 0, \ \forall \ell, s, t \tag{6.36g}$$

$$\underline{\kappa}_{n,s,t} \geq 0, \overline{\kappa}_{n,s,t} \geq 0, \ \phi^{c}_{n,s,t} \geq 0, \ \forall n, s, t \tag{6.36h}$$

$$\rho \geq 0 \tag{6.36i}$$

$$\lambda_{n,s,t} \ \text{u.r.s.}, \ \forall n, s, t \tag{6.36j}$$

$$\mu_{\ell,s,t} \ \text{u.r.s.}, \ \forall \ell, s, t \tag{6.36k}$$

where $\Omega^{\text{DV}} \equiv \{\beta_{i,n,s,t,u}, \beta^{\text{up}}_{i,n,s,t,u}, \beta^{\text{down}}_{i,n,s,t,u}, \phi^{y}_{i,n,s,t,u}, \underline{\mu}_{\ell,s,t}, \overline{\mu}_{\ell,s,t}, \underline{\kappa}_{n,s,t}, \overline{\kappa}_{n,s,t}, \phi^{c}_{n,s,t}, \lambda_{n,s,t}, \mu_{\ell,s,t}, \rho\}$ are lower-level dual variables. For example, (6.36a) is the dual constraint related to RE generation such that the marginal revenue, $\lambda_{n,s,t} - W_s D^{\text{slp}}_{n,s,t} \sum_{u' \in \mathcal{U}_{i,n}} y_{i,n,s,t,u'} + W_s \left(1 - \sum_{j \in \mathcal{J}} Q_j x_j\right) \rho$, equals the operating cost, $W_s C^{\text{opr}}_{i,n,u}$, plus any "shadow prices," $\beta_{i,n,s,t,u} + \beta^{\text{up}}_{i,n,s,t,u} - \beta^{\text{down}}_{i,n,s,t,u} - \beta^{\text{up}}_{i,n,s,t+1,u} + \beta^{\text{down}}_{i,n,s,t+1,u} - \phi^{y}_{i,n,s,t,u}$. The $-W_s D^{\text{slp}}_{n,s,t} \sum_{u' \in \mathcal{U}_{i,n}} y_{i,n,s,t,u'}$ term reflects how increased generation would lower the price for a Cournot firm and is removed from marginal revenue in case of a price taker. Similarly, (6.36b) equates the marginal revenue and cost for NRE generation, where $W_s \left(1 - \sum_{j \in \mathcal{J}} Q_j x_j\right) \rho$ in the marginal revenue is replaced by $-W_s \sum_{j \in \mathcal{J}} Q_j x_j \rho$ to reflect the fact that the REC price is an implicit tax for NRE.

In order to obtain the strong-duality equality, we first derive the dual objective function. From QP duality [5], it is known that the dual objective function includes quadratic terms from (6.35a) as well as the products of the dual variables and the constant terms in constraints (6.28b)–(6.28e), $\forall i \in \mathcal{I}$, (6.29b)–(6.29h), and (6.35b). Following [11] to preserve convexity, we implement the strong-duality expression as an inequality such that the primal objective is greater than or equal to the dual objective:

$$\sum_{s\in\mathcal{S}} W_s \sum_{n\in\mathcal{N}} \sum_{t\in\mathcal{T}} \left[D^{\mathrm{int}}_{n,s,t} c_{n,s,t} - \frac{1}{2} D^{\mathrm{slp}}_{n,s,t} c^2_{n,s,t} - \sum_{i\in\mathcal{I}} \sum_{u\in\mathcal{U}_{i,n}} C^{\mathrm{opr}}_{i,n,u} y_{i,n,s,t,u} \right.$$
$$\left. -\frac{1}{2} D^{\mathrm{slp}}_{n,s,t} \sum_{i\in\mathcal{I}} \left(\sum_{u\in\mathcal{U}_{i,n}} y_{i,n,s,t,u} \right)^2 \right]$$
$$\geq \frac{1}{2} \sum_{s\in\mathcal{S}} W_s \sum_{n\in\mathcal{N}} \sum_{t\in\mathcal{T}} D^{\mathrm{slp}}_{n,s,t} c^2_{n,s,t} + \frac{1}{2} \sum_{s\in\mathcal{S}} W_s \sum_{n\in\mathcal{N}} \sum_{t\in\mathcal{T}} D^{\mathrm{slp}}_{n,s,t} \sum_{i\in\mathcal{I}} \left(\sum_{u\in\mathcal{U}_{i,n}} y_{i,n,s,t,u} \right)^2$$
$$+ \sum_{i\in\mathcal{I}} \sum_{n\in\mathcal{N}} \sum_{s\in\mathcal{S}} \sum_{t\in\mathcal{T}} \sum_{u\in\mathcal{U}_{i,n}} K^{\mathrm{gen}}_{i,n,u} T_t \left(A_{n,s,t,u} \beta_{i,n,s,t,u} + R^{\mathrm{up}}_u \beta^{\mathrm{up}}_{i,n,s,t,u} + R^{\mathrm{down}}_u \beta^{\mathrm{down}}_{i,n,s,t,u} \right)$$
$$+ \sum_{\ell\in\mathcal{L}} \sum_{s\in\mathcal{S}} \sum_{t\in\mathcal{T}} K^{\mathrm{trn}}_{\ell} \left(\underline{\mu}_{\ell,s,t} + \overline{\mu}_{\ell,s,t} \right) + \sum_{n\in\mathcal{N}} \sum_{s\in\mathcal{S}} \sum_{t\in\mathcal{T}} \pi \left(\underline{\kappa}_{n,s,t} + \overline{\kappa}_{n,s,t} \right) \tag{6.37}$$

The resulting mathematical program with primal and dual constraints (MPPDC) comprises the objective function (6.24a) subject to upper-level constraints (6.34a)–(6.34b), lower-level primal constraints (6.28b)–(6.28e), $\forall i \in \mathcal{I}$, (6.29b)–(6.29h), and (6.35b), lower-level dual constraints (6.36a)–(6.36k), and the strong-duality expression (6.37). Note that the presence of the extended-cost terms, $\frac{1}{2} \sum_{s\in\mathcal{S}} W_s \sum_{n\in\mathcal{N}} \sum_{t\in\mathcal{T}} D^{\mathrm{slp}}_{n,s,t} \sum_{i\in\mathcal{I}} \left(\sum_{u\in\mathcal{U}_{i,n}} y_{i,n,s,t,u} \right)^2$, in (6.37) accurately captures Cournot behavior. However, this MPPDC cannot be readily tackled by off-the-shelf solvers because of non-linearities in the primal constraint (6.35b) and dual constraints (6.36a)–(6.36b). Specifically, (6.35b) includes bilinear terms for x_j and $y_{i,n,s,t,u}$, while (6.36a)–(6.36b) have bilinear terms for x_j and ρ.

We use the approach of [1] to linearize bilinear terms in (6.35b) via auxiliary variables g_j and w_j:

$$\sum_{s\in\mathcal{S}} W_s \sum_{i\in\mathcal{I}} \sum_{n\in\mathcal{N}} \sum_{t\in\mathcal{T}} \sum_{u\in\mathcal{U}^{\mathrm{R}}_{i,n}} y_{i,n,s,t,u} - \sum_{j\in\mathcal{J}} w_j \geq 0 \tag{6.38a}$$

$$w_j - Q_j \sum_{s\in\mathcal{S}} W_s \sum_{i\in\mathcal{I}} \sum_{n\in\mathcal{N}} \sum_{t\in\mathcal{T}} \sum_{u\in\mathcal{U}_{i,n}} y_{i,n,s,t,u} + g_j = 0, \ \forall j \tag{6.38b}$$

$$x_j \underline{M}^{\mathrm{y}} Q_j \leq w_j \leq x_j \overline{M}^{\mathrm{y}} Q_j, \ \forall j \tag{6.38c}$$

$$\left(1 - x_j\right) \underline{M}^{\mathrm{y}} Q_j \leq g_j \leq \left(1 - x_j\right) \overline{M}^{\mathrm{y}} Q_j, \ \forall j \tag{6.38d}$$

$$g_j \text{ u.r.s.}, \ \forall j \tag{6.38e}$$

$$w_j \text{ u.r.s.}, \ \forall j \tag{6.38f}$$

Similarly, (6.36a)–(6.36b) may be linearized as follows using auxiliary variables e_j and r_j:

$$W_s C^{\text{opr}}_{i,n,u} + \beta_{i,n,s,t,u} + \beta^{\text{up}}_{i,n,s,t,u} - \beta^{\text{down}}_{i,n,s,t,u} - \beta^{\text{up}}_{i,n,s,t+1,u} + \beta^{\text{down}}_{i,n,s,t+1,u}$$

$$- \lambda_{n,s,t} + W_s D^{\text{slp}}_{n,s,t} \sum_{u' \in \mathcal{U}_{i,n}} y_{i,n,s,t,u'} - \phi^{y}_{i,n,s,t,u} + W_s \left(\sum_{j \in \mathcal{J}} r_j - \rho \right) = 0,$$

$$\forall i, n, s, t, u \in \mathcal{U}^{\text{R}}_{i,n} \tag{6.39a}$$

$$W_s C^{\text{opr}}_{i,n,u} + \beta_{i,n,s,t,u} + \beta^{\text{up}}_{i,n,s,t,u} - \beta^{\text{down}}_{i,n,s,t,u} - \beta^{\text{up}}_{i,n,s,t+1,u} + \beta^{\text{down}}_{i,n,s,t+1,u}$$

$$- \lambda_{n,s,t} + W_s D^{\text{slp}}_{n,s,t} \sum_{u' \in \mathcal{U}_{i,n}} y_{i,n,s,t,u'} - \phi^{y}_{i,n,s,t,u} + W_s \sum_{j \in \mathcal{J}} r_j = 0,$$

$$\forall i, n, s, t, u \in \mathcal{U}^{\text{C}}_{i,n} \tag{6.39b}$$

$$r_j - Q_j \rho + e_j = 0, \ \forall j \tag{6.39c}$$

$$x_j \underline{M}^{\rho} Q_j \le r_j \le x_j \overline{M}^{\rho} Q_j, \ \forall j \tag{6.39d}$$

$$\left(1 - x_j\right) \underline{M}^{\rho} Q_j \le e_j \le \left(1 - x_j\right) \overline{M}^{\rho} Q_j, \ \forall j \tag{6.39e}$$

$$e_j \text{ u.r.s.}, \ \forall j \tag{6.39f}$$

$$r_j \text{ u.r.s.}, \ \forall j \tag{6.39g}$$

Given these linearizations, the MPPDC that represents the bi-level problem of the policymaker's RPS target setting in a deregulated electricity industry is rendered as the following MIQCQP:

$$\underset{\{x_j\} \cup \Omega^{\text{LL}} \cup \Omega^{\text{DV}}}{\text{Maximize}} \quad (6.24\text{a})$$

$$\begin{aligned} \text{s.t.} \quad & (6.34\text{a})\text{–}(6.34\text{b}) \\ & (6.28\text{b})\text{–}(6.28\text{e}), \ \forall i \in \mathcal{I} \\ & (6.29\text{b})\text{–}(6.29\text{h}) \\ & (6.36\text{c})\text{–}(6.36\text{k}) \\ & (6.38\text{a})\text{–}(6.38\text{f}) \\ & (6.39\text{a})\text{–}(6.39\text{g}) \\ & (6.37) \end{aligned}$$

where $\Omega^{\text{LL}} \equiv \overline{\Omega}^{\text{LL}} \cup \{e_j, g_j, r_j, w_j\}$ is the set of all lower-level decision variables.

Illustrative Example 6.7 *Welfare-maximizing MIQCQP for optimal RPS target in a deregulated electricity industry.*

We again use the same data as in Illustrative Example 6.5 and vary Z over $[0, 0.02]$. The problem instances under perfect competition are implemented by removing the extended-cost term, $\frac{1}{2}\sum_{s\in\mathcal{S}} W_s \sum_{n\in\mathcal{N}} \sum_{t\in\mathcal{T}} D^{\text{slp}}_{n,s,t} \sum_{i\in\mathcal{I}} \left(\sum_{u\in\mathcal{U}_{i,n}} y_{i,n,s,t,u}\right)^2$, from the lower-level objective function (6.35a). This means that the MPPDC should delete (i) the $W_s D^{\text{slp}}_{n,s,t} \sum_{u'\in\mathcal{U}_{i,n}} y_{i,n,s,t,u'}$ terms in (6.36a)–(6.36b), cf. (6.39a)–(6.39b) and (ii) the $\frac{1}{2}\sum_{s\in\mathcal{S}} W_s \sum_{n\in\mathcal{N}} \sum_{t\in\mathcal{T}} D^{\text{slp}}_{n,s,t} \sum_{i\in\mathcal{I}} \left(\sum_{u\in\mathcal{U}_{i,n}} y_{i,n,s,t,u}\right)^2$ terms from both sides of the strong-duality expression (6.37). Figure 6.11 indicates the optimal RPS target under perfect competition and Cournot oligopoly. The *implied* RPS target under central planning is also given. Since a policymaker who faces a perfectly competitive power sector under deregulation cannot induce a curb in consumption, it instead boosts the fraction of RE output. By contrast, a policymaker sets a lower RPS target when facing an oligopolistic power sector in order to avoid enhancing its market power. However, the incentive to withhold generation affects not only the electricity price but also the REC price. Indeed, in Fig. 6.12, the REC price under Cournot oligopoly increases to above that under perfect competition when $Z = 0.005$.

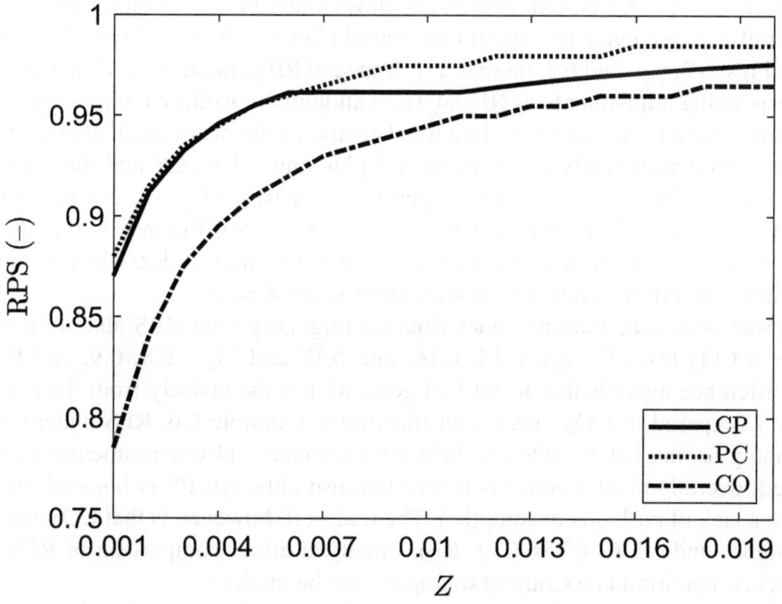

Fig. 6.11 RPS target with respect to Z

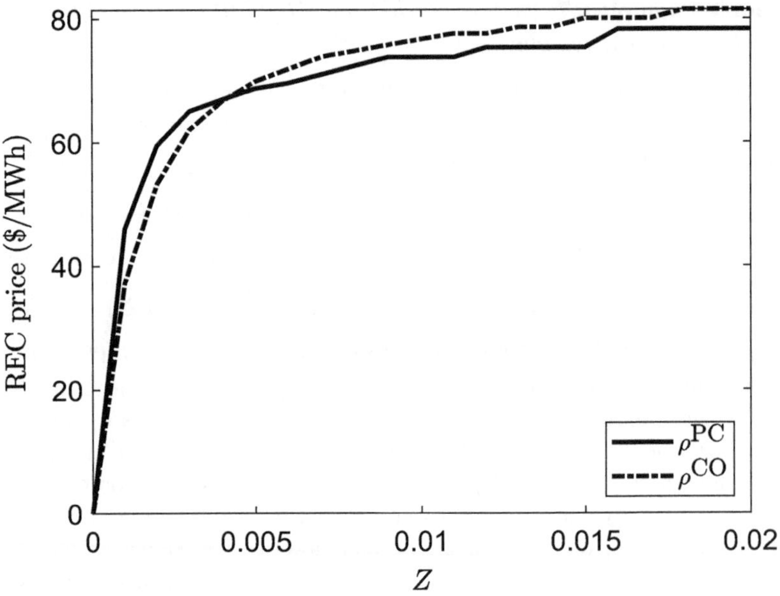

Fig. 6.12 REC price with respect to Z

In terms of power-system operations, those under perfect competition with RPS are similar in aggregate to those under central planning (Figs. 6.13, 6.15, and 6.17). As in Figs. 6.3, 6.4, and 6.5, there is a shift toward RE generation as Z increases with corresponding adjustments to NI and TF. Although the welfare components behave similarly, there is an overall welfare loss because of the distortion that consumption is not curbed sufficiently as under central planning. Thus, CS and the PS of firm $i = 2$ are higher under perfect competition with RPS vis-à-vis central planning, albeit at the cost of lower PS for firm $i = 1$. Another difference is that the REC price is never high enough to induce a switch in the merit order, which means that gas-fired generation is never used apart from when $Z = 0$.

Power-system operations under Cournot oligopoly with RPS also mirror those under a CO_2 tax, cf. Figs. 6.14, 6.16, and 6.18 and Figs. 6.8, 6.9, and 6.10. A key difference again is that fossil-fuel generation is exclusively from the coal-fired plant. Compared to CO_2 taxation in Illustrative Example 6.6, RPS under Cournot oligopoly seems better suited to balance economic and environmental concerns. Indeed, overall social welfare is higher because although PS is boosted, so is CS due to a lack of curb on consumption. The trade-off, however, is that CO_2 emissions are higher under a CO_2 tax (Fig. 6.6). Finally, a direct comparison of RPS under perfect competition and Cournot oligopoly can be made:

- Social welfare is higher under perfect competition, cf. Figs. 6.13 and 6.14, with a transfer from consumers to producers under Cournot oligopoly.

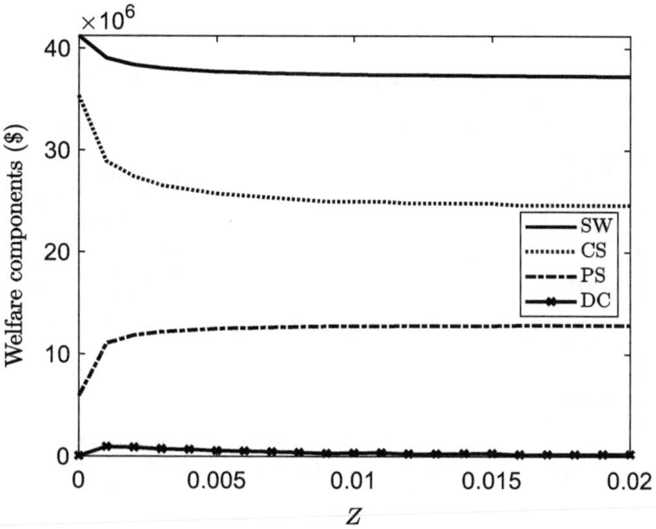

Fig. 6.13 Welfare components under perfect competition and RPS with respect to Z

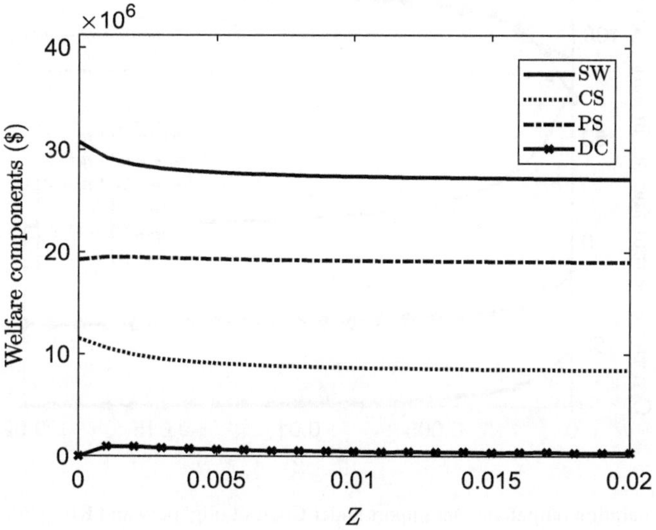

Fig. 6.14 Welfare components under Cournot oligopoly and RPS with respect to Z

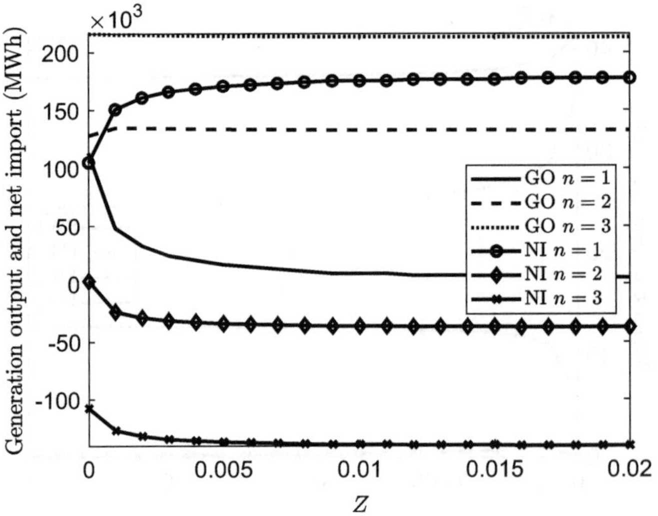

Fig. 6.15 Generation output and net import under perfect competition and RPS with respect to Z

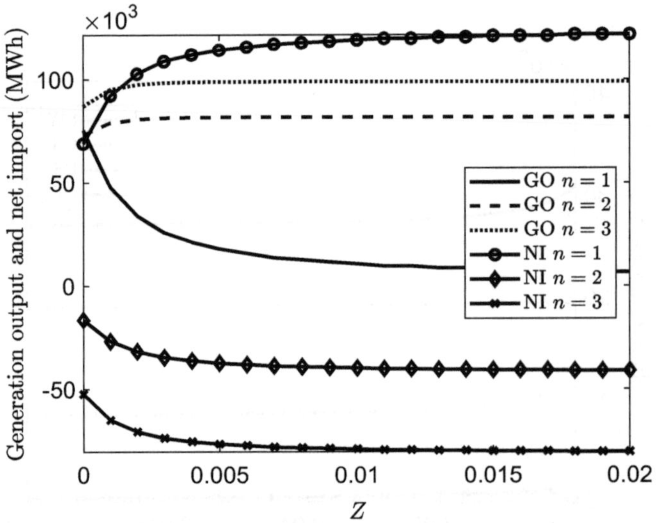

Fig. 6.16 Generation output and net import under Cournot oligopoly and RPS with respect to Z

- Generation output is generally higher under perfect competition, cf. Figs. 6.15 and 6.16, although node $n = 2$ is already a net exporter under Cournot oligopoly even with $Z = 0$ due to the exertion of market power.
- Transmission flows are generally higher under perfect competition, cf. Figs. 6.17 and 6.18, which reflects the curbed consumption under Cournot oligopoly.

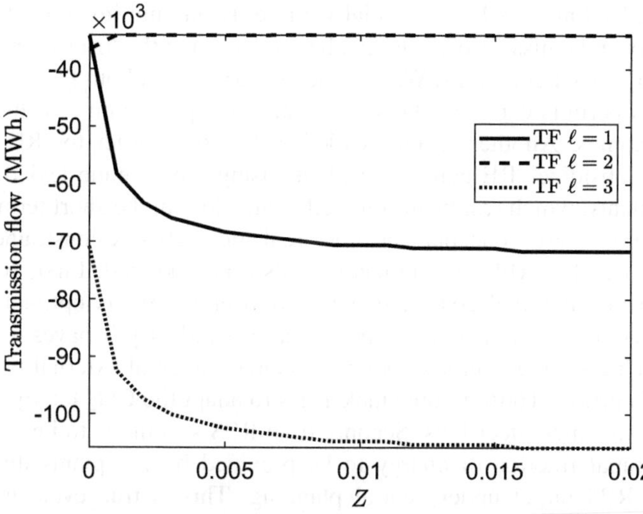

Fig. 6.17 Transmission flow under perfect competition and RPS with respect to Z

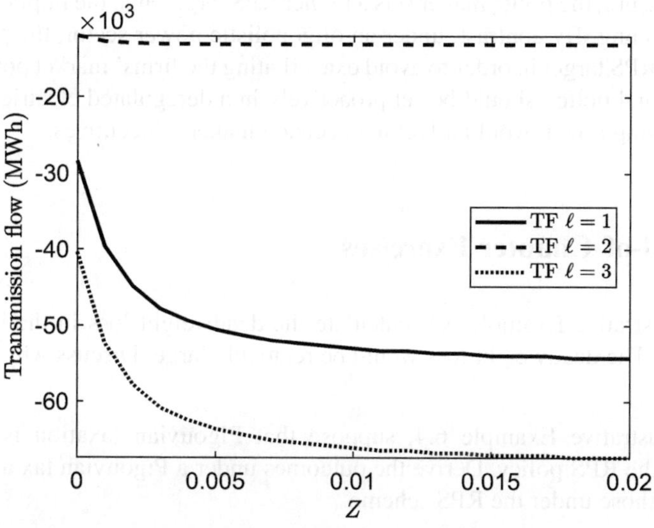

Fig. 6.18 Transmission flow under Cournot oligopoly and RPS with respect to Z

6.5 Summary

In this chapter, we have discussed the issues of negative externalities, focusing on examples of CO_2 emissions. A negative externality occurs when firms face only their private costs of production but not the social costs inclusive of the damage cost from CO_2 emissions. If no environmental regulation is implemented, then the market fails, leading to a loss of social welfare. Economic instruments, such as a Pigouvian tax and emission permits, can be used to force the firms to internalize the cost of damage from emissions. We have demonstrated that both Pigouvian taxation and emission permits can have the same effects in equilibrium to achieve socially optimal outcomes. Another scheme called RPS sets a target for RE generation. RPS policy subsidizes RE generation plants using the revenue levied from NRE generation plants, which results in some efficiency loss in the short term.

We illustrate these concepts via more realistic, network-constrained problem instances in which VRES intermittency is also incorporated. First, while a CO_2 tax equal to the marginal cost of damage from emissions is optimal if industry is perfectly competitive, it may not be the case if industry behaves à la Cournot. In effect, such a setting exhibits not only an environmental externality but also an economic distortion. Thus, a policymaker has to adapt the CO_2 tax by anticipating the power companies' decisions. Second, if an RPS scheme is to be implemented, then the optimal fraction of energy to be provided by RE plants diverges from the implied RPS target under central planning. This is true even under perfect competition because the cost of the environmental externality cannot be directly internalized by consumers to reduce quantity demanded. Consequently, as a countervailing measure, the policymaker sets a higher RPS target than the implied one under central planning. By contrast, under an oligopolistic power sector, the policymaker lowers the RPS target in order to avoid exacerbating the firms' market power. Hence, environmental policy should be set proactively in a deregulated electricity industry by considering how it would affect the decision makers' incentives.

6.6 End-of-Chapter Exercises

6.1 In Illustrative Example 6.1, calculate the deadweight loss in the business-as-usual case. The deadweight loss would be relatively large. Discuss why it would be so.

6.2 In Illustrative Example 6.4, suppose that Pigouvian taxation is introduced instead of the RPS policy. Derive the outcomes under a Pigouvian tax and compare them with those under the RPS scheme.

6.3 In Illustrative Example 6.4, vary the RPS target, Q, between 0 and 1. Calculate the social welfare inclusive of the cost of damage with the varying target. Confirm that the RPS scheme cannot achieve the social optimum.

6.4 Modify the bi-level model in Sect. 6.4.2 such that the upper-level decision is a cap on CO_2 emissions, r^{cap} (in t). This cap is then treated as a parameter at the lower level, which will require an equilibrium constraint of the form $\sum_{s \in \mathcal{S}} W_s \sum_{t \in \mathcal{T}} \sum_{n \in \mathcal{N}} \sum_{i \in \mathcal{I}} \sum_{u \in \mathcal{U}_{i,n}} E_u y_{i,n,s,t,u} \leq r^{\text{cap}}$ with a corresponding dual variable ρ^{cap} (in \$/t). Consequently, each firm i takes ρ^{cap} as an exogenous price of CO_2 permits in its objective function (6.28a), i.e., effectively replacing the CO_2 tax, r^{tax}, in Sect. 6.4.2. Implement problem instances for this revised formulation using data from Illustrative Example 6.6. How are the results affected?

6.5 Modify the bi-level model in Sect. 6.4.3 such that the upper-level decision is a feed-in premium (FiP) on RE, r^{fip} (in \$/MWh). This FiP is the revenue earned by RE technologies on top of the market-clearing price of electricity and treated as a parameter at the lower level, which will require an extra term of the form $\sum_{s\in\mathcal{S}} W_s \sum_{t\in\mathcal{T}} \sum_{n\in\mathcal{N}} \sum_{i\in\mathcal{I}} \sum_{u\in\mathcal{U}_{i,n}^{\text{R}}} r^{\text{fip}} y_{i,n,s,t,u}$ in the lower-level objective function (6.35a). Moreover, the RPS constraint (6.35b) should be deleted from the lower-level optimization problem. Implement problem instances for this revised formulation using data from Illustrative Example 6.7. How are the results affected? Keep in mind that the government revenue, i.e., precisely the negative of the FiP payment to RE technologies, will need to be accounted for in the overall calculation of social welfare.

6.7 GAMS Codes

Here, we present GAMS codes for solving selected examples numerically. The following code solves Illustrative Example 6.1:

```
* Welfare-maximizing QP with a quadratic damage function

Sets
I generators /I1*I2/;

* Intercept of inverse demand

Scalar A /100/;

* Slope parameter of inverse demand

Scalar B /1/;

* Damage parameter

Scalar Z /0.1/;

Parameters
C(I)       Cost coefficients
/ I1        0.25
  I2        1/

E(I)       Emission rates
/ I1        4
  I2        2/;

Variables
OF          Objective function value
```

```
;

Positive variables
y(I)      Output
;

Equations
Objective
;

Objective.. OF =E= (A-0.5*B*SUM(I, y(I)))*SUM(I, y(I))-SUM(I, C(I
    )*y(I)**2)-0.5*Z*SUM(I, E(I)*y(I))**2;

MODEL SPD /ALL/;

SOLVE SPD USING NLP MAXIMIZING OF;
```

The following code solves Illustrative Example 6.2:

```
* MCP for emission tax

Sets
I generators /I1*I2/;

Alias(I,II);

* Intercept of inverse demand

Scalar A /100/;

* Slope parameter of inverse demand

Scalar B /1/;

* Emission tax

Scalar T /12.3288/;

Parameters
C(I)     Cost coefficients
/ I1      0.25
  I2      1/

E(I)     Emission rates
/ I1      4
  I2      2/;

Positive variables
y(I)     Output
;

Equations
KKT(I)
;
```

```
KKT(I).. -(A-B*SUM(II, y(II)))+2*C(I)*y(I)+E(I)*T =G= 0;

MODEL ET
      /
       KKT.y
      /;

SOLVE ET USING mcp;
```

The following code solves Illustrative Example 6.3:

```
* MCP for emission permits

Sets
I generators /I1*I2/;

Alias(I,II);

* Intercept of inverse demand

Scalar A /100/;

* Slope parameter of inverse demand

Scalar B /1/;

* Emission cap

Scalar G /123.2877/;

Parameters
C(I)      Cost coefficients
/ I1       0.25
  I2       1/

E(I)      Emission rates
/ I1       4
  I2       2/;

Positive variables
y(I)      Output
rho       Permit price
;

Equations
KKT(I)
ECap
;

KKT(I).. -(A-B*SUM(II, y(II)))+2*C(I)*y(I)+E(I)*rho =G= 0;
ECap..  G-SUM(I, E(I)*y(I)) =G= 0;

MODEL EP
```

```
      /
       KKT.y
       ECap.rho
      /;

SOLVE EP USING mcp;
```

The following code solves Illustrative Example 6.4:

```
* MCP for RPS

Sets
I generators /I1*I2/
R(I) RE generator /I1/
N(I) NRE generator /I2/
;

Alias(I,II);

* Intercept of inverse demand

Scalar A /100/;

* Slope parameter of inverse demand

Scalar B /1/;

* RPS level

Scalar Q /0.4/;

Parameters
C(I)      Cost coefficients
/ I1       0
  I2       1/

K(I)      Generation capacity
/ I1       15
  I2       50/

E(I)      Emission rates
/ I1       0
  I2       2/
;

Positive variables
y(I)      Output
beta(I)   Dual for generation capacity
rho       REC price
;

Equations
KKT(I)
Limit(I)
```

```
REC
;

KKT(I).. -(A-B*SUM(II, y(II)))+2*C(I)*y(I)+Q*rho-rho$R(I)+beta(I)
     =G= 0;
Limit(I).. K(I)-y(I) =G= 0;
REC.. SUM(I, y(I)$R(I))-Q*SUM(I, y(I)) =G= 0;

MODEL RPS
      /
       KKT.y
       Limit.beta
       REC.rho
      /;

SOLVE RPS USING mcp;
```

For the sake of numerical scaling, especially for the bi-level problem instances, modeling is implemented on a single-day basis. The annual quantities may be obtained *ex post* by summing up the results, e.g., generation output, and multiplying them by the number of days in each season, i.e., 183. The following file contains the common data used in the problem instances for all Illustrative Examples 6.5, 6.6, and 6.7:

```
* EX_data.gms: Data for operations with externalities problem
    instances

* Set definitions

Sets
i Firms                                 /i1*i2/
j RPS levels                            /j1*j201/
l Transmission lines                    /l1*l3/
n Nodes                                 /n1*n3/
s Seasons                               /s1*s2/
t Periods                               /t1*t3/
u Generation units                      /u1*u4/
c_u(u) Conventional generation units /u3*u4/
r_u(u) Renewable generation units /u1*u2/
itontou(I,N,U) Firm-to-node-to-unit relation  /i1.n1.u3, i1.n1.u4
    , i2.n2.u1, i2.n3.u2/
;

Alias(N,NN);
Alias(I,II);
Alias(U,UU);

* RPS levels
Parameters Q(j);
Q('j1')=0;
loop ((j) $ (ord( j ) le card(j)) ,
Q(j+1) = Q(j)+0.005;);
```

```
Set TL Transmission line characteristics
/Susceptance, Capacity/
;

* Time parameters

Parameters
TT(T)       Length of each period in hours
/ t1        8
  t2        8
  t3        8/

W(S)        Weight of each season
/ s1        1
  s2        1/
;

* Number of days per season

Scalar Days /183/
;

* Power line parameters

Table Incidence(L,N) Matches power lines with nodes
        n1      n2      n3
l1      1       -1       0
l2      0        1      -1
l3      1        0      -1
;

TABLE LineOpt (L, TL) Transmission line information
    Susceptance Capacity
l1  5100        48.8
l2  5100        48.8
l3  5100        48.8
;

Parameter K_trn(l) Maximum thermal capacity of power line;
K_trn(l) = LineOpt(L, 'Capacity');

Parameter B(l) Transmission line susceptance;
B(l) = LineOpt(L, 'Susceptance');

Parameter
LPlus(L,N)
/
l1.n1 1
l2.n2 1
l3.n1 1
/

LMinus(L,N)
/
```

```
l1.n2 1
l2.n3 1
l3.n3 1
/
;

Parameter
NPlus(L,N)
/
l1.n1 1
l3.n1 1
l2.n2 1
/

NMinus(L,N)
/
l1.n2 1
l2.n3 1
l3.n3 1
/
;

* Demand parameters

Table DemandData(N,*) Demand data by node
      INT  SLP
n1    220   1
n2    140   1
n3    120   1
;

Parameter
D_int(N,S,T)    Demand intercept,
D_slp(N,S,T)    Demand slope
;

D_int(N,S,T)=   DemandData(N, 'INT');
D_slp(N,S,T)=   DemandData(N, 'SLP');

* Power generation parameters

Parameters

R(U)        Ramping limit of each technology
/ u1        1
  u2        1
  u3        0.3
  u4        0.6
/


E(U)        Emission rate of each technology
/ u1        0
  u2        0
```

```
  u3       0.9
  u4       0.5
/
;

Table

A(N,S,T,U)   Maximum availability factor for each technology at each node by season and by period
              u1      u2         u3       u4
n1.s1.t1     0        0          1        1
n1.s1.t2     0        0          1        1
n1.s1.t3     0        0          1        1
n1.s2.t1     0        0          1        1
n1.s2.t2     0        0          1        1
n1.s2.t3     0        0          1        1
n2.s1.t1     0.20     0          1        1
n2.s1.t2     0.10     0          1        1
n2.s1.t3     0.05     0          1        1
n2.s2.t1     0.25     0          1        1
n2.s2.t2     0.50     0          1        1
n2.s2.t3     0.75     0          1        1
n3.s1.t1     0        0.20       1        1
n3.s1.t2     0        0.40       1        1
n3.s1.t3     0        0.50       1        1
n3.s2.t1     0        1.00       1        1
n3.s2.t2     0        0.75       1        1
n3.s2.t3     0        0.10       1        1
;

Table C_opr(I,N,U) Operating cost of generation unit type u at node n owned by firm i
            u1    u2    u3    u4
i1.n1       0     0     20    50
i2.n2       0     0     20    50
i2.n3       0     0     20    50
;

Table K_gen(I,N,U) Installed generation capacity of generation type u at node n owned by firm i
              u1       u2       u3       u4
i1.n1         0        0        35       40
i2.n2         50       0        0        0
i2.n3         0        50       0        0
;

Display B;

Scalar Pi /3.14159/;

Scalar Z /0/;

Scalar M_trn /14500/;
```

```
Scalar M_y /3000/;

Scalar M_beta /3000/;

Scalar M_beta_down /3000/;

Scalar M_beta_up /3000/;

Scalar M_c /3000/;

Scalar M_gamma_d /14500/;

Scalar M_gamma_u /14500/;

Scalar M_mu_down /14500/;

Scalar M_mu_up /14500/;

Scalar M_kappa_down /3000/;

Scalar M_kappa_up /3000/;

Scalar M_v /14500/;

Scalar M_mu /14500/;

Scalar M_rho /521.80/;

Scalar Mrhod lowest possible REC value /0/;

Scalar Mrhou highest possible REC value /800/;

Scalar Myd lowest possible output /0/;

Scalar Myu highest possible output /3000/;
```

The following code solves Illustrative Example 6.5 to determine the first-best welfare-maximizing power-system operations under central planning in presence of externalities:

```
* CP_EX.gms: Three-node central-planning operational dispatch
   under externalities QP implementation

$INCLUDE PSE/EX_data.gms

Scalar starttime;
starttime = jnow;

* Variable definition

Variables
f_hat(L,S,T) Realized power flow on line l in season s and period
    t
```

```
v(N,S,T) Voltage angle at node n in season s and period t
OF Objective function;

Positive variables
c(N,S,T) Consumption at node n in season s and period t
y(I,N,S,T,U) Generation output from unit u at node n owned by
    firm i in season s and period t
;

Equations OF_SW, CP_EQ2, CP_EQ3a, CP_EQ3b, CP_EQ4a, CP_EQ4b,
    CP_EQ5, CP_EQ6, CP_EQ7, CP_EQ8;
* Maximize social welfare inclusive of the cost of externality
OF_SW.. SUM(S, W(S)*(SUM((N,T), D_int(N,S,T)*c(N,S,T) - 0.5*D_slp
    (N,S,T)*c(N,S,T)*c(N,S,T) - SUM(I, SUM(U, C_opr(I,N,U)*y(I,N,
    S,T,U)) ) ) ) ) -0.5*Days*Z*(SUM(S, W(S)*(SUM((N,T), SUM(I,
    SUM(U, E(U)*y(I,N,S,T,U))) ))))*(SUM(S, W(S)*(SUM((N,T), SUM(
    I, SUM(U, E(U)*y(I,N,S,T,U))) ))) ) -OF =E= 0;
* Power flow on line L in season S and period T
CP_EQ2(L,S,T).. f_hat(L,S,T) - B(L)*(SUM(N$LPlus(L,N),v(N,S,T)) -
     SUM(N$LMinus(L,N),v(N,S,T))) =E= 0;
* Transmission capacity constraint on line L in season S and
    period T
CP_EQ3a(L,S,T).. K_trn(L)-f_hat(L,S,T)  =G= 0;
* Transmission capacity constraint on line L in season S and
    period T
CP_EQ3b(L,S,T).. K_trn(L)+f_hat(L,S,T)  =G= 0;
* Voltage angle limit at node N in season S and period T
CP_EQ4a(N,S,T).. -v(N,S,T) + Pi =G= 0;
* Voltage angle limit at node N in season S and period T
CP_EQ4b(N,S,T).. v(N,S,T) + Pi =G= 0;
* Power balance at node N in season S and period T
CP_EQ5(N,S,T).. c(N,S,T)- SUM(I, SUM(U, y(I,N,S,T,U))) + TT(T)*
    SUM(L$NPlus(L,N), f_hat(L,S,T)) -  TT(T)*SUM(L$NMinus(L,N),
    f_hat(L,S,T)) =E= 0;
* Generation capacity constraint for firm I at node N in season S
     and period T using unit U
CP_EQ6(I,N,S,T,U).. -y(I,N,S,T,U) + TT(T)*A(N,S,T,U)*K_gen(I,N,U)
     =G= 0;
* Generation up-ramping constraint for firm I at node N in season
     S and period T using unit U
CP_EQ7(I,N,S,T,U).. R(U)*TT(T)*K_gen(I,N,U) - y(I,N,S,T,U) + y(I,
    N,S,T-1,U) =G= 0;
* Generation down-ramping constraint for firm I at node N in
    season S and period T using unit U
CP_EQ8(I,N,S,T,U).. R(U)*TT(T)*K_gen(I,N,U) + y(I,N,S,T,U)- y(I,N
    ,S,T-1,U) =G= 0;

****Producers****
y.fx(I,N,S,T,U)$(NOT itontou(I,N,U))=0;

Model  CP_QP_EX
         /
ALL
         /
```

```
;
option optcr=0;
option reslim = 3000000;
Option Iterlim=100000;
Option QCP = Cplex;

Solve CP_QP_EX maximizing OF using qcp ;
```

The following code solves Illustrative Example 6.6 to determine bi-level CO_2 taxation:

```
* BL_tax.gms: Three-node bi-level operational dispatch under tax
    MIQP implementation

$INCLUDE PSE/EX_data.gms

Scalar starttime;
starttime = jnow;

* Allow market power by setting 'CO' equal to '1'

Scalar CO /1/;

* Variable definition

Variables
f_hat(L,S,T) Realized power flow on line l in season s and period
    t
v(N,S,T) Voltage angle at node n in season s and period t
c(N,S,T) Consumption at node n in season s and period t
y(I,N,S,T,U) Generation output from unit u at node n owned by
    firm i in season s and period t
mu(L,S,T) Dual for voltage law on line l in season s and period t
lambda(N,S,T) Dual for energy balance at node n in season s and
    period t
r_tax  Carbon tax set by the policymaker
OF Objective function
;

Positive variables
phi_c(N,S,T) Dual for non-negativity of consumption at node n in
    season s and period t
phi_y(I,N,S,T,U) Dual for non-negativity of generation from unit
    u at node n owned by firm i in season s and period t
beta(I,N,S,T,U) Dual for generation capacity from unit u at node
    n owned by firm i in season s and period t
beta_up(I,N,S,T,U) Dual for generation up-ramping capacity from
    unit u at node n owned by firm i in season s and period t
beta_down(I,N,S,T,U) Dual for generation down-ramping capacity
    from unit u at node n owned by firm i in season s and period
    t
mu_up(L,S,T) Dual for positive transmission capacity on line l in
     season s and period t
```

```
mu_down(L,S,T) Dual for negative transmission capacity on line l
    in season s and period t
kappa_up(N,S,T) Dual for positive voltage angle limit at node n
    in season s and period t
kappa_down(N,S,T) Dual for negative voltage angle limit at node n
    in season s and period t
;

Binary variables
x_c(N,S,T) BV for KKT condition for c at node n in season s and
    period t
x_y(I,N,S,T,U) BV for KKT condition for y from unit u at node n
    owned by firm i in season s and period t
x_beta(I,N,S,T,U) BV for KKT condition for beta from unit u at
    node n owned by firm i in season s and period t
x_beta_up(I,N,S,T,U) BV for KKT condition for beta_up from unit u
    at node n owned by firm i in season s and period t
x_beta_down(I,N,S,T,U) BV for KKT condition for beta_udown from
    unit u at node n owned by firm i in season s and period t
x_kappa_up(N,S,T) BV for KKT condition for kappa_up at node n in
    season s and period t
x_kappa_down(N,S,T) BV for KKT condition for kappa_down at node n
    in season s and period t
x_mu_up(L,S,T) BV for KKT condition for mu_up on line l in season
    s and period t
x_mu_down(L,S,T) BV for KKT condition for mu_down on line l in
    season s and period t
;

Equations OF_SW, UL_EQ, YD_EQ, CD_EQ, FD_EQ, VD_EQ, CP_EQ2,
    CP_EQ5, Phi_Y_EQa, Phi_Y_EQb, Phi_Y_EQc, Beta_EQa, Beta_EQb,
    Beta_EQc, Beta_Up_EQa, Beta_Up_EQb, Beta_Up_EQc,
    Beta_Down_EQa, Beta_Down_EQb, Beta_Down_EQc, Mu_Down_EQa,
    Mu_Down_EQb, Mu_Down_EQc, Mu_Up_EQa, Mu_Up_EQb, Mu_Up_EQc,
    Kappa_Down_EQa, Kappa_Down_EQb, Kappa_Down_EQc, Kappa_Up_EQa,
    Kappa_Up_EQb, Kappa_Up_EQc, Phi_C_EQa, Phi_C_EQb, Phi_C_EQc;
* Maximize social welfare inclusive of the cost of externality
OF_SW.. SUM(S, W(S)*(SUM((N,T), D_int(N,S,T)*c(N,S,T) - 0.5*D_slp
    (N,S,T)*c(N,S,T)*c(N,S,T) - SUM(I, SUM(U, C_opr(I,N,U)*y(I,N,
    S,T,U)) ) ) ) ) -0.5*Days*Z*(SUM(S, W(S)*(SUM((N,T), SUM(I,
    SUM(U, E(U)*y(I,N,S,T,U))) ))))*(SUM(S, W(S)*(SUM((N,T), SUM(
    I, SUM(U, E(U)*y(I,N,S,T,U))) ))) ) -OF =E= 0;
* Non-negativity of ETS cap
UL_EQ.. -r_tax =L= 0;
* KKT condition for y
YD_EQ(I,N,S,T,U)$(itontou(i,n,u)).. W(S)*C_opr(I,N,U) + W(S)*E(U)
    *r_tax + beta(I,N,S,T,U) + beta_up(I,N,S,T,U) - beta_down(I,N
    ,S,T,U) - beta_up(I,N,S,T+1,U) + beta_down(I,N,S,T+1,U) - W(S
    )*(D_int(N,S,T) - D_slp(N,S,T)*(SUM(II, SUM(UU, y(II,N,S,T,UU
    ))) -TT(T)*SUM(L$NPlus(L,N), f_hat(L,S,T)) + TT(T)*SUM(
    L$NMinus(L,N), f_hat(L,S,T))) ) - phi_y(I,N,S,T,U) + W(S)*
    D_slp(N,S,T)*(SUM(UU , y(I,N,S,T,UU)))$(CO) =E= 0;
* KKT condition for c
```

```
CD_EQ(N,S,T).. -W(S)*(D_int(N,S,T) - D_slp(N,S,T)*c(N,S,T)) +
     lambda(N,S,T) - phi_c(N,S,T) =E= 0;
* KKT condition for f_hat
FD_EQ(L,S,T).. mu(L,S,T) + mu_up(L,S,T)  - mu_down(L,S,T) + TT(T)
     *SUM(N$LPlus(L,N), lambda(N,S,T)) - TT(T)*SUM(N$LMinus(L,N),
     lambda(N,S,T)) =E= 0;
* KKT condition for v
VD_EQ(N,S,T).. -SUM(L$NPlus(L,N), B(L)*mu(L,S,T) ) + SUM(L$NMinus
     (L,N), B(L)*mu(L,S,T) ) + kappa_up(N,S,T) - kappa_down(N,S,T)
      =E= 0;
* Power flow on line L in season S and period T
CP_EQ2(L,S,T).. f_hat(L,S,T) - B(L)*(SUM(N$LPlus(L,N),v(N,S,T)) -
     SUM(N$LMinus(L,N),v(N,S,T))) =E= 0;
* Power balance at node N in season S and period T
CP_EQ5(N,S,T).. c(N,S,T)- SUM(I, SUM(U, y(I,N,S,T,U))) + TT(T)*
     SUM(L$NPlus(L,N), f_hat(L,S,T)) -  TT(T)*SUM(L$NMinus(L,N),
     f_hat(L,S,T)) =E= 0;
* Disjunctive constraints for phi_y
Phi_Y_EQa(I,N,S,T,U).. -y(I,N,S,T,U) =L= 0;
Phi_Y_EQb(I,N,S,T,U)..  y(I,N,S,T,U) - M_y*x_y(I,N,S,T,U) =L= 0;
Phi_Y_EQc(I,N,S,T,U)..  phi_y(I,N,S,T,U) - M_y*(1-x_y(I,N,S,T,U))
     =L= 0;
* Disjunctive constraints for beta
Beta_EQa(I,N,S,T,U).. y(I,N,S,T,U) - TT(T)*A(N,S,T,U)*K_gen(I,N,U
     ) =L= 0;
Beta_EQb(I,N,S,T,U).. -y(I,N,S,T,U) + TT(T)*A(N,S,T,U)*K_gen(I,N,
     U) - M_beta*x_beta(I,N,S,T,U) =L= 0;
Beta_EQc(I,N,S,T,U)..  beta(I,N,S,T,U) - M_beta*(1-x_beta(I,N,S,T
     ,U)) =L= 0;
* Disjunctive constraints for beta_up
Beta_Up_EQa(I,N,S,T,U).. y(I,N,S,T,U) - y(I,N,S,T-1,U) - TT(T)*R(
     U)*K_gen(I,N,U) =L= 0;
Beta_Up_EQb(I,N,S,T,U).. -y(I,N,S,T,U) + y(I,N,S,T-1,U) + TT(T)*R
     (U)*K_gen(I,N,U) - M_beta_up*x_beta_up(I,N,S,T,U) =L= 0;
Beta_Up_EQc(I,N,S,T,U)..  beta_up(I,N,S,T,U) - M_beta_up*(1-
     x_beta_up(I,N,S,T,U)) =L= 0;
* Disjunctive constraints for beta_down
Beta_Down_EQa(I,N,S,T,U).. -y(I,N,S,T,U) + y(I,N,S,T-1,U) - TT(T)
     *R(U)*K_gen(I,N,U) =L= 0;
Beta_Down_EQb(I,N,S,T,U).. y(I,N,S,T,U) - y(I,N,S,T-1,U) + TT(T)*
     R(U)*K_gen(I,N,U) - M_beta_down*x_beta_down(I,N,S,T,U) =L= 0;
Beta_Down_EQc(I,N,S,T,U)..  beta_down(I,N,S,T,U) - M_beta_down
     *(1-x_beta_down(I,N,S,T,U)) =L= 0;
* Disjunctive constraints for mu_down
Mu_Down_EQa(L,S,T).. -K_trn(L) - f_hat(L,S,T) =L= 0;
Mu_Down_EQb(L,S,T).. K_trn(L) + f_hat(L,S,T) - M_mu_down*
     x_mu_down(L,S,T) =L= 0;
Mu_Down_EQc(L,S,T)..  mu_down(L,S,T) - M_mu_down*(1-x_mu_down(L,S
     ,T)) =L= 0;
* Disjunctive constraints for mu_up
Mu_Up_EQa(L,S,T).. -K_trn(L) + f_hat(L,S,T) =L= 0;
Mu_Up_EQb(L,S,T).. K_trn(L) - f_hat(L,S,T) - M_mu_up*x_mu_up(L,S,
     T) =L= 0;
```

```
Mu_Up_EQc(L,S,T)..  mu_up(L,S,T) - M_mu_up*(1-x_mu_up(L,S,T)) =L=
     0;
* Disjunctive constraints for kappa_down
Kappa_Down_EQa(N,S,T).. -Pi - v(N,S,T) =L= 0;
Kappa_Down_EQb(N,S,T).. Pi + v(N,S,T) - M_kappa_down*x_kappa_down
     (N,S,T) =L= 0;
Kappa_Down_EQc(N,S,T)..  kappa_down(N,S,T) - M_kappa_down*(1-
     x_kappa_down(N,S,T)) =L= 0;
* Disjunctive constraints for kappa_up
Kappa_Up_EQa(N,S,T).. -Pi + v(N,S,T) =L= 0;
Kappa_Up_EQb(N,S,T).. Pi - v(N,S,T) - M_kappa_up*x_kappa_up(N,S,T
     ) =L= 0;
Kappa_Up_EQc(N,S,T)..  kappa_up(N,S,T) - M_kappa_up*(1-x_kappa_up
     (N,S,T)) =L= 0;
* Disjunctive constraints for phi_c
Phi_C_EQa(N,S,T).. -c(N,S,T) =L= 0;
Phi_C_EQb(N,S,T)..  c(N,S,T) - M_c*x_c(N,S,T) =L= 0;
Phi_C_EQc(N,S,T)..  phi_c(N,S,T) - M_c*(1-x_c(N,S,T)) =L= 0;

****Producers****
y.fx(I,N,S,T,U)$(NOT itontou(I,N,U))=0;

Model  BL_tax
        /
ALL
        /
;
option optcr=0;
option reslim = 3000000;
Option Iterlim=100000;
Option MIQCP = Cplex;

Solve BL_tax maximizing OF using miqcp ;
```

The following code solves Illustrative Example 6.7 to determine bi-level RPS targeting:

```
* BL_RPS.gms: Three-node bi-level operational dispatch under RPS
    MIQCQP implementation

$INCLUDE PSE/EX_data.gms

Scalar starttime;
starttime = jnow;

* Allow market power by setting 'CO' equal to '1'

Scalar CO /1/;

* Variable definition

Variables
```

```
f_hat(L,S,T) Realized power flow on line l in season s and period
    t
v(N,S,T) Voltage angle at node n in season s and period t
c(N,S,T) Consumption at node n in season s and period t
y(I,N,S,T,U) Generation output from unit u at node n owned by
    firm i in season s and period t
mu(L,S,T) Dual for voltage law on line l in season s and period t
lambda(N,S,T) Dual for energy balance at node n in season s and
    period t
rr(j) RPS revenue at level j
ww(j) RE production requirement at level j
ee(j) Auxiliary variable to calculate RPS revenue at level j
gg(j) Auxiliary variable to calculate RE production requirement
    at level j
OF Objective function
;

Positive variables
rho REC price
phi_c(N,S,T) Dual for non-negativity of consumption at node n in
    season s and period t
phi_y(I,N,S,T,U) Dual for non-negativity of generation from unit
    u at node n owned by firm i in season s and period t
beta(I,N,S,T,U) Dual for generation capacity from unit u at node
    n owned by firm i in season s and period t
beta_up(I,N,S,T,U) Dual for generation up-ramping capacity from
    unit u at node n owned by firm i in season s and period t
beta_down(I,N,S,T,U) Dual for generation down-ramping capacity
    from unit u at node n owned by firm i in season s and period
    t
mu_up(L,S,T) Dual for positive transmission capacity on line l in
    season s and period t
mu_down(L,S,T) Dual for negative transmission capacity on line l
    in season s and period t
kappa_up(N,S,T) Dual for positive voltage angle limit at node n
    in season s and period t
kappa_down(N,S,T) Dual for negative voltage angle limit at node n
    in season s and period t
;

Binary variables
x(J) RPS selection at level j;

Equations OF_SW, UL_EQ, CP_EQ2, CP_EQ3a, CP_EQ3b, CP_EQ4a,
    CP_EQ4b, CP_EQ5, CP_EQ6, CP_EQ7, CP_EQ8, CP_EQ9, CP_EQ10a,
    CP_EQ10b, CP_EQ10c, CP_EQ10d, CP_EQ10e, CP_EQ11, CP_EQ12,
    SD_EQ, YD_EQ, YD_EQa, YD_EQb, YD_EQc, YD_EQd, YD_EQe, CD_EQ,
    FD_EQ, VD_EQ;
* Maximize social welfare inclusive of the cost of externality
OF_SW.. SUM(S, W(S)*(SUM((N,T), D_int(N,S,T)*c(N,S,T) - 0.5*D_slp
    (N,S,T)*c(N,S,T)*c(N,S,T) - SUM(I, SUM(U, C_opr(I,N,U)*y(I,N,
    S,T,U)) ) ) ) ) -0.5*Days*Z*(SUM(S, W(S)*(SUM((N,T), SUM(I,
    SUM(U, E(U)*y(I,N,S,T,U))) ))))*(SUM(S, W(S)*(SUM((N,T), SUM(
    I, SUM(U, E(U)*y(I,N,S,T,U))) ))) ) -OF =E= 0;
```

```
* Only one RPS level may be selected
UL_EQ.. SUM(J, x(J)) =E= 1;
* Power flow on line L in season S and period T
CP_EQ2(L,S,T).. f_hat(L,S,T) - B(L)*(SUM(N$LPlus(L,N),v(N,S,T)) - SUM(N$LMinus(L,N),v(N,S,T))) =E= 0;
* Transmission capacity constraint on line L in season S and period T
CP_EQ3a(L,S,T).. -K_trn(L) + f_hat(L,S,T)  =L= 0;
* Transmission capacity constraint on line L in season S and period T
CP_EQ3b(L,S,T).. -K_trn(L) - f_hat(L,S,T)  =L= 0;
* Voltage angle limit at node N in season S and period T
CP_EQ4a(N,S,T).. -v(N,S,T) - Pi =L= 0;
* Voltage angle limit at node N in season S and period T
CP_EQ4b(N,S,T).. v(N,S,T) - Pi =L= 0;
* Power balance at node N in season S and period T
CP_EQ5(N,S,T).. c(N,S,T)- SUM(I, SUM(U, y(I,N,S,T,U))) + TT(T)*SUM(L$NPlus(L,N), f_hat(L,S,T)) -  TT(T)*SUM(L$NMinus(L,N), f_hat(L,S,T)) =E= 0;
* Generation capacity constraint for firm I at node N in season S and period T using unit U
CP_EQ6(I,N,S,T,U).. y(I,N,S,T,U) - TT(T)*A(N,S,T,U)*K_gen(I,N,U) =L= 0;
* Generation up-ramping constraint for firm I at node N in season S and period T using unit U
CP_EQ7(I,N,S,T,U).. -R(U)*TT(T)*K_gen(I,N,U) + y(I,N,S,T,U) - y(I,N,S,T-1,U) =L= 0;
* Generation down-ramping constraint for firm I at node N in season S and period T using unit U
CP_EQ8(I,N,S,T,U).. -R(U)*TT(T)*K_gen(I,N,U) - y(I,N,S,T,U) + y(I,N,S,T-1,U) =L= 0;
* RPS constraint
CP_EQ9.. SUM(s, W(s)*(SUM(i, SUM(n, SUM(t, SUM(u$r_u(u), y(i,n,s,t,u)))))))- SUM(j, ww(j)) =G= 0;
* RPS linearization at level j
CP_EQ10a(j).. ww(j) - Q(j)*SUM(s, W(s)*(SUM(i, SUM(n, SUM(t, SUM(u, y(i,n,s,t,u))))))) + gg(j) =E= 0;
CP_EQ10b(j,s).. ww(j) - Q(j)*Myd*x(j) =G= 0;
CP_EQ10c(j,s).. -ww(j) + Q(j)*Myu*x(j) =G= 0;
CP_EQ10d(j,s).. gg(j) - Q(j)*Myd*(1-x(j)) =G= 0;
CP_EQ10e(j,s).. -gg(j) + Q(j)*Myu*(1-x(j)) =G= 0;
* Non-negativity of consumption
CP_EQ11(N,S,T).. -c(N,S,T) =L= 0;
* Non-negativity of generation
CP_EQ12(I,N,S,T,U).. -y(I,N,S,T,U) =L= 0;
* Strong-duality expression
SD_EQ.. SUM(S, W(S)*(SUM((N,T), D_int(N,S,T)*c(N,S,T) - D_slp(N,S,T)*c(N,S,T)*c(N,S,T) - SUM(I, SUM(U, C_opr(I,N,U)*y(I,N,S,T,U)) )  ) ) ) - SUM(S, W(S)*(SUM((N,T), D_slp(N,S,T)*(SUM(I, SUM(U, y(I,N,S,T,U))*SUM(U, y(I,N,S,T,U))$(CO)   )  ) )  ) ) - (SUM(I, SUM(N, SUM(S, SUM(T, SUM(U, TT(T)*K_gen(I,N,U)*(A(N,S,T,U)*beta(I,N,S,T,U) + R(U)*beta_up(I,N,S,T,U) + R(U)*beta_down(I,N,S,T,U) )  ) )  )  ) ) + SUM(L, SUM(S, SUM(T,
```

```
    K_trn(L)*(mu_up(L,S,T)+ mu_down(L,S,T))) )   ) +SUM(N, SUM(S,
    SUM(T, Pi*(kappa_up(N,S,T)+kappa_down(N,S,T))) ) ) ) =G= 0;
* Dual constraint related to y
YD_EQ(I,N,S,T,U)$(itontou(i,n,u)).. W(S)*C_opr(I,N,U) + beta(I,N,
    S,T,U) + beta_up(I,N,S,T,U) - beta_down(I,N,S,T,U) - beta_up(
    I,N,S,T+1,U) + beta_down(I,N,S,T+1,U) - lambda(N,S,T) - phi_y
    (I,N,S,T,U) + W(S)*D_slp(N,S,T)*SUM(UU, y(I,N,S,T,UU))$(CO) +
     W(S)*SUM(j, rr(j))-rho$(r_u(u)) =E= 0;
* RPS revenue linearization at level j
YD_EQa(j).. rr(j) - Q(j)*rho + ee(j) =E= 0;
YD_EQb(j).. rr(j) - Q(j)*Mrhod*x(j) =G= 0;
YD_EQc(j).. -rr(j) + Q(j)*Mrhou*x(j) =G= 0;
YD_EQd(j).. ee(j) - Q(j)*Mrhod *(1-x(j)) =G= 0;
YD_EQe(j).. -ee(j) + Q(j)*Mrhou *(1-x(j)) =G= 0;
* Dual constraint related to c
CD_EQ(N,S,T).. -W(S)*(D_int(N,S,T) - D_slp(N,S,T)*c(N,S,T)) +
    lambda(N,S,T) - phi_c(N,S,T) =E= 0;
* Dual constraint related to f_hat
FD_EQ(L,S,T).. mu(L,S,T) + mu_up(L,S,T)  - mu_down(L,S,T) + TT(T)
    *SUM(N$LPlus(L,N), lambda(N,S,T)) - TT(T)*SUM(N$LMinus(L,N),
    lambda(N,S,T)) =E= 0;
* Dual constraint related to v
VD_EQ(N,S,T).. -SUM(L$NPlus(L,N), B(L)*mu(L,S,T) ) + SUM(L$NMinus
     (L,N), B(L)*mu(L,S,T) ) + kappa_up(N,S,T) - kappa_down(N,S,T)
     =E= 0;

****Producers****
y.fx(I,N,S,T,U)$(NOT itontou(I,N,U))=0;

Model  BL_RPS
        /
ALL
        /
;
option optcr=0;
option reslim = 3000000;
Option Iterlim=100000;
Option MIQCP = Cplex;

Solve BL_RPS maximizing OF using miqcp ;
```

References

1. Baringo, L., Conejo, A.J.: Transmission and wind power investment. IEEE Trans. Power Syst. **27**, 885–893 (2012)
2. Barnett, A.H.: The Pigouvian tax rule under monopoly. Am. Econ. Rev. **70**, 1037–1041 (1980)
3. Chen, Y., Siddiqui, A.S., Tanaka, M.: Analysis of Environmental Policy in the Power Sector. Springer, Cham (2020)
4. Conejo, A.J., Carrión, M., Morales, J.M.: Decision Making Under Uncertainty in Electricity Markets. Springer, New York (2010)

5. Dorn, W.S.: Duality in quadratic programming. Q. Appl. Math. **18**, 155–162 (1960)
6. Energy Information Administration: Sources of Greenhouse Gas Emissions (2019). https://www.epa.gov/ghgemissions/sources-greenhouse-gas-emissions
7. Fortuny-Amat, J., McCarl, B.: A representation and economic interpretation of a two-level programming problem. J. Oper. Res. Soc. **9**, 783–792 (1981)
8. Gabriel, S.A., Conejo, A.J., Fuller, J.D., Hobbs, B.F., Ruiz, C.: Complementarity Modeling in Energy Markets. Springer, New York (2013)
9. Hashimoto, H.: A spatial Nash equilibrium model. In: Harker, P.T. (ed.) Spatial Price Equilibria: Advances in Theory, Computation, and Application. Springer, New York (1985)
10. Hobbs, B.F.: Linear complementarity models of Nash-Cournot competition in bilateral and POOLCO power markets. IEEE Trans. Power Syst. **16**, 194–202 (2001)
11. Huppmann, D., Egerer, J.: National-strategic investment in European power transmission capacity. Eur. J. Oper. Res. **247**, 191–203 (2015)
12. Kile, H., Uhlen, K., Warland, L., Kjølle, G.: A comparison of AC and DC power flow models for contingency and reliability analysis. In: 2014 Power Systems Computation Conference, Wroclaw (2014)
13. Nicholson, W., Snyder, C.: Microeconomic Theory: Basic Principles and Extensions. Cengage Learning, Boston (2016)
14. Reichenberg, L., Siddiqui, A.S., Wogrin, S.: Policy implications of downscaling the time dimension in power system planning models to represent variability in renewable output. Energy **159**, 870–877 (2018)
15. Requate, T.: Environmental policy under imperfect competition. In: Tietenberg, T., Folmer, H. (eds.) The International Yearbook of Environmental and Resource Economics 20 06/20 07: A Survey of Current Issues. Edward Elgar Publishing, Cheltenham (2006)
16. Siddiqui, A.S., Tanaka, M., Chen, Y.: Are targets for renewable portfolio standards too low? The impact of market structure on energy policy. Eur. J. Oper. Res. **250**, 328–341 (2016)
17. Tanaka, M., Chen, Y.: Market power in renewable portfolio standards. Energy Econ. **39**, 187–196 (2013)
18. Varian, H.R.: Microeconomic Analysis. W.W. Norton & Company, New York (1992)

Chapter 7
Investment

7.1 Introduction

Given ambitious targets for power-sector decarbonization, increased investment in variable renewable energy sources (VRES) will be required. Although levelized costs of VRES have decreased to the extent that they are at parity with fossil-fueled alternatives, their integration into the power sector is complicated by their intermittent output and remote locations from demand centers.[1] These drawbacks may be mitigated by complementary deployment of flexible assets such as fast-ramping plants, energy storage, demand response, and transmission interconnections. Toward this end, conventional optimization methods for generation expansion [10] could be used. However, their straightforward application is not suitable for the current paradigm with increased supply-side volatility and a decentralized industry. The former aspect requires a more sophisticated treatment of temporal variation than conventional load slicing, e.g., clustering procedures [20]. As for the latter attribute, conflicting objectives among distinct agents may reduce the effectiveness of a central-planning investment strategy, thereby necessitating the use of bi-level modeling [28].

In this chapter, we explore investment decisions in a decentralized electricity industry with high VRES penetration. First, in Sect. 7.2, we investigate transmission planning, which will be required by both the remote locations of promising VRES sites and variability management. As a benchmark, we will use a single-agent model for adding transmission capacity to accommodate VRES capacity expansion. Next, we will use a bi-level model to reflect deregulated power systems' separation of ownership, viz. transmission lines are added by regulated transmission system

[1] Although VRES has come to refer to solar and wind power because of those technologies' uncontrollable availabilities, thermal plants' outputs may also be at the whim of weather conditions [29].

M. Tanaka et al., *Economics of Power Systems*, International Series
in Operations Research & Management Science 327,
https://doi.org/10.1007/978-3-030-92871-1_7

operators (TSOs) while generation output is the responsibility of profit-maximizing power companies. The TSO may be regarded as a leader and power companies as followers in a Stackelberg framework. Furthermore, if power companies are price takers, then the bi-level model typically collapses to a single-level one as there are no distortions from the exertion of market power, i.e., manipulation of generation output in order to cause prices to deviate from marginal costs. However, market power has been documented to occur in at least some price zones during specific time periods even in largely competitive electricity markets such as Nord Pool [31]. Subsequent need for generation flexibility induced by greater VRES penetration could actually enhance the leverage of the owners of flexible assets, e.g., gas-fired plants or storage. Toward this end, we will present a bi-level model in which the TSO at the upper level may be able to anticipate the strategic behavior, i.e., as Cournot oligopolists, of power companies at the lower level and take countervailing decisions in the form of welfare-enhancing transmission investments.

Next, in Sect. 7.3, we address investment in generation capacity. Mirroring the structure of Sect. 7.2, we begin with a benchmark central-planning approach, i.e., proceeding as if a single welfare-maximizing entity were responsible for all generation-capacity expansion and output decisions. In order to focus on investment in generation capacity and its consequences for operations, we fix the transmission capacity. Since power companies may have enough market share in deregulated electricity industries to behave strategically, we subsequently develop a bi-level, i.e., Stackelberg [33], model. Here, a single strategic power company makes its generation-capacity expansion decision at the upper level in anticipation of lower-level market-clearing decisions by an ISO and price-taking market operations. Follower firms at the lower level may also add capacity but are unable to anticipate their decisions' impact on prices. By concentrating strategic generation-investment decisions in the hands of a single dominant firm, we isolate the economic distortions from the exercise of market power.[2] Finally, Sect. 7.4 summarizes the chapter's contents, while Sects. 7.5 and 7.6 provide end-of-chapter exercises and GAMS codes for selected examples, respectively.

7.2 Transmission Expansion

Although many member countries belonging to the Organisation for Economic Co-operation and Development (OECD) [17] have deregulated their electricity industries, transmission planning remains under the auspices of state-regulated entities. Since the transmission sector is a natural monopoly, it is justifiable to separate its operations from those of the generation and retail sectors, where

[2] Competition among multiple Stackelberg leaders is also possible and modeled as an equilibrium problem with equilibrium constraints (EPEC) [15, 35].

Fig. 7.1 Two-node network

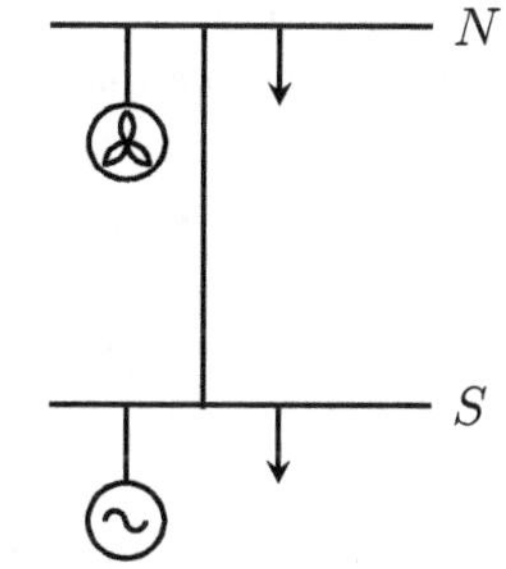

competition has been introduced.[3] In a similar vein, the distribution network is typically kept state regulated. Given this paradigm, we will take the perspective of a welfare-maximizing TSO that invests in transmission lines.[4] Meanwhile, profit-maximizing power companies decide on generation capacity and output at the lower level, and a surplus-maximizing ISO controls power flows in order to maintain energy balance at every node. Such a setup naturally lends itself to a bi-level framework for decision analysis. However, it is also useful to establish a single-level central-planning model as a benchmark against which to compare all decentralized results. We do so in Sect. 7.2.1 before moving on to the bi-level model for transmission planning in Sect. 7.2.2.

7.2.1 Transmission Expansion Under Central Planning

We first develop economic intuition via a stylized two-node, single-period model in which a central planner makes all transmission and generation decisions. Although such a model abstracts from real-world details, viz. VRES intermittency, it, nevertheless, provides insight about the tradeoffs inherent in transmission planning. Based on [28], the model has a north and a south node, $j = N, S$. Both nodes have linear inverse-demand functions, $A_j - B_j x_j$, where A_j (in \$/MW) and B_j (in \$/MW^2) are positive parameters related to the maximum willingness to pay for power and price elasticity of demand at node j, respectively. Here, x_j (in MW) is the consumption at node j. Node S is the load center and has only thermal generation, while node N has relatively little demand but ample VRES capacity, i.e., $A_S > A_N$ (Fig. 7.1). Assuming constant long-run marginal costs for the technologies, $C_j > 0$

[3] Profit-maximizing merchant investors are also responsible for some DC interconnections.

[4] In the U.S., transmission planners are usually referred to as regional transmission organizations (RTOs).

(in \$/MW), along with fixed a transmission capacity of K (in MW), the welfare-maximizing optimal dispatch is:

$$\begin{aligned}
\underset{y_N \geq 0, y_S \geq 0, f}{\text{Maximize}}\ & A_N (y_N + f) - \frac{1}{2} B_N (y_N + f)^2 + A_S (y_S - f) - \frac{1}{2} B_S (y_S - f)^2 \\
& - C_N y_N - C_S y_S && (7.1a) \\
\text{s.t. } & \lambda^- : -K \leq f \leq K : \lambda^+ && (7.1b) \\
& y_N + f \geq 0 : \beta_N && (7.1c) \\
& y_S - f \geq 0 : \beta_S && (7.1d)
\end{aligned}$$

where y_j (in MW) is the generation output at node j and f is the transmission flow from node S to N. We restrict generation to be non-negative and assume that capacity is not binding. The objective function (7.1a) is simply to maximize social welfare comprising consumer surplus, producer surplus, and merchandising surplus.[5] Constraints (7.1b) limit the transmission flow in either direction, while constraints (7.1c)–(7.1d) require non-negativity of consumption at each node. Since (7.1a)–(7.1d) is a quadratic program (QP) with a concave objective function and linear constraints, its following KKT conditions are also necessary and sufficient for optimality:

$$\begin{aligned}
& 0 \leq y_N \perp -[A_N - B_N (y_N + f)] + C_N - \beta_N \geq 0 && (7.2a) \\
& 0 \leq y_S \perp -[A_S - B_S (y_S - f)] + C_S - \beta_S \geq 0 && (7.2b) \\
& f \text{ u.r.s.}, \ - A_S + B_S (y_S - f) + A_N - B_N (y_N + f) \\
& \qquad - \lambda^+ + \lambda^- + \beta_N - \beta_S = 0 && (7.2c) \\
& 0 \leq \lambda^+ \perp K - f \geq 0 && (7.2d) \\
& 0 \leq \lambda^- \perp K + f \geq 0 && (7.2e) \\
& 0 \leq \beta_N \perp y_N + f \geq 0 && (7.2f) \\
& 0 \leq \beta_S \perp y_S - f \geq 0 && (7.2g)
\end{aligned}$$

Assuming that consumption at each node is strictly positive, i.e., $\beta_j = 0$ in (7.2f)–(7.2g), and power flows from node S to node N at its rated capacity, i.e., $\lambda^{-,*} = 0$ in (7.2e) and $f^* = K$ in (7.2d), we can show that the market-clearing price at each node j is simply equal to marginal cost, C_j, from (7.2a)–(7.2b). Consequently,

---

[5] Consumer surplus is gross consumer surplus, $\int_0^{y_N+f} (A_N - B_N x_N)\, dx_N + \int_0^{y_S-f} (A_S - B_S x_S)\, dx_S$, minus the cost of consumption, $p_N (y_N + f) + p_S (y_S - f)$. Producer surplus is revenue from sales, $p_N y_N + p_S y_S$, minus generation cost, $C_N y_N + C_S y_S$. Merchandising surplus is $(p_N - p_S) f$.

from (7.2c), we obtain the result that $\lambda^{+,*} = C_N - C_S$, viz. the marginal value of an infinitesimal increase in the transmission capacity. This finding makes economic sense as long as the north node has a higher long-run marginal cost ($C_N \geq C_S$), i.e., it is welfare enhancing to transmit power from the relatively cheaper node. More important, it indicates that the marginal value of expanding the transmission line, $\lambda^{+,*}$, is precisely equal to the net benefit from being able to supplant costly generation output at node N with that from node S.[6] Hence, at its essence, welfare-enhancing transmission investment entails comparing such marginal benefits with marginal costs of expansion.

Given this perspective, we now proceed to a more detailed framework for assessing transmission expansion under central planning. The approach is similar to that of [8] in that a single transmission planner adds lines to the network given the generation capacities. However, we allow for price-responsive demand in order to incorporate possible market power once we transition to a bi-level model [16]. In particular, we assume that the power system has a set of nodes $\mathcal{N}$, each of which has an inverse-demand function, $D^{int}_{n,s,t} - D^{\text{slp}}_{n,s,t} c_{n,s,t}$, where $D^{\text{int}}_{n,s,t}$ (in \$/MWh) and $D^{\text{slp}}_{n,s,t}$ (in \$/MWh^2) are the intercept and slope parameters, respectively, at node $n \in \mathcal{N}$ during season $s \in \mathcal{S}$ and period $t \in \mathcal{T}$. The concept of seasons and periods is similar to that in Chap. 2, i.e., representative seasons with unitless weights W_s and periods with lengths T_t (in h), while $c_{n,s,t}$ (in MWh) is a decision variable that indicates the quantity of energy consumed at node $n \in \mathcal{N}$ during season $s \in \mathcal{S}$ and period $t \in \mathcal{T}$. Each node $n \in \mathcal{N}$ also has installed generation capacity $K^{\text{gen}}_{i,n,u}$ (in MW) of technology $u \in \mathcal{U}_{i,n}$ that constrains generation output, $y_{i,n,s,t,u}$ (in MWh).[7] Operating costs for technologies are $C^{\text{opr}}_{i,n,u}$ (in \$/MWh), which are comparatively low for VRES and assumed to be zero for simplicity. VRES availabilities may be captured via unitless parameters $A_{n,s,t,u}$, which are between 0 and 1.[8] The flexibility of non-VRES technologies is reflected by maximum up- and down-ramping rates, R^{up}_u and R^{down}_u, respectively.

Connecting the nodes are transmission lines $\ell \in \mathcal{L}$, which are available for adoption at levels $j \in \mathcal{J}_\ell$ by the central planner in order to manage system variability in a welfare-enhancing manner. Assuming a lossless DC load-flow approximation in which Kirchhoff's laws are enforced, the power flow on line ℓ at level j in season s and period t, $f_{j,\ell,s,t}$ (in MW), is proportional to the difference in nodal voltage angles, $v_{n,s,t}$ (in rad), between the line's sending and receiving points. Thus, by choosing the size of each transmission line via binary variables $x_{j,\ell}$, the transmission planner effectively selects not only the capacity, $K^{\text{trn}}_{j,\ell}$ (in MW), but also

[6] The simple framework here ignores economic distortions from the exercise of market power and the social costs of emissions from thermal generation at node S, which would alter the aforementioned analysis [28].

[7] The index $i \in \mathcal{I}$ is superfluous for now because it refers to firms. However, its use will become relevant in the bi-level framework of Sect. 7.2.2.

[8] These parameters are set to 1 for non-VRES technologies.

the susceptance, $B_{j,\ell}$ (in S).[9] Hence, although line susceptance changes with the capacity size, it is possible to treat this dependence in a linear manner by summing up the flows over all levels to obtain the realized flows, $\hat{f}_{\ell,s,t} = \sum_{j \in \mathcal{J}_\ell} f_{j,\ell,s,t}$ (in MW).

The notation for the subsequent problem formulation is similar to that used in Chap. 2.

Indices and Sets

$i \in \mathcal{I}$	Firms.
$j \in \mathcal{J}_\ell$	Discrete capacity levels of transmission investment on line ℓ.
$\ell \in \mathcal{L}$	Transmission lines.
$\mathcal{L}_n^+, \mathcal{L}_n^-$	Transmission lines sending from/receiving at node n.
$n \in \mathcal{N}$	Nodes.
n_ℓ^+, n_ℓ^-	Node index for sending/receiving node of line ℓ.
$s \in \mathcal{S}$	Seasons.
$t \in \mathcal{T}$	Time periods.
$u \in \mathcal{U}_{i,n}$	Generating units belonging to firm i at node n.

Parameters

$A_{n,s,t,u}$	Maximum availability factor for technology u at node n in season s and period t [–].
$B_{j,\ell}$	Susceptance of transmission line ℓ at level $j \in \mathcal{J}_\ell$ [S].
$C_{i,n,u}^{\text{opr}}$	Operating cost of generation unit $u \in \mathcal{U}_{i,n}$ at node n belonging to firm i [\$/MWh].
$C_{j,\ell}^{\text{trn}}$	Amortized investment cost of transmission line ℓ at level $j \in \mathcal{J}_\ell$ [\$].
$D_{n,s,t}^{\text{int}}$	Intercept of inverse demand at node n in season s and period t [\$/MWh].
$D_{n,s,t}^{\text{slp}}$	Slope of inverse demand at node n in season s and period t [\$/MWh^2].
$K_{i,n,u}^{\text{gen}}$	Installed generation capacity of generation unit $u \in \mathcal{U}_{i,n}$ at node n belonging to firm i [MW].
$K_{j,\ell}^{\text{trn}}$	Capacity of transmission line ℓ at level $j \in \mathcal{J}_\ell$ [MW].
M^{trn}	Large positive constant used to linearize power flows [–].
R_u^{up}	Maximum up-ramping rate of generation unit u [–].
R_u^{down}	Maximum down-ramping rate of generation unit u [–].
T_t	Length of period t [h].
W_s	Weight of season s [–].

[9] Here, "S" is the SI unit "siemens".

Binary Variables

$x_{j,\ell}$ Binary variable that is equal to 1 if discrete capacity level $j \in \mathcal{J}_\ell$ is selected for line ℓ and 0 otherwise.

Continuous Variables

$c_{n,s,t}$ Energy consumption at node n in season s and period t [MWh].
$f_{j,\ell,s,t}$ Power flow on line ℓ at capacity level $j \in \mathcal{J}_\ell$ in season s and period t [MW].
$\hat{f}_{\ell,s,t}$ Realized power flow on line ℓ in season s and period t [MW].
$v_{n,s,t}$ Voltage angle at node n in season s and period t [rad].
$y_{i,n,s,t,u}$ Generation from unit $u \in \mathcal{U}_{i,n}$ at node n belonging to firm i in season s and period t [MWh].

$$\underset{\Omega^{\text{CP}}}{\text{Maximize}} \sum_{s\in\mathcal{S}} W_s \sum_{t\in\mathcal{T}} \sum_{n\in\mathcal{N}} \left[\left(D^{\text{int}}_{n,s,t} c_{n,s,t} - \frac{1}{2} D^{\text{slp}}_{n,s,t} c^2_{n,s,t} \right) \right.$$

$$\left. - \sum_{i\in\mathcal{I}} \sum_{u\in\mathcal{U}_{i,n}} C^{\text{opr}}_{i,n,u} y_{i,n,s,t,u} \right] - \sum_{\ell\in\mathcal{L}} \sum_{j\in\mathcal{J}_\ell} C^{\text{trn}}_{j,\ell} x_{j,\ell} \tag{7.3a}$$

$$\text{s.t. } x_{j,\ell} \in \{0, 1\}, \forall \ell, j \in \mathcal{J}_\ell \tag{7.3b}$$

$$\sum_{j\in\mathcal{J}_\ell} x_{j,\ell} = 1, \forall \ell \tag{7.3c}$$

$$-(1 - x_{j,\ell}) M^{\text{trn}} \le f_{j,\ell,s,t} - B_{j,\ell} \left(v_{n^+_\ell,s,t} - v_{n^-_\ell,s,t} \right) \le (1 - x_{j,\ell}) M^{\text{trn}},$$
$$\forall \ell, s, t, j \in \mathcal{J}_\ell \tag{7.3d}$$

$$-K^{\text{trn}}_{j,\ell} x_{j,\ell} \le f_{j,\ell,s,t} \le K^{\text{trn}}_{j,\ell} x_{j,\ell}, \forall \ell, s, t, j \in \mathcal{J}_\ell \tag{7.3e}$$

$$\hat{f}_{\ell,s,t} = \sum_{j\in\mathcal{J}_\ell} f_{j,\ell,s,t}, \forall \ell, s, t \tag{7.3f}$$

$$-\pi \le v_{n,s,t} \le \pi, \forall n, s, t \tag{7.3g}$$

$$c_{n,s,t} - \sum_{i\in\mathcal{I}} \sum_{u\in\mathcal{U}_{i,n}} y_{i,n,s,t,u} + T_t \sum_{\ell\in\mathcal{L}^+_n} \hat{f}_{\ell,s,t} - T_t \sum_{\ell\in\mathcal{L}^-_n} \hat{f}_{\ell,s,t} = 0,$$
$$\forall n, s, t \tag{7.3h}$$

$$y_{i,n,s,t,u} \le T_t A_{n,s,t,u} K^{\text{gen}}_{i,n,u}, \forall i, n, s, t, u \in \mathcal{U}_{i,n} \tag{7.3i}$$

$$y_{i,n,s,t,u} - y_{i,n,s,t-1,u} \le T_t R^{\text{up}}_u K^{\text{gen}}_{i,n,u}, \forall i, n, s, t, u \in \mathcal{U}_{i,n} \tag{7.3j}$$

$$- y_{i,n,s,t,u} + y_{i,n,s,t-1,u} \leq T_t R_u^{\text{down}} K_{i,n,u}^{\text{gen}}, \ \forall i, n, s, t, u \in \mathcal{U}_{i,n} \tag{7.3k}$$

$$c_{n,s,t} \geq 0, \ \forall n, s, t \tag{7.3l}$$

$$y_{i,n,s,t,u} \geq 0, \ \forall i, n, s, t, u \in \mathcal{U}_{i,n} \tag{7.3m}$$

$$f_{j,\ell,s,t} \text{ u.r.s.}, \ \forall \ell, s, t, j \in \mathcal{J}_\ell \tag{7.3n}$$

$$\hat{f}_{\ell,s,t} \text{ u.r.s.}, \ \forall \ell, s, t \tag{7.3o}$$

$$v_{n,s,t} \text{ u.r.s.}, \ \forall n, s, t \tag{7.3p}$$

where $\Omega^{\text{CP}} \equiv \left\{c_{n,s,t}, f_{j,\ell,s,t}, \hat{f}_{\ell,s,t}, v_{n,s,t}, x_{j,\ell}, y_{i,n,s,t,u}\right\}$ are the optimization variables. The objective function (7.3a) is to maximize social welfare, which comprises consumer surplus, producer surplus, the ISO's merchandising surplus, and the TSO's investment cost. Assuming endogenously determined equilibrium prices, $p_{n,s,t}$, that are paid (earned) by consumers (producers) at node n in season s and period t, we can decompose social welfare as follows:

- Consumer surplus is the gross surplus minus the cost of purchasing energy, i.e., $\sum_{n\in\mathcal{N}}\sum_{s\in\mathcal{S}}\sum_{t\in\mathcal{T}} W_s \left(D_{n,s,t}^{\text{int}} c_{n,s,t} - \frac{1}{2} D_{n,s,t}^{\text{slp}} c_{n,s,t}^2 - p_{n,s,t} c_{n,s,t}\right)$.
- Producer surplus is the revenue earned by firms minus the generation cost, i.e., $\sum_{i\in\mathcal{I}}\sum_{n\in\mathcal{N}}\sum_{s\in\mathcal{S}}\sum_{t\in\mathcal{T}}\sum_{u\in\mathcal{U}_{i,n}} W_s \left(p_{n,s,t} - C_{i,n,u}^{\text{opr}}\right) y_{i,n,s,t,u}$.
- Merchandising surplus is the net revenue from energy imports across the nodes, i.e., $\sum_{n\in\mathcal{N}}\sum_{s\in\mathcal{S}}\sum_{t\in\mathcal{T}} W_s T_t p_{n,s,t} \left(\sum_{\ell\in\mathcal{L}_n^-} \hat{f}_{\ell,s,t} - \sum_{\ell\in\mathcal{L}_n^+} \hat{f}_{\ell,s,t}\right)$.
- Investment cost is $\sum_{\ell\in\mathcal{L}}\sum_{j\in\mathcal{J}_\ell} C_{j,\ell}^{\text{trn}} x_{j,\ell}$.

Note that via the energy-balance constraint (7.3h), the consumer payment, $p_{n,s,t} c_{n,s,t}$, equals the generation revenue, $\sum_{i\in\mathcal{I}}\sum_{u\in\mathcal{U}_{i,n}} p_{n,s,t} y_{i,n,s,t,u}$, plus the merchandising surplus, $T_t p_{n,s,t} \left(\sum_{\ell\in\mathcal{L}_n^-} \hat{f}_{\ell,s,t} - \sum_{\ell\in\mathcal{L}_n^+} \hat{f}_{\ell,s,t}\right)$. Hence, these terms cancel in the objective function.

The objective of maximizing social welfare in the mixed-integer quadratic program (MIQP) (7.3a)–(7.3p) is subject to several constraints. First, investment in transmission lines is a binary choice, viz. each combination of line ℓ and level $j \in \mathcal{J}_\ell$ can be either selected or not (7.3b), and only a single-level $j \in \mathcal{J}_\ell$ must be selected for each line ℓ (7.3c). Second, power flows on transmission lines are modeled by (7.3d)–(7.3g). Actually, (7.3d)–(7.3e) may be rendered more directly as $f_{j,\ell,s,t} = x_{j,\ell} B_{j,\ell} \left(v_{n_\ell^+,s,t} - v_{n_\ell^-,s,t}\right)$, $\forall \ell, s, t, j \in \mathcal{J}_\ell$ and $-K_{j,\ell}^{\text{trn}} \leq f_{j,\ell,s,t} \leq K_{j,\ell}^{\text{trn}}$, $\forall \ell, s, t, j \in \mathcal{J}_\ell$, respectively. However, the former equation is non-linear since $x_{j,\ell}$ is multiplied by $v_{n,s,t}$. It is linearized via (7.3d)–(7.3e) as follows: if $x_{j,\ell} = 1$, then line ℓ is built at level $j \in \mathcal{J}_\ell$, which collapses (7.3d)–(7.3e) to $f_{j,\ell,s,t} = B_{j,\ell} \left(v_{n_\ell^+,s,t} - v_{n_\ell^-,s,t}\right)$, $\forall \ell, s, t, j \in \mathcal{J}_\ell$ and $-K_{j,\ell}^{\text{trn}} \leq f_{j,\ell,s,t} \leq K_{j,\ell}^{\text{trn}}$, $\forall \ell, s, t, j \in \mathcal{J}_\ell$ as desired. By contrast, if $x_{j,\ell} = 0$, then $f_{j,\ell,s,t} = 0$

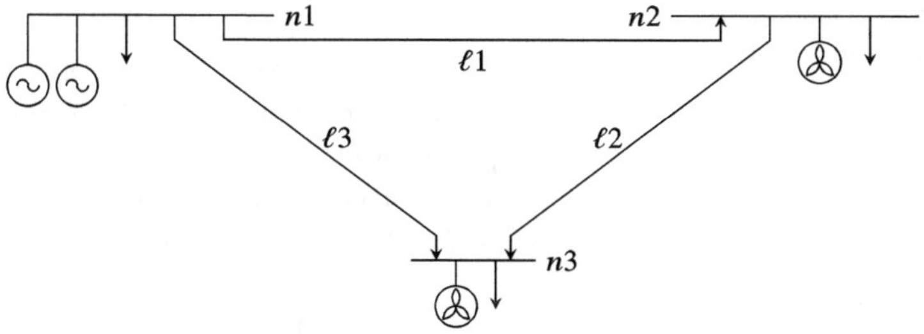

Fig. 7.2 Three-node test network

Table 7.1 Demand parameters for all (s, t)

	Node		
Parameter	$n = 1$	$n = 2$	$n = 3$
$D^{\text{int}}_{n,s,t}$ (\$/MWh)	220	140	120
$D^{\text{slp}}_{n,s,t}$ (\$/MWh^2)	1	1	1

via (7.3e), while (7.3d) is non-binding. Based on these disjunctive constraints,[10] the realized power flow for line ℓ is obtained in (7.3f) by summing over all of the levels $j \in \mathcal{J}_{\ell}$. (7.3g) constrains voltage angles to be in $[-\pi, \pi]$. Third, energy balance at every node n is enforced in each in season s and period t by equating the consumption with the local generation and net imports (7.3h). Fourth, generation output is constrained by available capacity (7.3i), while generation ramping is limited as a proportion of the installed capacity (7.3j)–(7.3k). Finally, the decision variables are classified as being either non-negative (7.3l)–(7.3m) (in case of consumption and generation) or unrestricted in sign, i.e., "u.r.s.," (7.3n)–(7.3p) (in case of power flows, realized power flows, and voltage angles).

Illustrative Example 7.1 *Welfare-maximizing MIQP for centrally planned transmission expansion.*

We implement the central-planning MIQP (7.3a)–(7.3p) for the three-node network in Fig. 7.2. Demand data given in Table 7.1 indicate that node $n = 1$ is the load center, while node $n = 3$ has relatively low consumption. There are two seasons and three periods within each season such that each season comprises 183 days, i.e., $W_s = 183$, and each period is eight-hours long, i.e., $T_t = 8$. Demand parameters do not vary by season or period for sake of simplicity. Instead, we focus on the heterogeneity among generation resources such that the fossil-fuel technologies, $u = 3$ (coal) and $u = 4$ (gas), are installed at node $n = 1$ and belong to firm $i = 1$ (Table 7.2) with operating costs based on Illustrative Example 2.1. By contrast, VRES are owned by firm $i = 2$ at the low-demand nodes, $n = 2$ and $n = 3$,

[10] Big-Ms in disjunctive constraints must be carefully specified. On the one hand, they should be large enough to avoid artificially limiting the constraints. On the other hand, they should be small enough to avoid scaling issues for numerical solvers [19].

Table 7.2 Generation costs, installed capacities, and ramp rates

	$i=1$	$i=1$	$i=2$	$i=2$
	$n=1$	$n=1$	$n=2$	$n=3$
Parameter	$u=3$	$u=4$	$u=1$	$u=2$
$C^{\text{opr}}_{i,n,u}$ (\$/MWh)	20	50	0	0
$K^{\text{gen}}_{i,n,u}$ (MW)	35	40	50	50
$R^{\text{up}}_u = R^{\text{down}}_u$ (–)	0.30	0.60	1	1

Table 7.3 Availability parameters for VRES technology $u = 1$ at node $n = 2$, $A_{n,s,t,u}$ (–)

	Period		
Season	$t=1$	$t=2$	$t=3$
$s=1$	0.20	0.10	0.05
$s=2$	0.25	0.50	0.75

Table 7.4 Availability parameters for VRES technology $u = 2$ at node $n = 3$, $A_{n,s,t,u}$ (–)

	Period		
Season	$t=1$	$t=2$	$t=3$
$s=1$	0.20	0.40	0.50
$s=2$	1.00	0.75	0.10

Table 7.5 Transmission-line parameters for all ℓ

	Attribute		
Level j	$B_{j,\ell}$ (S)	$K^{\text{trn}}_{j,\ell}$ (MW)	$C^{\text{trn}}_{j,\ell}$ (\$)
1	0	0	0
2	1200	3.7	104,529.6
3	1500	6.1	173,923.2
4	1700	12.2	348,724.8
5	2000	18.3	522,648.0
6	2300	24.4	696,571.2
7	2800	30.5	870,494.4
8	3600	36.6	1,045,296.0
9	4900	42.7	1,219,219.2
10	5100	48.8	1,393,142.4

with availability parameters, $A_{n,s,t,u}$, given in Tables 7.3 and 7.4. From these data, VRES technology $u = 1$ may be thought of as an on-shore one, while $u = 2$ can be considered as the off-shore one. Although the generation technologies have installed capacities given in Table 7.2, we assume initially that no transmission lines exist. Instead, the central planner may construct transmission lines based on the candidates given in Table 7.5. These data are based on the lower range of estimates from [22] such that the annual amortized costs correspond roughly to \$335/(MW-km). For example, a line of length 85 km with a capacity of 48.8 MW has an annual amortized cost of \$1,393,142.4. The discrete capacity levels' susceptances are based on calculations from [21].

Given the input data, it is optimal to build transmission lines $\ell = 1$, $\ell = 2$, and $\ell = 3$ in capacities of 12.2, 12.2, and 18.3 MW, respectively. The aggregate welfare results given in Table 7.6 indicate that the benefits of this transmission plan accrue

Table 7.6 Welfare results (in $) with and without transmission investment for centrally planned transmission expansion

Component	Transmission investment	No transmission investment
CS	34,377,804	29,170,201
PS	5,957,193	6,719,759
MS	810,715	0
TC	1,220,098	0
SW	39,925,614	35,889,960

Table 7.7 Operational results (in MWh) with and without transmission investment for centrally planned transmission expansion

Attribute	Node (or line)	Transmission investment	No transmission investment
Consumption	$n = 1$	214,598	197,640
	$n = 2$	128,902	95,160
	$n = 3$	108,602	109,800
Generation	$n = 1$	114,719	197,640
	$n = 2$	133,735	95,160
	$n = 3$	203,647	109,800
Net imports	$n = 1$	99,879	0
	$n = 2$	−4834	0
	$n = 3$	−95,045	0
Energy flows	$\ell = 1$	−31,484	0
	$\ell = 2$	−26,651	0
	$\ell = 3$	−68,394	0

principally to consumers since consumer surplus (CS) increases by approximately 18%. Although there is a 12% loss in producer surplus (PS) vis-à-vis not investing, the overall increase in social welfare (SW) is 11%. It is worthwhile to note that the revenues collected by a *notional* transmission owner in the form of merchandising surplus (MS) would not be enough to cover the transmission cost (TC) [18]. In effect, it is acceptable for one sector of the electricity industry to make a loss under central planning in order to obtain a net increase in social welfare.[11]

The difference in the operations of the power system facilitated by transmission investment is worth investigating further in Table 7.7. In general, the transmission lines allow node $n = 1$ to exploit the full potential of VRES at nodes $n = 2$ and especially $n = 3$. Energy is imported by node $n = 1$, thereby enabling an increase in consumption where it is valued the most while supplanting fossil-fuel generation by VRES output. Although average prices decrease at nodes $n = 1$ and $n = 2$, they actually increase at node $n = 3$ due to the possibility to export off-shore wind output

[11] There may be other reasons for constructing transmission lines at a loss for a *notional* transmission owner. For example, it may be necessary to do so in order to reduce CO_2 emissions [28] and to increase VRES output [16].

Table 7.8 Nodal prices (\$/MWh) for centrally planned transmission expansion

Node	Season	Period $t = 1$	$t = 2$	$t = 3$
$n = 1$	$s = 1$	50	37.33	20
	$s = 2$	20	0	20
$n = 2$	$s = 1$	50	37.33	20
	$s = 2$	10	0	18.29
$n = 3$	$s = 1$	50	37.33	20
	$s = 2$	0	0	19.21

Table 7.9 Generation output (MWh) for centrally planned transmission expansion

Node	Season	Period $t = 1$	$t = 2$	$t = 3$
$n = 1$	$s = 1$	170	168	200
	$s = 2$	6.38	0	82.50
$n = 2$	$s = 1$	80	40	20
	$s = 2$	100	190.79	300
$n = 3$	$s = 1$	80	160	200
	$s = 2$	343.62	289.21	40

to consumers with a higher willingness to pay. Thus, although a *notional* firm $i = 1$ has a lower PS with transmission investment, a *notional* firm $i = 2$ with a VRES fleet ends up with a higher PS under the optimal transmission plan.

It is also instructive to scrutinize the results at the seasonal level in order to understand how transmission investment affects system operations. Since there is no linking constraint between the seasons, it is actually possible to analyze the operational results of each season separately.[12] We begin with season $s = 1$, in which VRES availability at node $n = 2$ is relatively low, while that at node $n = 3$ is moderately high, cf. Tables 7.3 and 7.4. Consequently, some non-VRES output is optimal in each period, and prices are equal across the nodes in each period, cf. Tables 7.8 and 7.9. This means that there is no transmission congestion in any period, and the price-setting technologies in periods $t = 1$, $t = 2$, and $t = 3$ are gas, coal, and coal, respectively. In particular, during period $t = 1$, coal's output is 84 MWh due to its up-ramping restrictions, which means that gas has to produce 86 MWh as the marginal technology, i.e., the market-clearing price equals the marginal cost of gas generation. During period $t = 2$, gas ramps down to 0 MWh, while coal ramps up to 168 MWh, i.e., it is again ramp-constrained, and it sets the market price on the basis of its ramping capability. Because the ramping constraint is binding, the market-clearing price is higher than coal's marginal cost of \$20/MWh. By contrast, during period $t = 3$, only 200 MWh of coal are needed, which is well within the limits of both the installed capacity and ramping rate. Thus, the market-clearing price is simply coal's marginal cost. During all periods, VRES dispatch is at its

[12] Examples of such constraints are annual caps on CO_2 emissions and inter-seasonal energy-balance requirements on storage.

Table 7.10 Net imports (MWh) for centrally planned transmission expansion

Node	Season	Period		
		$t = 1$	$t = 2$	$t = 3$
$n = 1$	$s = 1$	0	14.67	0
	$s = 2$	193.62	220	117.50
$n = 2$	$s = 1$	10	62.67	100
	$s = 2$	30	−50.79	−178.29
$n = 3$	$s = 1$	−10	−77.33	−100
	$s = 2$	−223.62	−169.21	60.79

available capacity. Finally, from Table 7.10, we note that node $n = 2$ is persistently an importer during season $s = 1$, node $n = 3$ is an exporter, and node $n = 1$ is self-sufficient except during period $t = 2$ when its ramp-constrained generation capacity necessitates imports.[13]

In contrast to season $s = 1$, season $s = 2$ has relatively high VRES availability during all periods except at node $n = 3$ in period $t = 3$. There is particularly high VRES availability at node $n = 3$ during period $t = 1$, which enables substantial VRES output and exports to both nodes $n = 1$ and $n = 2$. In fact, so high is VRES availability at $n = 3$ that line $\ell = 3$ is congested during period $t = 1$. The resulting prices at nodes $n = 1, n = 2$, and $n = 3$ are set by coal, capacity-constrained VRES, and unconstrained VRES, respectively. Thus, the price at node $n = 2$ is positive to reflect the marginal value of installed capacity, whereas that at node $n = 3$ is zero to reflect the marginal cost of VRES. Meanwhile, in period $t = 2$, VRES availability is plentiful at both nodes $n = 2$ and $n = 3$, which enables sufficient exports to $n = 1$ to obviate fossil-fuel generation there. Since VRES is the marginal technology, VRES capacity limits are not reached, and no transmission lines are congested, prices at all nodes are zero. The situation in period $t = 3$ is markedly different since VRES availability is almost non-existent at node $n = 3$, which necessitates its importing energy. Instead, VRES output at node $n = 2$ operates at its available capacity to export energy to both nodes $n = 1$ and $n = 3$. Line $\ell = 1$ becomes congested, which leads to distinct nodal prices set by unconstrained coal generation (node $n = 1$) and capacity-constrained VRES output (both nodes $n = 2$ and $n = 3$).

7.2.2 Bi-Level Transmission Expansion

In contrast to a centrally planned electricity industry, power-system operations are the purview of profit-maximizing firms and a welfare-maximizing ISO that are distinct from the regulated TSO. Since the TSO's transmission-expansion decisions

[13] For ease of interpretation, we present the disaggregated results in Tables 7.9 and 7.10 on a daily basis. In order to obtain the annual quantities reported in Table 7.7, the disaggregated quantities should be summed up and multiplied by the number of days in each season, i.e., 183.

anticipate those of the firms and the ISO, a bi-level framework is appropriate for analyzing transmission investment and operations [7, 16]. In particular, the upper level comprises the TSO's welfare-maximization problem with decisions $x_{j,\ell}$ that are constrained by the lower-level problems of the firms and the ISO. At the lower level, each firm $i \in \mathcal{I}$ determines generation dispatch, $y_{i,n,s,t,u}$, while the ISO decides upon consumption, $c_{n,s,t}$, power flows, $f_{j,\ell,s,t}$, realized power flows, $\hat{f}_{\ell,s,t}$, and voltage angles, $\upsilon_{n,s,t}$. It is important to emphasize that each of these lower-level agents takes not only $x_{j,\ell}$ but also the decisions of the other agents as given.[14]

The notation follows from that in Sect. 7.2.1 along with the following additions:

Dual Variables

$\beta_{i,n,s,t,u}$	Marginal value of maximum generation for firm i at node n in season s and period t for unit $u \in \mathcal{U}_{i,n}$ [\$/MWh].
$\beta^{\text{up}}_{i,n,s,t,u}/\beta^{\text{down}}_{i,n,s,t,u}$	Marginal value of up-/down-ramping generation for firm i at node n in season s and period t for unit $u \in \mathcal{U}_{i,n}$ [\$/MWh].
$\mu_{j,\ell,s,t}$	Marginal value of power flow on line ℓ at capacity level $j \in \mathcal{J}_\ell$ in season s and period t [\$/MW].
$\hat{\mu}_{j,\ell,s,t}$	Auxiliary variable for marginal value of power flow on line ℓ at capacity level $j \in \mathcal{J}_\ell$ in season s and period t [\$/MW].
$\underline{\mu}_{j,\ell,s,t}/\overline{\mu}_{j,\ell,s,t}$	Marginal value of minimum/maximum transmission capacity on line ℓ at capacity level $j \in \mathcal{J}_\ell$ in season s and period t [\$/MW].
$\psi_{\ell,s,t}$	Marginal value of realized power flow on line ℓ in season s and period t [\$/MW].
$\underline{\kappa}_{n,s,t}/\overline{\kappa}_{n,s,t}$	Marginal value of minimum/maximum voltage angle limit at node n in season s and period t [\$/rad].
$\lambda_{n,s,t}$	Marginal value of energy consumption at node n in season s and period t [\$/MWh].
$\phi^{c}_{n,s,t}$	Marginal value of non-negativity of consumption at node n in season s and period t [\$/MWh].
$\phi^{y}_{i,n,s,t,u}$	Marginal value of non-negativity of generation output by firm i at node n in season s and period t for unit $u \in \mathcal{U}_{i,n}$ [\$/MWh].

The upper-level problem of the TSO is as follows:

$$\underset{x_{j,\ell}}{\text{Maximize}} \sum_{s\in\mathcal{S}} W_s \sum_{t\in\mathcal{T}} \sum_{n\in\mathcal{N}} \Bigg[\left(D^{\text{int}}_{n,s,t} c_{n,s,t} - \frac{1}{2} D^{\text{slp}}_{n,s,t} c^2_{n,s,t} \right) - \sum_{i\in\mathcal{I}} \sum_{u\in\mathcal{U}_{i,n}} C^{\text{opr}}_{i,n,u} y_{i,n,s,t,u} \Bigg] - \sum_{\ell\in\mathcal{L}} \sum_{j\in\mathcal{J}_\ell} C^{\text{trn}}_{j,\ell} x_{j,\ell} \tag{7.4a}$$

[14] For example, firm $i' \in \mathcal{I}$ takes the following variables as given: $c_{n,s,t}$, $f_{j,\ell,s,t}$, $\hat{f}_{\ell,s,t}$, $\upsilon_{n,s,t}$, $x_{j,\ell}$, and $y_{i,n,s,t,u}$, $\forall i \neq i'$. Likewise, the ISO takes $x_{j,\ell}$ and $y_{i,n,s,t,u}$ as given.

$$\text{s.t. } x_{j,\ell} \in \{0,1\}, \forall \ell, j \in \mathcal{J}_\ell \quad (7.4b)$$

$$\sum_{j \in \mathcal{J}_\ell} x_{j,\ell} = 1, \forall \ell \quad (7.4c)$$

As can be readily seen, the TSO's objective function (7.4a) is identical to that from central planning (7.3a). Likewise, constraints (7.4b)–(7.4c) are the same as (7.3b)–(7.3c) from central planning. However, the important difference is that the remaining decisions about power-system operations are made by distinct agents at the lower level.

First, each firm $i \in \mathcal{I}$ determines dispatch in order to maximize its operational profit:

$$\underset{y_{i,n,s,t,u}}{\text{Maximize}} \sum_{s \in \mathcal{S}} W_s \sum_{n \in \mathcal{N}} \sum_{t \in \mathcal{T}} \sum_{u \in \mathcal{U}_{i,n}} \left(D^{\text{int}}_{n,s,t} - D^{\text{slp}}_{n,s,t} \left(\sum_{i' \in \mathcal{I}} \sum_{u' \in \mathcal{U}_{i',n}} y_{i',n,s,t,u'} \right.\right.$$

$$\left.\left. - T_t \left(\sum_{\ell \in \mathcal{L}_n^+} \hat{f}_{\ell,s,t} - \sum_{\ell \in \mathcal{L}_n^-} \hat{f}_{\ell,s,t} \right)\right) - C^{\text{opr}}_{i,n,u} \right) y_{i,n,s,t,u} \quad (7.5a)$$

$$\text{s.t. } y_{i,n,s,t,u} \le T_t A_{n,s,t,u} K^{\text{gen}}_{i,n,u} : \beta_{i,n,s,t,u}, \forall n, s, t, u \in \mathcal{U}_{i,n} \quad (7.5b)$$

$$y_{i,n,s,t,u} - y_{i,n,s,t-1,u} \le T_t R^{\text{up}}_u K^{\text{gen}}_{i,n,u} : \beta^{\text{up}}_{i,n,s,t,u}, \forall n, s, t, u \in \mathcal{U}_{i,n} \quad (7.5c)$$

$$- y_{i,n,s,t,u} + y_{i,n,s,t-1,u} \le T_t R^{\text{down}}_u K^{\text{gen}}_{i,n,u} : \beta^{\text{down}}_{i,n,s,t,u},$$

$$\forall n, s, t, u \in \mathcal{U}_{i,n} \quad (7.5d)$$

$$y_{i,n,s,t,u} \ge 0 : \phi^{y}_{i,n,s,t,u}, \forall n, s, t, u \in \mathcal{U}_{i,n} \quad (7.5e)$$

The objective of firm $i \in \mathcal{I}$ is to maximize its profit (or, equivalently, producer surplus since we ignore fixed costs), which is given in (7.5a). As alluded to in Sect. 7.2.1, it comprises sales revenue minus operating costs, i.e., $\sum_{n \in \mathcal{N}} \sum_{s \in \mathcal{S}} \sum_{t \in \mathcal{T}} \sum_{u \in \mathcal{U}_{i,n}} W_s \left(p_{n,s,t} - C^{\text{opr}}_{i,n,u} \right) y_{i,n,s,t,u}$. The only difference between the latter expression and the one in (7.5a) is that the electricity price, $p_{n,s,t}$, is replaced by the inverse-demand function, $\left(D^{\text{int}}_{n,s,t} - D^{\text{slp}}_{n,s,t} c_{n,s,t} \right)$, to reflect the influence of firm i's generation on the equilibrium price as in a Nash-Cournot framework [11]. This is further emphasized by the replacement of $c_{n,s,t}$ by local generation, $\sum_{i' \in \mathcal{I}} \sum_{u' \in \mathcal{U}_{i',n}} y_{i',n,s,t,u'}$, plus net imports, $-T_t \sum_{\ell \in \mathcal{L}_n^+} \hat{f}_{\ell,s,t} + T_t \sum_{\ell \in \mathcal{L}_n^-} \hat{f}_{\ell,s,t}$. By contrast, a price-taking firm would not have this substitution in its objective function because it would not be able to perceive the impact of its decisions on the equilibrium. The next three constraints, (7.5b)–(7.5d), limit generation output and ramping based on installed capacity and ramp rates, respectively, analogous to (7.3i)–(7.3k). Finally, (7.5e) imposes non-negativity restrictions on generation output, cf. (7.3m), and the lower-case Greek letters after the semi-colons are dual variables associated with the constraints.[15]

Second, the ISO's surplus-maximization problem is:

$$\underset{\substack{c_{n,s,t}, f_{j,\ell,s,t},\\ \hat{f}_{\ell,s,t}, v_{n,s,t}}}{\text{Maximize}} \sum_{s \in \mathcal{S}} W_s \sum_{t \in \mathcal{T}} \sum_{n \in \mathcal{N}} \left(D^{\text{int}}_{n,s,t} c_{n,s,t} - \frac{1}{2} D^{\text{slp}}_{n,s,t} c^2_{n,s,t} \right) \tag{7.6a}$$

$$\text{s.t. } f_{j,\ell,s,t} - B_{j,\ell} x_{j,\ell} \left(v_{n^+_\ell,s,t} - v_{n^-_\ell,s,t} \right) = 0 : \mu_{j,\ell,s,t}, \forall \ell, s, t, j \in \mathcal{J}_\ell \tag{7.6b}$$

$$\underline{\mu}_{j,\ell,s,t} : -K^{\text{trn}}_{j,\ell} \leq f_{j,\ell,s,t} \leq K^{\text{trn}}_{j,\ell} : \overline{\mu}_{j,\ell,s,t}, \forall \ell, s, t, j \in \mathcal{J}_\ell \tag{7.6c}$$

$$\hat{f}_{\ell,s,t} = \sum_{j \in \mathcal{J}_\ell} f_{j,\ell,s,t} : \psi_{\ell,s,t}, \forall \ell, s, t \tag{7.6d}$$

$$\underline{\kappa}_{n,s,t} : -\pi \leq v_{n,s,t} \leq \pi : \overline{\kappa}_{n,s,t}, \forall n, s, t \tag{7.6e}$$

$$c_{n,s,t} - \sum_{i \in \mathcal{I}} \sum_{u \in \mathcal{U}_{i,n}} y_{i,n,s,t,u} + T_t \sum_{\ell \in \mathcal{L}^+_n} \hat{f}_{\ell,s,t} - T_t \sum_{\ell \in \mathcal{L}^-_n} \hat{f}_{\ell,s,t} = 0 :$$

$$\lambda_{n,s,t}, \forall n, s, t \tag{7.6f}$$

$$c_{n,s,t} \geq 0 : \phi^c_{n,s,t}, \forall n, s, t \tag{7.6g}$$

$$f_{j,\ell,s,t} \text{ u.r.s.}, \forall \ell, s, t, j \in \mathcal{J}_\ell \tag{7.6h}$$

$$\hat{f}_{\ell,s,t} \text{ u.r.s.}, \forall \ell, s, t \tag{7.6i}$$

$$v_{n,s,t} \text{ u.r.s.}, \forall n, s, t \tag{7.6j}$$

The ISO's objective (7.6a) is to maximize the gross surplus from consumption, $\sum_{s \in \mathcal{S}} W_s \sum_{t \in \mathcal{T}} \sum_{n \in \mathcal{N}} \left(D^{\text{int}}_{n,s,t} c_{n,s,t} - \frac{1}{2} D^{\text{slp}}_{n,s,t} c^2_{n,s,t} \right)$. Since generation and transmission plans are taken as given from the ISO's perspective, their associated costs are constant and, therefore, not necessary to include in (7.6a), cf. (7.4a). The ISO's constraints on grid operations follow directly from those in central planning with the exception that it is not necessary to linearize Kirchhoff's laws in (7.6b)–(7.6c), cf. (7.3d)–(7.3e), because $x_{j,\ell}$ is treated as a parameter. Thus, from the perspective of the ISO, (7.6b)–(7.6c) are already linear. Furthermore, (7.6d)–(7.6j) match (7.3f)–(7.3h), (7.3l), and (7.3n)–(7.3p).

The bi-level model comprising the upper-level problem (7.4a)–(7.4c) constrained by the lower-level ones, (7.5a)–(7.5e), $\forall i \in \mathcal{I}$, and (7.6a)–(7.6j), is typically resolved by rendering it into single-level optimization problem. Since each lower-level problem is convex, it is sufficient to replace it by its Karush–Kuhn–Tucker

[15] Alternatively, the dual variables may be interpreted as the marginal values associated with relaxing the corresponding constraints.

(KKT) conditions. The resulting mathematical program with equilibrium constraints (MPEC) is a single-level optimization problem but is non-convex due to the presence of complementarity conditions. Although these may be handled via disjunctive constraints [5], the problem instances from the resulting MIQP may prove to be intractable due to the large number of binary variables. Another resolution method to the bi-level problem is to reformulate the lower-level problems as a single optimization problem and replace the latter by (1) its primal constraints, (2) its dual constraints, and (3) strong duality. The resulting mathematical program with primal and dual constraints (MPPDC) may yield problem instances that require fewer binary variables to resolve non-convexities, and it is the route that we pursue.

First, we reformulate the lower-level equilibrium problems, (7.5a)–(7.5e), $\forall i \in \mathcal{I}$, and (7.6a)–(7.6j), as a single-agent QP. Such a reformulation is possible because the demand and supply functions are linear and the transmission costs are proportional to the distance covered [9].

$$\underset{\Omega^{\text{LL}}}{\text{Maximize}} \sum_{s\in\mathcal{S}} W_s \sum_{t\in\mathcal{T}} \sum_{n\in\mathcal{N}} \Bigg[D^{\text{int}}_{n,s,t} c_{n,s,t} - \frac{1}{2} D^{\text{slp}}_{n,s,t} c^2_{n,s,t} - \sum_{i\in\mathcal{I}} \sum_{u\in\mathcal{U}_{i,n}} C^{\text{opr}}_{i,n,u} y_{i,n,s,t,u}$$

$$-\frac{1}{2} D^{\text{slp}}_{n,s,t} \sum_{i\in\mathcal{I}} \Bigg(\sum_{u\in\mathcal{U}_{i,n}} y_{i,n,s,t,u} \Bigg)^2 \Bigg] \tag{7.7a}$$

$$\text{s.t. } f_{j,\ell,s,t} - B_{j,\ell} x_{j,\ell} \left(v_{n^+_\ell,s,t} - v_{n^-_\ell,s,t} \right) = 0 : \mu_{j,\ell,s,t}, \forall \ell, s, t, j \in \mathcal{J}_\ell \tag{7.7b}$$

$$\underline{\mu}_{j,\ell,s,t} : -K^{\text{trn}}_{j,\ell} \leq f_{j,\ell,s,t} \leq K^{\text{trn}}_{j,\ell} : \overline{\mu}_{j,\ell,s,t}, \forall \ell, s, t, j \in \mathcal{J}_\ell \tag{7.7c}$$

$$\hat{f}_{\ell,s,t} = \sum_{j\in\mathcal{J}_\ell} f_{j,\ell,s,t} : \psi_{\ell,s,t}, \forall \ell, s, t \tag{7.7d}$$

$$\underline{\kappa}_{n,s,t} : -\pi \leq v_{n,s,t} \leq \pi : \overline{\kappa}_{n,s,t}, \forall n, s, t \tag{7.7e}$$

$$c_{n,s,t} - \sum_{i\in\mathcal{I}} \sum_{u\in\mathcal{U}_{i,n}} y_{i,n,s,t,u} + T_t \sum_{\ell\in\mathcal{L}^+_n} \hat{f}_{\ell,s,t} - T_t \sum_{\ell\in\mathcal{L}^-_n} \hat{f}_{\ell,s,t} = 0 :$$

$$\lambda_{n,s,t}, \forall n, s, t \tag{7.7f}$$

$$y_{i,n,s,t,u} \leq T_t A_{n,s,t,u} K^{\text{gen}}_{i,n,u} : \beta_{i,n,s,t,u}, \forall i, n, s, t, u \in \mathcal{U}_{i,n} \tag{7.7g}$$

$$y_{i,n,s,t,u} - y_{i,n,s,t-1,u} \leq T_t R^{\text{up}}_u K^{\text{gen}}_{i,n,u} : \beta^{\text{up}}_{i,n,s,t,u},$$

$$\forall i, n, s, t, u \in \mathcal{U}_{i,n} \tag{7.7h}$$

$$- y_{i,n,s,t,u} + y_{i,n,s,t-1,u} \leq T_t R^{\text{down}}_u K^{\text{gen}}_{i,n,u} : \beta^{\text{down}}_{i,n,s,t,u},$$

$$\forall i, n, s, t, u \in \mathcal{U}_{i,n} \tag{7.7i}$$

$$y_{i,n,s,t,u} \geq 0 : \ \phi^{y}_{i,n,s,t,u}, \ \forall i, n, s, t, u \in \mathcal{U}_{i,n} \tag{7.7j}$$

$$c_{n,s,t} \geq 0 : \ \phi^{c}_{n,s,t}, \ \forall n, s, t \tag{7.7k}$$

$$f_{j,\ell,s,t} \text{ u.r.s.}, \ \forall \ell, s, t, j \in \mathcal{J}_\ell \tag{7.7l}$$

$$\hat{f}_{\ell,s,t} \text{ u.r.s.}, \ \forall \ell, s, t \tag{7.7m}$$

$$v_{n,s,t} \text{ u.r.s.}, \ \forall n, s, t \tag{7.7n}$$

Here, $\Omega^{\text{LL}} \equiv \left\{c_{n,s,t}, f_{j,\ell,s,t}, \hat{f}_{\ell,s,t}, v_{n,s,t}, y_{i,n,s,t,u}\right\}$. Note that $x_{j,\ell}$ is not a decision variable at the lower level. The objective function (7.7a) is similar to the social surplus in the ISO's objective function (7.6a) with the exception of the operating cost, $-\sum_{s\in\mathcal{S}} W_s \sum_{t\in\mathcal{T}} \sum_{n\in\mathcal{N}} \sum_{i\in\mathcal{I}} \sum_{u\in\mathcal{U}_{i,n}} C^{\text{opr}}_{i,n,u} y_{i,n,s,t,u}$, and the extended-cost term, $-\frac{1}{2}\sum_{s\in\mathcal{S}} W_s \sum_{t\in\mathcal{T}} \sum_{n\in\mathcal{N}} D^{\text{slp}}_{n,s,t} \sum_{i\in\mathcal{I}} \left(\sum_{u\in\mathcal{U}_{i,n}} y_{i,n,s,t,u}\right)^2$, which adjusts for the Cournot behavior of firms. If the latter term is excluded, then all firms are price takers.

Second, since (7.7a)–(7.7n) is a QP given $x_{j,\ell}$ and, thus, a convex problem, it may be replaced by its primal constraints, dual constraints, and the strong-duality equality. The primal constraints are simply (7.7b)–(7.7n), while the dual constraints are related to the QP's KKT conditions:

$$W_s C^{\text{opr}}_{i,n,u} + \beta_{i,n,s,t,u} + \beta^{\text{up}}_{i,n,s,t,u} - \beta^{\text{down}}_{i,n,s,t,u} - \beta^{\text{up}}_{i,n,s,t+1,u} + \beta^{\text{down}}_{i,n,s,t+1,u}$$
$$- \lambda_{n,s,t} + W_s D^{\text{slp}}_{n,s,t} \sum_{u'\in\mathcal{U}_{i,n}} y_{i,n,s,t,u'} - \phi^{y}_{i,n,s,t,u} = 0, \forall i, n, s, t, u \in \mathcal{U}_{i,n} \tag{7.8a}$$

$$- W_s \left(D^{\text{int}}_{n,s,t} - D^{\text{slp}}_{n,s,t} c_{n,s,t}\right) + \lambda_{n,s,t} - \phi^{c}_{n,s,t} = 0, \ \forall n, s, t \tag{7.8b}$$

$$\mu_{j,\ell,s,t} + \overline{\mu}_{j,\ell,s,t} - \underline{\mu}_{j,\ell,s,t} - \psi_{\ell,s,t} = 0, \ \forall \ell, s, t, j \in \mathcal{J}_\ell \tag{7.8c}$$

$$\psi_{\ell,s,t} + T_t \lambda_{n^+_\ell,s,t} - T_t \lambda_{n^-_\ell,s,t} = 0, \ \forall \ell, s, t \tag{7.8d}$$

$$- \sum_{\ell\in\mathcal{L}^+_n} \sum_{j\in\mathcal{J}_\ell} x_{j,\ell} B_{j,\ell} \mu_{j,\ell,s,t} + \sum_{\ell\in\mathcal{L}^-_n} \sum_{j\in\mathcal{J}_\ell} x_{j,\ell} B_{j,\ell} \mu_{j,\ell,s,t} + \overline{\kappa}_{n,s,t} - \underline{\kappa}_{n,s,t} = 0,$$
$$\forall n, s, t \tag{7.8e}$$

$$\beta_{i,n,s,t,u} \geq 0, \beta^{\text{up}}_{i,n,s,t,u} \geq 0, \beta^{\text{down}}_{i,n,s,t,u} \geq 0, \phi^{y}_{i,n,s,t,u} \geq 0, \ \forall i, n, s, t, u \in \mathcal{U}_{i,n} \tag{7.8f}$$

$$\underline{\mu}_{j,\ell,s,t} \geq 0, \overline{\mu}_{j,\ell,s,t} \geq 0, \ \forall \ell, s, t, j \in \mathcal{J}_\ell \tag{7.8g}$$

$$\underline{\kappa}_{n,s,t} \geq 0, \overline{\kappa}_{n,s,t} \geq 0, \phi^{c}_{n,s,t} \geq 0, \ \forall n, s, t \tag{7.8h}$$

$$\lambda_{n,s,t} \text{ u.r.s.}, \ \forall n, s, t \tag{7.8i}$$

$$\mu_{j,\ell,s,t} \text{ u.r.s.}, \forall \ell, s, t, j \in \mathcal{J}_\ell \tag{7.8j}$$

$$\psi_{\ell,s,t} \text{ u.r.s.}, \forall \ell, s, t \tag{7.8k}$$

Meanwhile, from QP duality [3], the dual objective function comprises the quadratic terms in (7.7a) along with the products of the dual variables and the constant terms in constraints (7.7b)–(7.7n). Keeping in line with [12], we represent the strong-duality expression as the following inequality in which the primal objective is constrained to being greater than or equal to the dual objective:

$$\sum_{s \in \mathcal{S}} W_s \sum_{n \in \mathcal{N}} \sum_{t \in \mathcal{T}} \left[D^{\text{int}}_{n,s,t} c_{n,s,t} - \frac{1}{2} D^{\text{slp}}_{n,s,t} c^2_{n,s,t} - \sum_{i \in \mathcal{I}} \sum_{u \in \mathcal{U}_{i,n}} C^{\text{opr}}_{i,n,u} y_{i,n,s,t,u} \right.$$
$$\left. - \frac{1}{2} D^{\text{slp}}_{n,s,t} \sum_{i \in \mathcal{I}} \left(\sum_{u \in \mathcal{U}_{i,n}} y_{i,n,s,t,u} \right)^2 \right]$$
$$\geq \frac{1}{2} \sum_{s \in \mathcal{S}} W_s \sum_{n \in \mathcal{N}} \sum_{t \in \mathcal{T}} D^{\text{slp}}_{n,s,t} c^2_{n,s,t} + \frac{1}{2} \sum_{s \in \mathcal{S}} W_s \sum_{n \in \mathcal{N}} \sum_{t \in \mathcal{T}} D^{\text{slp}}_{n,s,t} \sum_{i \in \mathcal{I}} \left(\sum_{u \in \mathcal{U}_{i,n}} y_{i,n,s,t,u} \right)^2$$
$$+ \sum_{i \in \mathcal{I}} \sum_{n \in \mathcal{N}} \sum_{s \in \mathcal{S}} \sum_{t \in \mathcal{T}} \sum_{u \in \mathcal{U}_{i,n}} K^{\text{gen}}_{i,n,u} T_t \left(A_{n,s,t,u} \beta_{i,n,s,t,u} + R^{\text{up}}_u \beta^{\text{up}}_{i,n,s,t,u} + R^{\text{down}}_u \beta^{\text{down}}_{i,n,s,t,u} \right)$$
$$+ \sum_{\ell \in \mathcal{L}} \sum_{s \in \mathcal{S}} \sum_{t \in \mathcal{T}} \sum_{j \in \mathcal{J}_\ell} K^{\text{trn}}_{j,\ell} \left(\underline{\mu}_{j,\ell,s,t} + \overline{\mu}_{j,\ell,s,t} \right) + \sum_{n \in \mathcal{N}} \sum_{s \in \mathcal{S}} \sum_{t \in \mathcal{T}} \pi \left(\underline{\kappa}_{n,s,t} + \overline{\kappa}_{n,s,t} \right) \tag{7.9}$$

It is now possible to reformulate the bi-level problem as a single-level MPPDC in which the lower level is replaced by the primal constraints (7.7b)–(7.7n), dual constraints (7.8a)–(7.8k), and the strong-duality expression (7.9). Prior to this step, however, non-linearities in (7.7b) and (7.8e) need to be treated. Specifically, these stem from the products of $x_{j,\ell}$ and $v_{n,s,t}$ in (7.7b) and $x_{j,\ell}$ and $\mu_{j,\ell,s,t}$ in (7.8e) because although $x_{j,\ell}$ is treated as a parameter at the lower level, it is, nevertheless, a variable for the MPPDC as a whole. Consequently, we replace (7.7b)–(7.7c) by (7.3d)–(7.3e) as explained in Sect. 7.2.1. As for (7.8e), we replace it with the following courtesy of the auxiliary variable $\hat{\mu}_{j,\ell,s,t}$ [1]:

$$- \sum_{\ell \in \mathcal{L}^+_n} \sum_{j \in \mathcal{J}_\ell} B_{j,\ell} \left(\mu_{j,\ell,s,t} - \hat{\mu}_{j,\ell,s,t} \right) + \sum_{\ell \in \mathcal{L}^-_n} \sum_{j \in \mathcal{J}_\ell} B_{j,\ell} \left(\mu_{j,\ell,s,t} - \hat{\mu}_{j,\ell,s,t} \right)$$
$$+ \overline{\kappa}_{n,s,t} - \underline{\kappa}_{n,s,t} = 0, \forall n, s, t \tag{7.10a}$$

$$- x_{j,\ell} M^{\text{trn}} \leq \mu_{j,\ell,s,t} - \hat{\mu}_{j,\ell,s,t} \leq x_{j,\ell} M^{\text{trn}}, \forall \ell, s, t, j \in \mathcal{J}_\ell \tag{7.10b}$$

$$-\left(1-x_{j,\ell}\right)M^{\text{trn}} \leq \hat{\mu}_{j,\ell,s,t} \leq \left(1-x_{j,\ell}\right)M^{\text{trn}},\ \forall \ell, s, t, j \in \mathcal{J}_\ell \tag{7.10c}$$

$$\hat{\mu}_{j,\ell,s,t} \text{ u.r.s.},\ \forall \ell, s, t, j \in \mathcal{J}_\ell \tag{7.10d}$$

Putting it all together, the MPPDC of the bi-level transmission-expansion problem may be rendered as the following mixed-integer quadratically constrained quadratic program (MIQCQP):

$$\begin{aligned} &\underset{\{x_{j,\ell}\}\cup\Omega^{\text{LL}}\cup\Omega^{\text{DV}}}{\text{Maximize}} \quad (7.4\text{a}) \\ &\qquad \text{s.t.}\ (7.4\text{b}) - (7.4\text{c}) \\ &\qquad\qquad (7.3\text{d}) - (7.3\text{e}),\ (7.7\text{d}) - (7.7\text{n}) \\ &\qquad\qquad (7.8\text{a}) - (7.8\text{d}),\ (7.8\text{f}) - (7.8\text{k}),\ (7.10\text{a}) - (7.10\text{d}) \\ &\qquad\qquad (7.9) \end{aligned}$$

Here, $\Omega^{\text{DV}} \equiv \{\beta_{i,n,s,t,u}, \beta^{\text{up}}_{i,n,s,t,u}, \beta^{\text{down}}_{i,n,s,t,u}, \phi^{y}_{i,n,s,t,u}, \underline{\mu}_{j,\ell,s,t}, \overline{\mu}_{j,\ell,s,t}, \underline{\kappa}_{n,s,t}, \overline{\kappa}_{n,s,t}, \phi^{c}_{n,s,t}, \lambda_{n,s,t}, \mu_{j,\ell,s,t}, \hat{\mu}_{j,\ell,s,t}, \psi_{\ell,s,t}\}$ is the set of dual variables from the lower level.

Illustrative Example 7.2 *Welfare-maximizing MIQCQP for bi-level transmission expansion under Cournot oligopoly.*

In order to illustrate bi-level transmission planning, we implement a numerical example with the same input data as in Illustrative Example 7.1, i.e., from Tables 7.1, 7.2, 7.3, 7.4, and 7.5. It should be noted that if the firms at the lower level are price takers, then the MIQCQP representing the bi-level problem instance will yield the same solution as the MIQP from central planning (7.3a)–(7.3p). This is because all of the terms in the lower-level objective function (7.7a) appear in the upper-level objective function (7.4a) once the extended-cost term $-\frac{1}{2}\sum_{s\in\mathcal{S}} W_s \sum_{t\in\mathcal{T}} \sum_{n\in\mathcal{N}} D^{\text{slp}}_{n,s,t} \sum_{i\in\mathcal{I}} \left(\sum_{u\in\mathcal{U}_{i,n}} y_{i,n,s,t,u}\right)^2$ is ignored. In case of perfect competition, this extended-cost term is dropped from both sides of the strong-duality expression (7.9), and its partial derivative with respect to $y_{i,n,s,t,u}$, i.e., $W_s D^{\text{slp}}_{n,s,t} \sum_{u'\in\mathcal{U}_{i,n}} y_{i,n,s,t,u'}$, is excluded from the corresponding dual constraint (7.8a). Intuitively, there is no conflict between the lower and upper levels [7]. However, in case of market power at the lower level or the presence of a damage cost at the upper level (even under perfect competition), the two functions would not be aligned [28]. Hence, we focus on results in which firms at the lower level behave à la Cournot.

As a benchmark, we compare aggregate results without transmission investment. Market power decreases social welfare by over 21%, cf. Tables 7.6 and 7.11. There is also a welfare transfer to producers as PS nearly triples due to the exertion of market power while CS contracts by a similar factor. This effect is due to the firms' withholding capacity such that marginal cost equals *marginal revenue* rather than *marginal utility*. For example, at node $n = 1$ during season $s = 1$ and period $t = 3$,

Table 7.11 Welfare results (in \$) with and without transmission investment for bi-level transmission expansion

Component	Transmission investment	No transmission investment
CS	11,466,595	8,751,975
PS	19,228,945	19,524,270
MS	50,527	0
TC	382,982	0
SW	30,363,085	28,276,245

coal capacity is neither ramp- nor capacity-constrained. Under perfect competition, it produces 200 MWh such that the resulting price of \$20/MWh matches its marginal cost. By contrast, under Cournot oligopoly, the coal plant generates up to the point such that its marginal cost matches marginal revenue, $220 - 2c_{1,1,3}$, which yields a dispatch of 100 MWh and a price of \$120/MWh. Likewise, at node $n = 3$ during season $s = 2$ and period $t = 1$, 400 MWh of VRES are available. Under perfect competition, 140 MWh of VRES are dispatched to yield a price of \$0/MWh. Since the marginal revenue at node $n = 3$ is $120 - 2c_{3,2,1}$, the optimal dispatch under market power is 60 MWh, thereby yielding a price of \$60/MWh even though the marginal cost is zero.

The optimal transmission plan with Cournot behavior at the lower level is rather distinct from that under central planning. Due to the producers' exertion of market power, less transmission capacity is required, viz. $\ell = 1$, $\ell = 2$, and $\ell = 3$ are built at levels 3.7, 3.7, and 6.1 MW, respectively. These capacities are just large enough to enhance economic efficiency. If the producers' market power were ignored and the optimal capacity sizes were set as in Illustrative Example 7.1, then overall social welfare would decrease from \$30,363,085.[16] Due to this limited scope for maneuver, the increase in welfare is relatively modest at 7%, most of which accrues to consumers (Table 7.11).

From the operational results in Table 7.12, transmission investment enables more of the VRES at nodes $n = 2$ and $n = 3$ to be sold at node $n = 1$ where the willingness to pay is highest. Coal generation at node $n = 1$ is reduced, and VRES output at nodes $n = 2$ and $n = 3$ is increased, thereby leading to a slight overall increase in generation (and consumption). The main beneficiaries are consumers at node $n = 1$, who enjoy higher consumption at lower prices, and firm $i = 2$, which increases sales at higher prices. Node $n = 1$ is a net importer, while the other two nodes are net exporters.

A closer examination of operations in Tables 7.13, 7.14, and 7.15 reveals that there is no transmission congestion in season $s = 1$, while line $\ell = 1$ is always congested in season $s = 2$. Although the equalization of market-clearing prices

[16] In particular, although both CS and PS would be higher than \$11,466,595 and \$19,228,945, respectively, MS would be zero and TC would be higher. Thus, the extra cost of higher transmission capacity would more than offset the increases in CS and PS.

Table 7.12 Operational results (in MWh) with and without transmission investment for bi-level transmission expansion

Attribute	Node (or Line)	Transmission investment	No transmission investment
Consumption	$n = 1$	143,732	104,310
	$n = 2$	56,990	62,220
	$n = 3$	34,420	62,220
Generation	$n = 1$	75,868	104,310
	$n = 2$	72,392	62,220
	$n = 3$	86,882	62,220
Net imports	$n = 1$	67,864	0
	$n = 2$	−15,402	0
	$n = 3$	−52,463	0
Energy flows	$\ell = 1$	−24,891	0
	$\ell = 2$	−9,489	0
	$\ell = 3$	−42,974	0

Table 7.13 Nodal prices ($/MWh) for bi-level transmission expansion

		Period		
Node	Season	$t = 1$	$t = 2$	$t = 3$
$n = 1$	$s = 1$	85	92	96
	$s = 2$	83.99	83.99	93.60
$n = 2$	$s = 1$	85	92	96
	$s = 2$	82.63	82.63	90.32
$n = 3$	$s = 1$	85	92	96
	$s = 2$	83.38	83.38	92.15

Table 7.14 Generation output (MWh) for bi-level transmission expansion

		Period		
Node	Season	$t = 1$	$t = 2$	$t = 3$
$n = 1$	$s = 1$	65	72	76
	$s = 2$	63.99	63.99	73.60
$n = 2$	$s = 1$	80	40	20
	$s = 2$	82.63	82.63	90.32
$n = 3$	$s = 1$	80	92	96
	$s = 2$	83.39	83.39	40

Table 7.15 Net imports (MWh) for bi-level transmission expansion

		Period		
Node	Season	$t = 1$	$t = 2$	$t = 3$
$n = 1$	$s = 1$	70	56	48
	$s = 2$	72.03	72.03	52.79
$n = 2$	$s = 1$	−25	8	24
	$s = 2$	−25.26	−25.26	−40.65
$n = 3$	$s = 1$	−45	−64	−72
	$s = 2$	−46.77	−46.77	−12.15

in season $s = 1$ is similar to the result in Illustrative Example 7.1, it is not the case here that node $n = 2$ is a persistent net importer. In fact, it exports energy during $t = 1$ when its resource availability is relatively high. By contrast, nodes $n = 1$ and $n = 3$ are persistent net importers and exporters, respectively. Nodal price differences arise in season $s = 2$ due to the persistent congestion of line $\ell = 1$. Nevertheless, the variations are not as marked as in Illustrative Example 7.1 because consumption and, by extension, energy flows are curbed due to the exercise of market power. Therefore, prices are slightly higher at node $n = 1$, which is a persistent net importer. Also in contrast to Illustrative Example 7.1 is the outcome that both nodes $n = 2$ and $n = 3$ are net exporters throughout this season, even in period $t = 3$ when VRES availability at node $n = 3$ is relatively low. Finally, the only generation dispatched at node $n = 1$ is coal.

7.3 Generation Expansion

Similar to investment planning in Sect. 2.3, we address generation expansion in power systems. Unlike the aforementioned treatment of transmission investment, we here focus on investment in generation capacity by a strategic firm. Assuming a given transmission network and continuous capacity-expansion decisions, this setup leads to a bi-level framework in which a strategic firm makes its generation-expansion decision at the upper level in anticipation of the decisions made by the follower firms and the ISO. Here, we treat the follower firms as if they made investment and operational decisions simultaneously, i.e., an open-loop assumption.[17] By contrast, a single-agent QP results if industry is centrally planned.

7.3.1 Generation Expansion Under Central Planning

The formulation and, thus, the nomenclature are similar to those for transmission expansion in Sect. 7.2.1. However, since the transmission network is fixed here, we suppress the $j \in \mathcal{J}_\ell$ index in the susceptance and capacity parameters, $B_{j,\ell}$ and $K^{\text{trn}}_{j,\ell}$, respectively. In a similar vein, transmission-investment costs are not included in the objective function to maximize social welfare, and the variable $f_{j,\ell,s,t}$ is also superfluous since $\hat{f}_{\ell,s,t}$ reflects the transmission flow on line ℓ. Instead, a new decision variable, $z_{i,n,u}$ (in MW), with corresponding parameter, $C^{\text{gen}}_{i,n,u}$ (in \$/MW), are introduced to reflect the new generation capacity and amortized investment cost for technology u added by firm i at node n.

[17] If multiple Stackelberg leaders competed [15, 35], then this would lead to a closed-loop formulation, i.e., an EPEC.

$$\underset{\Omega^{\text{CP}}}{\text{Maximize}} \sum_{s \in \mathcal{S}} W_s \sum_{t \in \mathcal{T}} \sum_{n \in \mathcal{N}} \left[\left(D^{\text{int}}_{n,s,t} c_{n,s,t} - \frac{1}{2} D^{\text{slp}}_{n,s,t} c^2_{n,s,t} \right) \right.$$

$$\left. - \sum_{i \in \mathcal{I}} \sum_{u \in \mathcal{U}_{i,n}} C^{\text{opr}}_{i,n,u} y_{i,n,s,t,u} \right] - \sum_{i \in \mathcal{I}} \sum_{n \in \mathcal{N}} \sum_{u \in \mathcal{U}_{i,n}} C^{\text{gen}}_{i,n,u} z_{i,n,u} \tag{7.11a}$$

$$\text{s.t. } \hat{f}_{\ell,s,t} - B_\ell \left(v_{n^+_\ell,s,t} - v_{n^-_\ell,s,t} \right) = 0, \ \forall \ell, s, t \tag{7.11b}$$

$$- K^{\text{trn}}_\ell \leq \hat{f}_{\ell,s,t} \leq K^{\text{trn}}_\ell, \ \forall \ell, s, t \tag{7.11c}$$

$$- \pi \leq v_{n,s,t} \leq \pi, \ \forall n, s, t \tag{7.11d}$$

$$c_{n,s,t} - \sum_{i \in \mathcal{I}} \sum_{u \in \mathcal{U}_{i,n}} y_{i,n,s,t,u} + T_t \sum_{\ell \in \mathcal{L}^+_n} \hat{f}_{\ell,s,t} - T_t \sum_{\ell \in \mathcal{L}^-_n} \hat{f}_{\ell,s,t} = 0,$$

$$\forall n, s, t \tag{7.11e}$$

$$y_{i,n,s,t,u} \leq T_t A_{n,s,t,u} \left(K^{\text{gen}}_{i,n,u} + z_{i,n,u} \right),$$

$$\forall i, n, s, t, u \in \mathcal{U}_{i,n} \tag{7.11f}$$

$$y_{i,n,s,t,u} - y_{i,n,s,t-1,u} \leq T_t R^{\text{up}}_u \left(K^{\text{gen}}_{i,n,u} + z_{i,n,u} \right),$$

$$\forall i, n, s, t, u \in \mathcal{U}_{i,n} \tag{7.11g}$$

$$- y_{i,n,s,t,u} + y_{i,n,s,t-1,u} \leq T_t R^{\text{down}}_u \left(K^{\text{gen}}_{i,n,u} + z_{i,n,u} \right),$$

$$\forall i, n, s, t, u \in \mathcal{U}_{i,n} \tag{7.11h}$$

$$c_{n,s,t} \geq 0, \ \forall n, s, t \tag{7.11i}$$

$$y_{i,n,s,t,u} \geq 0, \ \forall i, n, s, t, u \in \mathcal{U}_{i,n} \tag{7.11j}$$

$$z_{i,n,u} \geq 0, \ \forall i, n, u \in \mathcal{U}_{i,n} \tag{7.11k}$$

$$\hat{f}_{\ell,s,t} \text{ u.r.s.}, \ \forall \ell, s, t \tag{7.11l}$$

$$v_{n,s,t} \text{ u.r.s.}, \ \forall n, s, t \tag{7.11m}$$

where $\Omega^{\text{CP}} \equiv \left\{ c_{n,s,t}, \hat{f}_{\ell,s,t}, v_{n,s,t}, y_{i,n,s,t,u}, z_{i,n,u} \right\}$ are the optimization variables. The objective function (7.11a) is to maximize social welfare inclusive of the cost of generation investment, i.e., it is identical to that for transmission expansion (7.3a) except for the deletion of the transmission-investment cost and inclusion of the generation-investment cost. Kirchhoff's laws are encapsulated by (7.11b)–(7.11d), where linearization is not required as in (7.3d)–(7.3e) because the transmission capacities (and susceptance levels) are fixed. Nodal energy balance is once again reflected by (7.11e), while (7.11f)–(7.11h) enforce capacity and ramping constraints, cf. (7.3i)–(7.3k), inclusive of existing and new installations.

Finally, (7.11i)–(7.11k) are non-negativity constraints, e.g., generation investment cannot be negative, while (7.11l)–(7.11m) indicate that power flows and voltage angles are unrestricted in sign.

Illustrative Example 7.3 *Welfare-maximizing QP for centrally planned generation expansion.*

Using the three-node test network in Fig. 7.2 and data from Illustrative Example 7.1, we implement the QP (7.11a)–(7.11m) for benchmark centrally planned generation expansion. In particular, demand data are given in Table 7.1, operating characteristics of generation are listed in Table 7.2, and availabilities of VRES are displayed in Tables 7.3 and 7.4.[18] The seasonal weight and period length are again $W_s = 183$ and $T_t = 8$, respectively. Since we focus on generation investment, we now fix the transmission capacities to 48.8 MW for all lines with the corresponding susceptances indicated in Table 7.5.[19] Moreover, the amortized costs of generation investment are \$1,265/kW, \$4,375/kW, \$3,676/kW, and \$1,084/kW for technologies $u = 1$ to $u = 4$, respectively. These correspond to the amortized costs of 200 MW on-shore wind, 400 MW off-shore wind, 650 MW coal, and 430 MW combined-cycle gas-fired plants, respectively [4]. Using the amortization procedure in Sect. 2.3.1 with a thirty-year period and a 5%/a interest rate, the annual amortized costs are \$82,290/MW, \$284,602/MW, \$239,120/MW, and \$70,510/MW, respectively.[20]

The socially optimal generation expansion is 91.04 MW of on-shore wind capacity ($u = 1$) at node $n = 2$ and 27.83 MW of gas-fired capacity ($u = 4$) at node $n = 1$. Since we start with no installed generation capacity and sufficient transmission capacity to prevent congestion, PS and MS are both equal to zero. In other words, *notional* firms' investment and operational decisions are such that their revenues exactly cover their amortized capital and operating costs.[21] Similarly, the lack of transmission congestion equalizes prices across the network, thereby yielding no revenues to a *notional* ISO. Therefore, the maximized social welfare equals the CS (Table 7.16). In terms of operations, all of the generation occurs at nodes $n = 1$ and $n = 2$ with the latter as a net exporter on aggregate (Table 7.17). By contrast, nodes $n = 1$ and $n = 3$ are net importers overall with energy flows to these two nodes from node $n = 2$ as well as some energy flow from node $n = 1$ to $n = 3$ along line $\ell = 3$.

Closer examination of the operational results provides further insights about seasonal dynamics. For example, in season $s = 1$, prices are set by the ramp-

[18] In order to focus on generation investment, we have no initial installed capacities for generation.

[19] The sunk cost of transmission investment is, therefore, excluded from the objective function.

[20] It would be more realistic to use discrete decisions for levels of generation investment. Such an assumption would fit better with the estimated amortized costs, which vary depending on the installed capacity. However, discrete investment levels are challenging to incorporate at the lower level, e.g., by follower firms as in Sect. 7.3.2. Therefore, we use the representative plants to estimate the amortized capital costs assuming no scale effects.

[21] We include amortized investment costs in PS.

Table 7.16 Welfare results (in \$) for generation expansion

Component	Central planning	Bi-level planning
CS	24,272,952	19,328,908
PS	0	3,865,903
MS	0	0
SW	24,272,952	23,194,811

Table 7.17 Operational results (in MWh) for generation expansion

Attribute	Node (or Line)	Central planning	Bi-level planning
Consumption	$n = 1$	187,488	174,393
	$n = 2$	99,648	86,553
	$n = 3$	77,688	64,593
Generation	$n = 1$	130,376	176,576
	$n = 2$	234,449	148,962
	$n = 3$	0	0
Net imports	$n = 1$	57,112	−2183
	$n = 2$	−134,800	−62,409
	$n = 3$	77,688	64,592
Energy flows	$\ell = 1$	−63,971	−20,075
	$\ell = 2$	70,830	42,334
	$\ell = 3$	6859	22,259

Table 7.18 Prices (\$/MWh) for centrally planned generation expansion

	Period		
Season	$t = 1$	$t = 2$	$t = 3$
$s = 1$	66.92	61.51	73.65
$s = 2$	54.78	38.62	0

Table 7.19 Generation output (MWh) for centrally planned generation expansion

		Period		
Node	Season	$t = 1$	$t = 2$	$t = 3$
$n = 1$	$s = 1$	133.58	222.64	222.64
	$s = 2$	133.58	0	0
$n = 2$	$s = 1$	145.66	72.83	36.42
	$s = 2$	182.08	364.15	480

constrained gas-fired plant and the capacity-constrained on-shore wind plant in period $t = 1$, while prices in periods $t = 2$ and $t = 3$ are set by capacity-constrained gas-fired and on-shore wind plants (Table 7.18). In order to understand this reasoning, note that in period $t = 1$ the gas-fired plant produces 133.58 MWh, which is 60% of its maximum output in accordance with its ramping capability, while the on-shore wind plant produces 145.66 MWh, which is 20% of its maximum output in accordance with its availability factor (Table 7.19). In periods $t = 2$ and $t = 3$, the gas-fired plant generates at its maximum possible output of 222.64 MWh, while the on-shore wind plant is similarly dispatched at 10 and 5%, respectively, of its maximum output based on its availability. Indeed, due to the relatively low

Table 7.20 Net imports (MWh) for centrally planned generation expansion

Node	Season	Period $t = 1$	$t = 2$	$t = 3$
$n = 1$	$s = 1$	19.50	−64.15	−76.29
	$s = 2$	31.64	181.39	220
$n = 2$	$s = 1$	−72.58	5.66	29.94
	$s = 2$	−96.86	−262.77	−340
$n = 3$	$s = 1$	53.08	58.49	46.35
	$s = 2$	65.22	81.38	120

availability factor for on-shore wind at node $n = 2$ during periods $t = 2$ and $t = 3$, node $n = 2$ is actually a net importer, while node $n = 1$ is a net exporter (Table 7.20). Consequently, energy flows in the positive direction on line $\ell = 1$ from node $n = 1$ to $n = 2$. However, during period $t = 1$, the situation is reversed due to the ramp-constrained gas-fired plant at node $n = 1$ and the relatively high wind availability at node $n = 2$, i.e., energy is exported from node $n = 2$ to $n = 1$. Finally, node $n = 3$ is always a net importer with positive flows on lines $\ell = 2$ and $\ell = 3$.

Due to higher wind availability at node $n = 2$ during season $s = 2$, the price and flow patterns are somewhat different. In fact, the gas-fired plant is dispatched only in period $t = 1$ and not deployed at all for the rest of the periods. Thus, the price in period $t = 1$ is set by the ramp-constrained gas-fired plant[22] and the capacity-constrained on-shore wind plant. Meanwhile, prices in periods $t = 2$ and $t = 3$ are set by the on-shore wind plant, viz. \$38.62/MWh and \$0/MWh, respectively, to reflect capacity-constrained and unconstrained dispatch. As a result, node $n = 2$ is a persistent net exporter, while nodes $n = 1$ and $n = 3$ are net importers throughout season $s = 2$. In contrast to season $s = 1$, energy generally flows from node $n = 3$ to $n = 1$ along line $\ell = 3$ except in period $t = 1$ when the gas-fired plant is dispatched.

7.3.2 Bi-Level Generation Expansion

We assess generation expansion in a deregulated electricity industry by assuming that one firm denoted i^* is strategic and has first-mover advantage [14]. Therefore, it behaves as a Stackelberg leader in capacity investment vis-à-vis follower firms, $\hat{i} \in \hat{I}$, where $i^* \cup \hat{I} = I$ and $i^* \cap \hat{I} = \emptyset$. Investment by the strategic firm i^* takes place at the upper level in anticipation of market clearing and followers' capacity additions at the lower level. In effect, the followers' investment and operational decisions are treated as open loop, i.e., as if they were made simultaneously. Furthermore, we do

[22] Actually, it is up-constrained in period $t = 1$ and down-constrained in period $t = 2$.

not allow for operational market power at the lower level in order to focus on the implications of strategic investment.

Correspondingly, the upper-level problem is that of generation expansion by the strategic firm i^*:

$$\underset{z_{i^*,n,u}}{\text{Maximize}} \sum_{s\in\mathcal{S}} W_s \sum_{n\in\mathcal{N}} \sum_{t\in\mathcal{T}} \sum_{u\in\mathcal{U}_{i^*,n}} \left(\frac{\lambda_{n,s,t}}{W_s} - C^{\text{opr}}_{i^*,n,u}\right) y_{i^*,n,s,t,u}$$

$$-\sum_{n\in\mathcal{N}} \sum_{u\in\mathcal{U}_{i^*,n}} C^{\text{gen}}_{i^*,n,u} z_{i^*,n,u} \tag{7.12a}$$

$$\text{s.t. } z_{i^*,n,u} \geq 0, \forall n, u \in \mathcal{U}_{i^*,n} \tag{7.12b}$$

The objective function (7.12a) is to maximize profit comprising revenue from sales minus operating costs and generation-expansion costs subject to non-negativity of investment (7.12b). It should be emphasized that the strategic firm's revenue, $\frac{\lambda_{n,s,t}}{W_s} y_{i^*,n,s,t,u}$, is a product of lower-level primal and dual variables. Thus, even though firm i^* does not directly control the market-clearing price, it can indirectly influence it via its investment decisions.

At the lower level, strategic firm i^* behaves as a price taker and has only $y_{i^*,n,s,t,u}$ as a decision variable:

$$\underset{y_{i^*,n,s,t,u}}{\text{Maximize}} \sum_{s\in\mathcal{S}} W_s \sum_{n\in\mathcal{N}} \sum_{t\in\mathcal{T}} \sum_{u\in\mathcal{U}_{i^*,n}} \left(\frac{\lambda_{n,s,t}}{W_s} - C^{\text{opr}}_{i^*,n,u}\right) y_{i^*,n,s,t,u}$$

$$-\sum_{n\in\mathcal{N}} \sum_{u\in\mathcal{U}_{i^*,n}} C^{\text{gen}}_{i^*,n,u} z_{i^*,n,u} \tag{7.13a}$$

$$\text{s.t. } y_{i^*,n,s,t,u} \leq T_t A_{n,s,t,u} \left(K^{\text{gen}}_{i^*,n,u} + z_{i^*,n,u}\right) : \beta_{i^*,n,s,t,u},$$

$$\forall n, s, t, u \in \mathcal{U}_{i^*,n} \tag{7.13b}$$

$$y_{i^*,n,s,t,u} - y_{i^*,n,s,t-1,u} \leq T_t R^{\text{up}}_u \left(K^{\text{gen}}_{i^*,n,u} + z_{i^*,n,u}\right) :$$

$$\beta^{\text{up}}_{i^*,n,s,t,u}, \forall n, s, t, u \in \mathcal{U}_{i^*,n} \tag{7.13c}$$

$$- y_{i^*,n,s,t,u} + y_{i^*,n,s,t-1,u} \leq T_t R^{\text{down}}_u \left(K^{\text{gen}}_{i^*,n,u} + z_{i^*,n,u}\right) :$$

$$\beta^{\text{down}}_{i^*,n,s,t,u}, \forall n, s, t, u \in \mathcal{U}_{i^*,n} \tag{7.13d}$$

$$y_{i^*,n,s,t,u} \geq 0 : \phi^{y}_{i^*,n,s,t,u}, \forall n, s, t, u \in \mathcal{U}_{i^*,n} \tag{7.13e}$$

The objective function (7.13a) is to maximize profit given the market-clearing price and generation investment, while constraints (7.13b)–(7.13e) are similar to (7.5b)–(7.5e) after adjusting for capacity expansion, $z_{i^*,n,u}$. Dual variables are once again given in lower-case Greek letters adjacent to relevant constraints.

Non-strategic firm $\hat{i} \in \hat{I}$ has a similar problem at the lower level to that of the strategic firm except that it also is able to invest in generation capacity:

$$\underset{y_{\hat{i},n,s,t,u}, z_{\hat{i},n,u}}{\text{Maximize}} \sum_{s \in \mathcal{S}} W_s \sum_{n \in \mathcal{N}} \sum_{t \in \mathcal{T}} \sum_{u \in \mathcal{U}_{\hat{i},n}} \left(\frac{\lambda_{n,s,t}}{W_s} - C^{\text{opr}}_{\hat{i},n,u} \right) y_{\hat{i},n,s,t,u}$$

$$- \sum_{n \in \mathcal{N}} \sum_{u \in \mathcal{U}_{\hat{i},n}} C^{\text{gen}}_{\hat{i},n,u} z_{\hat{i},n,u} \tag{7.14a}$$

$$\text{s.t. } y_{\hat{i},n,s,t,u} \leq T_t A_{n,s,t,u} \left(K^{\text{gen}}_{\hat{i},n,u} + z_{\hat{i},n,u} \right) : \beta_{\hat{i},n,s,t,u},$$

$$\forall n, s, t, u \in \mathcal{U}_{\hat{i},n} \tag{7.14b}$$

$$y_{\hat{i},n,s,t,u} - y_{\hat{i},n,s,t-1,u} \leq T_t R^{\text{up}}_u \left(K^{\text{gen}}_{\hat{i},n,u} + z_{\hat{i},n,u} \right) :$$

$$\beta^{\text{up}}_{\hat{i},n,s,t,u}, \ \forall n, s, t, u \in \mathcal{U}_{\hat{i},n} \tag{7.14c}$$

$$- y_{\hat{i},n,s,t,u} + y_{\hat{i},n,s,t-1,u} \leq T_t R^{\text{down}}_u \left(K^{\text{gen}}_{\hat{i},n,u} + z_{\hat{i},n,u} \right) :$$

$$\beta^{\text{down}}_{\hat{i},n,s,t,u}, \ \forall n, s, t, u \in \mathcal{U}_{\hat{i},n} \tag{7.14d}$$

$$y_{\hat{i},n,s,t,u} \geq 0 : \ \phi^{y}_{\hat{i},n,s,t,u}, \ \forall n, s, t, u \in \mathcal{U}_{\hat{i},n} \tag{7.14e}$$

$$z_{\hat{i},n,u} \geq 0 : \ \phi^{z}_{\hat{i},n,u}, \ \forall n, u \in \mathcal{U}_{\hat{i},n} \tag{7.14f}$$

Due to the presence of the capacity-expansion decision at the lower level, $z_{\hat{i},n,u}$, constraint (7.14f) is included in the non-strategic firm's problem.

Managing consumer surplus and transmission flows in the network is once again the responsibility of the ISO. Thus, its optimization problem is similar to the one observed earlier (7.6a)–(7.6j) in Sect. 7.2.2:

$$\underset{c_{n,s,t}, \hat{f}_{\ell,s,t}, \upsilon_{n,s,t}}{\text{Maximize}} \sum_{s \in \mathcal{S}} W_s \sum_{t \in \mathcal{T}} \sum_{n \in \mathcal{N}} \left(D^{\text{int}}_{n,s,t} c_{n,s,t} - \frac{1}{2} D^{\text{slp}}_{n,s,t} c^2_{n,s,t} \right) \tag{7.15a}$$

$$\text{s.t. } \hat{f}_{\ell,s,t} - B_\ell \left(\upsilon_{n^+_\ell,s,t} - \upsilon_{n^-_\ell,s,t} \right) = 0 : \ \mu_{\ell,s,t}, \forall \ell, s, t \tag{7.15b}$$

$$\underline{\mu}_{\ell,s,t} : -K^{\text{trn}}_\ell \leq \hat{f}_{\ell,s,t} \leq K^{\text{trn}}_\ell : \ \overline{\mu}_{\ell,s,t}, \forall \ell, s, t \tag{7.15c}$$

$$\underline{\kappa}_{n,s,t} : -\pi \leq \upsilon_{n,s,t} \leq \pi : \ \overline{\kappa}_{n,s,t}, \forall n, s, t \tag{7.15d}$$

$$c_{n,s,t} - \sum_{i \in \mathcal{I}} \sum_{u \in \mathcal{U}_{i,n}} y_{i,n,s,t,u} + T_t \sum_{\ell \in \mathcal{L}^+_n} \hat{f}_{\ell,s,t}$$

$$- T_t \sum_{\ell \in \mathcal{L}^-_n} \hat{f}_{\ell,s,t} = 0 : \ \lambda_{n,s,t}, \forall n, s, t \tag{7.15e}$$

$$c_{n,s,t} \geq 0 : \ \phi^{c}_{n,s,t}, \ \forall n, s, t \tag{7.15f}$$

$$\hat{f}_{\ell,s,t} \text{ u.r.s.}, \ \forall \ell, s, t \tag{7.15g}$$

$$v_{n,s,t} \text{ u.r.s.}, \ \forall n, s, t \tag{7.15h}$$

Since transmission capacities are fixed, the variable $f_{j,\ell,s,t}$ is no longer necessary. Otherwise, the ISO has the same objective function, i.e., to maximize gross consumer surplus (7.15a), as that in (7.6a). Likewise, constraints on Kirchhoff's laws (7.15b), transmission capacities (7.15c), voltage angles (7.15d), nodal energy balance (7.15e), and variables (7.15f)–(7.15h) parallel those from Sect. 7.2.2.

Overall, the bi-level model consists of the upper-level problem of strategic firm i^* (7.12a)–(7.12b) constrained by (1) the lower-level operational problem of strategic firm i^* (7.13a)–(7.13e), (2) the lower-level open-loop investment and operational problems of non-strategic firms $\hat{i} \in \hat{\mathcal{I}}$ (7.14a)–(7.14f), and (3) the ISO's surplus-maximization problem (7.15a)–(7.15h).

It may seem appropriate to reformulate this bi-level model via the MPPDC approach deployed in Sect. 7.2.2. In that case, the lower-level problems would be first reformulated as a single-agent QP and then equivalently expressed in terms of the resulting QP's (1) primal constraints, (2) dual constraints, and (3) strong-duality expression. However, two complications arise in this endeavor. First, the upper-level objective function (7.12a) has bilinear terms $\lambda_{n,s,t} y_{i^*,n,s,t,u}$ that are products of a dual variable and a primal variable from the lower level. These would require linearization via either binary expansion or the use of strong duality from the strategic firm's lower-level LP (7.13a)–(7.13e). Second, the strong-duality expression for the lower-level QP would include bilinear terms $\beta_{i^*,n,s,t,u} z_{i^*,n,u}$, $\beta^{\text{up}}_{i^*,n,s,t,u} z_{i^*,n,u}$, and $\beta^{\text{down}}_{i^*,n,s,t,u} z_{i^*,n,u}$ because $z_{i^*,n,u}$ is not a variable at the lower level. These would also require binary expansion for linearization.

While the aforementioned MPPDC approach may be undertaken, the need for linearization of the SDE via binary variables may not be computationally tractable for realistic problem instances [34]. Instead, it may be more appealing to resort to an MPEC approach to reformulate the bi-level model as an MIQP. Specifically, we replace each lower-level problem by its KKT conditions. Although it requires linearization of the bilinear terms in (7.12a) via strong duality and linearization of KKT conditions via binary variables [5, 6], there is no quadratic constraint with bilinear terms as in the MIQCQP arising from the MPPDC approach.

The KKT conditions corresponding to the lower-level optimization problem of strategic firm i^* (7.13a)–(7.13e) are:

$$W_s C^{\text{opr}}_{i^*,n,u} + \beta_{i^*,n,s,t,u} + \beta^{\text{up}}_{i^*,n,s,t,u} - \beta^{\text{down}}_{i^*,n,s,t,u} - \beta^{\text{up}}_{i^*,n,s,t+1,u}$$

$$+ \beta^{\text{down}}_{i^*,n,s,t+1,u} - \lambda_{n,s,t} - \phi^{y}_{i^*,n,s,t,u} = 0, \forall n, s, t, u \in \mathcal{U}_{i^*,n} \tag{7.16a}$$

$$0 \leq \phi^{y}_{i^*,n,s,t,u} \perp y_{i^*,n,s,t,u} \geq 0, \ \forall n, s, t, u \in \mathcal{U}_{i^*,n} \tag{7.16b}$$

$$0 \leq \beta_{i^*,n,s,t,u} \perp T_t A_{n,s,t,u} \left(K^{\text{gen}}_{i^*,n,u} + z_{i^*,n,u} \right) - y_{i^*,n,s,t,u} \geq 0,$$

$$\forall n, s, t, u \in \mathcal{U}_{i^*,n} \tag{7.16c}$$

$$0 \leq \beta^{\text{up}}_{i^*,n,s,t,u} \perp T_t R^{\text{up}}_u \left(K^{\text{gen}}_{i^*,n,u} + z_{i^*,n,u}\right) - y_{i^*,n,s,t,u} + y_{i^*,n,s,t-1,u} \geq 0,$$

$$\forall n, s, t, u \in \mathcal{U}_{i^*,n} \qquad (7.16\text{d})$$

$$0 \leq \beta^{\text{down}}_{i^*,n,s,t,u} \perp T_t R^{\text{down}}_u \left(K^{\text{gen}}_{i^*,n,u} + z_{i^*,n,u}\right) + y_{i^*,n,s,t,u} - y_{i^*,n,s,t-1,u} \geq 0,$$

$$\forall n, s, t, u \in \mathcal{U}_{i^*,n} \qquad (7.16\text{e})$$

Likewise, non-strategic firms have a similar set of KKT conditions corresponding to optimization problem (7.14a)–(7.14f):

$$W_s C^{\text{opr}}_{\hat{i},n,u} + \beta_{\hat{i},n,s,t,u} + \beta^{\text{up}}_{\hat{i},n,s,t,u} - \beta^{\text{down}}_{\hat{i},n,s,t,u} - \beta^{\text{up}}_{\hat{i},n,s,t+1,u}$$

$$+ \beta^{\text{down}}_{\hat{i},n,s,t+1,u} - \lambda_{n,s,t} - \phi^{y}_{\hat{i},n,s,t,u} = 0, \forall \hat{i} \in \hat{\mathcal{I}}, n, s, t, u \in \mathcal{U}_{\hat{i},n} \qquad (7.17\text{a})$$

$$0 \leq \phi^{y}_{\hat{i},n,s,t,u} \perp y_{\hat{i},n,s,t,u} \geq 0, \ \forall \hat{i} \in \hat{\mathcal{I}}, n, s, t, u \in \mathcal{U}_{\hat{i},n} \qquad (7.17\text{b})$$

$$0 \leq \beta_{\hat{i},n,s,t,u} \perp T_t A_{n,s,t,u} \left(K^{\text{gen}}_{\hat{i},n,u} + z_{\hat{i},n,u}\right) - y_{\hat{i},n,s,t,u} \geq 0,$$

$$\forall \hat{i} \in \hat{\mathcal{I}}, n, s, t, u \in \mathcal{U}_{\hat{i},n} \qquad (7.17\text{c})$$

$$0 \leq \beta^{\text{up}}_{\hat{i},n,s,t,u} \perp T_t R^{\text{up}}_u \left(K^{\text{gen}}_{\hat{i},n,u} + z_{\hat{i},n,u}\right) - y_{\hat{i},n,s,t,u} + y_{\hat{i},n,s,t-1,u} \geq 0,$$

$$\forall \hat{i} \in \hat{\mathcal{I}}, n, s, t, u \in \mathcal{U}_{\hat{i},n} \qquad (7.17\text{d})$$

$$0 \leq \beta^{\text{down}}_{\hat{i},n,s,t,u} \perp T_t R^{\text{down}}_u \left(K^{\text{gen}}_{\hat{i},n,u} + z_{\hat{i},n,u}\right) + y_{\hat{i},n,s,t,u} - y_{\hat{i},n,s,t-1,u} \geq 0,$$

$$\forall \hat{i} \in \hat{\mathcal{I}}, n, s, t, u \in \mathcal{U}_{\hat{i},n} \qquad (7.17\text{e})$$

$$C^{\text{gen}}_{\hat{i},n,u} - \sum_{s \in \mathcal{S}} \sum_{t \in \mathcal{T}} T_t A_{n,s,t,u} \beta_{\hat{i},n,s,t,u} - \sum_{s \in \mathcal{S}} \sum_{t \in \mathcal{T}} T_t R^{\text{up}}_u \beta^{\text{up}}_{\hat{i},n,s,t,u}$$

$$- \sum_{s \in \mathcal{S}} \sum_{t \in \mathcal{T}} T_t R^{\text{down}}_u \beta^{\text{down}}_{\hat{i},n,s,t,u} - \phi^{z}_{\hat{i},n,u} = 0, \forall \hat{i} \in \hat{\mathcal{I}}, n, u \in \mathcal{U}_{\hat{i},n} \qquad (7.17\text{f})$$

$$0 \leq \phi^{z}_{\hat{i},n,u} \perp z_{\hat{i},n,u} \geq 0, \ \forall \hat{i} \in \hat{\mathcal{I}}, n, u \in \mathcal{U}_{\hat{i},n} \qquad (7.17\text{g})$$

KKT conditions (7.17a)–(7.17e) are analogous to (7.16a)–(7.16e) for the strategic firm i^*. Moreover, since non-strategic firm $\hat{i} \in \hat{\mathcal{I}}$ also has to choose generation capacity at the lower level, it has two additional KKT conditions (7.17f)–(7.17g) corresponding to $z_{\hat{i},n,u}$. For example, (7.17g) states that if $z_{\hat{i},n,u} > 0$, then $\phi^{z}_{\hat{i},n,u} = 0$. Consequently, from (7.17f), it must be the case that the amortized investment cost of technology $u \in \mathcal{U}_{\hat{i},n}$ at node n is exactly covered by the capacity and ramping rents.

In a similar vein, the KKT conditions for the ISO's optimization problem (7.15a)–(7.15h) are:

$$-W_s\left(D^{\text{int}}_{n,s,t} - D^{\text{slp}}_{n,s,t} c_{n,s,t}\right) + \lambda_{n,s,t} - \phi^c_{n,s,t} = 0, \ \forall n, s, t \tag{7.18a}$$

$$\mu_{\ell,s,t} + \overline{\mu}_{\ell,s,t} - \underline{\mu}_{\ell,s,t} + T_t \lambda_{n^+_\ell,s,t} - T_t \lambda_{n^-_\ell,s,t} = 0, \ \forall \ell, s, t \tag{7.18b}$$

$$-\sum_{\ell \in \mathcal{L}^+_n} B_\ell \mu_{\ell,s,t} + \sum_{\ell \in \mathcal{L}^-_n} B_\ell \mu_{\ell,s,t} + \overline{\kappa}_{n,s,t} - \underline{\kappa}_{n,s,t} = 0, \ \forall n, s, t \tag{7.18c}$$

$$\mu_{\ell,s,t} \text{ u.r.s.}, \ \hat{f}_{\ell,s,t} - B_\ell\left(v_{n^+_\ell,s,t} - v_{n^-_\ell,s,t}\right) = 0, \ \forall \ell, s, t \tag{7.18d}$$

$$0 \le \underline{\mu}_{\ell,s,t} \perp \hat{f}_{\ell,s,t} + K^{\text{trn}}_\ell \ge 0, \ \forall \ell, s, t \tag{7.18e}$$

$$0 \le \overline{\mu}_{\ell,s,t} \perp -\hat{f}_{\ell,s,t} + K^{\text{trn}}_\ell \ge 0, \ \forall \ell, s, t \tag{7.18f}$$

$$0 \le \underline{\kappa}_{n,s,t} \perp v_{n,s,t} + \pi \ge 0, \ \forall n, s, t \tag{7.18g}$$

$$0 \le \overline{\kappa}_{n,s,t} \perp -v_{n,s,t} + \pi \ge 0, \ \forall n, s, t \tag{7.18h}$$

$$\lambda_{n,s,t} \text{ u.r.s.}, \ c_{n,s,t} - \sum_{i \in \mathcal{I}} \sum_{u \in \mathcal{U}_{i,n}} y_{i,n,s,t,u} + T_t \sum_{\ell \in \mathcal{L}^+_n} \hat{f}_{\ell,s,t}$$
$$- T_t \sum_{\ell \in \mathcal{L}^-_n} \hat{f}_{\ell,s,t} = 0, \ \forall n, s, t \tag{7.18i}$$

$$0 \le \phi^c_{n,s,t} \perp c_{n,s,t} \ge 0, \ \forall n, s, t \tag{7.18j}$$

Using these KKT conditions to replace the lower-level problems, the bi-level model may be expressed as the following MPEC:

$$\underset{\{z_{i*,n,u}\} \cup \Omega^{\text{LL}} \cup \Omega^{\text{DV}}}{\text{Maximize}} \quad (7.12\text{a})$$
$$\text{s.t.} \quad (7.12\text{b})$$
$$(7.16\text{a}) - (7.16\text{e})$$
$$(7.17\text{a}) - (7.17\text{g})$$
$$(7.18\text{a}) - (7.18\text{j})$$

where $\Omega^{\text{LL}} \equiv \{c_{n,s,t}, \hat{f}_{\ell,s,t}, v_{n,s,t}, y_{i,n,s,t,u}, z_{\hat{i},n,u}\}$ and $\Omega^{\text{DV}} \equiv \{\beta_{i,n,s,t,u}, \beta^{\text{up}}_{i,n,s,t,u}, \beta^{\text{down}}_{i,n,s,t,u}, \phi^y_{i,n,s,t,u}, \phi^z_{\hat{i},n,u}, \underline{\mu}_{\ell,s,t}, \overline{\mu}_{\ell,s,t}, \underline{\kappa}_{n,s,t}, \overline{\kappa}_{n,s,t}, \phi^c_{n,s,t}, \lambda_{n,s,t}, \mu_{\ell,s,t}\}$. Note that this MPEC is non-linear because of (1) bilinear terms $\lambda_{n,s,t} y_{i*,n,s,t,u}$ in the objective function (7.12a) and (2) complementarity conditions in (7.16b)–(7.16e), (7.17b)–(7.17e) and (7.17g), and (7.18e)–(7.18h) and (7.18j).

We reformulate the MPEC for strategic generation investment by using (1) strong duality for the non-strategic firm's LP (7.14a)–(7.14f) and the ISO's QP (7.15a)–

(7.15h) from the lower level to linearize the bilinear terms $\lambda_{n,s,t} y_{i^*,n,s,t,u}$ [23] in the objective function (7.12a) and (2) disjunctive constraints [5] to resolve complementarity conditions in (7.16b)–(7.16e), (7.17b)–(7.17e) and (7.17g), and (7.18e)–(7.18h) and (7.18j). First, we apply LP strong duality to (7.14a)–(7.14f), which holds for all $\hat{i} \in \hat{\mathcal{I}}$:

$$\sum_{s\in\mathcal{S}} W_s \sum_{n\in\mathcal{N}} \sum_{t\in\mathcal{T}} \sum_{u\in\mathcal{U}_{\hat{i},n}} \left(\frac{\lambda_{n,s,t}}{W_s} - C^{\text{opr}}_{\hat{i},n,u}\right) y_{\hat{i},n,s,t,u} - \sum_{n\in\mathcal{N}} \sum_{u\in\mathcal{U}_{\hat{i},n}} C^{\text{gen}}_{\hat{i},n,u} z_{\hat{i},n,u}$$
$$= \sum_{n\in\mathcal{N}} \sum_{s\in\mathcal{S}} \sum_{t\in\mathcal{T}} \sum_{u\in\mathcal{U}_{\hat{i},n}} T_t K^{\text{gen}}_{\hat{i},n,u} \left(A_{n,s,t,u} \beta_{\hat{i},n,s,t,u} + R^{\text{up}}_u \beta^{\text{up}}_{\hat{i},n,s,t,u} + R^{\text{down}}_u \beta^{\text{down}}_{\hat{i},n,s,t,u}\right)$$
$$\Rightarrow \sum_{s\in\mathcal{S}} \sum_{n\in\mathcal{N}} \sum_{t\in\mathcal{T}} \sum_{u\in\mathcal{U}_{\hat{i},n}} \lambda_{n,s,t} y_{\hat{i},n,s,t,u}$$
$$= \sum_{s\in\mathcal{S}} \sum_{n\in\mathcal{N}} \sum_{t\in\mathcal{T}} \sum_{u\in\mathcal{U}_{\hat{i},n}} W_s C^{\text{opr}}_{\hat{i},n,u} y_{\hat{i},n,s,t,u} + \sum_{n\in\mathcal{N}} \sum_{u\in\mathcal{U}_{\hat{i},n}} C^{\text{gen}}_{\hat{i},n,u} z_{\hat{i},n,u}$$
$$+ \sum_{n\in\mathcal{N}} \sum_{s\in\mathcal{S}} \sum_{t\in\mathcal{T}} \sum_{u\in\mathcal{U}_{\hat{i},n}} T_t K^{\text{gen}}_{\hat{i},n,u} \left(A_{n,s,t,u} \beta_{\hat{i},n,s,t,u} + R^{\text{up}}_u \beta^{\text{up}}_{\hat{i},n,s,t,u} + R^{\text{down}}_u \beta^{\text{down}}_{\hat{i},n,s,t,u}\right) \tag{7.19}$$

Likewise, applying QP strong duality to (7.15a)–(7.15h) yields:

$$\sum_{s\in\mathcal{S}} W_s \sum_{n\in\mathcal{N}} \sum_{t\in\mathcal{T}} \left(D^{\text{int}}_{n,s,t} c_{n,s,t} - D^{\text{slp}}_{n,s,t} c^2_{n,s,t}\right)$$
$$= \sum_{\ell\in\mathcal{L}} \sum_{s\in\mathcal{S}} \sum_{t\in\mathcal{T}} K^{\text{trn}}_{\ell} \left(\underline{\mu}_{\ell,s,t} + \overline{\mu}_{\ell,s,t}\right) + \sum_{n\in\mathcal{N}} \sum_{s\in\mathcal{S}} \sum_{t\in\mathcal{T}} \pi \left(\underline{\kappa}_{n,s,t} + \overline{\kappa}_{n,s,t}\right)$$
$$+ \sum_{n\in\mathcal{N}} \sum_{s\in\mathcal{S}} \sum_{t\in\mathcal{T}} \lambda_{n,s,t} \left(\sum_{\hat{i}\in\hat{\mathcal{I}}} \sum_{u\in\mathcal{U}_{\hat{i},n}} y_{\hat{i},n,s,t,u} + \sum_{u\in\mathcal{U}_{i^*,n}} y_{i^*,n,s,t,u}\right)$$
$$\Rightarrow \sum_{n\in\mathcal{N}} \sum_{s\in\mathcal{S}} \sum_{t\in\mathcal{T}} \sum_{u\in\mathcal{U}_{i^*,n}} \lambda_{n,s,t} y_{i^*,n,s,t,u}$$
$$= \sum_{s\in\mathcal{S}} W_s \sum_{n\in\mathcal{N}} \sum_{t\in\mathcal{T}} \left(D^{\text{int}}_{n,s,t} c_{n,s,t} - D^{\text{slp}}_{n,s,t} c^2_{n,s,t}\right)$$
$$- \sum_{\ell\in\mathcal{L}} \sum_{s\in\mathcal{S}} \sum_{t\in\mathcal{T}} K^{\text{trn}}_{\ell} \left(\underline{\mu}_{\ell,s,t} + \overline{\mu}_{\ell,s,t}\right) - \sum_{n\in\mathcal{N}} \sum_{s\in\mathcal{S}} \sum_{t\in\mathcal{T}} \pi \left(\underline{\kappa}_{n,s,t} + \overline{\kappa}_{n,s,t}\right)$$
$$- \sum_{\hat{i}\in\hat{\mathcal{I}}} \sum_{n\in\mathcal{N}} \sum_{s\in\mathcal{S}} \sum_{t\in\mathcal{T}} \sum_{u\in\mathcal{U}_{\hat{i},n}} \lambda_{n,s,t} y_{\hat{i},n,s,t,u} \tag{7.20}$$

where we have used the fact that $y_{i,n,s,t,u}$ is not a decision variable in the ISO's optimization problem and $\sum_{i\in\mathcal{I}}\sum_{u\in\mathcal{U}_{i,n}} y_{i,n,s,t,u} = \sum_{\hat{i}\in\hat{\mathcal{I}}}\sum_{u\in\mathcal{U}_{\hat{i},n}} y_{\hat{i},n,s,t,u} + \sum_{u\in\mathcal{U}_{i*,n}} y_{i*,n,s,t,u}$. Next, we sum up (7.19) over all $\hat{i}\in\hat{\mathcal{I}}$ and insert it into (7.20) to obtain the following convex expression for $\sum_{n\in\mathcal{N}}\sum_{s\in\mathcal{S}}\sum_{t\in\mathcal{T}}\sum_{u\in\mathcal{U}_{i*,n}} \lambda_{n,s,t} y_{i*,n,s,t,u}$:

$$\sum_{s\in\mathcal{S}} W_s \sum_{n\in\mathcal{N}}\sum_{t\in\mathcal{T}} \left(D^{\text{int}}_{n,s,t} c_{n,s,t} - D^{\text{slp}}_{n,s,t} c^2_{n,s,t}\right)$$
$$-\sum_{\ell\in\mathcal{L}}\sum_{s\in\mathcal{S}}\sum_{t\in\mathcal{T}} K^{\text{trn}}_{\ell}\left(\underline{\mu}_{\ell,s,t} + \overline{\mu}_{\ell,s,t}\right) - \sum_{n\in\mathcal{N}}\sum_{s\in\mathcal{S}}\sum_{t\in\mathcal{T}} \pi\left(\underline{\kappa}_{n,s,t} + \overline{\kappa}_{n,s,t}\right)$$
$$-\sum_{\hat{i}\in\hat{\mathcal{I}}}\sum_{s\in\mathcal{S}}\sum_{n\in\mathcal{N}}\sum_{t\in\mathcal{T}}\sum_{u\in\mathcal{U}_{\hat{i},n}} W_s C^{\text{opr}}_{\hat{i},n,u} y_{\hat{i},n,s,t,u} - \sum_{\hat{i}\in\hat{\mathcal{I}}}\sum_{n\in\mathcal{N}}\sum_{u\in\mathcal{U}_{\hat{i},n}} C^{\text{gen}}_{\hat{i},n,u} z_{\hat{i},n,u}$$
$$-\sum_{\hat{i}\in\hat{\mathcal{I}}}\sum_{n\in\mathcal{N}}\sum_{s\in\mathcal{S}}\sum_{t\in\mathcal{T}}\sum_{u\in\mathcal{U}_{\hat{i},n}} T_t K^{\text{gen}}_{\hat{i},n,u}\left(A_{n,s,t,u}\beta_{\hat{i},n,s,t,u} + R^{\text{up}}_u \beta^{\text{up}}_{\hat{i},n,s,t,u} + R^{\text{down}}_u \beta^{\text{down}}_{\hat{i},n,s,t,u}\right) \tag{7.21}$$

Hence, the strategic firm's objective function (7.12a) may be written as:

$$\sum_{s\in\mathcal{S}} W_s \sum_{n\in\mathcal{N}}\sum_{t\in\mathcal{T}} \left(D^{\text{int}}_{n,s,t} c_{n,s,t} - D^{\text{slp}}_{n,s,t} c^2_{n,s,t}\right)$$
$$-\sum_{\ell\in\mathcal{L}}\sum_{s\in\mathcal{S}}\sum_{t\in\mathcal{T}} K^{\text{trn}}_{\ell}\left(\underline{\mu}_{\ell,s,t} + \overline{\mu}_{\ell,s,t}\right) - \sum_{n\in\mathcal{N}}\sum_{s\in\mathcal{S}}\sum_{t\in\mathcal{T}} \pi\left(\underline{\kappa}_{n,s,t} + \overline{\kappa}_{n,s,t}\right)$$
$$-\sum_{\hat{i}\in\hat{\mathcal{I}}}\sum_{s\in\mathcal{S}}\sum_{n\in\mathcal{N}}\sum_{t\in\mathcal{T}}\sum_{u\in\mathcal{U}_{\hat{i},n}} W_s C^{\text{opr}}_{\hat{i},n,u} y_{\hat{i},n,s,t,u} - \sum_{\hat{i}\in\hat{\mathcal{I}}}\sum_{n\in\mathcal{N}}\sum_{u\in\mathcal{U}_{\hat{i},n}} C^{\text{gen}}_{\hat{i},n,u} z_{\hat{i},n,u}$$
$$-\sum_{\hat{i}\in\hat{\mathcal{I}}}\sum_{n\in\mathcal{N}}\sum_{s\in\mathcal{S}}\sum_{t\in\mathcal{T}}\sum_{u\in\mathcal{U}_{\hat{i},n}} T_t K^{\text{gen}}_{\hat{i},n,u}\left(A_{n,s,t,u}\beta_{\hat{i},n,s,t,u} + R^{\text{up}}_u \beta^{\text{up}}_{\hat{i},n,s,t,u}\right.$$
$$\left. + R^{\text{down}}_u \beta^{\text{down}}_{\hat{i},n,s,t,u}\right)$$
$$-\sum_{s\in\mathcal{S}} W_s \sum_{n\in\mathcal{N}}\sum_{t\in\mathcal{T}}\sum_{u\in\mathcal{U}_{i*,n}} C^{\text{opr}}_{i*,n,u} y_{i*,n,s,t,u} - \sum_{n\in\mathcal{N}}\sum_{u\in\mathcal{U}_{i*,n}} C^{\text{gen}}_{i*,n,u} z_{i*,n,u} \tag{7.22}$$

As for disjunctive constraints, we first devise them for complementarity conditions (7.16b)–(7.16e) and (7.17b)–(7.17e) corresponding to all firms' decisions:

$$0 \le y_{i,n,s,t,u} \le M^{\text{y}} x^{\text{y}}_{i,n,s,t,u}, \ \forall i, n, s, t, u \in \mathcal{U}_{i,n} \tag{7.23a}$$

$$0 \le \phi^{\text{y}}_{i,n,s,t,u} \le M^{\text{y}}\left(1 - x^{\text{y}}_{i,n,s,t,u}\right), \ \forall i, n, s, t, u \in \mathcal{U}_{i,n} \tag{7.23b}$$

$$0 \leq T_t A_{n,s,t,u} \left(K^{\text{gen}}_{i,n,u} + z_{i,n,u} \right) - y_{i,n,s,t,u} \leq M^{\beta} x^{\beta}_{i,n,s,t,u},$$

$$\forall i, n, s, t, u \in \mathcal{U}_{i,n} \tag{7.23c}$$

$$0 \leq \beta_{i,n,s,t,u} \leq M^{\beta} \left(1 - x^{\beta}_{i,n,s,t,u} \right), \ \forall i, n, s, t, u \in \mathcal{U}_{i,n} \tag{7.23d}$$

$$0 \leq T_t R^{\text{up}}_u \left(K^{\text{gen}}_{i,n,u} + z_{i,n,u} \right) - y_{i,n,s,t,u} + y_{i,n,s,t-1,u}$$

$$\leq M^{\beta^{\text{up}}} x^{\beta^{\text{up}}}_{i,n,s,t,u}, \ \forall i, n, s, t, u \in \mathcal{U}_{i,n} \tag{7.23e}$$

$$0 \leq \beta^{\text{up}}_{i,n,s,t,u} \leq M^{\beta^{\text{up}}} \left(1 - x^{\beta^{\text{up}}}_{i,n,s,t,u} \right), \ \forall i, n, s, t, u \in \mathcal{U}_{i,n} \tag{7.23f}$$

$$0 \leq T_t R^{\text{down}}_u \left(K^{\text{gen}}_{i,n,u} + z_{i,n,u} \right) + y_{i,n,s,t,u} - y_{i,n,s,t-1,u}$$

$$\leq M^{\beta^{\text{down}}} x^{\beta^{\text{down}}}_{i,n,s,t,u}, \ \forall i, n, s, t, u \in \mathcal{U}_{i,n} \tag{7.23g}$$

$$0 \leq \beta^{\text{down}}_{i,n,s,t,u} \leq M^{\beta^{\text{down}}} \left(1 - x^{\beta^{\text{down}}}_{i,n,s,t,u} \right), \ \forall i, n, s, t, u \in \mathcal{U}_{i,n} \tag{7.23h}$$

$$x^{\text{y}}_{i,n,s,t,u} \in \{0, 1\}, \ x^{\beta}_{i,n,s,t,u} \in \{0, 1\}, \ x^{\beta^{\text{up}}}_{i,n,s,t,u} \in \{0, 1\},$$

$$x^{\beta^{\text{down}}}_{i,n,s,t,u} \in \{0, 1\}, \ \forall i, n, s, t, u \in \mathcal{U}_{i,n} \tag{7.23i}$$

where M^{y} is a large positive constant and $x^{\text{y}}_{i,n,s,t,u}$ is a binary variable that equals 1 if $y_{i,n,s,t,u} > 0$, for example, which renders $\phi^{\text{y}}_{i,n,s,t,u} = 0$.[23] Other binary variables in (7.23i) and big-Ms are defined similarly. Since non-strategic firms also have the complementarity conditions (7.17g) related to generation investment at the lower level, we similarly linearize those via the following disjunctive constraints:

$$0 \leq z_{\hat{i},n,u} \leq M^{\text{z}} x^{\text{z}}_{\hat{i},n,u}, \ \forall \hat{i} \in \hat{\mathcal{I}}, n, u \in \mathcal{U}_{\hat{i},n} \tag{7.24a}$$

$$0 \leq \phi^{\text{z}}_{\hat{i},n,u} \leq M^{\text{z}} \left(1 - x^{\text{z}}_{\hat{i},n,u} \right), \ \forall \hat{i} \in \hat{\mathcal{I}}, n, u \in \mathcal{U}_{\hat{i},n} \tag{7.24b}$$

$$x^{\text{z}}_{\hat{i},n,u} \in \{0, 1\}, \ \forall \hat{i} \in \hat{\mathcal{I}}, n, u \in \mathcal{U}_{\hat{i},n} \tag{7.24c}$$

[23] These so-called big-Ms must be tuned in a manner that they are large enough to avoid artificial limits on the underlying constraints yet small enough not to introduce scaling issues for numerical solvers. The results of the central-planning problem instances may be used to inform these values. Alternatively, they may be selected based on knowledge of other parameters, e.g., $M^{\text{y}} = 1000$ corresponding to the maximum generation output in any period [19].

where M^{z} is a large positive constant and $x^{z}_{\hat{i},n,u}$ is a binary variable that equals 1 if $z_{\hat{i},n,u} > 0$. Finally, we use the following disjunctive constraints to linearize the ISO's complementarity conditions (7.18e)–(7.18h) and (7.18j):

$$0 \leq \hat{f}_{\ell,s,t} + K^{\text{trn}}_{\ell} \leq M^{\underline{\mu}} x^{\underline{\mu}}_{\ell,s,t}, \ \forall \ell, s, t \tag{7.25a}$$

$$0 \leq \underline{\mu}_{\ell,s,t} \leq M^{\underline{\mu}} \left(1 - x^{\underline{\mu}}_{\ell,s,t}\right), \ \forall \ell, s, t \tag{7.25b}$$

$$0 \leq -\hat{f}_{\ell,s,t} + K^{\text{trn}}_{\ell} \leq M^{\overline{\mu}} x^{\overline{\mu}}_{\ell,s,t}, \ \forall \ell, s, t \tag{7.25c}$$

$$0 \leq \overline{\mu}_{\ell,s,t} \leq M^{\overline{\mu}} \left(1 - x^{\overline{\mu}}_{\ell,s,t}\right), \ \forall \ell, s, t \tag{7.25d}$$

$$0 \leq v_{n,s,t} + \pi \leq M^{\underline{\kappa}} x^{\underline{\kappa}}_{n,s,t}, \ \forall n, s, t \tag{7.25e}$$

$$0 \leq \underline{\kappa}_{n,s,t} \leq M^{\underline{\kappa}} \left(1 - x^{\underline{\kappa}}_{n,s,t}\right), \ \forall n, s, t \tag{7.25f}$$

$$0 \leq -v_{n,s,t} + \pi \leq M^{\overline{\kappa}} x^{\overline{\kappa}}_{n,s,t}, \ \forall n, s, t \tag{7.25g}$$

$$0 \leq \overline{\kappa}_{n,s,t} \leq M^{\overline{\kappa}} \left(1 - x^{\overline{\kappa}}_{n,s,t}\right), \ \forall n, s, t \tag{7.25h}$$

$$0 \leq c_{n,s,t} \leq M^{\text{c}} x^{\text{c}}_{n,s,t}, \ \forall n, s, t \tag{7.25i}$$

$$0 \leq \phi^{\text{c}}_{n,s,t} \leq M^{\text{c}} \left(1 - x^{\text{c}}_{n,s,t}\right), \ \forall n, s, t \tag{7.25j}$$

$$x^{\underline{\mu}}_{\ell,s,t} \in \{0, 1\}, \ x^{\overline{\mu}}_{\ell,s,t} \in \{0, 1\}, \ \forall \ell, s, t \tag{7.25k}$$

$$x^{\underline{\kappa}}_{n,s,t} \in \{0, 1\}, \ x^{\overline{\kappa}}_{n,s,t} \in \{0, 1\}, \ x^{\text{c}}_{n,s,t} \in \{0, 1\}, \ \forall n, s, t \tag{7.25l}$$

Ultimately, the MPEC corresponding to the bi-level generation-expansion problem may be rendered as the following MIQP:

$$\begin{aligned}
&\underset{\{z_{i*,n,u}\} \cup \Omega^{\text{LL}} \cup \Omega^{\text{DV}} \cup \Omega^{\text{BV}}}{\text{Maximize}} \quad (7.22)\\
&\qquad \text{s.t.} \quad (7.12\text{b})\\
&\qquad \qquad (7.16\text{a})\\
&\qquad \qquad (7.17\text{a}), \ (7.17\text{f})\\
&\qquad \qquad (7.18\text{a}) - (7.18\text{d}), \ (7.18\text{i})\\
&\qquad \qquad (7.23\text{a}) - (7.23\text{i})\\
&\qquad \qquad (7.24\text{a}) - (7.24\text{c})\\
&\qquad \qquad (7.25\text{a}) - (7.25\text{l})
\end{aligned}$$

where $\Omega^{\text{BV}} \equiv \{x^{\text{y}}_{i,n,s,t,u}, x^{\beta}_{i,n,s,t,u}, x^{\beta^{\text{up}}}_{i,n,s,t,u}, x^{\beta^{\text{down}}}_{i,n,s,t,u}, x^{\text{z}}_{\hat{i},n,u}, x^{\underline{\mu}}_{\ell,s,t}, x^{\overline{\mu}}_{\ell,s,t}, x^{\underline{\kappa}}_{n,s,t}, x^{\overline{\kappa}}_{n,s,t}, x^{\text{c}}_{n,s,t}\}$ is the set of binary variables used in the disjunctive constraints.

Table 7.21 Prices (\$/MWh) for bi-level generation expansion

	Period		
Season	$t = 1$	$t = 2$	$t = 3$
$s = 1$	77.24	56.28	63.62
$s = 2$	69.90	50	50

It should be emphasized that constraints (7.12b) and (7.16a) apply only to the strategic firm, (7.17a), (7.17f), and (7.24a)–(7.24c) apply only to non-strategic firms, and (7.23a)–(7.23i) apply to all firms.

Illustrative Example 7.4 *Profit-maximizing MIQP for bi-level generation expansion.*

A profit-maximizing strategic firm $i = 2$ adopts on-shore wind capacity at node $n = 2$ like its non-strategic counterpart in Illustrative Example 7.3. However, the capacity adopted is only 55 MW in contrast to the 91.04 MW installed in the centrally planned model. This withholding of investment is done to increase the market-clearing prices at the lower level in order to boost the strategic firm's profit. At the same time, the non-strategic firm $i = 1$ expands its capacity addition at node $n = 1$ of technology $u = 4$ to 33.39 MW from 27.83 MW in response to the price signal. Consequently, vis-à-vis the CS under central planning, that in a bi-level framework decreases by over 20% (Table 7.16), while PS[24] increases from zero to nearly \$4 million for the strategic firm. Since the increase in PS is not enough to offset the loss in CS, there is an overall loss in welfare of almost 5%. The aggregate operational results are similar to those for central planning (Table 7.17) with the difference that consumption decreases at every node and gas-fired generation output increases to replace the share vacated by on-shore wind plants. Hence, node $n = 1$ actually becomes a net exporter overall to compensate for some of the reduced output from node $n = 2$.

By reducing its generation investment, strategic firm $i = 2$ is successful at increasing market-clearing prices in most (but not all) periods. For example, in season $s = 1$, prices are higher than those under central planning only in period $t = 1$ (Table 7.21). Indeed, non-strategic firm $i = 1$ expands its generation capacity at node $n = 1$, which keeps prices in check during periods $t = 2$ and $t = 3$ when VRES availability is limited (Table 7.22). The price is also higher in period $t = 3$ vis-à-vis period $t = 2$ due to lower VRES availability. During these two periods, the gas-fired plant at node $n = 1$ operates at its rated capacity, and it is only its ramping restriction in period $t = 1$ that yields the higher prices desired by the strategic firm. Thus, the price is set by ramp-constrained gas generation and capacity-constrained VRES generation in period $t = 1$. This renders node $n = 2$ into a net importer (except in period $t = 1$), while node $n = 1$ ($n = 3$) is a net exporter (net importer) during all periods (Table 7.23).

[24] We include amortized investment costs in this metric.

Table 7.22 Generation output (MWh) for bi-level generation expansion

Node	Season	Period		
		$t = 1$	$t = 2$	$t = 3$
$n = 1$	$s = 1$	160.29	267.15	267.15
	$s = 2$	160.29	110	0
$n = 2$	$s = 1$	88	44	22
	$s = 2$	110	220	330

Table 7.23 Net imports (MWh) for bi-level generation expansion

Node	Season	Period		
		$t = 1$	$t = 2$	$t = 3$
$n = 1$	$s = 1$	−17.53	−103.44	−110.77
	$s = 2$	−10.20	60	170
$n = 2$	$s = 1$	−25.24	39.72	54.38
	$s = 2$	−39.90	−130	−240
$n = 3$	$s = 1$	42.76	63.72	56.38
	$s = 2$	50.10	70	70

In contrast to season $s = 1$, generally higher VRES availability enables the strategic firm to dictate terms in season $s = 2$. Prices across all periods are higher than those under central planning. Specifically, gas-fired generation at node $n = 1$ is actually below capacity during periods $t = 2$ and $t = 3$, which enables the on-shore wind plant at node $n = 2$ to set the price by being dispatched at capacity. In effect, on-shore wind capacity is set strategically in order to permit it to supplant the gas plant, which would have cleared the market at a price of \$50/MWh. Thus, node $n = 2$ ($n = 3$) is a net exporter (net importer) during all periods, whereas node $n = 1$ is a net importer except in period $t = 1$ when VRES availability is at its lowest.

7.4 Summary

Decarbonization of the power sector will require new investment in VRES technologies. Over the past decade, policy measures such as feed-in tariffs and renewable portfolio standards have incentivized power companies to phase in VRES. The resulting economies of scale have brought down capital costs of on-shore wind turbines to parity with those of gas-fired plants as mentioned in Chap. 2. Nevertheless, the remote locations and intermittent output of such VRES technologies pose a challenge to power systems along with existing issues related to market power.

In this chapter, we have devised and implemented models for analyzing investment in both transmission and generation capacity. The former takes the perspective of a welfare-maximizing TSO that must anticipate the possible exertion of market power by firms when investing in new lines to integrate VRES. Compared to a central-planning paradigm, a deregulated one with firms behaving à la Cournot in market operations requires a bi-level framework for analysis that invariably leads to a distinct transmission-expansion plan. As for generation investment, we compare the capacity adopted by a benchmark welfare-maximizing central planner with that of a strategic firm behaving as a Stackelberg leader. In this case, the strategic firm withholds capacity investment in order to boost market-clearing prices, thereby maximizing its own profit at the expense of social welfare.

Given the ambitious climate targets of most OECD countries, ignoring such real-world complications in setting policy could jeopardize not only economic but also environmental objectives. The framework for analysis in this chapter provides a basis to quantify welfare losses and to explore countervailing mechanisms to align public and private incentives better. For example, in the case of transmission investment, the TSO is proactive in anticipating the Cournot behavior of power companies at the lower level. This perspective could be extended to the problem of strategic generation investment with a welfare-maximizing TSO in a tri-level model [24, 25] that anticipates the strategic investment at the middle level and market clearing at the lowest level. Alternatively, even in a bi-level model, the entity at the upper level could be a policymaker that decides upon a VRES or an emission target that becomes a binding constraint at the lower level [27, 30]. Moreover, the bi-level models presented in this chapter could be adapted to investigate incentives for investment in energy storage [34] or prosumer behavior more generally [26]. Finally, more realistic models would require careful representation of spatio-temporal variations [20, 32] and strategic equilibria among several generators [15, 35] or transmission planners [12] in an EPEC as well as enhanced solution methods for solving large-scale bi-level problem instances [2, 13].

7.5 End-of-Chapter Exercises

7.1 Assuming interior solutions, find closed-form expressions for all primal and dual variables in the stylized QP (7.1a)–(7.1d) by using the KKT conditions (7.2a)–(7.2g). Hint: It may be helpful to partition the set of solutions into distinct cases depending on which way power flows and which plants are dispatched, cf. [28]. Perform comparative statics on the primal and dual variables with respect to the size of the transmission line, K.

7.2 Gather relevant data in order to implement Illustrative Examples 7.1 and 7.2 that are tailored to your jurisdiction. How do the transmission-expansion plans compare with those envisaged in policy documents?

7.3 In Illustrative Example 7.2, we mentioned that maximized welfare would actually be lower if the transmission-expansion plan from central planning in Illustrative Example 7.1 were used. Verify that this is, indeed, the case by executing the GAMS code for Illustrative Example 7.2 while fixing the upper-level decisions to those from Illustrative Example 7.1.

7.4 Implement Illustrative Example 7.4 but with the roles of the two firms swapped, i.e., make firm $i = 1$ as the strategic firm that makes profit-maximizing generation-investment decisions at the upper level. How does the strategy of such a firm with a fossil-fuel portfolio compare with that of a VRES-dominated firm?

7.5 Gather relevant data in order to implement Illustrative Examples 7.3 and 7.4 that are tailored to your jurisdiction. How do the generation-expansion plans compare with those envisaged in policy documents?

7.6 GAMS Codes

Here, we present GAMS codes for solving selected examples numerically. For sake of numerical scaling, especially for the bi-level problem instances, modeling is implemented on a single-day basis. The annual quantities may be obtained *ex post* by summing up the results, e.g., generation output, and multiplying them by the number of days in each season, i.e., 183. The following file contains the common data used in the problem instances for transmission expansion, i.e., Illustrative Examples 7.1 and 7.2.

```
* TEP_data.gms: Data for transmission planning problem instances

* Set definitions

Sets
i Firms                                   /i1*i2/
j Discrete transmission levels            /j1*j10/
l Transmission lines                      /l1*l3/
n Nodes                                   /n1*n3/
s Seasons                                 /s1*s2/
t Periods                                 /t1*t3/
u Generation units                        /u1*u4/
itontou(I,N,U) Firm-to-node-to-unit relation  /i1.n1.u3, i1.n1.u4
    , i2.n2.u1, i2.n3.u2/
;

Set TL Transmission line characteristics
/Susceptance, Capacity, Cost/
;

Alias(N,NN);
Alias(I,II);
Alias(U,UU);

* Time parameters

Parameters
TT(T)       Length of each period in hours
/ t1        8
  t2        8
```

```
  t3       8/

W(S)       Weight of each season
/ s1       1
  s2       1/
;

* Number of days per season

Scalar Days /183/
;

* Power line parameters

Table Incidence(L,N) Matches power lines with nodes
      n1      n2      n3
l1    1       -1       0
l2    0        1      -1
l3    1        0      -1
;

TABLE LineOpt (J, TL) Transmission line information
          Susceptance   Capacity       Cost
j1         0             0             0
j2         1200          3.7           11.9
j3         1500          6.1           19.8
j4         1700          12.2          39.7
j5         2000          18.3          59.5
j6         2300          24.4          79.3
j7         2800          30.5          99.1
j8         3600          36.6          119.0
j9         4900          42.7          138.8
j10        5100          48.8          158.6
;

Parameter  K_trn(J,L) Maximum thermal capacity of power line;
K_trn(J,L) =  LineOpt(J, 'Capacity');

Parameter C_trn(J,L) Amortized investment cost;
C_trn(J,L) = SUM(S, SUM(T, W(S)*TT(T)*LineOpt(J, 'Cost')));

Parameter B(J,L) Transmission line susceptance;
B(J,L) = LineOpt(J, 'Susceptance');

Parameter
LPlus(L,N)
/
l1.n1 1
l2.n2 1
l3.n1 1
/

LMinus(L,N)
/
```

```
l1.n2 1
l2.n3 1
l3.n3 1
/
;

Parameter
NPlus(L,N)
/
l1.n1 1
l3.n1 1
l2.n2 1
/

NMinus(L,N)
/
l1.n2 1
l2.n3 1
l3.n3 1
/
;

* Demand parameters

Table DemandData(N,*) Demand data by node
      INT  SLP
n1    220   1
n2    140   1
n3    120   1
;

Parameter
D_int(N,S,T)    Demand intercept,
D_slp(N,S,T)    Demand slope
;

D_int(N,S,T)=   DemandData(N, 'INT');
D_slp(N,S,T)=   DemandData(N, 'SLP');

* Power generation parameters

Parameters

R(U)       Ramping limit of each technology
/ u1       1
  u2       1
  u3       0.3
  u4       0.6
/
;

Table
```

```
A(N,S,T,U)   Maximum availability factor for each technology at
    each node by season and by period
                u1      u2       u3      u4
n1.s1.t1      0       0        1       1
n1.s1.t2      0       0        1       1
n1.s1.t3      0       0        1       1
n1.s2.t1      0       0        1       1
n1.s2.t2      0       0        1       1
n1.s2.t3      0       0        1       1
n2.s1.t1      0.20    0        1       1
n2.s1.t2      0.10    0        1       1
n2.s1.t3      0.05    0        1       1
n2.s2.t1      0.25    0        1       1
n2.s2.t2      0.50    0        1       1
n2.s2.t3      0.75    0        1       1
n3.s1.t1      0       0.20     1       1
n3.s1.t2      0       0.40     1       1
n3.s1.t3      0       0.50     1       1
n3.s2.t1      0       1.00     1       1
n3.s2.t2      0       0.75     1       1
n3.s2.t3      0       0.10     1       1
;

Table C_opr(I,N,U) Operating cost of generation unit type u at
    node n owned by firm i
              u1   u2   u3   u4
i1.n1         0    0    20   50
i2.n2         0    0    20   50
i2.n3         0    0    20   50
;

Table K_gen(I,N,U) Installed generation capacity of generation
    type u at node n owned by firm i
                u1      u2       u3      u4
i1.n1         0       0        35      40
i2.n2         50      0        0       0
i2.n3         0       50       0       0
;

Parameter K_gen_vres(I,N,U);

K_gen_vres('i2','n2','u1')=K_gen('i2','n2','u1');
K_gen_vres('i2','n3','u2')=K_gen('i2','n3','u2');

Display B, C_trn;

Scalar Pi /3.14159/;

Scalar M_trn /14500/;
```

The following code solves Illustrative Example 7.1 to determine welfare-maximizing transmission expansion under central planning.

```
* CP_TEP.gms: Three-node central-planning transmission-expansion planning MIQP implementation

$INCLUDE PSE/TEP_data.gms

Scalar starttime;
starttime = jnow;

* Variable definition

Variables
f(J,L,S,T) Potential power flow on line l at capacity level j in season s and period t
f_hat(L,S,T) Realized power flow on line l in season s and period t
v(N,S,T) Voltage angle at node n in season s and period t
OF Objective function;

Positive variables
c(N,S,T) Consumption at node n in season s and period t
y(I,N,S,T,U) Generation output from unit u at node n owned by firm i in season s and period t
;

Binary variables
x(J,L) Investment decision on line l at capacity level j;

Equations OF_SW, CP_EQ3, CP_EQ4a, CP_EQ4b, CP_EQ5a, CP_EQ5b, CP_EQ6, CP_EQ7a, CP_EQ7b, CP_EQ8, CP_EQ9, CP_EQ10, CP_EQ11;
* Maximize social welfare
OF_SW.. SUM(S, W(S)*(SUM((N,T), D_int(N,S,T)*c(N,S,T) - 0.5*D_slp(N,S,T)*c(N,S,T)*c(N,S,T) - SUM(I, SUM(U, C_opr(I,N,U)*y(I,N,S,T,U)) ) ) ) ) - SUM((J,L), C_trn(J,L)*x(J,L))-OF =E= 0;
* Only one capacity level may be selected for each line L
CP_EQ3(L).. SUM(J, x(J,L)) =E= 1;
* Power flow on line L at level J in season S and period T
CP_EQ4a(J,L,S,T).. (1-x(J,L))*M_trn - f(J,L,S,T) + B(J,L)*(SUM(N$LPlus(L,N),v(N,S,T)) - SUM(N$LMinus(L,N),v(N,S,T))) =G= 0;
* Power flow on line L at level J in season S and period T
CP_EQ4b(J,L,S,T).. (1-x(J,L))*M_trn + f(J,L,S,T) - B(J,L)*(SUM(N$LPlus(L,N),v(N,S,T)) - SUM(N$LMinus(L,N),v(N,S,T))) =G= 0;
* Transmission capacity constraint on line L at level J in season S and period T
CP_EQ5a(J,L,S,T).. K_trn(J,L)*x(J,L)-f(J,L,S,T)  =G= 0;
* Transmission capacity constraint on line L at level J in season S and period T
CP_EQ5b(J,L,S,T).. K_trn(J,L)*x(J,L)+f(J,L,S,T)  =G= 0;
* Realized power flow on line L in season S and period T
CP_EQ6(L,S,T).. f_hat(L,S,T) - SUM(J,f(J,L,S,T)) =E= 0;
* Voltage angle limit at node N in season S and period T
CP_EQ7a(N,S,T).. -v(N,S,T) + Pi =G= 0;
* Voltage angle limit at node N in season S and period T
CP_EQ7b(N,S,T).. v(N,S,T) + Pi =G= 0;
* Power balance at node N in season S and period T
```

```
CP_EQ8(N,S,T).. c(N,S,T)- SUM(I, SUM(U, y(I,N,S,T,U))) + TT(T)*
    SUM(L$NPlus(L,N), f_hat(L,S,T)) -  TT(T)*SUM(L$NMinus(L,N),
    f_hat(L,S,T)) =E= 0;
* Generation capacity constraint for firm I at node N in season S
    and period T using unit U
CP_EQ9(I,N,S,T,U).. -y(I,N,S,T,U) + TT(T)*A(N,S,T,U)*K_gen(I,N,U)
    =G= 0;
* Generation up-ramping constraint for firm I at node N in season
    S and period T using unit U
CP_EQ10(I,N,S,T,U).. R(U)*TT(T)*K_gen(I,N,U) - y(I,N,S,T,U) + y(I
    ,N,S,T-1,U) =G= 0;
* Generation down-ramping constraint for firm I at node N in
    season S and period T using unit U
CP_EQ11(I,N,S,T,U).. R(U)*TT(T)*K_gen(I,N,U) + y(I,N,S,T,U)- y(I,
    N,S,T-1,U) =G= 0;

****Producers****
y.fx(I,N,S,T,U)$(NOT itontou(I,N,U))=0;

Model  CP_MIQP_TEP
        /
ALL
        /
;
option optcr=0;
option reslim = 3000000;
Option Iterlim=100000;
Option MIQCP = Cplex;

Solve CP_MIQP_TEP maximizing OF using miqcp ;
```

The following code solves Illustrative Example 7.2 to determine bi-level transmission expansion.

```
* BL_TEP.gms: Three-node bi-level transmission-expansion planning
    MIQCQP implementation

$INCLUDE PSE/TEP_data.gms

Scalar starttime;
starttime = jnow;

* Allow market power by setting 'CO' equal to '1'

Scalar CO /1/;

* Variable definition

Variables
c(N,S,T) Consumption at node n in season s and period t
y(I,N,S,T,U) Generation output from unit u at node n owned by
    firm i in season s and period t
```

```
f(J,L,S,T) Potential power flow on line l at capacity level j in season s and period t
f_hat(L,S,T) Realized power flow on line l in season s and period t
v(N,S,T) Voltage angle at node n in season s and period t
mu(J,L,S,T) Dual for voltage law on line l at capacity level j in season s and period t
lambda(N,S,T) Dual for energy balance at node n in season s and period t
psi(L,S,T) Dual for realized power flow on line l in season s and period t
mu_hat(J,L,S,T) Auxiliary variable for voltage law on line l at capacity level j in season s and period t
OF Objective function
;

Positive variables
phi_c(N,S,T) Dual for non-negativity of consumption at node n in season s and period t
phi_y(I,N,S,T,U) Dual for non-negativity of generation from unit u at node n owned by firm i in season s and period t
beta(I,N,S,T,U) Dual for generation capacity from unit u at node n owned by firm i in season s and period t
beta_up(I,N,S,T,U) Dual for generation up-ramping capacity from unit u at node n owned by firm i in season s and period t
beta_down(I,N,S,T,U) Dual for generation down-ramping capacity from unit u at node n owned by firm i in season s and period t
mu_up(J,L,S,T) Dual for positive transmission capacity on line l at capacity level j in season s and period t
mu_down(J,L,S,T) Dual for negative transmission capacity on line l at capacity level j in season s and period t
kappa_up(N,S,T) Dual for positive voltage angle limit at node n in season s and period t
kappa_down(N,S,T) Dual for negative voltage angle limit at node n in season s and period t
;

Binary variables
x(J,L) Investment decision on line l at capacity level j;

Equations OF_SW, CP_EQ3, CP_EQ4a, CP_EQ4b, CP_EQ5a, CP_EQ5b, CP_EQ6, CP_EQ7a, CP_EQ7b, CP_EQ8, CP_EQ9, CP_EQ10, CP_EQ11, CP_EQ12, CP_EQ13, SD_EQ, YD_EQ, CD_EQ, FD_EQ, HD_EQ, VD_EQa, VD_EQb, VD_EQc, VD_EQd, VD_EQe;
* Maximize social welfare
OF_SW.. SUM(S, W(S)*(SUM((N,T), D_int(N,S,T)*c(N,S,T) - 0.5*D_slp(N,S,T)*c(N,S,T)*c(N,S,T) - SUM(I, SUM(U, C_opr(I,N,U)*y(I,N,S,T,U)) ) ) ) ) - SUM((J,L), C_trn(J,L)*x(J,L))-OF =E= 0;
* Only one capacity level may be selected for each line L
CP_EQ3(L).. SUM(J, x(J,L)) =E= 1;
* Power flow on line L at level J in season S and period T
CP_EQ4a(J,L,S,T).. -(1-x(J,L))*M_trn + f(J,L,S,T) - B(J,L)*(SUM(N$LPlus(L,N),v(N,S,T)) - SUM(N$LMinus(L,N),v(N,S,T))) =L= 0;
```

```
* Power flow on line L at level J in season S and period T
CP_EQ4b(J,L,S,T).. -(1-x(J,L))*M_trn - f(J,L,S,T) + B(J,L)*(SUM(
    N$LPlus(L,N),v(N,S,T)) - SUM(N$LMinus(L,N),v(N,S,T))) =L= 0;
* Transmission capacity constraint on line L at level J in season
     S and period T
CP_EQ5a(J,L,S,T).. -K_trn(J,L)*x(J,L) + f(J,L,S,T)  =L= 0;
* Transmission capacity constraint on line L at level J in season
     S and period T
CP_EQ5b(J,L,S,T).. -K_trn(J,L)*x(J,L) - f(J,L,S,T)  =L= 0;
* Realized power flow on line L in season S and period T
CP_EQ6(L,S,T).. f_hat(L,S,T) - SUM(J,f(J,L,S,T)) =E= 0;
* Voltage angle limit at node N in season S and period T
CP_EQ7a(N,S,T).. -v(N,S,T) - Pi =L= 0;
* Voltage angle limit at node N in season S and period T
CP_EQ7b(N,S,T).. v(N,S,T) - Pi =L= 0;
* Power balance at node N in season S and period T
CP_EQ8(N,S,T).. c(N,S,T)- SUM(I, SUM(U, y(I,N,S,T,U))) +  TT(T)*
    SUM(L$NPlus(L,N), f_hat(L,S,T)) -  TT(T)*SUM(L$NMinus(L,N),
    f_hat(L,S,T)) =E= 0;
* Generation capacity constraint for firm I at node N in season S
     and period T using unit U
CP_EQ9(I,N,S,T,U).. y(I,N,S,T,U) - TT(T)*A(N,S,T,U)*K_gen(I,N,U)
    =L= 0;
* Generation up-ramping constraint for firm I at node N in season
     S and period T using unit U
CP_EQ10(I,N,S,T,U).. -R(U)*TT(T)*K_gen(I,N,U) + y(I,N,S,T,U) - y(
    I,N,S,T-1,U) =L= 0;
* Generation down-ramping constraint for firm I at node N in
    season S and period T using unit U
CP_EQ11(I,N,S,T,U).. -R(U)*TT(T)*K_gen(I,N,U) - y(I,N,S,T,U) + y(
    I,N,S,T-1,U) =L= 0;
* Non-negativity of consumption
CP_EQ12(N,S,T).. -c(N,S,T) =L= 0;
* Non-negativity of generation
CP_EQ13(I,N,S,T,U).. -y(I,N,S,T,U) =L= 0;
* Strong-duality expression
SD_EQ.. SUM(S, W(S)*(SUM((N,T), D_int(N,S,T)*c(N,S,T) - D_slp(N,S
    ,T)*c(N,S,T)*c(N,S,T) - SUM(I, SUM(U, C_opr(I,N,U)*y(I,N,S,T,
    U)) )  ) ) ) - SUM(S, W(S)*(SUM((N,T), D_slp(N,S,T)*(SUM(I,
    SUM(U, y(I,N,S,T,U))*SUM(U, y(I,N,S,T,U))$(CO)   )  ) )  ) )
    - (SUM(I, SUM(N, SUM(S, SUM(T, SUM(U, TT(T)*K_gen(I,N,U)*(A(N
    ,S,T,U)*beta(I,N,S,T,U) + R(U)*beta_up(I,N,S,T,U) + R(U)*
    beta_down(I,N,S,T,U) )  ) )  )  ) ) + SUM(L, SUM(S, SUM(T,
    SUM(J, K_trn(J,L)*(mu_up(J,L,S,T)+ mu_down(J,L,S,T))) )  ) )
    +SUM(N, SUM(S, SUM(T, Pi*(kappa_up(N,S,T)+kappa_down(N,S,T)))
     ) ) ) =G= 0;
* Dual constraint related to y
YD_EQ(I,N,S,T,U)$(itontou(i,n,u)).. W(S)*C_opr(I,N,U) + beta(I,N,
    S,T,U) + beta_up(I,N,S,T,U) - beta_down(I,N,S,T,U) - beta_up(
    I,N,S,T+1,U) + beta_down(I,N,S,T+1,U) - lambda(N,S,T) - phi_y
    (I,N,S,T,U) + W(S)*D_slp(N,S,T)*SUM(UU, y(I,N,S,T,UU))$(CO) =
    E= 0;
* Dual constraint related to c
```

```
CD_EQ(N,S,T).. -W(S)*(D_int(N,S,T) - D_slp(N,S,T)*c(N,S,T)) +
    lambda(N,S,T) - phi_c(N,S,T) =E= 0;
* Dual constraint related to f
FD_EQ(J,L,S,T).. mu(J,L,S,T)+mu_up(J,L,S,T)-mu_down(J,L,S,T)-psi(
    L,S,T) =E= 0;
* Dual constraint related to f_hat
HD_EQ(L,S,T).. psi(L,S,T) + TT(T)*SUM(N$LPlus(L,N), lambda(N,S,T)
    ) - TT(T)*SUM(N$LMinus(L,N), lambda(N,S,T)) =E= 0;
* Dual constraint related to v
VD_EQa(N,S,T).. -SUM(L$NPlus(L,N), SUM(J, B(J,L)*(mu(J,L,S,T)-
    mu_hat(J,L,S,T)) ) ) + SUM(L$NMinus(L,N), SUM(J, B(J,L)*(mu(J
    ,L,S,T)-mu_hat(J,L,S,T)) ) ) + kappa_up(N,S,T) - kappa_down(N
    ,S,T) =E= 0;
* Dual constraint related to v
VD_EQb(J,L,S,T).. -x(J,L)*M_trn + (mu(J,L,S,T)-mu_hat(J,L,S,T)) =
    L= 0;
* Dual constraint related to v
VD_EQc(J,L,S,T).. -x(J,L)*M_trn - (mu(J,L,S,T)-mu_hat(J,L,S,T)) =
    L= 0;
* Dual constraint related to v
VD_EQd(J,L,S,T).. -(1-x(J,L))*M_trn + mu_hat(J,L,S,T) =L= 0;
* Dual constraint related to v
VD_EQe(J,L,S,T).. -(1-x(J,L))*M_trn - mu_hat(J,L,S,T) =L= 0;

****Producers****
y.fx(I,N,S,T,U)$(NOT itontou(I,N,U))=0;

Model  BL_MIQCQP_TEP
         /
ALL
         /
;
option optcr=0;
option reslim = 3000000;
Option Iterlim=100000;
Option MIQCP = Cplex;

Solve BL_MIQCQP_TEP maximizing OF using miqcp ;
```

The following file contains the common data used in the problem instances for generation expansion, i.e., Illustrative Examples 7.3 and 7.4.

```
* GEP_data.gms: Data for generation planning problem instances

* Set definitions

Sets
i Firms                         /i1*i2/
is(i)  Strategic firms          / i2 /
ins(i) Fringe firms             / i1 /
l Transmission lines            /l1*l3/
n Nodes                         /n1*n3/
s Seasons                       /s1*s2/
```

```
t Periods                            /t1*t3/
u Generation units                   /u1*u4/
itontou(I,N,U) Firm-to-node-to-unit relation  /i1.n1.u3, i1.n1.u4
     , i2.n2.u1, i2.n3.u2/
;

Set TL Transmission line characteristics
/Susceptance, Capacity/
;

Alias(N,NN);
Alias(I,II);
Alias(U,UU);

* Time parameters

Parameters
TT(T)       Length of each period in hours
/ t1        8
  t2        8
  t3        8/

W(S)        Weight of each season
/ s1        1
  s2        1/
;

* Number of days per season

Scalar Days /183/
;

* Power line parameters

Table Incidence(L,N) Matches power lines with nodes
         n1      n2      n3
l1       1       -1       0
l2       0        1      -1
l3       1        0      -1
;

TABLE LineOpt (L, TL) Transmission line information
    Susceptance Capacity
l1 5100         48.8
l2 5100         48.8
l3 5100         48.8
;

Parameter K_trn(l) Maximum thermal capacity of power line;
K_trn(l) = LineOpt(L, 'Capacity');

Parameter B(l) Transmission line susceptance;
B(l) = LineOpt(L, 'Susceptance');
```

```
Parameter
LPlus(L,N)
/
l1.n1 1
l2.n2 1
l3.n1 1
/

LMinus(L,N)
/
l1.n2 1
l2.n3 1
l3.n3 1
/
;

Parameter
NPlus(L,N)
/
l1.n1 1
l3.n1 1
l2.n2 1
/

NMinus(L,N)
/
l1.n2 1
l2.n3 1
l3.n3 1
/
;

* Demand parameters

Table DemandData(N,*) Demand data by node
        INT  SLP
n1      220   1
n2      140   1
n3      120   1
;

Parameter
D_int(N,S,T)    Demand intercept,
D_slp(N,S,T)    Demand slope
;

D_int(N,S,T)=   DemandData(N, 'INT');
D_slp(N,S,T)=   DemandData(N, 'SLP');

* Power generation parameters

Parameters
```

```
R(U)        Ramping limit of each technology
/ u1        1
  u2        1
  u3        0.3
  u4        0.6
/
;

Table

A(N,S,T,U)    Maximum availability factor for each technology at
    each node by season and by period
             u1      u2      u3     u4
n1.s1.t1     0       0       1      1
n1.s1.t2     0       0       1      1
n1.s1.t3     0       0       1      1
n1.s2.t1     0       0       1      1
n1.s2.t2     0       0       1      1
n1.s2.t3     0       0       1      1
n2.s1.t1     0.20    0       1      1
n2.s1.t2     0.10    0       1      1
n2.s1.t3     0.05    0       1      1
n2.s2.t1     0.25    0       1      1
n2.s2.t2     0.50    0       1      1
n2.s2.t3     0.75    0       1      1
n3.s1.t1     0       0.20    1      1
n3.s1.t2     0       0.40    1      1
n3.s1.t3     0       0.50    1      1
n3.s2.t1     0       1.00    1      1
n3.s2.t2     0       0.75    1      1
n3.s2.t3     0       0.10    1      1
;

Table C_opr(I,N,U) Operating cost of generation unit type u at
    node n owned by firm i
            u1   u2   u3   u4
i1.n1       0    0    20   50
i2.n2       0    0    20   50
i2.n3       0    0    20   50
;

Table K_gen(I,N,U) Installed generation capacity of generation
    type u at node n owned by firm i
             u1      u2      u3     u4
i1.n1        0       0       0      0
i2.n2        0       0       0      0
i2.n3        0       0       0      0
;

Table C_gen(i,n,u) Amortized investment cost of generation type u
     at node n owned by firm i
        u1     u2     u3      u4
i1.n1  449.76 1555.2 1306.56 385.44
i2.n2  449.76 1555.2 1306.56 385.44
```

```
i2.n3  449.76 1555.2 1306.56 385.44
;

Parameter K_gen_vres(I,N,U);

K_gen_vres('i2','n2','u1')=K_gen('i2','n2','u1');
K_gen_vres('i2','n3','u2')=K_gen('i2','n3','u2');

Display B, C_gen;

Scalar Pi /3.14159/;

*Scalar M_trn /14500/;

Scalar M_y /1000/;

Scalar M_beta /3000/;

Scalar M_beta_down /3000/;

Scalar M_beta_up /3000/;

Scalar M_c /1000/;

Scalar M_z /1000/;

*Scalar M_gamma_d /14500/;

*Scalar M_gamma_u /14500/;

Scalar M_mu_down /14500/;

Scalar M_mu_up /14500/;

Scalar M_kappa_down /3000/;

Scalar M_kappa_up /3000/;
```

The following code solves Illustrative Example 7.3 to determine welfare-maximizing generation expansion under central planning.

```
* CP_GEP.gms: Three-node central-planning generation-expansion
    planning QP implementation

$INCLUDE PSE/GEP_data.gms

Scalar starttime;
starttime = jnow;

* Variable definition

Variables
```

```
f_hat(L,S,T) Realized power flow on line l in season s and period
    t
v(N,S,T) Voltage angle at node n in season s and period t
OF Objective function;

Positive variables
c(N,S,T) Consumption at node n in season s and period t
y(I,N,S,T,U) Generation output from unit u at node n owned by
    firm i in season s and period t
z(I,N,U) Generation investment in unit u at node n owned by firm
    i
;

Equations OF_SW, CP_EQ2, CP_EQ3a, CP_EQ3b, CP_EQ4a, CP_EQ4b,
    CP_EQ5, CP_EQ6, CP_EQ7, CP_EQ8;
* Maximize social welfare
OF_SW.. SUM(S, W(S)*(SUM((N,T), D_int(N,S,T)*c(N,S,T) - 0.5*D_slp
    (N,S,T)*c(N,S,T)*c(N,S,T) - SUM(I, SUM(U, C_opr(I,N,U)*y(I,N,
    S,T,U)) ) ) ) ) - SUM(I, SUM(N, SUM(U, C_gen(I,N,U)*z(I,N,U)
    ) ) ) - OF =E= 0;
* Power flow on line L in season S and period T
CP_EQ2(L,S,T).. f_hat(L,S,T) - B(L)*(SUM(N$LPlus(L,N),v(N,S,T)) -
     SUM(N$LMinus(L,N),v(N,S,T))) =E= 0;
* Transmission capacity constraint on line L in season S and
    period T
CP_EQ3a(L,S,T).. K_trn(L)-f_hat(L,S,T)  =G= 0;
* Transmission capacity constraint on line L in season S and
    period T
CP_EQ3b(L,S,T).. K_trn(L)+f_hat(L,S,T)  =G= 0;
* Voltage angle limit at node N in season S and period T
CP_EQ4a(N,S,T).. -v(N,S,T) + Pi =G= 0;
* Voltage angle limit at node N in season S and period T
CP_EQ4b(N,S,T).. v(N,S,T) + Pi =G= 0;
* Power balance at node N in season S and period T
CP_EQ5(N,S,T).. c(N,S,T)- SUM(I, SUM(U, y(I,N,S,T,U))) + TT(T)*
    SUM(L$NPlus(L,N), f_hat(L,S,T)) -  TT(T)*SUM(L$NMinus(L,N),
    f_hat(L,S,T)) =E= 0;
* Generation capacity constraint for firm I at node N in season S
     and period T using unit U
CP_EQ6(I,N,S,T,U).. -y(I,N,S,T,U) + TT(T)*A(N,S,T,U)*(K_gen(I,N,U
    )+z(I,N,U)) =G= 0;
* Generation up-ramping constraint for firm I at node N in season
     S and period T using unit U
CP_EQ7(I,N,S,T,U).. R(U)*TT(T)*(K_gen(I,N,U)+z(I,N,U)) - y(I,N,S,
    T,U) + y(I,N,S,T-1,U) =G= 0;
* Generation down-ramping constraint for firm I at node N in
    season S and period T using unit U
CP_EQ8(I,N,S,T,U).. R(U)*TT(T)*(K_gen(I,N,U)+z(I,N,U)) + y(I,N,S,
    T,U)- y(I,N,S,T-1,U) =G= 0;

****Producers****
y.fx(I,N,S,T,U)$(NOT itontou(I,N,U))=0;
z.fx(I,N,U)$(NOT itontou(I,N,U))=0;
```

```
Model   CP_QP_GEP
        /
ALL
        /
;
option optcr=0;
option reslim = 3000000;
Option Iterlim=100000;
Option QCP = Cplex;

Solve CP_QP_GEP maximizing OF using qcp ;
```

The following code solves Illustrative Example 7.4 to determine bi-level generation expansion with a profit-maximizing strategic firm at the upper level.

```
* BL_GEP.gms: Three-node bi-level generation-expansion planning
    MIQP implementation

$INCLUDE PSE/GEP_data.gms

Scalar starttime;
starttime = jnow;

* Variable definition

Variables
f_hat(L,S,T) Realized power flow on line l in season s and period
    t
v(N,S,T) Voltage angle at node n in season s and period t
c(N,S,T) Consumption at node n in season s and period t
y(I,N,S,T,U) Generation output from unit u at node n owned by
    firm i in season s and period t
z(I,N,U) Generation investment in unit u at node n owned by firm
    i
mu(L,S,T) Dual for voltage law on line l in season s and period t
lambda(N,S,T) Dual for energy balance at node n in season s and
    period t
OF Objective function
;

Positive variables
phi_c(N,S,T) Dual for non-negativity of consumption at node n in
    season s and period t
phi_y(I,N,S,T,U) Dual for non-negativity of generation from unit
    u at node n owned by firm i in season s and period t
phi_z(INS,N,U) Dual for non-negativity of generation from unit u
    at node n owned by non-strategic firm ins
beta(I,N,S,T,U) Dual for generation capacity from unit u at node
    n owned by firm i in season s and period t
beta_up(I,N,S,T,U) Dual for generation up-ramping capacity from
    unit u at node n owned by firm i in season s and period t
beta_down(I,N,S,T,U) Dual for generation down-ramping capacity
    from unit u at node n owned by firm i in season s and period
    t
```

```
mu_up(L,S,T) Dual for positive transmission capacity on line l in season s and period t
mu_down(L,S,T) Dual for negative transmission capacity on line l in season s and period t
kappa_up(N,S,T) Dual for positive voltage angle limit at node n in season s and period t
kappa_down(N,S,T) Dual for negative voltage angle limit at node n in season s and period t
;

Binary variables
x_c(N,S,T) BV for KKT condition for c at node n in season s and period t
x_y(I,N,S,T,U) BV for KKT condition for y from unit u at node n owned by firm i in season s and period t
x_z(INS,N,U) BV for KKT condition for z from unit u at node n owned by non-strategic firm ins
x_beta(I,N,S,T,U) BV for KKT condition for beta from unit u at node n owned by firm i in season s and period t
x_beta_up(I,N,S,T,U) BV for KKT condition for beta_up from unit u at node n owned by firm i in season s and period t
x_beta_down(I,N,S,T,U) BV for KKT condition for beta_udown from unit u at node n owned by firm i in season s and period t
x_kappa_up(N,S,T) BV for KKT condition for kappa_up at node n in season s and period t
x_kappa_down(N,S,T) BV for KKT condition for kappa_down at node n in season s and period t
x_mu_up(L,S,T) BV for KKT condition for mu_up on line l in season s and period t
x_mu_down(L,S,T) BV for KKT condition for mu_down on line l in season s and period t
;

Equations OF_SP, UL_EQ, YD_EQ, ZD_EQ, CD_EQ, FD_EQ, VD_EQ, CP_EQ2, CP_EQ5, Phi_Y_EQa, Phi_Y_EQb, Phi_Y_EQc, Beta_EQa, Beta_EQb, Beta_EQc, Beta_Up_EQa, Beta_Up_EQb, Beta_Up_EQc, Beta_Down_EQa, Beta_Down_EQb, Beta_Down_EQc, Phi_Z_EQa, Phi_Z_EQb, Phi_Z_EQc, Mu_Down_EQa, Mu_Down_EQb, Mu_Down_EQc, Mu_Up_EQa, Mu_Up_EQb, Mu_Up_EQc, Kappa_Down_EQa, Kappa_Down_EQb, Kappa_Down_EQc, Kappa_Up_EQa, Kappa_Up_EQb, Kappa_Up_EQc, Phi_C_EQa, Phi_C_EQb, Phi_C_EQc;
* Maximize strategic firm's profit
OF_SP.. SUM(S, W(S)*(SUM((N,T), D_int(N,S,T)*c(N,S,T) - D_slp(N,S,T)*c(N,S,T)*c(N,S,T) - SUM(I, SUM(U, C_opr(I,N,U)*y(I,N,S,T,U)) ) ) ) ) - SUM(I, SUM(N, SUM(U, C_gen(I,N,U)*z(I,N,U) ) ) ) - (SUM(INS, SUM(N, SUM(S, SUM(T, SUM(U, TT(T)*K_gen(INS,N,U)*(A(N,S,T,U)*beta(INS,N,S,T,U) + R(U)*beta_up(INS,N,S,T,U) + R(U)*beta_down(INS,N,S,T,U) ) ) ) ) ) ) + SUM(L, SUM(S, SUM(T, K_trn(L)*(mu_up(L,S,T)+ mu_down(L,S,T))) ) ) +SUM(N, SUM(S, SUM(T, Pi*(kappa_up(N,S,T)+kappa_down(N,S,T))) ) ) ) - OF =E= 0;
* Non-negativity of strategic firm's investment decision
UL_EQ(IS,N,U).. -z(IS,N,U) =L= 0;
* KKT condition for y
```

```
YD_EQ(I,N,S,T,U)$(itontou(i,n,u)).. W(S)*C_opr(I,N,U) + beta(I,N,
    S,T,U) + beta_up(I,N,S,T,U) - beta_down(I,N,S,T,U) - beta_up(
    I,N,S,T+1,U) + beta_down(I,N,S,T+1,U) - lambda(N,S,T) - phi_y
    (I,N,S,T,U) =E= 0;
* KKT condition for z
ZD_EQ(INS,N,U)$(itontou(ins,n,u)).. C_gen(INS,N,U) - SUM(S, SUM(T
    , TT(T)*A(N,S,T,U)*beta(INS,N,S,T,U) ) ) - SUM(S, SUM(T, TT(T
    )*R(U)*beta_up(INS,N,S,T,U) ) ) - SUM(S, SUM(T, TT(T)*R(U)*
    beta_down(INS,N,S,T,U) ) ) - phi_z(INS,N,U) =E= 0;
* KKT condition for c
CD_EQ(N,S,T).. -W(S)*(D_int(N,S,T) - D_slp(N,S,T)*c(N,S,T)) +
    lambda(N,S,T) - phi_c(N,S,T) =E= 0;
* KKT condition for f_hat
FD_EQ(L,S,T).. mu(L,S,T) + mu_up(L,S,T)  - mu_down(L,S,T) + TT(T)
    *SUM(N$LPlus(L,N), lambda(N,S,T)) - TT(T)*SUM(N$LMinus(L,N),
    lambda(N,S,T)) =E= 0;
* KKT condition for v
VD_EQ(N,S,T).. -SUM(L$NPlus(L,N), B(L)*mu(L,S,T) ) + SUM(L$NMinus
    (L,N), B(L)*mu(L,S,T) ) + kappa_up(N,S,T) - kappa_down(N,S,T)
    =E= 0;
* Power flow on line L in season S and period T
CP_EQ2(L,S,T).. f_hat(L,S,T) - B(L)*(SUM(N$LPlus(L,N),v(N,S,T)) -
    SUM(N$LMinus(L,N),v(N,S,T))) =E= 0;
* Power balance at node N in season S and period T
CP_EQ5(N,S,T).. c(N,S,T)- SUM(I, SUM(U, y(I,N,S,T,U))) + TT(T)*
    SUM(L$NPlus(L,N), f_hat(L,S,T)) - TT(T)*SUM(L$NMinus(L,N),
    f_hat(L,S,T)) =E= 0;
* Disjunctive constraints for phi_y
Phi_Y_EQa(I,N,S,T,U).. -y(I,N,S,T,U) =L= 0;
Phi_Y_EQb(I,N,S,T,U)..  y(I,N,S,T,U) - M_y*x_y(I,N,S,T,U) =L= 0;
Phi_Y_EQc(I,N,S,T,U)..  phi_y(I,N,S,T,U) - M_y*(1-x_y(I,N,S,T,U))
    =L= 0;
* Disjunctive constraints for beta
Beta_EQa(I,N,S,T,U).. y(I,N,S,T,U) - TT(T)*A(N,S,T,U)*(K_gen(I,N,
    U)+z(I,N,U)) =L= 0;
Beta_EQb(I,N,S,T,U).. -y(I,N,S,T,U) + TT(T)*A(N,S,T,U)*(K_gen(I,N
    ,U)+z(I,N,U)) - M_beta*x_beta(I,N,S,T,U) =L= 0;
Beta_EQc(I,N,S,T,U)..  beta(I,N,S,T,U) - M_beta*(1-x_beta(I,N,S,T
    ,U)) =L= 0;
* Disjunctive constraints for beta_up
Beta_Up_EQa(I,N,S,T,U).. y(I,N,S,T,U) - y(I,N,S,T-1,U) - TT(T)*R(
    U)*(K_gen(I,N,U)+z(I,N,U)) =L= 0;
Beta_Up_EQb(I,N,S,T,U).. -y(I,N,S,T,U) + y(I,N,S,T-1,U) + TT(T)*R
    (U)*(K_gen(I,N,U)+z(I,N,U)) - M_beta_up*x_beta_up(I,N,S,T,U)
    =L= 0;
Beta_Up_EQc(I,N,S,T,U)..  beta_up(I,N,S,T,U) - M_beta_up*(1-
    x_beta_up(I,N,S,T,U)) =L= 0;
* Disjunctive constraints for beta_down
Beta_Down_EQa(I,N,S,T,U).. -y(I,N,S,T,U) + y(I,N,S,T-1,U) - TT(T)
    *R(U)*(K_gen(I,N,U)+z(I,N,U)) =L= 0;
Beta_Down_EQb(I,N,S,T,U).. y(I,N,S,T,U) - y(I,N,S,T-1,U) + TT(T)*
    R(U)*(K_gen(I,N,U)+z(I,N,U)) - M_beta_down*x_beta_down(I,N,S,
    T,U) =L= 0;
```

```
Beta_Down_EQc(I,N,S,T,U).. beta_down(I,N,S,T,U) - M_beta_down *(1-x_beta_down(I,N,S,T,U)) =L= 0;
* Disjunctive constraints for phi_z
Phi_Z_EQa(INS,N,U).. -z(INS,N,U) =L= 0;
Phi_Z_EQb(INS,N,U).. z(INS,N,U) - M_z*x_z(INS,N,U) =L= 0;
Phi_Z_EQc(INS,N,U).. phi_z(INS,N,U) - M_z*(1-x_z(INS,N,U)) =L= 0;
* Disjunctive constraints for mu_down
Mu_Down_EQa(L,S,T).. -K_trn(L) - f_hat(L,S,T) =L= 0;
Mu_Down_EQb(L,S,T).. K_trn(L) + f_hat(L,S,T) - M_mu_down* x_mu_down(L,S,T) =L= 0;
Mu_Down_EQc(L,S,T).. mu_down(L,S,T) - M_mu_down*(1-x_mu_down(L,S,T)) =L= 0;
* Disjunctive constraints for mu_up
Mu_Up_EQa(L,S,T).. -K_trn(L) + f_hat(L,S,T) =L= 0;
Mu_Up_EQb(L,S,T).. K_trn(L) - f_hat(L,S,T) - M_mu_up*x_mu_up(L,S,T) =L= 0;
Mu_Up_EQc(L,S,T).. mu_up(L,S,T) - M_mu_up*(1-x_mu_up(L,S,T)) =L= 0;
* Disjunctive constraints for kappa_down
Kappa_Down_EQa(N,S,T).. -Pi - v(N,S,T) =L= 0;
Kappa_Down_EQb(N,S,T).. Pi + v(N,S,T) - M_kappa_down*x_kappa_down(N,S,T) =L= 0;
Kappa_Down_EQc(N,S,T).. kappa_down(N,S,T) - M_kappa_down*(1-x_kappa_down(N,S,T)) =L= 0;
* Disjunctive constraints for kappa_up
Kappa_Up_EQa(N,S,T).. -Pi + v(N,S,T) =L= 0;
Kappa_Up_EQb(N,S,T).. Pi - v(N,S,T) - M_kappa_up*x_kappa_up(N,S,T) =L= 0;
Kappa_Up_EQc(N,S,T).. kappa_up(N,S,T) - M_kappa_up*(1-x_kappa_up(N,S,T)) =L= 0;
* Disjunctive constraints for phi_c
Phi_C_EQa(N,S,T).. -c(N,S,T) =L= 0;
Phi_C_EQb(N,S,T).. c(N,S,T) - M_c*x_c(N,S,T) =L= 0;
Phi_C_EQc(N,S,T).. phi_c(N,S,T) - M_c*(1-x_c(N,S,T)) =L= 0;

****Producers****
y.fx(I,N,S,T,U)$(NOT itontou(I,N,U))=0;
z.fx(I,N,U)$(NOT itontou(I,N,U))=0;


Model BL_MIQP_GEP
      /
ALL
      /
;
option optcr=0;
option reslim = 3000000;
Option Iterlim=100000;
Option MIQCP = Cplex;

Solve BL_MIQP_GEP maximizing OF using miqcp ;
```

References

1. Baringo, L., Conejo, A.J.: Transmission and wind power investment. IEEE Trans. Power Syst. **27**, 885–893 (2012)
2. Bylling, H., Gabriel, S.A., Boomsma, T.K.: A parametric programming approach to bilevel optimisation with lower-level variables in the upper level. J. Oper. Res. Soc. **71**, 846–865 (2020)
3. Dorn, W.S.: Duality in quadratic programming. Quart. Appl. Math. **18**, 155–162 (1960)
4. Energy Information Administration: Capital cost and performance characteristic estimates for utility scale electric power generating technologies (2020). https://www.eia.gov/analysis/studies/powerplants/capitalcost/pdf/capital_cost_AEO2020.pdf
5. Fortuny-Amat, J., McCarl, B.: A representation and economic interpretation of a two-level programming problem. J. Oper. Res. Soc. **9**, 783–792 (1981)
6. Gabriel, S.A., Conejo, A.J., Fuller, J.D., Hobbs, B.F., Ruiz, C.: Complementarity Modeling in Energy Markets. Springer, New York (2013)
7. Garcés, L.P., Conejo, A.J., García-Bertrand, R., Romero, R.: A bilevel approach to the transmission expansion planning within a market environment. IEEE Trans. Power Syst. **24**, 1513–1522 (2009)
8. Garver, L.L.: Transmission network estimation using linear programming. IEEE Trans. Power Apparat. Syst. **89**, 1688–1697 (1970)
9. Hashimoto, H.: A spatial Nash equilibrium model. In: Harker, P.T. (ed.) Spatial Price Equilibria: Advances in Theory, Computation, and Application. Springer, Berlin (1985)
10. Hobbs, B.F.: Optimization methods for electric utility resource planning. Eur. J. Oper. Res. **83**, 1–20 (1995)
11. Hobbs, B.F.: Linear complementarity models of Nash-Cournot competition in bilateral and POOLCO power markets. IEEE Trans. Power Syst. **16**, 194–202 (2001)
12. Huppmann, D., Egerer, J.: National-strategic investment in European power transmission capacity. Eur. J. Oper. Res. **247**, 191–203 (2015)
13. Kazempour, J., Conejo, A.J.: Strategic generation investment under uncertainty via Benders decomposition. IEEE Trans. Power Syst. **27**, 424–432 (2012)
14. Kazempour, J., Conejo, A.J., Ruiz, C.: Strategic generation investment using a complementarity approach. IEEE Trans. Power Syst. **26**, 940–948 (2011)
15. Kazempour, J., Conejo, A.J., Ruiz, C.: Generation investment equilibria with strategic producers–Part I: formulation. IEEE Trans. Power Syst. **28**, 2613–2622 (2013)
16. Maurovich-Horvat, L., Boomsma, T.K., Siddiqui, A.S.: Transmission and wind investment in a deregulated electricity industry. IEEE Trans. Power Syst. **30**, 1633–1643 (2015)
17. Organisation for Economic Co-operation and Development (2021). https://www.oecd.org/
18. Pérez-Arriaga, I.J., Rubio, F.J., Puerta, J.F., Arceluz, J., Marín, J.: Marginal pricing of transmission services: an analysis of cost recovery. In: Einhorn, M., Siddiqi, R. (eds.) Electricity Transmission Pricing and Technology. Springer, Berlin (1996)
19. Pineda, S., Morales, J.M.: Solving linear bilevel problems using big-Ms: not all that glitters is gold. IEEE Trans. Power Syst. **34**, 2469–2471 (2019)
20. Reichenberg, L., Siddiqui, A.S., Wogrin, S.: Policy implications of downscaling the time dimension in power system planning models to represent variability in renewable output. Energy **159**, 870–877 (2018)
21. Reta-Hernández, M.: Transmission line parameters. In: Grigsby, L.L. (ed.) Electric Power Generation, Transmission, and Distribution. CRC Press, Boca Raton (2012)
22. Rodríguez-Sarasty, J.A., Debia, S., Pineau, P.-O.: Deep decarbonization in Northeastern North America: the value of electricity market integration and hydropower. Ener. Pol. **152**, 112210 (2021)
23. Ruiz, C., Conejo, A.J.: Pool strategy of a producer with endogenous formation of locational marginal prices. IEEE Trans. Power Syst. **24**, 1855–1866 (2009)

24. Sauma, E.E., Oren, S.S.: Proactive planning and valuation of transmission investments in restructured electricity markets. J. Reg. Econ. **30**, 261–290 (2006)
25. Sauma, E.E., Oren, S.S.: Economic criteria for planning transmission investment in restructured electricity markets. IEEE Trans. Power Syst. **22**, 1394–1405 (2007)
26. Schittekatte, T., Momber, I., Meeus, L.: Future-proof tariff design: recovering sunk grid costs in a world where consumers are pushing back. Ener. Econ. **70**, 484–498 (2018)
27. Siddiqui, A.S., Tanaka, M., Chen, Y.: Are targets for renewable portfolio standards too low? The impact of market structure on energy policy. Eur. J. Oper. Res. **250**, 328–341 (2016)
28. Siddiqui, A.S., Tanaka, M., Chen, Y.: Sustainable transmission planning in imperfectly competitive electricity industries: balancing economic and environmental outcomes. Eur. J. Oper. Res. **275**, 208–223 (2019)
29. Storrow, B.: Why the deep freeze caused Texas to lose power. Sci. Amer (2021). https://www.scientificamerican.com/article/why-the-deep-freeze-caused-texas-to-lose-power/
30. Tanaka, M., Chen, Y., Siddiqui, A.S.: Regulatory jurisdiction and policy coordination: a bi-Level modeling approach for performance-based environmental policy. J. Oper. Res. Soc. https://doi.org/10.1080/01605682.2020.1843980
31. Tangerås, T.P., Mauritzen, J.: Real-time versus day-ahead market power in a hydro-based electricity market. J. Ind. Econ. **66**, 904–941 (2018)
32. Tejada-Arango, D.A., Domeshek, M., Wogrin, S., Centeno, E.: Enhanced representative days and system states modeling for energy storage investment analysis. IEEE Trans. Power Syst. **33**, 6534–6544 (2018)
33. Varian, H.R.: Microeconomic Analysis. W.W. Norton, New York (1992)
34. Virasjoki, V., Siddiqui, A.S., Oliveira, F., Salo, A.: Utility-scale energy storage in an imperfectly competitive power sector. Ener. Econ. **88**, 104716 (2020)
35. Wogrin, S., Hobbs, B.F., Ralph, D., Centeno, E., Barquin, J.: Open versus closed loop capacity equilibria in electricity markets under perfect and oligopolistic competition. Math. Prog. **140**, 295–322 (2013)

Index

B
Benefit, 19
  aggregation, 24
  constant marginal benefit, 26
  gross benefit, 2, 19, 20
  marginal benefit, 19, 25, 26
  willingness-to-pay, 19, 25, 26
Bi-level model
  carbon taxation, 213, 220, 222, 225
  generation investment, 256, 277, 284, 286, 290, 291
  renewable portfolio standard, 225, 226, 230, 231
  Stackelberg game, 213, 256, 277, 281, 293
  transmission investment, 256, 257, 268, 270, 271, 274

C
Consumer surplus, 2, 19–21
  aggregation, 24
  surplus maximization, 2, 22, 25
Cost
  constant marginal cost, 64
  damage cost, 198
  external cost, 198
  linear marginal cost, 64
  long-run marginal cost, 58
  marginal cost, 27, 38, 43, 44
  marginal cost of damage, 210, 212, 213, 222
  private cost, 198
  private marginal cost, 198, 199
  social cost, 198
  social marginal cost, 199

D
Deadweight loss, 29, 157, 159, 199
Demand, 7
  aggregation, 22
  complements, 12
  demand curve, 12
  demand function, 2, 7, 8
  demand response, 2, 27
  inverse-demand function, 8
  inverse-market-demand function, 23
  law of demand, 8, 10
  linear demand function, 2, 8, 9, 15
  linear inverse-demand function, 9, 15
  market-demand function, 2, 23
  power rating limits, 25
  substitutes, 12

E
Elasticity, 13
  constant price elasticity of demand, 17
  elastic, 14
  inelastic, 14
  perfectly elastic, 16, 17
  perfectly inelastic, 15, 17
  price elasticity of demand, 2, 14, 15, 158, 169

M. Tanaka et al., *Economics of Power Systems*, International Series in Operations Research & Management Science 327,
https://doi.org/10.1007/978-3-030-92871-1

Energy storage, 36, 48, 55, 56, 75
Externalities, 197, 198, 206, 207
  cap-and-trade program, 201
  carbon taxation, 207, 213, 217–220, 222, 223, 225, 226, 232
  central planning, 199, 207, 211
  emission permits, 197, 200, 201, 203, 236
  EU Emissions Trading System, 37, 38
  market-based mechanism, 200, 209, 213
  market failure, 197
  negative externalities, 197
  Pigouvian tax, 197, 200–202, 236
  Regional Greenhouse Gas Initiative, 37, 38
  renewable energy certificates, 204, 225, 226, 228, 231, 232
  renewable portfolio standard, 197, 200, 204, 205, 207, 213, 223, 225, 226, 230, 232, 236

G
Game theory, 160
  best-response function, 161
  Nash equilibrium, 161
Greenhouse gas emissions, 36, 197
  CO_2, 197, 207–213, 218, 222, 223, 226, 232
  NOx, 197
  SO_2, 197

I
Investment
  generation, 256, 277
    bi-level, 281
    central planning, 277, 279
  transmission, 255, 256
    bi-level, 259, 267
    central planning, 257, 259, 263
Investor-owned utility, 35

L
Load-duration curve, 48, 51, 53, 55, 56

M
Marginal pricing
  basic clearing formulation, 129
  congested clearing, 127
  investment-cost recovery, 117
  multi-period general formulation, 148
  multi-period marginal pricing, 145
  non-convexities, 131, 135
  optimal control, 118
  perfect competition, 122
  short-term efficiency, 124
  two-stage clearing formulation, 143
  two-stage pricing, 137
  un-congested clearing, 124
Market clearing
  day-ahead market, 98
  futures market, 112
  intra-day market, 112
  network-constrained multi-period auction, 108
  network-constrained single-period auction, 105
  single-node multi-period auction, 101
  single-node single-period auction, 98
  stochastic auction, 112
Market power, 156, 158
  average Lerner index, 169
  Lerner index, 158, 169
  monopoly, 156, 163
  monopsony, 158, 159
  price-cost markup, 158, 169
  price maker, 156
  price setter, 156
Mathematical program
  binary expansion, 284
  complementarity problem, 203
  disjunctive constraints, 220, 222, 263, 271, 287–290
  Karush-Kuhn-Tucker condition, 25, 165, 167, 202, 218–220, 226
  linear program, 42, 44, 58, 60, 62, 68, 73, 80
    duality, 286, 287
  mathematical program with equilibrium constraints, 220, 222, 226, 271, 284, 286, 290
  mathematical program with primal and dual constraints, 226, 229, 230, 271, 273, 274, 284
  mixed-complementarity problem, 218, 226
  mixed-integer quadratic program, 207, 222, 262, 263, 271, 274, 284, 290, 291
    quadratically constrained, 207, 230, 231, 274, 284
  quadratic program, 210, 211, 218, 227, 258, 271, 272, 277, 279, 284, 293
    duality, 226–229, 272, 273, 284, 286, 287

O
Oligopoly, 160, 161
- best-response function, 162, 164
- Cournot duopoly, 162
- Cournot oligopoly, 161, 162, 222, 256, 269, 272, 274, 275, 292, 293
- Herfindahl-Hirschman index (HHI), 168
- leader-follower oligopoly, 171
- market clearing, 172
- market clearing: dual problem, 174
- market clearing: optimality conditions, 175
- market clearing: primal problem, 173
- multiple leaders, 172, 183
- Nash-Cournot equilibrium, 163, 165–167, 218, 226
- Stackelberg oligopoly, 170

P
Perfect competition, 156, 159, 163
- price taker, 156, 158

Power flow
- Kirchhoff's laws, 210, 259, 270, 278, 284

Pricing
- dynamic pricing, 29
- time-varying pricing, 27, 29

Prosumer, 2, 30

R
Renewable energy, 200, 204
- hydropower, 35
- photovoltaics, 30
- renewable energy technologies, 210–212, 223, 225, 228
- solar power, 36
- variable, 36, 38, 48, 51, 53, 55, 56, 70, 211, 212, 255–257, 259, 263–267, 275, 277, 279, 292–294
- wind power, 36

S
Supply
- constant marginal cost, 64
- emission costs, 36–38
- fuel costs, 36–38
- heat rate, 37, 38
- investment costs, 36, 47
- investment planning, 55
- levelized cost, 36, 47, 48, 51
- linear marginal cost, 64
- long-run marginal cost, 58
- marginal cost, 38, 43, 44
- operating costs, 36–39, 44, 46, 47
- profit maximization, 36, 60, 66
- ramping, 36, 55, 56
- screening curve, 36, 48, 50, 51, 53, 55, 56
- supply curve, 38, 64
- unit commitment, 55
- variable O&M costs, 36, 38

U
Utility, 1–3
- Cobb-Douglas utility function, 1, 3
- marginal utility, 3, 6
- quadratic utility function, 1, 5, 8
- quasilinear utility function, 9, 21
- utility function, 1, 3
- utility maximization, 2, 7, 22

MIX
Papier aus verantwortungsvollen Quellen
Paper from responsible sources
FSC® C105338

If you have any concerns about our products,
you can contact us on
ProductSafety@springernature.com

In case Publisher is established outside the EU,
the EU authorized representative is:
Springer Nature Customer Service Center GmbH
Europaplatz 3, 69115 Heidelberg, Germany

Printed by Libri Plureos GmbH
in Hamburg, Germany